Waine's World

The Best of
B. Waine Kong's
Five Years of Weekly Columns

The Upson Beacon
Thomaston, Georgia
(2016 - 2021)

minna PRESS

All proceeds from the sale of this book
go to the ZÖe Pediatrics Foundation.

Thank you for contributing to this worthy cause.

ISBN: 978-1-7353069-6-4

Editor: Lena Joy Rose

Layout and cover design: Mark Weinberger

Image of Basil Waine Kong: Luke Haney

Printed in United States of America

Ordering Information:
Quantity (Bulk) Sales. Special discounts are available on quantity
(bulk) purchases by corporations, associations, and others.
For details email: bwaine@ZÖepeds.com

Foreword

In 2016, I invited Dr. Kong to contribute a weekly column, to which he enthusiastically accepted. I labeled his columns "Waine's World," and it turned out to be a positive addition to our local newspaper. He is a gifted writer.

Dr. Kong is relatively new to the community, many of his columns are refreshing reminders of what an amazing community we are blessed to live in and be a part of. Dr. Kong never seems to run out of complimentary things to say about our community.

Through his columns, over the past six years, Dr. Kong has become a popular figure in our community. He not only doesn't mind people stopping to chat about one thing or another, he welcomes it.

I am a "Waine's World" fan. I hope you will enjoy re-reading some of his columns and sharing his book with neighbors near and far.

It is his wish that this compilation of his columns and writings will be preserved for future generations. In addition, all proceeds from the sale of this book go to the ZÖe Pediatrics Foundation, a fantastic cause that will help children in this service area. Happy reading!

Debbie McClain
Publisher and Co-Owner
The Upson Beacon
Thomaston, Georgia

Contents

Foreword   iii

Introduction   11

—2016—

1. An Ode to Spring Thomaston is Full of It! "Hanami!"   16
2. Thomaston is a Special Place   19
3. Moving to Thomaston was a Great Call! I Dropped Anchor   20
4. For Thomaston to Prosper, Our Children Must Do Well.   22
5. How Does Thomaston Stack up?   25
6. Retiring in Thomaston   27
7. Raising Our Children for Export   29
8. Advice, Like Youth, is Probably Wasted on the Young   31
9. Economic Development in Thomaston   35
10. TUAC (Thomaston-Upson Arts Council)
    Thomaston's version of the National Endowment for the Arts   37
11. Heroes In Our Midst: The Four Harvey Brothers   39
12. Seven Steps to a Lifetime of Good Health   41
13. One Man's Journey: The Alton Harris Story   44
14. And Yet We Rise   47
15. Good Neighbors Enrich Our Lives   49
16. We Have Good Schools in Thomaston   51
17. Let Freedom Ring!   54
18. Rev. Albert Simmons: A Searcher of Truth and a Believer in Simple Generosity   55
19. Sweet Tea: A Southern Tradition   58
20. Freemasons Among Us   60
21. Meet An Amazing Young Man: Will Hernandez   62
22. The Raintree Rascals   64
23. Miss Betty: The Mother Teresa of Thomaston   65
24. Usain Bolt: The Greatest of All Time   68
25. A Parent's Guide to a Great Year at School   70
26. Being Happy in Thomaston   71
27. Human Propensities: Contemplating Human Nature in the Garden of Good and Evil   74
28. How Freud Thought of Human Nature   76
29. Serving Two Years as the President of the Thomaston Kiwanis   78
30. A Tribute to Grandparents   80
31. The Americanization of the World   82

Contents

32. If You Love, You Are a Reflection of God   84

33. The Thomaston–Upson Senior Center: A Great Place to Hang-Out   85

34. The Downside of Our Incredible Technological Innovations   87

35. Brilliantly Educated and Exceptional Young Ladies   89

36. The James Anthony Searcy Story: And Yet We Rise   91

37. Promote Democracy   93

38. My Relationship with the Great Architect of the Universe   94

39. Forget Me Not, O Gentle Savior   96

40. The Challenge of Making Each Hour Count   97

41. The Lord Loves a Cheerful Giver   99

—2017—

42. Blessed Be the Tie That Binds: If My Brother Succeeds, I Succeed; If He Fails, I Fail.   101

43. A Tribute to Martin Luther King Jr. (January 15, 1929- April 4, 1968)   103

44. Is There Any Good in Goodbye? (Coping With Separation)   104

45. *Noblesse Oblige*   106

46. Doing the Right Thing   108

47. The Poor Do Not Have to be With Us Always?   110

48. Shakespeare Anonymous?   112

49. We Need a Healthcare System that Promotes Health   113

50. It Takes a Village   114

51. Our Commitment to Diversity is a Commitment to Excellence   115

52. Your Integrity Matters   118

53. Beauty is in the Eye of the Beholder   119

54. Invest Generously in Long-Term Genetic Success   122

55. Out of School Stories of Dr. Stephanie Kong, The Pediatrician   124

56. The Self-Fulfilling Prophecy   125

57. Happy Mother's Day!   127

58. The Hope of Sudden Salvation: Will He Ever Straighten Up and Fly Right?   128

59. Does Regular Church Attendance Reduce Crime?   130

60. The Poisonwood Bible   131

61. The Importance of Fathers   133

62. The Thomaston-Upson County Airport: An Important Asset   135

63. Would You Place Your Party's Interests Above the Interests of Your Country?   137

64. How Is Your Compassion?   139

65. Cultivating Successful Children: Raising Soaring Eagles in Your Household   139

Contents

66. I Woke Up Not Dead Again in Thomaston 142

67. Our Iceland Adventure: A Land of Wonder, Beauty and a Lot to Do 144

68. Call Me Deacon 146

69. The Consequences of Associating with Hateful People 148

70. How We Got Here 149

71. A Tribute to Heather Heyer 150

72. The Upson County Ministerial Association Celebrating 45 Years! 151

73. The Impermanence of All Things 153

74. Birthday Traditions 154

75. The Joy of Exercise 156

76. The Embarrassment of Losing My Memory 158

77. We Are a Nation of Immigrants 160

78. Myths About the Common Cold 161

79. Our Fourth Amendment Rights 164

80. Freedom And Justice for All 166

81. A Godless Prophet: Jim Zeigler's Defense of Judge Moore 168

82. Are you Curious About Cuba? 170

83. Are We Witnessing the End of Morality? 172

84. A Cure for Winter Blues 174

85. Be Lifted Up Rather Than Be Pulled Down 177

—2018—

86. People in Need Offers an Opportunity to Please God 180

87. What's America to Me? 182

88. Promises To Keep and No Time to Waste 185

89. The Business of Being Human 187

90. Demographics of the World 188

91. Human Achievements and Limitations 189

92. A Brief Comparison of American and French Law 191

93. How to Kill Your Husband 192

94. And Yet We Rise 197

95. The Free State of the Isthmus 199

96. The Arc of Time Bends Toward Progress: Better Must Come! 201

97. Being Married 203

98. Blowing Smoke and Other Arcane Medical Practices: Sometimes Facts Don't Matter 206

99. About People Who Hate 208

Contents

100. We Are Held Together by Integrity: Do You Walk the Walk?   209

101. Teachers: Arsonists of the Mind (Speech to the Retired Teachers Association)   211

102. What's the Meaning of Southern Hospitality?   213

103. Small Towns are the Happiest Places to Live   214

104. A Leaning Tree is Not Always the First to Fall   215

105. Yes, I am a Bleeding Heart for Children   217

106. Being Devoted Doesn't Mean I think Our Country is Perfect—Just That I Love It   219

107. High Falls State Park: A Wonderful Place to Visit   220

108. Failure is a Prerequisite to Victory   221

109. A Family is Not a Sprint!   223

110. If Lincoln's Mother Came Back as a Ghost   224

111. Where Would You Prefer to Retire?   226

112. Kindness May Be More Important Than Love   228

113. The Lord Moves in Mysterious Ways   230

114. The Fluidity of Truth: For Every Truth the Opposite May Also Be True   232

115. Redemption: What a Concept!   235

116. Improving the Health of All Our Citizens   237

117. Crime Does Not Pay   239

118. The Bystander Effect: Birds of a Feather Flock Together   241

119. Snowmen Fall from Heaven Unassembled   244

120. Courage Over Adversity: In Defense of Bullies   246

121. Our Future Depends on What We Do in the Next Minute   248

122. Winning The Lottery Mostly Makes People Big Losers   250

123. When The Parent-Child Roles Are Reversed   252

124. Disappearing Islands Are No Myth   254

125. The Harder the Conflict, the More Glorious the Triumph   255

126. You Are Wealthier Than You Think   257

127. Sometimes the Apple Falls Far from the Tree   258

128. Christmas Comes But Once Per Year…   260

129. Go Easy on The Pie This Holiday Season   261

—2019—

130. Sound the Alarm: Our Life Expectancy is Now Decreasing   263

131. Paying Back China for Its Contributions to Our Quality of Life   265

132. We Have So Much More in Common Than What is Different   266

133. Child Naming Conventions Around the World   267

Contents

134. What I Stand For   269

135. Truth Decay   270

136. The Divine Symmetry and the Christian Story   272

137. Wedding Traditions   274

138. His Eye Is on The Sparrow...And I Know He Watches Me!   275

139. His Eye is on the Sparrow…My Hospitalization (Part 2)   277

140. American Aviation: Look How Far We Have Come in Less Than 100 Years   279

141. Thinking Like a Lawyer   281

142. Preventing Cardiovascular Disease   282

143. You Don't Have to Be Perfect to Be a Champion   285

144. Something Wonderful is Going on at Gordon State College   287

145. Moral Development: Our Conscience is the Glue that Binds Us   288

146. Casual Relationships Nourishes the Soul: Why Exchanging Pleasantries is Important   290

147. A Sense of Purpose is Essential for Happiness   292

148. There is Such a Thing as Too Much Information   294

149. When Your Children Graduate from High School?   296

150. Do We All Lie?   298

151. Celebrating the Emancipation Proclamation   299

152. I am Sorry, It Is Just Evil to Abuse Children   301

153. Euphoric Moments   303

154. My Visit to Portugal   304

155. Traveling Makes You Richer and Wiser   306

156. Does the Politics of Hate Jive with Southern Hospitality?   309

157. Becoming a Successful Leader   312

158. Mr. Rogers on Making Goodness Attractive   314

159. Nobody Blames Themselves   316

160. Can Change in a Moment (Man Proposes but God Disposes)   318

161. Our Fractured Politics: Let's not Buy into the Binary   319

162. You Don't Need a Weatherman to Know Which Way the Wind Blows   322

163. Are Community Churches Facing Extinction?   324

164. Nature Versus Nurture: Both Matter   326

165. Spirit Of the Heart Awards Banquet 2019   328

166. Loyalty Never Ends: Is Loyalty Important to You?   331

167. The Fragility of Life   332

168. The Fragility of Life Again?   334

Contents

169. Atonement, Justice and Grace 336

170. Avoid the Temptation to Dismiss Scholars 338

171. I Would Rather Have Jesus than Power, Silver or Gold 341

172. The Attack on Women: Train Your Children to Be Respectful 343

173. A Baby Can Make All the Difference in the World 346

—2020—

174. Does It Take a Great Sinner to Make a Great Saint? 348

175. Let's Go for a Walk 351

176. Meet Mr. Dannie Smith, a Renaissance Man 353

177. My Brother Left Us Too Soon (Reflections: Earl DeCarlton Kong) 355

178. Was Christianity a Secret Society in its Early Days? 359

179. Why Does the Flu Virus Spread in Winter? 361

180. What Does the LORD Require of You? 363

181. Transitions: What a Difference A Day Makes! 366

182. Regarding the Novel Coronavirus and COVID-19 368

183. Being A "Know It All" President Is Not Helping 370

184. Surviving the Pandemic (Everybody Needs Everybody) 372

185. The Looming Crisis: Welcome to the World of Microbes 375

186. Making Good Decisions 377

187. *Force Majeure*: When Circumstances Are Unforeseeable and Unavoidable 379

188. Being Grief Stricken 380

189. An Open Letter to Alan Landers. Is it time to give up on "The Great Agitator?" 381

190. My Ignorance is to be Respected as Much as Your Knowledge 383

191. Eating Our Young: An Open Letter to Police Chief Mike Richardson 384

192. A Pandemic of the Soul 386

193. Lessons I Learned from My Mother 387

194. Change is Gonna Come 389

195. Meet Colonel Bill Anderson: One Tough Marine and Vietnam Veteran 390

196. The Courage of Cordy Tindel (CT) Vivian (1924-2020) 392

197. Ex-Urban Migration: Living Off the Grid 393

198. Mathematics: The Language of God 395

199. All are Welcome to Thomaston 396

200. Global Warming: The Pandemic X 1,000 Percent 398

201. The Roots of Our Discontent 399

202. Projecting Our Deficits onto Others: Are You Talking About Me or Yourself? 401

Contents

203. Responsive Reading for Churches ... 402

204. What Would it Take for You to Stand Against a Tide? ... 404

205. Standing Positive and COVID-19 Negative ... 405

206. The Wages of Sin: You Reap What You Sow, the Harvest can be Hard to Bear ... 406

207. Suicide Threat from COVID-19 (The Number of People in Crisis is Increasing) ... 408

208. Where Does It End? (Do Not Be Overcome by Evil, But Overcome Evil with Good ... 410

209. Arrogant Boastful Know-It-Alls: Do You Have All the Answers? ... 411

210. Discrimination Hurts Everyone
(Whether You are the Victim or the One Dishing it Out) ... 413

211. Let Women Stay at Home and Hold Their Peace
("Seven against Thebes" Aeschylus, 467 B.C.) ... 415

212. Hold on, Help is on the Way ... 418

213. The Contributions of Immigrants (Confessions of an Immigrant) ... 420

214. The Young Black Woman Who Developed the COVID-19 Vaccine Platform Technology ... 422

215. Christmas In Jamaica When I Was 14 ... 424

216. Verily I Say unto You: "When You Save a Child, You Save the World" ... 427

—2021—

217. My Tribute to Dr. Lemuel Julian Haywood ... 429

218. Organizing a "White House Conference on Children" in 2022 ... 430

219. If You Aspire to Be Happy, Strive Not for Fame and Fortune but To Have a Servant's Heart ... 432

220. Paradise Lost: An Epic History of the World ... 433

221. Value of Rethinking, Joy of Being Wrong ... 435

222. How Will We Enjoy a Prosperous Future Living in the Past? ... 438

223. Crossing the Rubicon: Doing the Right Thing is Always the Best Thing ... 440

224. Guess Who is Playing Nice...Luke Combs ... 442

225. A Thing of Beauty is a Joy Forever ... 443

226. Sherry Farr, R.N.A Nurse on a Mission ... 445

227. Jealousy: The Ugly Emotion Known as the Green-Eyed Monster ... 447

228. Happiness and a Good Life is Built on the Quality of Your Relationships ... 449

Acknowledgements ... 452

Introduction

Thirty-five years ago, Dr. Stephanie Williamson became Dr. Stephanie Kong. After my retirement in 2012 (When I turned 68 years old), we moved to Thomaston to open "ZÖe Pediatrics" and I served as her business manager. Not every pediatrician can have a psychologist/lawyer at their beck and call. In doing so, however, I lost my name—not my good name, just my last name. It became confusing to staff and patients when "Dr. Kong" was summoned, so I agreed to be called "Dr. Waine" (notice the British spelling for Wayne). In 2016, I accepted the invitation to write a weekly column for the Upson Beacon, a weekly community newspaper in Georgia and my editor (Debbie McClain) designated it "Waine's World".

In this compilation, I selected columns that were previously published in the newspaper and recommend that you use this book as a daily reader (one for each workday, take off weekends). So, whether you sit in an "outhouse", a bidet, or on a throne, instead of wasting five minutes while you are taking care of your business, you can be entertained. You can have a little chuckle (I have been known to be funny from time to time); cry (I am compassionate and sympathetic); contemplate (I marvel at the universe and the human beings God placed here); rail at my politics; be inspired, or even gain some insights about our condition. I write from the heart. I chose the columns that I hope will still be relevant in the coming years. There are lessons to be learned and even some cathartic moments. As you read through this compilation, you may find some repeated aphorisms, or examples, but these are intentional to make my point in these weekly columns.

My favorite writer of all time is Mark Twain. I am not as smart as he was, but you probably know that he embargoed most of what he wrote to be published one hundred years after his death. He did not mind offending dead people but was more considerate of the living. So, the entire works of Mark Twain were finally published in 2008 and, because my wife knew about my passion for his stories, she bought the entire collection (a Christmas present) that took me the entire year to read. Since I don't believe you can read all 100,000 pages, without some of it rubbing off, get ready for a little bit of Twain's wit as I purposefully try to emulate his style. Every boy should read, *The Prince and the Pauper* and every girl should read, *Joan of Arc* for starters.

I lived in Columbia, Maryland for 20 years. That is exactly halfway between Washington D.C. and Baltimore, so I was a regular subscriber to *The Washington Post* as well as *The Baltimore Sun*. Even then, I was an avid reader of opinions. Can you imagine being able to read Art Buchwald daily? I also made a point of reading H.L. Mencken's, (*Baltimore Sun*) columns even though he preceded me by a hundred years. Those were the days, when having several cups of coffee and reading newspapers was everyone's routine. I am not sure I ever missed a day of reading *The Washington Post* in the morning and *The Baltimore Sun* each evening. Arthur Buchwald (1925 – 2007) was a humorist of the first order. I wouldn't be surprised if he also got his sense of humor from Mark Twain. I remember that he had been on dialysis for ten years and finally making peace over his passing, decided to end the damned nuisance. So, he pulled the plug and found out that he didn't need it after all and lived several years after that without the dreaded catheter. He also had a brother whose salary was $40,000 per year but could save $50,000 of it. His brother was able to accomplish this impossible feat by pricing the luxury model of a car, hotel room, clothes, and restaurant items, buying the more reasonable items and marking down the difference in his "savings book". The price of a BMW is $75,000, he bought a Ford instead and saved $40,000. Go figure!

I am now 78 years old (Born July 18, 1943, Victoria Jubilee Hospital, Kingston, Jamaica). Since I believe there are no old fools, I have hopefully picked up some wisdom along the way and I would love nothing better than to pass on "everything" that has ever made sense to me. My wish is that you enjoy reading these nuggets as much as I enjoyed writing them.

As a lawyer, I write about interesting legal issues. As a psychologist, I address issues of the mind. (What were you thinking?). As a Deacon at Greater Mount Zion Baptist Church (Rev. Charles Reeves), I attempt to address spiritual issues. (Did you know that just regularly going to a place of worship contributes to your sense of well-being and years to your life?)

I have been married for over 50 years, claim membership in a lodge, fraternity, Kiwanis and various social clubs. I have learned a thing or two about relationships, and, having raised four amazing children, I am blessed to enjoy a wonderful relationship with them as well. Having been the CEO of the Association of Black Cardiologists as well as a local president of the American Heart Association, I share what I know about heart disease (our number one killer). Because my wife is a physician, I keep up to speed on general health issues and pediatrics in particular.

As a resident of this little piece of Heaven we call Thomaston, I designated myself our most fervent cheerleader. Loving nature as much as I do, we are fortunate to live in this amazing place where there are no hurricanes, tornadoes, volcanoes, droughts, floods, forest fires, earthquakes, tsunamis, extreme hot or cold weather. Given our abundance of tall Georgia pines, flowering trees and magnolias, I found it interesting to learn that most people in the world cannot see a tree from where they live. We don't endure rush-hour traffic—even when there are accidents, things get cleared up in a jiffy. Everyone is hospitable and I enjoy seeing cows feasting in the green pastures and playing golf throughout the year. As I get to know more and more of the wonderful people who live here, I also feature their stories. Having visited over 100 countries, I love to talk about how other cultures handle births, deaths, marriages, how they nourish their minds and souls as well as ponder why we are the wealthiest people on earth but suffer from depression, unhappiness, and suicides more than those who are forced to live in poverty.

When I was 15 years old, I migrated to the United States. My mother is Black and my father Chinese. While uncommon here, my heritage is not unusual in Jamaica. I wish I had his skills as a golfer, but I am not what Tiger famously called "Cablinasian." I made a purposeful decision to be Black as defined by law. Other than my genes and name, I have had almost no Asian influence. So, this has led to some interesting situations. When I was negotiating a contract with the City of Atlanta 20 years ago, I had to prove that I was Black. So, I had to prepare a package showing family photographs, certified that I go to a Black church (Providence Missionary Baptist Church), belong to a Black fraternity (Alpha Phi Alpha), a Black lodge and worked almost exclusively for Black organizations (professor at the University of the District of Columbia, Vice President of Provident Hospital, Director of the Urban Cardiology Research Center and CEO of the Association of Black Cardiologists. The reviewer finally said, "Ok, Ok, Ok" and the deal was done. When we arrived in Thomaston and joined Greater Mount Zion Baptist Church, I was met with curious stares, and I am sure I am the cause of some amusement when I get happy. But I still get asked, "What are you?" and the answer is, my last name and appearance notwithstanding, we are a Black family.

I never thought I would live this long and also enjoy good health. I don't recommend my diet (I eat too much ice-cream and drink too much single malt scotch) but I can still do 30 push-ups and take time to go for a swim daily. The fountain of youth is swimming. My youngest son built a pool for us so my wife and I exit our back door and jump in—just lovely!

I trust you will not only purchase copies for the bathrooms of all your many families and friends in your world but make ZÖe Pediatrics Foundation one of your favorite charities. We do a lot of good and 100% of the proceeds from the sale of this book will go to the Foundation.

Children from poor families in middle and South Georgia: Ten Counties—Lamar, Upson, Spaulding, Pike, Troup, Marion, Talbot, Harris, Taylor, Meriwether, and Chattahoochee have limited access to dental care. With your help, we would like to close this gap by outfitting a "Mobile Pediatric Dental Office" to include a dentist and dental hygienist and make it available to this population. Very few pediatric dentists practice in these counties.

Tooth decay has been a preventable disease for over 50 years when the only options were extractions and false teeth. The public health formula that led to the dramatic improvement in dental health was threefold:

1. Fluoridate drinking water (preventing a third of cavities)
2. Preventive check-ups (twice per year)
3. Brushing and flossing daily.

As a result, dentists migrated from just pulling teeth and fitting false teeth to preventive dentistry, endodontics, periodontics, prosthodontics, and prosthodontics.

While dental care has seen a dramatic improvement, the dental needs of our community continues to lag. Rural areas are dependent upon well-water and bottled water for drinking; affordable dental care is still out of reach for most of the population; and lack of education regarding proper dental hygiene continues to frustrate an end to scourge of tooth decay.

Pediatric dentists provide specialized care for children through adolescence. They are trained to recognize and treat dental problems that are specific to children even though it is a preventable childhood disease that inflicts pain from infections that further handicaps the unfortunate victim's nutrition, speech and missing school leading to under-achievement. Poor children have three times the rate of untreated tooth decay as their better-off schoolmates.

The ZÖe Pediatrics Foundation is an independent 501(c)(3) not-for-profit Foundation, Tax ID: 47-5083340. It is the not-for-profit affiliate of ZÖe Pediatrics Inc., a for-profit Limited Liability Company. ZÖe Pediatrics provides medical care to over 200 patients per day and supports the Foundation as dental referrals are difficult to access in these counties.

A well-equipped dental van will provide us the portability so we can enhance our ability to serve a population that is clearly in need. There are just too many children with no access to dental services. We will offer our services primarily through schools. After the usual formalities and approvals, we will announce our arrival in advance and make appointments (thru the school nurse) for students. We will then park our van in the parking lot of each school (on a rotating basis in the ten counties) and offer a free dental health education and check-up to ALL students. Those who have dental carries will either be treated by our in-house pediatric dentist and dental hygienists or referred to another dentist for follow-up.

Our mission is vital. Please partner with us to make this a reality. Even $100 will help. Your donations will go directly to the implementation of the Dental Van. The cost associated with hiring personnel will be sustained by reimbursement from the federal government. Thank you in advance.

—Basil Waine Kong

1.
An Ode to Spring.
Thomaston is Full of It!
"Hanami!"

May 30, 2016

While you may want to be in Colorado in winter, New England during the fall, the best place to celebrate spring is Thomaston, Georgia. After a difficult winter, I am so excited to welcome sunshine. For those who flock to Washington D.C. to see the Japanese cherry tree blossoms around the Tidal Basin, that is fine and yes, they are spectacular, but springtime in Thomaston is more stunning. As I walk about my neighborhood with a camera in hand and a broad smile on my face, there is so much to take in and so little time. It passes quickly. Every week the channel changes—new colors appear. We are treated to daffodils, tulips, snow drifts, begonias, hibiscus, iris, plums, cherries, crab apple, peach, crepe myrtle, quince, lantanas, hydrangeas, and an amazing variety of azaleas. If you are sentimental, several varieties of magnolias are also on the menu. The beautiful purple wisteria makes Poplar Street the Christmas Lane of Spring. Are you seeing what I am seeing? These are amazing gifts from our creator. Can we all together say: "Thank you Lord?" Yes, spring is in the air and even for an old man, the sap is running, and I again feel the passions of my youth. According to Leo Tolstoy, "Every man and every living creature has a sacred right to the gladness of springtime." So, even though our allergies may be acting up as the trees pollinate, spring is still a feast for our watery eyes.

Atlanta (Piedmont Park) is one of the most colorful places to welcome spring, but we are just a little ahead of them. So, go ahead, walkabout (as they say in Australia) and see for yourself. When nature shows off like this with fruit trees heavy with blossoms, I blush inside even though I know our driveways will soon be painted yellow and there will be long lines at Tidal Wave Car Wash.

I drove past Anthony South's farm out on Moore's Crossing recently. I could just imagine fish jumping around in his lake and I hope he will allow me to fish this summer with my grandkids. I saw fat cows grazing in the meadow and green grass growing on rolling hills. If you are lucky enough to see his land when the morning mist is rising, you will want to commit the scene to a canvas, but definitely to your long-term memory. Hidden from the city, his farm seems to be surrounded by riches with his family enjoying an enviable life. I hope he planted strawberries again this year. The ice cream and shakes are truly delightful and to die for. There is no countryside more appealing.

If the bucolic countryside is not enough, tune into the Masters. Even if you hate golf or never played, during spring, it is the most beautiful golf course on earth—a majestic cathedral! It may be 365 acres but it's *God's Half Acre* to me. If the blooms try to come out too early, I am told they will pack ice around the roots to make sure "Master's Week" takes place when the surroundings are at the height of their beauty. I have been fortunate enough to have attended this tournament several times, and not only for the magnificent golfing skills, but for the display of flowers bordering an endless green manicured lawn. According to Dave Zurbuch, "It's breathtaking. You see the azaleas in large clusters, and that tells me this course has a lot of history to it. If these trees or bushes could only speak."

Of course, if you wanted to see more of the blooms of spring in Georgia, the fabulous Callaway Gardens in Pine Mountain is only 30 miles away. In addition to the butterfly house, while there, you can also traipse around in the woods and find toadstools, lichen, thistles, ferns, tendrils, and even colorful slime. If you are lucky, you may even come across my favorite—the wildflower *Macbridea alba*, known as "white birds in a nest," which, strangely enough, is a member of the mint family.

And do enjoy the magnificent sunsets on display. God is showing off! How can anyone be sad living in a place like this? Buds are swelling and blooming; lilies are emerging from their sleep; fruit trees awaken with the promise of a good harvest; songbirds, especially cardinals, are frittering about singing their hearts out seducing mates; the bees are sucking nectar; and butterflies take wing. Buds are shooting with the promise of cherries, apples, peaches and home-grown tomatoes, corn, radishes, sweet pea, and cucumbers will soon grace our tables.

The hot dogs with mustard and relish are waiting for you. Will you make it to the Braves opening game? I sure hope they make it to the World Series again.

Turn off the heater and air conditioner. Open the doors and windows all day and air out your house; open your car and pick-up truck windows when you drive. The cool breeze and sunshine will warm you inside and out. God is in his Heaven and all's right with the world.

According to the comedian, Robin Williams, "Spring is nature's way of saying let's party." But what is it that gets you pumped up and inspired? What puts a grin on your face that just doesn't want to go away? Watching whales? Going on a trip to some exotic location? Seeing your child walk for the first time? Going on a hot date? Getting a hole in one? Going out for ice cream?

Please join me in celebrating this new beginning. While the earth is being rejuvenated, so can we—a fresh start! It is a new season for us to relish. Wave to your neighbor as they come out from hibernation to smell the roses. Did you forget that you had neighbors? Whatever you may find to complain about, spring shouldn't be one of them. When I meet Him face to face, I will thank Him for awarding us so much goodness and mercy.

The greatest event of spring is, of course, Easter. Yes, Christ the Lord is risen. Hallelujah! Can I point out that Gandhi was born, lived a significant life, died, and was buried. Period. Full stop. George Washington was born, became the father of our country, died, and was buried. Period. Full stop. Buddha was born, founded a religion, died, and was buried. Period. Full stop. Muhammad was born, is revered as a prophet, died, and was buried. Period. Full stop. In fact, everyone in the world will come into the world, live, die and will be disposed of in various ways. But our Lord and Savior Jesus Christ was born in a manger, lived the life of a saint, was crucified at Calvary, died for our sins, and was buried in a sepulcher. But, after three days, the stone was rolled away; He ROSE again. He lives! Isn't that something to celebrate? This is the greatest story ever told and should humble us as Christians. I am awestruck with the promise of our salvation.

May His light guide your path; May His love grace your heart; And may His sacrifice strengthen your soul!

2.

Thomaston is a Special Place

March 2, 2016

In many communities, politicians play environmental roulette sanctioning (implicitly or explicitly) the ill-advised use of pesticides, cyanide from mining operations and pollution of the air, land and water. The result is rapacious devastation of the communities' natural resources and a devastating impact on their quality of life. No bird's sing and fruit trees deny them a harvest. Due to responsible management of our environment with sensible regulations, Thomaston is a place where birds sing, the land is fertile, and we are rewarded with abundant trees, vegetables, and flowers. What a great place to raise children!

There are many heads of departments, elected officials, and bureaucrats in many cities but few leaders. Thomaston is fortunate to have responsible individuals in government who are conscientious leaders and protective guardians who do the right things and make sure the right things get done. I am proud to live in a community where our elected officials make preservation of our natural resources and the protection of our environment their priority.

The concerted campaign to rid our community of virus carrying mosquitoes is a good example. Just be aware that the animal that is responsible for the most human suffering and death are not lions, tigers, hippos, or snakes; it is mosquitoes! Let us join the campaign to empty all containers around our yards that hold water and stock fish in every pond. Fish just love mosquito larvae.

While our politicians hire good people and make sure that every department has the resources, they need to accomplish their objectives, we are the envy of similar cities for the talent we have attracted. It requires vigilant citizens to hold their feet to the fire as public servants and not always virtuous. So, if you have issues with anyone in government, you are encouraged to call our city manager.

In addition, each citizen can help to:
1. Be respectful of our laws and courteous to those who must enforce our ordinances.
2. Do not discard oils, chemicals, paints and paint thinners, bleach and unused medication down your drain and toilets.
3. Discard old tires, batteries, appliances, and computers appropriately.

4. Reduce the burning of trash, wood, and leaves—this includes fireplaces.

5. Reach out with a helping hand to those less fortunate and demonstrate kindness and southern hospitality in all our transactions.

6. Support our churches, civic organizations and institutions.

7. Most importantly, do not litter. Let's show off a really beautiful city.

There is only so much our environment can endure. Enlightened self-interest should tell us that we all live under the same tent. We are in the process of transforming our city, from the closing of our factories and mills, resulting in high unemployment. While we cannot yet claim economic prosperity, we are on the mend.

3.

Moving to Thomaston was a Great Call! I DROPPED ANCHOR

March 9, 2016

With reference to these columns, I was once asked, "So, what's the point?" I am grateful to all of you for talking to me about my characterization of Thomaston and offering ideas for future columns. Typically, what is said is that it takes an outsider to "see" and "appreciate" the abundance of wealth we take for granted in Thomaston.

I am reminded of Alexis-Charles-Henri Clérel de Tocqueville, a French sociologist and political scientist who visited the United States in the 19th Century and wrote a wonderful book on Democracy in America in which he described a stable and prosperous democracy that could only have been seen through the lens of an outsider.

But to get back to "what's the point?" I think that Thomaston is ripe with possibilities right under our noses. The internet has opened the world for products we take for granted locally that are prized and sought after in China, Japan, Europe, and the rest of the world. I will share some of the possibilities:

1. **Could Thomaston become a tourist attraction?** Our Historical society has done a marvelous job collecting and displaying our history and so many people enjoy seeing and learning about this stuff. Can we take the next step and have tours? I received a copy of the *History of Thomaston* and taken on a grand guided tour. It was a great treat. Lots of people would pay for that experience if it were developed and marketed. I am seeing a horse-drawn carriage.

2. This experience would be greatly enhanced **if the City of Thomaston bought the Raintree Golf Course, added a hotel, and attracted golfers** who just want to get out of Atlanta. The Raintree property has tremendous potential.

3. **Could we develop a world class bakery?** I am addicted to home-made peach cobblers, buttermilk, pecan pies and red velvet cakes. When Ms. Geneva McDaniels favors me with one of her pies, it's a heavenly experience and they quickly disappear from our kitchen counter. It makes me a little sad that store-bought cakes and pies are served at most of our restaurants.

4. Like they do in Chicago for barbeque, **can we have a good old-fashioned pie contest and use the best recipes to bake and sell "Thomaston Pies?"** For that matter, people in Japan would probably love to have some of our amazing Big Chic fried chicken shipped to them. When I visited Japan, my host treated us with the best food and accommodations he could muster but the one item he said he wanted me to send back was "Sarsaparilla". He said he, his family and friends all loved it but could not get it in Japan. So, we sent them several cases. Could we find a way to feed this hunger?

5. With our reputation for southern hospitality, abundance of caring people who need jobs, mild weather, and low crime rate, **why isn't Thomaston a mecca for retirees?** Can we spread the word that we are neighborly people who would welcome elderly people to Thomaston?

6. With large tracts of land reasonably priced, we are an ideal location for manufacturing. Are we doing enough to bring jobs to Thomaston? **How are we positioning ourselves for the green energy explosion?**

7. **With the popularity of "vanity mailboxes" we could certainly use one of our empty buildings to cater to this demand.** Do you know how many

mailboxes there are in the world? Everyone wants to express themselves with customized mailboxes!

8. As our schools are no longer offering arithmetic, spelling, handwriting, history, ethics, and etiquette, I believe there is still a demand for these subjects. It's fine to say that we now have adding machines and spell check but what if there is no computer on hand. I find it embarrassing that graduates of our schools cannot make change if the cash register is out of commission. I really wish we wouldn't be so dependent on computers. Are we going back to signing our names with an "X"? Personally, I appreciate good penmanship—even if you are a doctor.

These are just a few ideas off the top of my head. As the saying goes, "Ladies and Gentlemen, there is gold in dem der hills." Without vision, the people suffer. Could our mayor be persuaded to designate a group of community leaders as a commission to consider business development for Thomaston?

4.

For Thomaston to Prosper, Our Children Must Do Well

March 23, 2016

If our children succeed, we all benefit; if they fail, we all fail. Our children are the canaries in our coal mine. If you want to judge the health and welfare of a community, look at the children. If we lose grandparents, we may lose our past, but if we lose our children, we lose our future.

Instead of greeting each other with "Hi, hello, what's going on? How you doing? Peace, respect and Namaste," Rev. Patrick O'Neill observed in 1991, that among the Maasai warriors of Kenya, their greeting to each other is: *Casserian Engari* which translates to, "How are the children?" The warriors are comforted if the answer is: *Sapati Ingera!* meaning, "All the children are well." If the children are well, then peace and prosperity is assured.

Imagine how we would each answer the question if it was put to us: How are the children of Thomaston? Would the answer be:

Some are doing great, but too many others are abused, neglected, go to bed hungry, sick, and just idle? Are they spending all their time on Twitter, Instagram, and Facebook? Are they lacking opportunity? And Jesus said, "Suffer the children to come unto me and forbid them not for as such is the Kingdom of Heaven."

What are you doing to advance the cause of our children? Every one of us can make a positive contribution to the health and welfare of our children and by extension, our community.

1. **Are you a volunteer or mentor in the schools?** Can we get together and spearhead a "Maker Space" in Thomaston?

2. **Are you a member of a civic organization that is dedicated to the welfare and uplifting of children?** The mission of Kiwanis is: "Serving the Children of the World". Care to join us?

3. **Are you a volunteer** for Girls' Scouts, Boys' Scout, Boys' and Girls Clubs, Big Brothers and Big Sisters, March of Dimes, Partnership for a Drug Free America, Special Olympics, Toys for Tots, soccer, or Little League? Wondering where to plug in? The Chamber of Commerce has a list.

4. **Do you teach Sunday school?** Are you guiding them in the path they should grow?

5. **Do you engage the children** you encounter on your rounds and make them feel special? Each year the Kiwanis donate funds to Mt. Moriah Baptist Church to sponsor their summer enrichment program. At the end of the summer, they attend one of our meetings to show off what they learned. As President, I always make the point that the City Fathers of Thomaston care about our children and make these funds available to improve the quality of their lives and advance their careers.

6. **Do you stand idly by while a child is being abused or harmed in any way?** Parents do not own their children. They belong to all of us, and it takes our entire village to raise them. Bright idle minds can just as well invent our next big breakthrough or become a hacker.

7. **Are you invested in making sure all our children are above average?** Are you willing to pay a little more property taxes to provide them a quality education?

Easter is coming. As many children parade before us at church or at the Rock Ranch in pretty duds, dresses, and hats, we may want to ask what books they are reading or have them show you the index cards they are using to memorize their words (vocabulary).

As the world becomes smaller, American children will not only be competing with each other, they will have to compete with high performing students around the world. Are you aware that 50% of the employees at Apple, Microsoft and IBM were born elsewhere because there are not enough Americans with these high-level skills? According to U.S. Department of Education Secretary Arne Duncan: "Our students today are competing against children in India, Japan, South Korea and China. Those students are going to school twenty-five to 30% longer than our children, consequently, children in the U.S. are at a competitive disadvantage. I think we're doing them a disservice." In addition, students in other countries are also more likely to receive tutoring and attend night classes.

Each person can make a difference. My wife makes a habit of asking young people, "What are your plans for the future?" With Kenya Sandifer's permission, I relay this story: Kenya was an orphan by the time she was five years old and was raised by her grandmother. She struggled through school.

When Kenya graduated from high school, she may have had plans but no direction. So, Dr. Kong offered her a part time job in our office just so she could become acquainted with the world of work. After the first week on the job, there were so many screw-ups and breakages prompting the appearance of several "No Kenya zone" signs on the desks of other employees. I made out bills and asked Kenya to address and mail them. As she had never mailed a letter, she mistakenly placed my address in the middle of the envelopes. A week later, the letters came back to me, and my bills were late. In her defense, she apologized and offered to reimburse us for the cost of late fees.

While that was not necessary, I failed to see the promise of this young lady, discussed the futility of the plan, and encouraged Dr. Kong to discontinue the program. She refused, reminding me and the staff that with all new beginnings, there will always be screw-ups and urged me to lean in and make this a priority. As the dutiful husband I am, I coached Kenya for an hour each day and to my surprise, she blossomed. I had her memorize three long difficult poems and she flawlessly recited them to the Kiwanis members to great applause.

She took the SAT's and the College Entrance Exams and exceeded her own expectations. She bought a car with the funds we paid her, her grandmother taught her to drive, and she scored 94 on her driver's test. She applied to Gordon College and was admitted without conditions (even with very poor grades from high school) and to her credit, she earned two "A's" and three "B's" for the five courses she took for her first semester. Kenya is one her way to becoming a pediatrician.

A gentleman once saw a woman picking up starfishes that had washed up on shore and throwing them back in the ocean and observed, "You don't seem to be making much progress, there are thousands of them." The lady simply answered, "I may not be able to save all of them, but I can save this one."

We will live a life of abundance if all the children are well, and we will reap a bitter harvest if they are not. Let us invest in the children so we can report, *Sapati Ingera!* All the children of Thomaston are well.

5.

How Does Thomaston Stack up?

March 30, 2016

Apparently, you can make a lot of money posting a list of "10" best or worse of anything. Any self-appointed group can attract a lot of eyeballs from publishing things like, "Ten Best Movies," "Ten Prettiest Women", "Ten Best Shots in Golf", "Ten Best Quarterbacks", "Ten Best Restaurants", "Ten Worst Cars", "Best and worst schools", and on and on. I found it amusing that when former Supreme Court justice Thomas Brennan sent questionnaires to a hundred of his fellow-lawyers, asking them to rank the top ten law schools, they ranked Penn State fifth even though there was no law school named "Penn State" and the State of Pennsylvania does not have a law school. On what basis did they make this ranking?

One rating service just published "The Ten Most Desirable Cities in Georgia" and had the audacity not to include Thomaston. They picked: Alpharetta, Roswell, Mountain Park, Sandy Springs, Decatur, Johns Creek, Druid Hills,

Wilmington Island, Suwanee, and Dunwoody. I have had the opportunity to visit all of these cities and I would put Thomaston ahead of all of them.

Here is some of the criteria they used:

- **Population Density.** They claim that the higher the density, the better. Really? I would rather think of it as the Three Bears, Goldilocks, and their porridge. Some cities are too small, some too large but Thomaston is just right. We do not live in a low-density community where it is difficult to find a good restaurant, shop, obtain medical services and get bank loans. We also do not live where you have to pay for parking, have traffic jams and have to deal with obnoxious big city people yelling at you. Thomaston is just right.

- **Lowest Unemployment Rates.** In other words, in communities with mostly retired or independently wealthy people who don't work, that city would be rated at the bottom and shipyard or coal mining communities with full employment would be rated first. While I think there is a lot of room for improvement (our unemployment rate is twice the national average), just be reminded that some people work slow, some people work fast, and some are half fast.

- **Highest Home Values.** I would rather live in a community where homes are affordable, in communities that are safe and people patient and kind. I would rather not live-in communities where people live in posh energy wasting 10,000 sq. ft. houses by themselves.

Ladies and gentlemen spread the word, "we have affordable housing". Our houses as well as property taxes cost about 30% for similar residences in Atlanta.

So, I would like to appoint myself "The Kong Rating Service for Quality of life for the best communities in Georgia" and rate Thomaston #1! We are really that good. While I am at it, my mother named me "Son #1"; On Father's Day my children never fail to give me the award for the "Greatest Father in the World", my wife thinks I am the "Best Husband!" Our employees tell us that we are the best employer in Georgia, and I have given myself the title of "Duke of Earl". You want to argue with me? What I learned is that who does the ranking determines who comes out on top. Better yet, "There is no such thing as the best place to live. One man's bread is another man's poison."

6.

Retiring in Thomaston

April 6, 2016

I am prompted to write this article because I recently had a conversation with a gentleman from Kansas who did an exhaustive search on the internet and finally decided to move to Thomaston because of the quality of life and affordability. He and his wife were not disappointed. Are the years piling up on you like leaves in late fall? I am 73 years old, and I readily confess that my wife and I live in a marvelous place.

The precision and significance of a fine timepiece or the Julian, Gregorian or Lunar calendar is lost if you retire to Thomaston. If you come here to live out your golden years; you may just find the fountain of youth or even an eternal spring. If you are living with weariness where you are, give up on that smoldering cauldron, stop crying out in futility and move out. Whether you want to pray, discover, feel safe, live among hospitable people, and enjoy good food (Brunswick Stew with corn chips) and good medical care, you too can live a life free from frustration and apprehensions by moving to this jewel that has been eluding you. Here are some things to consider about Thomaston:

Haven't you always wanted to get away from traffic jams? We have never had one and there is never a problem parking for free wherever your destination happens to be. And here is something unique. Bankers and lawyers make house calls. If you have difficulty getting out, they will send someone to your house and take care of your business. The postman also delivers the mail to my door.

We have wonderful nursing homes (Golden Living Center, Riverside Nursing Home, and Providence Nursing Home). If you live in the West Village Retirement Center in Silvertown and crane your neck a little, there are always children playing in the fabulous Greatest Generation Park, (especially at the dancing fountains) as well as people walking about the duck pond and under tall Georgia Pines. Visitors to our many parks enjoy sitting on the lovely park benches and visiting a spell. By the way, we don't tolerate grumpy people so go ahead and "speak" to anyone you encounter. If they ignore you, they are from out of town.

Houses cost about two thirds less than Atlanta. Here is a secret about Thomaston. Not long ago, Thomaston Mills hired about 4,000 people to manufacture cloth and cords for tires but cheap labor in China put them out of business. So, most employees had to relocate elsewhere, leaving a lot of quality housing at very affordable prices. You won't believe the deals—including low property taxes!

Do you want to pray, meditate, listen to inspirational sermons, and church music that is guaranteed to uplift your spirits and save your soul? You can choose from over 150 churches and any and all of them will welcome you with a warm embrace. This is a very friendly place, especially in our houses of worship.

Is your personal safety important to you? Not only are the citizens respectful and honest, our public servants are the best and will be there to serve you in your hour of need. The story is told of a criminal-minded individual who came to town with the intent of taking advantage of these trusting people and banks that don't have security guards. But when he arrived, everyone, including the police and the Sheriff treated him so well, he could not bear the thought of hurting them, so he changed his sinful ways and converted to become an upstanding citizen. The truth is that when most of the people break the law, it is impossible to fight crime but when only a few people are criminals, it is not difficult to identify them, convert them or arrest them. You will immediately notice how law-abiding our citizens are by how conscientious they are of obeying the speed limit and stop signs. Unlike big cities, they will patiently wait until it is safe to make their move into traffic.

Is the natural beauty of where you live important? Whatever the season, there are always flowers blooming—especially in winter. The sunrise and sunsets will linger long after it took your breath away.

We have first class doctors who take pride in providing excellent medical care whether it's at our medical center or at the offices of our community docs. If you need a higher level of care, Atlanta, Macon, or Columbus is only an hour away. Wellness care is also a priority. The Upson Regional Medical Center Wellness Center is a quality health club where a trainer or rehab nurse will work with you. I mostly use the wonderful swimming pools for my workouts.

What's your passion? If it's bridge, drop by The Archived and they will welcome you. While you are there, learn about the history of the city. If it's golf, you can have all the joy the game has to offer at the Raintree Golf Club. Join a group or just show up. No tee time is necessary. I love my sticks and don't ignore them.

Is solitude important? Sometimes the sweetest sound is silence interrupted by the rustling of leaves, the rippling of water cascading down the Flint River, children playing and the chirping of birds—music to my ears. When your mind is at peace, your thoughts are free to wander where your feet can no longer take you. Your juices flow freely giving you the courage to try new experiences and discover that you can get used to this. This may be the secret cure to stave off Alzheimer's.

Finally, as I get older, my need to serve and leave the world a better place grows. There are many opportunities to volunteer either by joining civic organizations or individually. We are waiting for you to join us. So, come to Thomaston, discard the barnacles and clutter from the hull of your mind. Life here is like good port wine, sweet, smooth, and rich. Come to visit or come to stay.

7.
Raising Our Children for Export

April 13, 2016

Our unemployment rate is twice the national average, if this current situation is allowed to continue, we will raise our children, educate them, and send them off to distant shores for work. I attended a Town Hall meeting and some of the discussion revolved around how we could entice more industry to Thomaston. The plan is to entice prospects with lots of cash, tax credits, roads, free land, and buildings as long as they bring jobs. Not a bad idea but, I think these incentives may be better invested developing home-grown industries.

The past offers us a rich database from which we can learn in order to keep succeeding. In 1925, Mr. O.B. Keller wrote an article in the *Atlanta Journal* praising R.E. Hightower and his sons "for their ongoing investment in their hometown and… defined Thomaston Mills as Georgia brains, Georgia training…and Georgia money, put right back into Thomaston." During R.E. Hightower's time, Georgia produced 60% of the county's tire fabric. Where are these men and women in 2016? Did the spirit and commitment of these builders of our great structures vanish? Why are we looking only to people from outside like the people in *Waiting for Godot* to rescue our economy? We may be starving to death with a loaf of bread under our arm.

In case you did not see or read the play by Samuel Beckett, it is about people waiting in vain for someone to rescue them when the solution to their woes was within their reach, if only they just had vision. Without vision, the people perish. We must also be careful that we don't get so focused on why we cannot attract industries to Thomaston that we lose sight of home-grown opportunities. What I heard was, we cannot get industries to move here because we are unable to compete with what other places are offering. I believe we have a lot to offer.

A few weeks ago, I wrote, "Could we develop a world class bakery? I am addicted to home-made peach cobblers, buttermilk, pecan pies and red velvet cakes. When Ms. Geneva McDaniels favors me with one of her pies, it's a heavenly experience and they quickly disappear from our kitchen counter.

Ms. Juliette Greivell Hightower wrote back in really eloquent style to advise, "While Dr. Kong's upbeat articles are wonderful, he missed the mark on one of his wishes for Thomaston: We already have a fantastic bakery: Cake House," which is owned by talented baker Deborah Culverhouse".

I immediately went looking for this elusive bakery. And yes, there it was on Main Street. I had a wonderful conversation with the owner who didn't understand how I could not have known she was there for so long. Unfortunately, I also found out that while she does make fabulous pies, cakes, and other baked goods, particularly cupcakes as Ms. Hightower described, her bakery is a one-woman operation. The pecan pie I ordered took five days. But, when it was delivered, it was warm right out of the oven. The taste was fantastic, I immediately ordered another one for the following week. Since all her goods are freshly baked to order and not frozen and de-thawed, it does cost more. Let's hear it for freshly baked goods. It is so worth it!

Many years ago, I was a consultant to a project in South Africa. We were trying to identify people (owners of small shops) who could be taught, funded, and motivated to expand their operations. In other words, a one-shop barber could be persuaded to have a dozen or more barbershops. What we discovered is that people were severely limited by their vision of themselves. If they are getting by with what they are doing they will be happy to keep doing it until they are persuaded to think bigger!

I was at the Meat Shop and ran into a couple from Tampa. They own a cabin in Thomaston and visit often to fish in the Flint River and enjoy the town. This is their idea of a good time. I wonder if those of us who live here take advantage of all this community has to offer or invite our friends far and near to join us in the fun. When they come, we all benefit.

My son and his family visited for Easter. He marveled that when the four of us teed off at Raintree we were the only ones on the course. As a low handicap golfer, my son thought the course had character and enjoyed the outing. The grandkids thoroughly enjoyed their stay. After the Easter egg hunt at the Rock Ranch, I took them for a long walk, throwing rocks and splashing around in the creek-bed at the end of Johnston Drive. I think the water in the creek rose a little bit because my grandkids waded in and threw a lot of rocks in the water. They enjoyed getting muddy in the process. I used to be able to skip rocks but seem to have lost that skill.

We need jobs in Thomaston so we can enjoy our grandkids!

8.
Advice, Like Youth, is Probably Wasted on the Young

April 20, 2016

I was invited to speak to the students at the alternative school recently about how to succeed, not only in school but in life. I started out with a nod to the greatness of these United States of America where "anyone with a little motivation" can get by and even reach greatness. But the truth is that there is no formula. Each person must find their own happiness and their way. It is a little scary to many students when they come to the realization that they have to take their own shower, get their own joke, eat their own hamburger, feel their own pain and die their own death. We may have a lot of people who love and want to help us make something of ourselves but, in the final analysis, everyone is alone. Mama may have, Papa may have, but God bless the child who has his own. However, I offered these seven principles to improve their chances.

1. **Recognize the possibilities.** You were born in the richest and most powerful country in the world in the best time in our history. To quote the Schuyler sisters in the award-winning new musical, "Hamilton," "Look around, look around at how lucky we are to be alive right now." Millions of people are trying to migrate to our shores because we are the land of opportunity. You can succeed with just a little effort. But you were also born into a time when

everywhere you look somebody is pointing out how the system is stacked against you. For example, your vote doesn't matter because of money in politics. Your savings and investments don't matter because the banks are too big to fail, and your merit doesn't matter because you are still going to be judged on your race or your sex or your neighborhood. It would be easy to let all of this news overwhelm you, suppress you, stop you from getting up in the morning and doing what you need to do. But recognize this constant barrage of negative information for the blessing that it is. It means you live in a country where we talk about our problems. It's only when the people on the news say everything's fine that you need to be cynical. Soon you will be putting your shoulder to the wheel and doing what you can to confront these problems and more.

2. **Don't let your mistakes define you**. If you can survive your teenage years without getting arrested, getting yourself or the woman in your life pregnant, or getting hooked on drugs, then you have made life easier for yourself. And even if you do these things, this is also a very forgiving country. In the U2 song, Bono sings to a person who got "stuck in a moment." He sings, "You've got to get yourself together." You've got stuck in a moment/And now you can't get out of it." The video shows a football player replaying that missed kick over and over in his head—the lost game, the angry teammates, the disappointed fans. But, if you don't get "stuck in the moment," you can "get out of it." You can make a lot of "mistakes" and still be on track to succeed whether your goal is a long healthy life, making money, being a scholar, doing something better than anyone else and being a force for good.

3. **Learn anything you can from anybody you can and never stop learning**. This doesn't always mean formal education. Education is highly sought after by most people but is not the only road to success. Children around the world marvel that American children have free education, and many do not take advantage of it. I am sure you have heard of the musician, "Fat Joe". Compare him with a gifted musician, who had been practicing the violin almost all her life, went to Julliard School of Music and eventually got her dream job making $50,000 per year with a great Orchestra. Fat Joe dropped out of high school, never took a music lesson, but made a hit song with two words, "Lean back," which he repeated over and over for three minutes and made ten million. Parents and teachers are consistent in their advice to be

respectful to others, get a good education and stop making a fool of yourself. We would never have had a Richard Pryor or Chris Rock if they followed that advice. So, be aware of your talents and develop to your highest potential.

4. **Try and try again.** Yes, only one in 300,000,000 win the lottery and there are very few accidental champions. You are probably never going to be discovered or win an Olympic medal by just showing up. If you want to be a world beater, you have to put in the time and effort under great coaching. There are some people who will answer the question: Can you do XYZ? with "let me try." Now, of course, even this "can do" attitude has its limits. If you have never done neurosurgery, don't try it. However, trying again is a good idea to follow at a task you believe in. Think of the stonecutter hammering away at his rock, perhaps 100 times without so much as a crack showing in it. Yet at the 101st blow it will split in two, and it was not that blow that did it, but all that had gone on before. So, keep hammering away.

5. **Don't get hung up on your title or your formal training.** In the book, *Rich Dad, Poor Dad*, Robert Kiyosaki compares his father, a highly educated professor to his uncle, an eighth-grade dropout. His educated father died in debt while his uncle became one of Hawaii's richest men by learning the art of making money. While he does not intend to denigrate education, he points out that you need more than education to accumulate wealth. In fact, very few of the billionaires of the world graduated from college. Bill Gates, Steve Jobs, Mark Zuckerberg, Tiger Woods, and Ted Turner famously dropped out or in the case of Bill Gates got kicked out of college. Although they can all be said to have committed the hours it takes to become the best in their field. Malcolm Gladwell has put forth the proposition that it takes ten thousand hours of concentrated effort to become expert at anything. What's the difference between a doctor and a janitor? One generation. A doctor can produce "ne'er do well" children and a janitor can produce children who make great contributions to society.

6. **Be nimble.** The definition of insanity is doing something repeatedly and expecting a different result. It would not be prudent to keep going back to watering holes that have dried up while squandering new opportunities. This is a new world reality that cannot be ignored. In 1998, Spencer Johnson wrote a parable entitled, "Who Moved My Cheese?" about a mouse who

kept going to the same spot in the maze looking for where the cheese used to be instead of using his nose to sniff out the cheese. From this little parable, he points out that the only certainty is change. We cannot continue to make horse drawn carriages and buggy whips when the demand for these products and services is gone. Don't prepare for work at the Mill, find a business that the world needs or become as indispensable as possible. In the movie "The Graduate," the main character's uncle advised him to get into plastics even though most people had no idea what that was. Instead of becoming victims of change, we can become agents of change. We can develop and market new products.

7. **The most important lesson I have learned in my 73 years on this planet is that "For every truth you learn in life, the opposite is also true"** (including this column). Simply, you may believe that "The early bird gets the worm" but also believe that "Good things come to those who wait." You may also believe that you have to be good looking and accomplished to get married, when most married people are neither extremely attractive nor greatly accomplished. You are always being advised to look "your best". But that would mean wearing the same outfit every day. How about the old truth that you should always spend less than you make? That would mean never going into debt but the road to wealth is to borrow and invest in something worthwhile like an education or some kind of business.

Most importantly, never be jealous or envious of anyone. As Mary Schmich wrote, "Don't waste your time on jealousy. Sometimes you're ahead, sometimes you're behind. The race is long and, in the end, it's only with yourself." Some may be better off but never better than you. You are incomparable and must eat your own supper. Looks are often deceiving. You will never know what is going on with another person. My thoughts are reflected in this thoughtful poem about "Richard Cory" by Edwin Arlington Robinson, "…And he was rich—yes, richer than a king—And admirably schooled in every grace. We thought that he was everything. To make us wish that we were in his place…And Richard Cory, one calm summer night, went home and put a bullet through his head."

9.

Economic Development in Thomaston

April 27, 2016

While we may disagree on how to achieve it, co-columnist Alan Landers and I are on the same page. Last week, he wrote, "The City and county officials, business leaders, community leaders and the man on the street are virtually unanimous in agreement; Economic Development is the most urgent priority for our community". That has been the theme of my columns as well. The unemployment rate is twice as high as the national average. I believe there is a great deal of home-grown potential if we just have vision. Can our mayor appoint a commission to look into it?

In the weeks to come, I plan to pay tribute to some of the individuals and organizations like Lions Club, Kiwanis and TUAC that help to make our community such a marvelous place. Consistent with the theme of Economic Development, this week I am singling out "Sonny Barfoot", President and CEO of Bell Creek Wood Products, for being an outstanding employer and contributor to the economic life of Thomaston.

Sonny's father, George Barfoot, worked for Martha Mills in the shipping department. He happened to notice that shipments went out on pallets. In his market research, he learned that the company paid a lot for pallets that he could make at home. So, he asked the BF Goodrich and Thomaston Mills if they would be willing to buy pallets for less than they were paying to the yonder supplier. When the answer came back yes, George applied for a $30,000 loan from C&S Bank. The officers of the bank, Jack Hunter, and Curt Johnson, saw the potential and loaned him the money with no collateral. George bought the machinery and asked his friends to come by after work and put in a couple hours making these pallets. Sonny was only 12 years old at the time, but a day did not go by when he did not help make pallets. Eventually George became the exclusive supplier of pallets to the Mill as well as Federal Paper Board and Thomaston Mills. Their business took off after that.

After Jack Hunter passed away and Kurt Johnson left the bank, the bank policy at C&S became more restrictive and George believed that banks use government regulations as an excuse to approve or deny loans. Some banks will only loan money to people who don't need it. He moved their banking business to West Central Georgia Bank and established a partnership with Eddie Rogers. Sonny is proud of his record of always paying his bills and, for that matter, never being late. He is even more proud that he has never missed a payroll.

"In case you are unfamiliar with the product, a pallet, sometimes called a skid, is a platform that supports heavy goods so they can be easily hoisted by a front loader, forklift or crane. When your refrigerator or washing machine was delivered, the pine pallet is the wooden form that your appliance sat on. Well, we make more than 100,000 units per year right here in Thomaston."

In 1981, Sonny's father died of cancer, and he inherited the business when he was 23 years old and has been at the helm for more than 30 years. He confessed that he has never traveled abroad or spent a great deal of time pursuing worldly pleasures. While he has three stepchildren with wife Leigh, this business is his life. When I visited him, he was preparing for a grueling OSHA inspection.

I first met Sonny when Mac Salter took me hunting for large rocks for a rock garden I was constructing and found them on Sonny's property. In the process, I saw about eight employees hard at work, half of them white and half black happily working together making these pallets. When I asked Sonny how he developed this amazing business and harmony among his employees, he said, "Without a college education, I do what I do because a higher power is always looking down and blessing me but also holding my feet to the fire to always do the right thing. This business takes all my attention."

I also asked him if he was interested in receiving a grant to hire more people and expand his operations. He said he plans to expand but does not want any charity from anyone. He can do it himself without being answerable to others. "There is a great demand for pallets, and I could sell twice as many if I could produce them." Finally, I asked if he could start up similar business-like axe or hammer handles, novelty mailboxes, toys, or even wooden spoons. He said he tried making broom and mop sticks, but he couldn't compete. But the pallet business is still good business.

Sonny Barfoot is a remarkable and compelling individual—as they say in Thomaston, "hand slapped, and cornbread fed". He loves Thomaston and promises he will die where he was born. "What I would like to see is more industry and a great bedroom community for people who have to work elsewhere."

According to Mr. Skelton, who has been employed by Bell Creek Wood Products for 20 years, "Mr. Barfoot is a good man who gets along with everybody and is fair to his employees. We often have a good laugh together."

10.

TUAC
(Thomaston-Upson Arts Council)
Thomaston's version of the
National Endowment for the Arts

May 4, 2016

As school systems across the country reduce and eliminate funding for art and music programs, we will have to depend more and more on private funding to close the gap. As funding for the arts are often viewed as superfluous, we should be grateful to those who value its place in our lives. Where would we be without drama? It's not like we are close to Broadway where we could pop over with the family to see a show. Yes, our lives would be drab indeed without live performances and the excitement of seeing the kids have fun and showing off their talents. Whether it is painting, singing, dancing, reciting, telling a story, editing and photography, it certainly makes my heart glad to experience them.

This leads me to TUAC (Thomaston-Upson Arts Council). They absolutely deserve our support. We should all become patrons of the arts and provide creative outlets for young people. I have supported the summer program for the past three years and plan to continue making funds available to continue this cherished tradition. Thanks to the Johnnie Caldwell family, TUAC has been doing a good job bringing arts education and various performances to our community for 30 years. Think about the idle hands that were kept busy building sets, learning lighting and sound, computer imaging, logistics and coordination! According to Jamie Myrick, "math is taught when a child is playing an instrument. English is taught when a child is reading or writing a script. Critical thinking is taught when a child is analyzing art."

The mission of TUAC is to "enrich the lives of all citizens by providing the highest quality arts programming possible". Specifically, they:

1. Emphasize the performing arts series and the arts-for-children program.

2. Provide opportunities and services to local arts and arts organizations; and

3. Pursue inclusion of the arts as integral in basic education.

Here are some other benefits for supporting TUAC and the arts in general:

1. Whether you are the performer, or the audience, music and dancing improve the quality of life for everyone.

2. Education in the arts improves the overall performance of students. (There is a powerful correlation between arts education and student achievement).

3. Creates opportunities for solid friendships.

4. Engenders an atmosphere of sharing (closer ties with peers).

5. Fosters concentration, excitement for learning and promotes confidence; (Do you want your children to overcome shyness?) Students who participate in arts programs are less likely to drop out of school.

6. Learning to sing or play an instrument will elevate students' status in their communities as they join church choirs, bands, and orchestras.

7. If you can play an instrument, you will never starve. (There will always be a demand for your musical talents and skills).

Some of these students will even grow up to be famous performers and bring credit to Thomaston, the place that fostered their gifts. Finally, as children become adults, it is important for them to answer the question, "What can I do? Who am I?" It is important for everyone to tell themselves that "at least I can sing, dance, tell jokes, perform, draw, recite Hamlet, and play the guitar, the violin, the harp, the trumpet. Do you want to know a great turn-on for the opposite sex? Playing the saxophone! My roommate in college had an abundance of girls making googly eyes at him. I was so jealous! All he had to do was play his saxophone. In fact, he was popular with everyone.

While you are thinking about it, go ahead, join TUAC and send them a check. Send it to 118 S Church St # A, Thomaston, GA 30286, and plan to attend their wonderful summer extravaganza. We have a wonderful space (Upson-Lee Arts Center), let's make good use of it. Do not allow this wonderful organization to fall by the wayside. What they do could transform our community and put a song in all our hearts. Children and perhaps all of us should have access to the arts. This is soul food at its best!

11.

Heroes In Our Midst: The Four Harvey Brothers

May 11, 2016

I just finished reading *The Brothers Karamazov*, by Fyodor Dostoevsky, acclaimed as a supreme achievement in world literature. It inspired me to dedicate this week's column to The Four Harvey Brothers. Together, they have compiled over 100 years of service in the U.S. Army. I met them four years ago when I first went to play golf at Raintree and we have been friends ever since. Part of the fun is that the group of us, including Willie Bee Traylor, all play about the same level. It is extremely competitive—no one is more dedicated to the rules. We enjoy great mental and physical health in our retirement because of our dedication to our God and our golf. I am told that you can increase your chances to end up in heaven by how many rounds of golf you play.

I assigned the names of the Brothers Karamazov (in parenthesis) to each of the four of them. Oldest brother Samuel (Dmitri), born in 1946, graduated from Drake High School here in Thomaston and was sworn into the Army in 1966 and honorably discharged in 2003 with the rank of E7 having served in Vietnam. He subsequently joined the Georgia National Guard Reserve for five years. After his marriage to the former Shirley Grant, they moved to Detroit where he worked for the Department of Military Affairs for the next 33 years. His passion is his God.

Second oldest brother, Randall (Ivan), was born in 1948, attended Cunningham Junior High, Drake High School and Crawford Training School and earned his GED in 1988. He attended Upson Vocational School where he received a diploma in cooling, heating, and welding. When he couldn't get a job, he joined the Army in 1976. His tour of duty took him to Korea, Germany, England and finally relocating to Detroit as a Sergeant E5 in 1979. He worked at Ford and Chrysler on their assembly lines and eventually became a foreman for the custodial staff with "Proin Management Corporation". He returned to Thomaston and was a long-distance trucker for 12 years for Hartland Express. He finally retired in 2003. He married Rosetta in 1969 and has two daughters, Nikeetia Rutherford and Sheila Ford. According to Junior, "Having seen the world with the Army, it was a joy to return to Thomaston where people treated me like a citizen. There is no place like home." His passion is golf, Musella Lodge 381 as well as a Deacon at Salem Baptist Church.

Third brother, Curtis (Alexei) was born 1952, went to Cunningham Junior High School in Yatesville and then to Drake High School. He attended Crawford County Training School, joined the Job Corp in 1970 and the Army in 1974. The Army sent him to St. Mary High School in Colorado Springs where he received his high school diploma. He then received special training in Missouri to repair heavy equipment as well as an ammunition specialist. Part of his cross-training was as a mess sergeant. He spent three years in Germany and 18 months at Fort Carson. He left the regular Army in 1979 and joined the Georgia National Army Reserve where he stayed for 18 years. During this time, he received special training in auto mechanics and auto body repair. He then worked at Georgia Highway Department for 20 years, finally retiring in 2000. He married the former Ms. Jayne Louise Walker in 2003 and divorced in 2006 without issue. He is an active member of Salem Baptist Church, loves golf and fishing. "Thomaston is a nice place for living".

Youngest brother Calvin, (Pavel) was born in 1954 and attended Yatesville High and joined the Georgia National Guard in 1976 where he stayed for two years. At the invitation of two of his brothers, he went to live in Detroit in 1979 and transferred to the Michigan National Guard. His day job in Detroit was smoking "Honey Baked" hams. The Army then assigned him to the Department of Defense where he worked for 29 years until his retirement in 2006 as a corporal. He worked for the inspection team specializing in hazardous materials. He married Celotis Nixon in 1994 but divorced in 1998 without issue. His passion is golf. "Thomaston is OK. You can make a life for yourself here."

It is remarkable that these four men were all inspired to serve their country. I am certainly in their debt as I am for all who put their lives on the line to preserve our American way of life. Like Dostoevsky, I may write their story someday.

Both parents (Randolph and Hattie Lee Fagan-Harvey) were very religious and strong disciplinarians who taught their sons the value of hard work. They worked hard so their children would enjoy a better life.

I am hoping that the VFW and the other Veterans organizations also reach out to these men as well. They have a lot to offer our community.

12.

Seven Steps to a Lifetime of Good Health

May 18, 2016

I read fellow columnist Bob Tribble's article last week and I believe we should be mindful of his messages:

- Even with a sharp decline over the past 20 years, each year, half of all deaths are cardiovascular related (heart attack, heart failure, strokes).
- Learn to recognize the signs and symptoms of a heart attack.
- The sooner you get to a source of care after the onset of chest pain, the better your chances of survival.
- I am adding a fourth caution, if you are having chest pain, do not drive your own automobile as there is a chance that you will black out before reaching the hospital.

While Bob believes that surviving a heart attack is the key to survival which is important, I have been preaching, cajoling, pleading, and begging everyone with whom I come in contract that "prevention" is the real key. The most important lesson we have learned over the past 20 years is that cardiovascular disease is preventable for 90% of us.

A risk factor is like running a stop sign. You may get away with it, but you increase your risk of an accident. A grandmother once told me that she couldn't buy her blood pressure pills because her granddaughter needed shoes. When you board an airplane, you are advised that, in case of emergency, put the oxygen mask on yourself first and then take care of others. If you are unable to function, you will not be able to take care of people who depend on you. Even the heart pumps blood to itself before sending it to the rest of your body. If you have scarce resources, buy the pills instead of the shoes.

The reason women have less heart disease is because they have fewer risk factors. As Dr. Salim Usef says with great passion, "If women live like men, they will die like men". In other words, if they smoke, don't exercise, and lead stressful lives, they will die at the same rate and from the same diseases as men. The reason women have more wealth than men is because husbands usually die first.

By promoting my "Seven Steps to Good Health" to your family and friends, you can live with the confidence that heart disease will not interfere with the quality of your life. You can't live forever, but you can dramatically reduce the chances that heart disease will be the cause of your demise. Helping our grandparents and our children live long productive lives depends on a radical shift toward prevention. It is never too early or too late to adopt a healthy lifestyle. The earlier children adopt these steps, the greater will be their chances of living to 100 years old. That is now a realistic goal!

1. **Be spiritually active.** Humans are spiritual beings. Meditation, prayers, joking and laughing, holding a grandchild, being in love, spending time with family and friends are uplifting and important for our spiritual development. We are almost required to continually feed our six senses— seeing, hearing, tasting, smelling, feeling, as well as our penchant to appreciate the beauty (our sixth sense) that is all around us including a sunrise or sunset, waterfalls and all the art and beauty of man and nature. Traveling, having adventures, visiting museums, star gazing, creating, listening to music or even the rustle of leaves should be a part of every child's experience. In addition, an important study from the University of Texas tells us that people, who attend church regularly, live seven to fourteen years longer than those who do not go to church. Apparently, the fellowship, good will, meditation, inspirational words and singing together increase our ability to cope. According to Dr. Malcolm Taylor, "If you have

God, family and friends, you may stumble, but you will never hit the ground."

2. **Take charge of your blood pressure.** Despite steady progress over the past 33 years, uncontrolled high blood pressure is projected to increase by 60% over the next 20 years. Tell your doctor you want to keep your blood pressure as close to goal (120/80 mm Hg) as possible.

3. **Control your cholesterol.** Keep your HDL high and your LDL low and total cholesterol low. High cholesterol leads to plaque, which restricts the flow of blood. Diet, exercise, and statin therapy are the keys to maintaining healthy cholesterol levels.

4. **Track your blood sugar and maintain ideal weight.** Obesity and diabetes track each other. As the rate of obesity goes up, so does diabetes. If you are overweight, you run a high risk of developing diabetes which increases your risk of heart attacks, strokes, blindness, amputations, and impotence. Why must sugar and fats accompany every expression of love and every celebration? Is it possible to have a birthday party, a wedding, or an anniversary party without a cake? By reducing obesity, we are taking a swing at diabetes. Three out of four diabetics will die from heart disease and stroke. If you experience fatigue, blurred vision, excessive thirst, frequent urination, unexplained weight loss and non-healing wounds and sores, consult a doctor immediately.

5. **Enjoy regular exercise** (60 minutes per day-every day), follow a sensible diet, and get a good night's sleep! Move those muscles. Increase your intake of fruits and vegetables, reduce fats and sugars, but most of all, eat less. Every little bit you do can either help or hurt your health a little bit. Don't be a fat maker by insisting that your kids "eat up" what they don't need and resist being a victim of a fat maker. Let's be more creative about demonstrating love for each other than to force feed the ones you most care about. If you don't sleep well, get a sleep study, and then follow your doctor's advice.

6. **Don't smoke.** Smoking is our most preventable cause of premature death. Nobody argues with this anymore, not even the smokers. Smoking constricts the arteries, increases carbon monoxide, lowers the good cholesterol, and is the primary cause of lung cancer. According to Benjamin Waterhouse (1754-1846): "Tobacco is a filthy weed, that from the devil

does proceed, it drains your purse, it burns your clothes, and makes a chimney of your nose."

7. **Access better health care.** Get a check-up and faithfully take your medication as prescribed. It is no longer acceptable for the most vulnerable among us to receive the worst care. Just because some of us are poor does not mean that we should be relegated to poor care. All members of society deserve to receive effective and respectful health care. More importantly, it does no good for you to be evaluated by a physician, have your condition diagnosed and medication prescribed if you do not then fill the prescription and take it as directed.

Being proactive about your health can add 10 more years to enjoy the company of our grandchildren and help guide them to lead happy, healthy, and productive lives. The nursery rhyme about *Humpty Dumpty* is illustrative of those who lazily sit on walls only to have great falls and heart attacks that no physician, no matter how skillful, can put together again. If Humpty was not sitting around watching television and playing video games, his risks of heart disease would have been reduced. We can take an important message from this nursery rhyme by understanding that no matter how good our reactive plans in medicine and surgery may be, it will never be as good as prevention. A good doctor cures disease, a really great doctor also prevents disease. If you are sick, you are not making money, you are spending it. Healthy people are much more likely to be wealthy people.

13.

One Man's Journey: The Alton Harris Story

May 25, 2016

This week, I wish to share one of the presentations at the Thomaston Kiwanis. I will not only invite you to a free lunch, but you are also welcomed to join us to listen to 20 minute (TED) talks on a variety of subjects. It is always enlightening.

Here was my introduction:

Our speaker of the hour is Mr. Alton Harris. I met him because his wife works for us at ZÖe Pediatrics. In talking with them, I was so impressed with what he had to say, I invited him to share what it was like for a black family living in Thomaston and working for Thomaston Mills in the 60s,70s and 80s. I've been trying to immerse myself in all the history I can from reading and talking with people in the know. I want to be informed as I write my weekly columns for *The Beacon*. Mr. Harris is 65 years old and has lived in Thomaston all his life.

Here is Mr. Alton Harris' speech:

I would like to thank Dr. Kong for inviting me to speak to you. I started at Thomaston Mills when I was 17. When I told my dad about the job, he was not happy and told me: "Boy, I want you to get an education. Don't cheat yourself." I responded, "Dad, don't worry. I will be alright." I started as a loom cleaner. Well, when I came home after my shift, my dad would want to know why I am so dirty. When I got my first paycheck it was $41 for the week. Mobility was important to me so when I figured it up and realized that I could now afford a car, I went out and bought a 1968 Ford on credit.

In a year, I went from a loom cleaner to a 'cloth dafer' and made five cents more per hour. In another six months I was moved up to a tiling helper. I felt proud of my progress and found this beautiful woman who I fell in love with and got married in 1971. We had our first child that same year and we have been together for 45 years.

In 1979, Mr. Chuck Store, the department manager of the weaver/slasher department told me: "Alton, I heard you were doing some crazy stuff down in the slasher room." What he meant was that when my shift supervisor, Mr. Ralph Black, left for the day, I would do the unthinkable and tried to run the machine even though I didn't know what I was doing. If no one was going to teach me, I was going to learn by doing. To be honest, I would start the slasher up and try to run it, I'm sorry, but I made a lot of bad yarn. So, Mr. Black told me: "You are a good worker but if you keep this up, I'm going to have to let you go." I told him: "When I walked into the department, I checked out the pay board and I saw that a slasher made a lot more than a sweeper. I want to be a Slasherman. So, Mr. Black said: "But you are not trained." I responded: "Then train me." So, he said: "What are you after?" and I said, "I want your job." He said, "Forget about that, you're not getting my job." Two and a half years later, I got the slasher operator job and became the shift foreman.

When Mr. Black got sick and had to retire, he recommended me, of all people, to take his place adding that I was already doing his work without his advice or consent. Mr. Grey asked: "Was he messing it up?" and Mr. Black (bless his soul) said: "Naw, he was doing it better than me." So, I did get Mr. Black's job after all. I believed it when my dad told me: "When you go out there in the world and get a job, be the best and don't let anyone tell you that you can't." I want to thank Mr. Black and the company for putting enough trust in me, to promote me from floor cleaner to supervisor. During the entire time, no one ever called me demeaning names or treated me harshly. I look back at my time with the Mill with great gratitude.

I must tell you this story. The friendliest guy at the Mill was Mr. George Hightower. He came through the plant at Christmas, shaking hands, wishing everyone a Merry Christmas. As he came into my department, there was some water on the floor. He slipped and cracked his head and back. Everyone was telling me that I was going to get fired. So, I was nervous and asked Mr. Black if I still had a job and he said, "Yes, as far as I know so let's go do inventory." Mr. George personally came to me all bandaged up, shook my hand, and told me: "It was entirely my fault, so don't you worry about it."

I was so relieved and then the next week I was actually promoted to department manager reporting to Mr. Russel Kellett. And if you know Mr. Kellett, he didn't let anyone get away with anything. He said: "You are the luckiest man in the world, you almost killed the president, and you get a promotion." So, I started plotting how to trip Mr. George again (just joking).

A few years later, Mr. Kellett, put his arm around my shoulders and said: "Alton, you are the best slasher man I ever had." Thomaston Mills also paid for my classes at Upson Tech and Georgia Tech.

I thank Thomaston Mills for giving me the wherewithal to take care of my family. I put two daughters through school. One of them has a master's in business from Mercer. My other daughter also has a degree in business from Gordon. I am testimony that Thomaston Mills took care of their employees and this community without prejudice. They treated everyone fairly. Compared to the brutal things that were going on in the rest of the country and even throughout Georgia, Thomaston was and is an exceptional place. Many employees didn't realize how good they had it until the doors closed.

The Hightowers are fine people. I hold in my hand a picture of Mrs. Annie Hightower. She's standing here at the altar of St. Mary AME Church. She would donate money to Saint Mary's every year during Christmas. If you go by Saint Mary, our education building came about because of the Hightowers. I sent Mr. Neal Hightower a letter saying we were trying to renovate the church and he generously contributed over $20,000.

In closing, I want to thank you again for allowing me to give you just a snippet of what this town has done for my family and what Thomaston Mills did for this community.

14.

And Yet We Rise

June 1, 2016

I just finished watching an inspired tennis match at Roland Garros (French Open) between Serena Williams and Teliana Pereira of Brazil. I found Pereira's rise to tennis greatness inspiring. It turns out that she grew up in severe poverty, in a mud hut, while her father worked as a janitor at a tennis camp. She loved to accompany him to work not only to help him empty the garbage, but to have the rare opportunity to play tennis. She fell in love with the game and found out that even without lessons and "borrowed" equipment, she could beat the pampered girls.

Eventually, she beat all the tennis pros in Brazil and with a win-loss record of 21-5 in professional tennis, (in 2015), she became the first Brazilian woman to win a World Tennis Association title. So, what's the difference between a janitor and a doctor, lawyer or professional tennis star? The answer is, "One generation!" It is also true that a doctor, lawyer, or tennis professional can produce criminals, drug addicts and under-achievers in the next generation.

So, I believe Maya Angelou said it best in her poem, "And Still I Rise"

You may shoot me with your words,

You may cut me with your eyes,

You may kill me with your hatefulness,

But still, like air, I'll rise.

My own father abandoned us when I was four years old. My mother deposited my brother and me with her mother and migrated to the United States, where she married, and started a new family. So, when I was 12 years old, if you had put both my mother and father in a police line-up, I would not have recognized either one of them. I have come this far by faith.

I did not read a book until I was 13 years old. I attended a one-room schoolhouse in the countryside of Jamaica. The elementary school I attended had no library and we did our work on "slates" that we washed after each exercise.

I joined my mother and her new family in the United States when I was 15 years old in 1959. Like a good Jamaican boy, I set a high school track record which helped a great deal with my transition and adjustment—especially with earning a scholarship to college. I would eventually earn a doctorate in psychology as well as become a lawyer.

In my first year of law school, as a history buff, I took an elective course on the "History of the Law". As the professor walked into our first class, he addressed us in Latin. If that was not intimidating enough, several students responded in Latin and the conversation continued between them for about three minutes. I felt completely out of place and wondered if I had made the wrong decision to pursue a law degree.

It got worse. As the professor discussed the various places around the world, books, tapestries and artifacts relating to origins of the law, there were always students who had been there and had firsthand knowledge. The only contribution to the discussion I could make had to do with the "Ten Commandments." Many of my fellow students not only had parents who were lawyers but had traveled extensively and attended the best schools and universities before studying the law. How was I to compete?

Well, I probably had to work harder, but I graduated and passed the Bar exam on my first attempt. The predictable formula for producing great students is to start with good genes, expose them to all the fields of human endeavor (music, art, literature, mathematics, science, geography, and history) take them on trips around the world so they see, feel and learn about other languages and cultures and give them good role models in a competitive environment.

But often, through ambition, hard work, a lot of help from teachers and mentors, students who lack all the above exceed the expectations of their communities and themselves. Don't give up on them. In the end, the harder the struggle, the sweeter the victory!

Like Pereira, the Williams Sisters came from the worst part of Los Angeles. Their father read a book about tennis and taught his daughters to play even if he could not play himself. They became world beaters. Serena is the best woman tennis professional in the entire world.

Do we have some of this greatness in Thomaston waiting to be nurtured?

15.

Good Neighbors Enrich Our Lives

June 8, 2016

Eleven years ago, a classmate from college (a foreign student) who had subsequently become a lawyer invited me to accompany him for a visit to his Tribal Village in Cameroon (Africa) and it was absolutely memorable. As the four of us drove into the small village, the children lined the street, waving tree branches and singing songs of welcome to their favorite son who had done good. They beamed with pride.

When we arrived, we were escorted to a reception hall, where the chiefs and elders in their finest robes were waiting. After offering us beer and palm wine, the Chief enthusiastically shouted, "Welcome Home", laughed heartily with his arms extended as if to embrace us all. The other village elders then individually shook hands with all of us and made us official members of their tribe (Tikar people). We were led into another room for a feast. Starting with peanut soup, we dined on barbecued beef kebabs, roast fish, curry chicken, crocodile, rice, yam, cassava, and bitter leaf greens. After we were all full and satisfied, we were offered honored seats for the show. The drummers and dancers took over for a really awesome performance. I didn't need an invitation to join the dancers to great applause.

Each time I visit my own village (Woodlands) in Jamaica, people are genuinely happy to welcome me back, eagerly reminding me of the role they played in raising me. I laugh with vigor as they hug and remind me about what I was like as a "little man". I indulge myself with whatever they offer, even if it was just a glass of water, but most often it was a drink of rum, carrot juice, sorrel, lemonade made with sour orange and fruits from the trees in their yard. As I go visiting from one house to the next, my teeth are never idle. So much food is offered, I worried that I was leaving a famine in my wake. And then on Sunday, I was asked to give an account of myself to the congregation from the pulpit. Among other things, I reminded them that the lessons they taught me served me well as I made my way through life. Even though I had to use a lot of imagination to remember the grove of trees from the remaining stumps, I felt completely at home.

Then five years ago, I was traveling through India with a group of 50 physicians visiting hospitals and learning about their culture. When we arrived in Jaipur, the capital of Rajasthan in Northern India, we were impressed that as our bus drove up to one of their palaces, they had covered the road to the entrance with marigolds. It was quite a sight! As we stopped, we were greeted by soldiers dressed in colorful uniforms on horseback, and then more soldiers on elephants and various other entertainers, musicians, dancers, and jugglers performing various acts as would be typical of a fair. I was particularly impressed with the man dressed like a horse.

We were then led to the food and what a feast it was! There were five food stations where chefs were ready to prepare whatever our hearts desired. In the background by the pool, a sitar-player played beautiful melodies during lunch. If that was not enough, after lunch, we were invited to play Elephant Polo. We were hoisted onto these huge animals and given long polo sticks as we tried to hit soccer balls into the goal. While we had difficulty making contact with the ball, the trained elephants helped us out by kicking the ball with their front legs. Goal! What a welcome!

In any case, my point is that here in Thomaston, when families visit, or when new people move to town, we may get a handshake or even a hug. We may even have a special dinner or welcome reception. Is it enough? We have had some absolutely wonderful people who will enrich our community moving here in the past few months, they include Tripp Penn, CEO of Upson Regional Medical Center; Mike

Richardson, Police Chief; Russell E. Thompson, Manager, City of Thomaston; Dr. Linda Gordon, (Pediatrician) and Dr. Nancy Butler (Ear, Nose and Throat).

Students and soldiers who have been away want assurance that they are with family who love and take pride in what they are doing. Newcomers want a tour and learn about our history and culture. Is there a welcome committee to visit and showcase what we have to offer? They are eager to find out about restaurants, hair stylists and banks. Do we even give them gifts of welcome and friendship?

When I moved here almost five years ago, I would have appreciated certificates for a chicken salad sandwich on rye from Country Cupboard, cookies from the Bake Shop, strawberry ice cream from the Rock Ranch, a car wash from Mike's or the WAVE, a round of golf at Raintree and a pass to the health club.

It doesn't take much effort to say, "You are welcome! *Mi casa es su casa!*"

16.
We Have Good Schools in Thomaston

June 15, 2016

Ever since I moved to Thomaston almost five years ago, I have heard that "Upson County has a horrible school system and Pike County is much better". I heard it so much that I began repeating it and even ill-advised one of our providers to buy a house in Pike County under the assumption that her children would have access to a better education.

I recently had the opportunity to tour all of our schools with Superintendent Maggie Shook (winner of the Georgia School Superintendents Association Bill Barr Leadership Award) as well as read the reports put out by various State agencies. It turned out that out of eight school systems comprising the Griffin Regional Education Service Agency (RESA), Thomaston-Upson ranked second on the "College and Career Ready Performance Index". Fayette County was the only school system that scored higher. Pike County ranked 4th and Lamar was 8th. Our graduation rate is an outstanding 85%. If you don't believe that is impressive, the rate in Atlanta is about 50%. Like the children that live around "Lake Wabigoon", all the indicators were above average. That is not bad folks. We actually have a school system we can be proud of. Let's sing it from the rafters. Let's stop perpetuating myths.

While we do not have 3D printers or a "Maker Space" for our kids to experiment, we have a one-to-one student to computer ratio. Please be assured that our students are not being left behind in the technology revolution. We are doing a lot with our computer/internet tutoring. I was most impressed with the inventiveness of the students in the high school class we attended.

All of our buildings are state-of-the-art, well designed and constructed as well as pleasant to the eye. There is not a dilapidated building anywhere on our campuses. Our playgrounds are functional and actually extremely well designed. We have a Fine Arts Center that opened a few years ago that is a state-of-the-art 900 seat facility that is serving our community and our students extremely well. I have attended several functions in the building and am delighted with both the function and its expression. It is a marvel.

On our superintendent's tour, I was particularly impressed with the various strategies being implemented at Upson-Lee South Elementary. Dr. LaSharon McClain, the principal, is a terrific leader. Her innovations are far reaching, and she has created an exciting learning environment. I saw pods of students seated in crescent shaped clusters facing the teacher. When the student's attention wanders, as they are prone to do, the teacher is able to touch the student and bring back his focus.

Now that I am convinced that we have a very good school system, I asked an acquaintance, Bob, "What do you think of our school system?" He answered, "I think it's horrible. As a taxpayer, we deserve better." "How did you come to that conclusion Bob?" I asked. "I judge them from how the kids that graduate perform on jobs and what they know. When I asked a few of them what time it is in California, the capital of NY, does the Sun revolve around the earth or does the earth revolve around the sun and what percent of the world's population lives in the United States? They have no clue. So, what does that say about the schools that graduate them?" I said, "Bob, you have a point, but compared to what? Maybe no high school student could answer your questions."

I have seen the light from my own observation as well as official, objective data and our students perform well above average. Coleman Kilby, for example, graduated from Upson-Lee High School this year. As the salutatorian, he gave an incredible speech to his classmates reinforcing the idea that it takes a village, and the students should always be grateful to the mentors in their lives. He won literature awards for four years, lettered in Cross-Country and won third place in a statewide science fair. He was also elected senior favorite and Prom King. He will be attending Swarthmore College on an academic scholarship. Our high school seniors received 53 scholarships, 48 were academic and five for sports. Montana Schug received a $96,000 scholarship to Denison University; Stensen Jordan received a $92,000 scholarship to Morehouse; Charlie Huff received an $80,000 scholarship to Mercer University. Over 100 will be eligible for the HOPE scholarship as they enter college this Fall.

Here is my only problem: When I walk the halls of our schools, you cannot miss the trophy cases full of awards honoring our heroes on various fields of battle—football, basketball, baseball, track and field, etc. I found nothing honoring our scholars. It turns out that when our scholars excel, they are given a piece of paper (certificates and plaques that they take home). Can we also have a display case in celebration of academic achievement? We need role models. I asked about the entertainers, writers, lawyers, doctors, religious leaders and all the graduates who excelled in their field. No one I asked could tell me their names but those who excelled in sports are generally known. Can we pay as much attention to academics as we do to sports?

Please be assured that our school system is diligently trying to provide a publicly funded education for every child within Upson County regardless of race, educational attainment, social class, family income, special needs, or personal characteristics. I believe the School Board, Dr. Shook, other administrators, and teachers provide quality education, adhering to statewide standards for teacher qualifications and other operational requirements, designed to provide ALL our students a safe and effective learning environment. You are doing God's work and doing it well. On behalf of the "Village," thank you!

Finally, the tour that Dr. Shook hosted is available to everyone. Just call and they will arrange it for you.

17.
Let Freedom Ring!

June 22, 2016

According to Wikipedia, Georgia under Governor James Oglethorpe was the only one of the original 13 British colonies to have banned slavery in 1735. It was reintroduced in 1751 by Royal Decree and with free labor, the invention of the cotton gin and fertile lands, the economy in Upson County, especially around Flint River, prospered for the next hundred years.

Upson County was founded in 1824. The City of Thomaston (a large producer of moonshine, mules, cotton, wheat, corn, cows, and pigs) came into being in 1825 as the seat of the county. By 1886, became (according to Penny Cliff), "one of the 100 Best Small Towns in America offering slow-paced Southern charm and hospitality."

President Lincoln signed the *Emancipation Proclamation* on Jan. 1, 1863, freeing all slaves, but as his authority did not extend to the Confederate States, there was a conspiracy to keep this information from the slaves and continue business as usual. As part of the Union Army's scorched earth policy to lay siege to the rebellious South, Wilson's Raiders Calvary coming up from Columbus burned almost everything in their path (the mills, all the agriculture, Double Churches Bridge and the railroad) reaching Thomaston on April 18, 1865. As the Union Army continued to Macon, on May 29, the plantation owners assembled their slaves around the courthouse and proclaimed that slavery was abolished. They were all free to go, wherever they liked, or stay on as sharecroppers.

General Lee surrendered on April 9, 1965, and with the Civil War settled, on July 13, Governor James Johnson made a public proclamation that "slavery is extinct, and involuntary servitude no longer exists in Georgia." In Texas, the word did not get to the slaves until June 19, 1965, so Freedom Day is celebrated as "Juneteenth" each year.

On the 29th of May 1866, the emancipated slaves in Thomaston, commemorated the occasion and started the tradition of an Emancipation Celebration that has continued unbroken for 150 years. The son of ex-slave and wealthy saddle-maker, (Mr. Guilford Speer), Mr. William Guilford is considered the visionary who organized the first emancipation celebration on May 29, 1866 until he left Thomaston in 1905. With the support of the city fathers and the community each year, Thomaston distinguishes itself by having the largest and longest running Emancipation Day Celebrations in these United States. And yes, it is celebrated each year on the Saturday before Memorial Day, and it is spectacular! It's a day of great celebration and family reunion when all past residents are expected back. Tents are pitched, fans are hooked up, horseshoe stakes are hammered into the ground 10 paces apart, card games are organized, the grill is lighted and kept going all day, grilling hot dogs, hamburgers, sausages, chicken, and steaks. Coolers are put out and everyone who stops by is offered libation of one sort or another. Everyone is in such high spirits and generous that it feels like Christmas in May!

The big parade starts on Bethel Street and ends at Lincoln Park and includes "Floats, horses, show cars, recreational vehicles and marching bands from Upson Lee High School, South Clayton High School, Greenville High School and Evans High School from Macon." Festivities are organized in each church making May 28, a day of music, prayers, speeches as well as the reading of the Emancipation Proclamation.

If you wish to participate, support, or contribute to next year's event, please call Rev. James McGill, 706-741-4068.

18.
Rev. Albert Simmons: A Searcher of Truth and a Believer in Simple Generosity

July 6, 2016

The Right Rev. Al Simmons is neither the famous baseball player nor the CEO of the Springfield Nuclear Power Plant (The Simpsons). He is the most lovable, erudite raconteur and generous spirit from the Highlands. Yes, even though he was born at Ft. McPherson in East Point, his grandmother was a "Fleming" from the Murray Clan, and you can readily get his attention with the sound of bagpipes. He wouldn't tell me what he wears under his Regal Kilts when he is in full dress attending the Highland Games in Culloden.

I once introduced Rev. Al Simmons as someone who had never attended a wedding where he was not the bride or a funeral where he was not the corpse. As unflattering as that sounds, I did not mean that he is egotistical or attention seeking. What he is, is a charismatic gentleman who always attracts attention because of the force of his confident personality and his infectious charm (when he wants to be).

As a very wise gentleman, wherever he shows up (at breakfast with the old guys at the Tasty Shoppe Café each morning; Kiwanis meetings Tuesdays; The Silver Circle on Wednesday afternoons, dinner at Aviano's with friends Desmond and Christy Dobbs on Wednesdays; the Family Supper Night on Fridays and definitely at church on Sundays) we are magnetically attracted to him and seek his insights and wisdom.

Personally, my soul is richer with every moment I spend in his company. I will also confess that there is a jockeying between Ruth, Linda, Ed, Tom, James and myself as to who will sit beside him, but I think he prefers the company of the women. When I moved to Thomaston five years ago, he was a neighbor and at his invitation, visited First Presbyterian but we became more acquainted when I became a fellow Kiwanian where he has been a member for 35 years.

If you tell him that it is good to see him, he will tell you that it is much better to be seen than viewed. He also believes that it is perfectly OK to eat your desert first as Jesus is coming. And this old chestnut, "Life is not a destiny after all, it is a journey." He also told me that no one wants to be 88 years old except when they reach 87. Such is the wisdom you would encounter if you read his columns in the *Thomaston Times*. For a very long time, he waxed eloquently on religious topics until he was switched to the opinion page. I had the opportunity to read some of his rants and they were always provocative.

He answered the call to become a presbyterian minister when he came under the influence of Rev. Charles Cowsert, who is now 100 years old. He idolized his mentor who once served apricot brandy for communion because he couldn't find the wine. Rev. Cowsert was very practical and spoke out boldly on social issues that occasionally got the ire of his congregants.

He met the love of his life (Mary Jean) at Union Theological Seminary in Richmond. After they married, she taught piano in their home wherever they lived. She directed the choirs and played the organ while her husband preached. He readily admitted that she was his better half. She was much better educated and talented than him and he encouraged all men to marry up. She is remembered for starting up the Thomaston Upson Arts Council (TUAC) along with Kay Hightower, and the Annual Choir Festival that unfortunately is no more due to her untimely death. Rev. Al and his wife have had a profound influence on Thomaston. If they did not come to Thomaston there would probably not be a Wellness Center at the hospital, soccer in our schools, a First-Generation Park, our Civic Center or the Performance and Art Center. As the first president of SPLOST, they developed a bucket list that has just about been accomplished.

Having been singled out to receive the honor of volunteer of the year by the Thomaston Chamber of Commerce, I don't believe Dr. Al ever said no to a genuine request. He is one of those people who would qualify for the description, "generous to a fault". Whatever the initiative is at Kiwanis, he is always the first to raise his hand and volunteer his funds. When I wanted to raise money for Rev. Secrecy's summer program, up went his hand with the first pledge. A generous soul. His mission in life is simple generosity and the uplifting of people, particularly people who can never repay him—always giving more than is prudent and taking less than he needs.

According to Rev. Al:

> Thomaston is a jewel and I love living here. It is a nice, pleasant community. My experience is that people care about each other here. However, we need jobs. Due to the shrinking of the middle class, trouble may be brewing if we don't bring industry here. Another alternative may be to attract more retired people to town. The nice but unemployed people can be offered to people who need to be looked after. With an aging population and the dramatic increase in Alzheimer's and other diseases of the old, we should jump on caring for them like a turkey on a June bug.

Each time my grandchildren come to visit and leave me worn out; I recite a poem Dr. Al taught me:

> I have seen the lights of Paris, But the lights I like best of all
> I have seen the lights of Rome. are the taillights of my grandchildren
>   going home.

As Rev. Al is 87 years old, the one request I would make is, "Rev. Al, please give up driving. I would be happy to be one of an army of people who would welcome the opportunity to take you places."

19.
Sweet Tea: A Southern Tradition

July 13, 2016

I was in the Thomaston Post Office recently and saw a woman wearing a T-shirt that read, "If sweet tea won't solve it, you have a problem." I laughed a little hysterically and got her attention. She said, "Whatever the question may be the answer is sweet tea." Then it occurred to me that since I moved to Thomaston five years ago, I not only added words like "that's a gooden", "How's your mama an 'em" and always "fixing" to do something or go somewhere and consuming gallons of sweet tea. I used to be a "gin and tonic" type of guy and even when I drank tea, it was unsweetened and hot. Now I drink frosty bottles and glasses of sweet tea and find it refreshing. Willie B Traylor always brings me a large bottle of Arizona brand sweet tea in his cooler. When I really want a treat, I add spearmint. Someone recommended that I add a shot of bourbon, but it detracted from the value and flavor of the tea. Mike Jones observed that at Kiwanis lunch meetings, "I see you always sit with a glass of sweet tea."

While there are lots of recipes, my favorite is "sun tea": Place six tea bags in a pitcher of cold water and place the pitcher on a windowsill in the hot sun for about four hours. When the water turns nice and brown, add a cup of sugar and several sprigs of mint or a spritz of lime, let it sit until it is cool and then place it into your refrigerator for guests or not. You may want to pour it over ice and enjoy it yourself. If you are up North and sweet tea is not on the menu, do not commit the SIN of just adding sugar, or worse, Splenda to hot water and Lipton. That is a good way to lose your spot in heaven.

If you dine in a Thai restaurant, you will notice that they serve "Thai iced tea". All you get is added sweet milk or sweetened condensed milk. The Arnold Palmer, by the way, is a mixing of two Southern favorites, equal parts lemonade, and sweet tea. Here are the rules of sweet tea:

    1. Sugar, syrup, or honey must be added while the tea is hot (a cup of sugar for each gallon), never after ice is added. Sugar dissolves poorly in cold liquids. This is one of the definite ways you can distinguish someone who is not

from the South. The other way to identify someone from up North is if they call lightning bugs "fireflies" or order "a grit" for breakfast.

2. The glass must be sweating before it is brought to your lips.

3. During the summer, it is against the law of Southern hospitality not to have a large pitcher of sweet tea chilling in your refrigerator to offer thirsty visitors.

4. While Arizona and Snapple brands are fine, sweet tea is never made with powder, stirred, or shaken.

According to Wikipedia:

The oldest known recipe for sweet iced tea was published in 1879 in a community cookbook called *Housekeeping in Old Virginia* by Marion Cabell Tyree, who was born in Texas... Sweet tea was once consumed as a punch mixed with hard liquor with flavorings of mint and cream, with mint julep being a close version of the punch drink with its similar ingredients...In 2003, supposedly as an April Fool's joke, the Georgia House introduced a Bill making it a "...misdemeanor of a high and aggravated nature" to sell iced tea in a restaurant that did not also offer sweet iced tea on the menu.

According to @LaurieSue:

Since so many of the early settlers of the South came from England and Ireland, the tradition of strong black tea came along with them. The heat and humidity of that region led to icing it. The ice was cut from the northern lakes in winter and shipped down in straw, then stored in ice houses which were often built sort of a berm to keep the hot outside temps from melting the ice.

Even before our country was unified, sweet tea brought us closer together. In the words of a woman known for her sweet words:

"Sweet tea is the house wine of the South" (Dolly Parton, *Steel Magnolias*).

20.
Freemasons Among Us

July 20, 2016

For the past 500 years, the Masons, otherwise known as Freemasons, have been shrouded in mystery because we pride ourselves in our secrets and as nature abhors a vacuum, there has been a great deal of speculation about our history, our rituals, and our practices. In the age of Google, not much is secret anymore. But this is nothing new. Information has always been readily available. Leo Tolstoy wrote arguably the greatest novel ever in 1865. According to a review by *Encyclopedia Britannica:* "No single English novel attains the universality of Leo Tolstoy's *War and Peace.*" I am giving you this background because, through one of his characters, (Pierre) revealed (in great detail) his introduction to Freemasonry, his initiation, and its impact on his life. I will not add much to his eloquent presentation as follows: "It is the teaching of Christianity freed from the bonds of State and Church, a teaching of equality, brotherhood, and love."

During the initiation ceremony, Pierre was admonished to:

> fly to a brother's aid whoever he may be, exhort him who goeth astray, raise him that falleth, never bear malice or enmity toward thy brother. Be kindly and courteous. Kindle in all hearts the flame of virtue. Share thy happiness with thy neighbor; and may envy never dim the purity of that bliss. Forgive thy enemy; do not avenge thyself except by doing him good. Thus, fulfilling the highest law, thou shall regain traces of the ancient dignity which thou have lost."

The Rector returned to inform the seeker of the seven virtues, corresponding to the seven steps of Solomon's temple, which every Freemason should cultivate in himself:

> (1) discretion, the keeping of the secrets of the Order; (2) Obedience to those of higher ranks in the order; (3) Morality; (4) Love of mankind; (5) Courage; (6) generosity; and (7) the love of death. In the seventh place, try, by the frequent thoughts of death to bring yourself to regard it not as a dreaded foe, but as a friend that frees the soul grown weary in the labors of virtue from this distressful life, and leads it to its place of recompense and peace.

Pierre tried to fathom the significance of the Square, one side of which symbolized God, another symbolized moral things, the third side, physical things, and the fourth a combination of these" and committed to giving all he encountered a square deal. After Pierre was initiated as a mason, coming from the darkness into the light and reborn to a new life, "something that was slumbering, something that was best within him, suddenly awoke, joyful and youthful in his soul. It immediately changed him, and he developed a new plan for his life. He sent for all his stewards to the head office and explained to them his intentions and wishes. He told them the steps would be taken immediately to free his serfs—until then, they were not to be over-burdened with labor, women while nursing their babies were not to be sent to work, assistance was to be given to the serfs, punishments were to be admonished… and hospitals, asylums, and schools were to be established."

Tolstoy writes:

> Freemasonry is the best expression of the best, the eternal aspects of humanity—the fraternity and equality of men who have virtuous aims… what does harm to another is wrong.

There are Masonic lodges in practically every town and hamlet throughout the world whose members take their oaths seriously. We often find each other in the most unlikely places.

The point is that in the tradition of Benjamin Franklin, John Hancock, Thomas Jefferson, Thomas Paine, Paul Revere, Daniel Webster, and George Washington, we are fortunate to have Masons in our community (both black and white), men of honor who have an unshakable belief in the power of reason, dedicated to brotherly love and equality and who aspire to do good without the expectation of a reward. Yes, we are known for our generosity, as we find enjoyment in giving, and remedying injustice is the only sure happiness.

21.
Meet An Amazing Young Man: Will Hernandez

July 27, 2016

Every trip I take to the golf course is an adventure. It was late in the afternoon last Wednesday and feeling a little unsettled, I decided to play a little golf to relax. It works every time! I made my way to Raintree and as I approached the first tee, I saw a young man about 16 years old ready to tee off. Upon seeing my approach, he invited me to go ahead of him or play together. "I already played and just wanted to work on some things." As I prefer not to play by myself, I accepted his invitation to play together, and it turned out to be one of the most entertaining nine holes I have played in a long time.

"I am Will Hernandez, and I am on the golf team at Upson-Lee High School," he said. We shook hands as I introduced myself. He responded, "Yes. I know about ZÖe Pediatrics. Nice meeting you." I immediately thought, "What a polite young man! They raise them right in Thomaston."

First of all, he drove the first green from the back tees (300 yards). I hit one of my best drives and was about 100 yards short. I was amazed at the skill and maturity of this young gentleman as he proceeded to score four under par (32) to my 44. He would have had to give me more than a stroke per hole for me to have a chance against him. I found no weaknesses in his game. As much as I (the older, wiser golfer, the student of 100 golf lessons) wanted to offer him some advice, I found nothing to improve. I was even impressed that he dutifully helped me find my wayward drives and took off his hat before shaking my hand at the end of our round. He could bomb it, his pitches and chips went the right distances and reading the greens were spot on. I, a veteran who has played golf for over sixty years, was humbled. How can you not love him?

Now, to be honest with you, becoming a pro is more difficult than winning the lottery. There are 7.3 billion people on the earth and about a million of them play golf and although thousands work in the golf industry, less than 500 in the entire world can make a living playing golf. Could Will become one of them? The odds are clearly against a kid from Thomaston making it as a pro, but he is that good and he has the discipline and integrity for greatness.

I began thinking about Zack Johnston, the famous pro from Iowa and the winner of the 2007 Masters and the 2015 Open Championship with over $100,000,000 in earnings. According to Wikipedia:

> The son of a chiropractor, Johnson was born in Iowa City, Iowa and raised in Cedar Rapids, the eldest of Dave and Julie Johnson's three children. Playing many sports as a youth (baseball, basketball, football, and soccer), Johnson took up golf at age 10 and developed his skills at Elmcrest Country Club. He played number two on the Regis High School golf team and led them to an Iowa 3A state championship in 1992, his sophomore year.
>
> Following graduation from high school in 1994, Johnson enrolled at Drake University in Des Moines. As the number two player on the Drake golf team, he led the Bulldogs to three NCAA regional meets and two Missouri Valley championships.

From here the story gets interesting. The citizens of the city of Cedar Rapids got together and agreed to back their favorite son. They assured him that he would have a good salary for ten years so he could pursue his dream. One of the town lawyers volunteered to be his lawyer and an accountant and others followed suit. Twenty-four "Friends of Zack" bought shares in him that Zack could surrender for double what they paid. It wasn't long before he paid them back in spades and he is now in the PGA Hall of Fame. Can you imagine what that felt like—the pride and sense of accomplishment for his backers?

Anyway, before I get too carried away, Will is a Jordan Spieth kind of guy, the son of Robert and Karla Hernandez who was born right here in Thomaston, May 6, 1999. He got interested in golf early as his father took him to the course and just made sure it was fun. As Will's love of golf increased so did his skills and before long, he was beating his father at the game. While he had an early interest in baseball, he gave that up a few years ago to concentrate on golf. Mr. Brian Oglesbee (golf coach) could not be happier as Will is his best golfer on the school team. He also takes regular lessons from Mr. Brewster Bassett, a PGA professional.

His favorite teacher at Upson Lee High School is Mr. Jim Grubb as his favorite subjects are Science and Mathematics. To keep in shape, and when he wants to get away from golf for a minute, he will run, swim, and play tennis.

Will, may the wind be always under your wings. A fabulous future awaits you.

22.
The Raintree Rascals

August 10, 2016

With The Southern Persuasion (Rick Parker, Steve Buchanan, and Leilani Durden), that terrific country music band playing nearby, it was a pleasure breaking bread (more like ingesting multiple slices of pizza) and imbibing our favorite libation with my fellow warriors and our wives last Friday evening. We are, of course, the Raintree Rascals, a golf club for seniors. Not that I needed an introduction as the Rascals will extend a welcome to anyone who desires to play with us. But in my case, Doyle Allen (Fellow Kiwanian) introduced me to the group two years ago and I regret every outing I have had to miss due to my other obligations. Jim Harrigan is fond of saying, "Waine, when you are not joking, you are smoking!" These are a great bunch of guys. Thomaston has a lot of great people.

The group started out with Dr. Mac Dallas and Mr. Bentley Adams a dozen years ago and whenever they met another golfer who had retired, an invitation was extended. We will even extend our welcome to those who are not retired.

Camaraderie is the main mission of our club but there are three main features:

1. On Mondays, Wednesdays, and Fridays, we divide into randomly selected teams and, using the Stableford format, tee it up and do battle for 18 holes with the winners taking home a fistful of dollars.

2. Each month, whoever is celebrating birthdays get together and throw a party for the group. Our favorite menu includes Brunswick Stew, Pizza, Chili and don't forget the cakes and pies.

3. On the second Monday of each month, we participate in a tournament with ten other clubs at one of the Canongate courses.

Obviously, with the affection we have for each other, there isn't a day when some of the group is not playing together. I look forward to Bob Gallman's funny emails and Bill Kelly's jokes and stories on the golf course. I even enjoy Bill Anderson's colorful exclamations that follow every mishit. The only way he could have a round without colorful language is if he played the perfect round, which he never will. This is a diverse group of friends.

Yes, the Raintree Rascals are BIG fun to be around but could be a tremendous asset to our city. I wonder if our mayor would consider assigning us a task that would help in Thomaston's future development. There are lots of resources at his disposal. A really great bunch of guys who used to do interesting things in their respective careers but who now spend their days hanging out with friends and chasing a little white ball around a field of dreams.

Congratulations to Billy Singer for his hole in one on Monday, Aug. 1 on hole number 15.

23.
Miss Betty:
The Mother Teresa of Thomaston

August 17, 2016

I first heard about Ms. Betty Goins and her husband Carey from Rev. Joey Smith, pastor of East Thomaston Baptist Church for the past 18 years and director of the Community Assistance Program for the "Upson County Ministerial Association." When he spoke to the Kiwanis Club recently about the wonderful work they do to help people in economic crises, (Community Assistance, Cancer Care and Transient Fund) I asked, "How are you able to raise enough money to carry out this work?" Rev. Smith responded, "There is only one answer: Ms. Betty. Through her mission to help the "least of these," Community Care Thrift Store is able to donate generously with a sustainable business model."

Ms. Betty draws her inspiration from Matthew 25, "For I was hungry and you gave me something to eat, I was thirsty and you gave me something to drink, I was a stranger and you invited me in, I needed clothes and you clothed me, I was sick and you looked after me, I was in prison and you came to visit me…Truly I tell you, whatever you did for one of the least of these brothers and sisters of mine, you did for me."

While this is not Calcutta, India, it is just as important to have a true advocate for the poor and for people who are down on their luck. Her mission field is Thomaston and Upson County. Born in 1939, Ms. Betty attended school in Columbus, married in her teens to Carey, in 1957, and they became parents of Lynda (Jones) and Marcus soon after that. The young couple moved to Thomaston in 1966 to take a job with Southern Natural Gas. They joined First Baptist Church and set down roots. For 13 years, she ran a craft and gift shop until her retirement in 2004.

After her retirement, she volunteered for "The House of Care" at First Baptist that was run by Mrs. Ann Ruff. She took on the assignment of distributing "clothing" that was being donated by members of the church and the community. When someone asked if they could buy the excess, overstocked and inappropriate donations and recycle them, Ms. Betty got the idea that she could accept donated items, organize, and repair them with the help of volunteers, sell them cheaply and donate the profits back to the community organizations that serve the poor. With diligent research from an "Entrepreneurial Kit" she got from the Chamber of Commerce and the internet, she wrote a business plan and applied to the IRS for a 501c3 that was successfully processed in record time. Obtaining not-for-profit status afforded contributors the opportunity to take a tax deduction for their donations regardless of the form it takes.

After incorporating and obtaining non-profit status, she moved operations out of the church and rented space that was being vacated by The Bargain Shop on Hightower Street and with no cost for inventory and working six days per week; she returned the $42,000 start-up grant to the Benevolent fund at First Baptist after just one year.

She then formed a Board of Directors that is completely independent. The current members are Ryan Tucker, Carole Martin, Sandra Miller, Janice Crutchfield, Nancy Allen, Denise Daniel, Sandy Kersey, Roger McClendon and Angela Pitts.

Having outgrown the space on Hightower Street, they were able to move into their current space at 108 Short E. Street in 2014.

According to Ms. Betty, "My mission came to me in my golden years. The Community Care Thrift Store is a blessing. Most importantly, it is an opportunity for well-meaning people to give something back, not only by donating items to the store but with their labor." To those who much is given, much is expected. According to the 50 or so volunteers, the satisfaction they receive from knowing that they make a difference in the lives of so many people is just awesome.

I believe that people in unfortunate circumstances offer us an opportunity to earn a blessing. My husband and I have never been happier or more blessed. Doing good deeds is like planting seeds for a future harvest. We also provide the opportunity for members of our community to buy quality, gently-used household items and clothing for very little money. A suit of clothes can be purchased for less than $10.00.

And then comes the good part: All the money we take in goes back to service organizations to help people who need a little hand holding. The organizations we support include: The Silvertown Soup Kitchen, Heritage Family Resource Center, Cancer Care Ministries, The Gilmore Center, the New Life Church Summer Program, the New Life Jail Ministry, Food for Thought, Empty Stocking Fund, First Methodist Church Thanksgiving dinner, Dementia Awareness (Teepa Snow), Back to School Bash, S.U.P.P.O.R.T. and Area Revival. Eventually, we will all be judged by how we took care of the less fortunate. Dr. Kong, it's not what we do, it's the difference we make. God is good and faithful.

In just the last year, in addition to her ardent fans and those who benefited from her largesse, Ms. Betty received the "Service to mankind" award from both the Thomaston Chamber of Commerce and the Sertoma Club. Ms. Betty, you are doing God's work 'toiling in the vineyard' keeping hope alive for the many people of Thomaston who would ordinarily have no hope. According to Rev. Al Simmons, "Ms. Betty is not only the Mother Theresa of Thomaston; she is an angel with a vision. She saw a need and filled it. She deserves everyone's support."

To donate, buy items from the store or volunteer: Please call (706) 646-4496. Their biggest need is for volunteers to help process donations, hang up clothes, straighten racks, etc. Spending a little time talking to Ms. Betty will also inspire you. She is full of goodness and mercy.

24.

Usain Bolt:
The Greatest of All Time

August 24, 2016

With all the doom and gloom predicted for the Rio Olympics, (Zika virus, unfinished construction, general unreadiness, crime, pestilence, sewage infested waters, political upheaval), though not perfect, Brazil pulled it off and it turned out to be most enjoyable. But as the Jamaican athletes excelled, maybe I had a little more fun than anyone else.

There is a little joke in Jamaica that goes like this: Four politicians are debating how to improve the dismal economy. One of the men came up with an idea: "Let's declare war on the United States. As Americans are prone to do, they will 'mash us up' but then invest billions of dollars developing our country like they did for Germany and Japan." Two others supported the idea but the fourth argued, "Suppose we win?" As preposterous as the idea may be, suppose there was a track meet between the United States and Jamaica, who do you think would prevail?

I was born in Jamaica and migrated to this great country when I was 15 years old. In the tradition of Jamaica, I enjoyed four years of high school participating and lettering in cross-country, wrestling, track and soccer. Because I had set a track record at Madison High School in New Jersey, I received a scholarship to attend Simpson College in Iowa. I never would have been able to attend college without this assistance.

The point is that I have always had a keen interest in sports while growing up in Jamaica. Even though I have settled into only playing golf in my old age, I once excelled at ping pong, swimming, tennis, badminton, racquetball, squash, volleyball, soccer, handball, skeet shooting, gymnastics, (I fell on my head doing the rings and passed out). I tried every sport to which I was introduced. However, I never got the hang of football.

As I was a fast runner, I was invited to try out for football. I thought it was hilarious that while I was running down the field with the ball, others were trying to tackle me. As I couldn't stop laughing, the coach invited me to turn in my gear and that was the end of my football career.

When my children invited me to go skiing, a sport that is far removed from Jamaica, (except for Jamaica Bobsled), without lessons, they took me to the highest peak at Keystone in Colorado. I didn't even have a ski jacket and only wore a heavy sweater. So, I started down and decided that I would purposely fall on my rump whenever I felt out of control. That happened to be every ten yards. While my children delighted at my incapacity and perfect strangers yelled at me, after several agonizing hours, I made it to the bottom without any broken bones and with my sweater caked with 20 pounds of ice. It was particularly therapeutic for my daughter as she said, "It was the first time in my life that I could do something better than you." With all my aches and pains, I thought I had accomplished something awesome.

Anyway, everyone marvels that Jamaica, a little island in the Caribbean with a population of about three million people could produce such amazing track stars. Is it their diet, attitude, coaching technique or maybe their genes? Each year, coaches from all over the world visit Jamaica to study the phenomenon and have yet to come up with an answer.

By what process could Jamaica produce the fastest human being that ever lived? Why do they have the fastest women? Legendary Usain St Leo Bolt won the 100m, 200m and the 4X100m relays with assistance from Asafa Powell, Yohan Blake and Nickel Ashmeade. The previous fastest woman in the world "Pocket Rocket" (Shelly Ann Frazier) passed the baton to Elaine Thompson who won gold in the 100 and silver in the 200 and in the 4X100m relay. Omar McLeod also won gold in the 110m hurdles and Shericka Jackson won the bronze in the women's 400m—a total of 11 medals. For the past 30 years, Jamaican men and women have dominated the sprint events. China has 500 times more people and Jamaica won twice as many medals in track and field.

The answer my friends is 'blowing in the wind'. I have participated in foot races since my first day of school. The most celebrated day of the school year at every school in Jamaica is "Sports Day." It's a day when local businesses contribute prizes in the form of a pocketknife, a spoon, a cup and saucer, a belt, a cap, etc. and children are the center of everyone's attention, and given a chance to show off what they can do.

My explanation for why Jamaicans excel at running is that there are not many opportunities to do anything else. As running fast is a high-status activity, it is not difficult to motivate children to practice. If any child, wherever they may live, wants to be a track star, the formula is very simple—run hard and often. You do best what you do most often.

25.
A Parent's Guide to a Great Year at School

August 31, 2016

All kids are nervous and excited about the first day of school. The challenges are many. But yes, it's evidence that they are growing up and in a few more years they will be leaving the nest, so cherish the memories. You are doing a wonderful job raising them. In the meantime, the most important gift you can bestow on your children is good health. If they have good health, they will be ready for anything.

So, be sure they are ready for the challenges at school. Take them to a pediatrician for a wellness child exam and update their immunizations. How is their vision and hearing? Do they have allergies? Do they drink plenty of water? Are they advised to avoid sugars and fats? (Sodas, bacon, sausages, hot dogs, chips, candy, doughnuts). Nutrition matters. A substantial breakfast will give your child the energy to do what a child has to do throughout the school day. Brain foods include salmon, eggs, peanuts, whole grains, honey, bananas, berries, beans, dairy products, lean meat, and chicken without the skin.

According to Bethany Thayer, spokeswoman for the American Dietetic Association (ADA),"Give the body junk food, and the brain is certainly going to suffer." Do they exercise vigorously and often? Children who exercise often have better memory and do better academically. Make sure the school nurse and your child's teacher know if your child is taking medication or prone to having seizures, allergies and other incidents requiring urgent attention.

Cleanliness is next to Godliness. Are your children used to washing their hands, brushing their teeth, coughing in their elbows, and bathing at least daily? Kids need it quiet when they study and when they sleep. "Early to bed, early to rise, makes a child healthy, wealthy and wise."

Teach them social skills and southern hospitality. This means they are respectful of others and speak to people they encounter. If it's no more than "good morning," "How are you?" "How's ya mama dem?" the weather, the latest news, did you hear the one about…? Maybe not for the victims but gossiping about teachers and other kids is actually a positive bonding exercise. More or less, we all do it.

Load them up with notes and flashcards, help them put the question on one side and the answer on the other and always have a stack with them to review in their down time. Use every spare moment to test them. It is the best aid to memorizing vocabulary and facts. There is a lot to know.

For older kids, you must alert them to the dangers of the internet. Whatever they send on Snapchat, Facebook and Twitter will be accessible forever. You have, I am certain, heard the horror stories of kids who sent nude pictures to friends they trusted, and they ended up committing suicide because their so-called friends made them public. There is no privacy on the internet. More importantly, their priority is learning and development, not to be on their phones and computers literally every minute. Let's just admit that it is a very difficult proposition to keep them from it.

Finally, rehearsing and role-playing is important. Take them to the school the day before and if other kids you know are headed in that direction, get them together and have a conversation about how they feel and why school is going to be fun. If it is the first day of school for your child, it will help to sit in a corner in the classroom for an hour where the child can see you. He or she will be comforted by your presence. A card or love note in their lunchbox or hidden in their notebook is good for a smile. Get them used to writing things down so they don't forget. This is a good habit for both children and old people.

Once an adult and twice a child.

26
Being Happy in Thomaston

September 7, 2016

You can find all the ingredients for personal happiness in Thomaston if you start with the premise that things don't have to be perfect for you to be happy. Happiness fluctuates, our perspectives change, and real happiness is about taking the good with the bad. Just remember that when you eat fish, you must always spit out a few bones. In Thomaston, the bones are digestible.

I confess to being happy. In fact, I am happier since moving to Thomaston five years ago. Last Thursday, after completing some meaningful work, I called Norm Kennedy and asked if he was interested in playing golf at 3 pm. He agreed. No tee time was necessary. Halfway through our round we noticed that in the silence of the afternoon, we had Raintree to ourselves (as we often do); a magnificent fresh cut lawn and trees embraced us, lakes reflecting the tall Georgia pines, birds darting about, and good company. We even admired the few remaining raintrees. I am one of Norm's many fans who admire his shot making. It doesn't get any better than this. It helps that both of us did significant work mingled with travel and adventures before we retired, (Norm was an Air Force Pilot and Traffic Controller and I was a psychology professor and lawyer). We married well, have great children and grandchildren, enjoy meaningful relationships, participate in community development, and love golf.

As positive talk and feelings lead to more positive talk and feelings, we decided that living in Thomaston is just grand. The people are kind and neighborly, there is never any traffic and parking is always easy and free. ALL of our public services work. When was the last time you had to conserve water, your garbage didn't get picked up, or the streets were not cleaned? Has any public official or employee ever been convicted for betraying the public trust? When the lights go out, isn't Cornelius Ivey on the case to get our power back almost immediately? And most importantly, the children are thriving.

As I write this, there is a devastating earthquake in Italy, fires raging in California, houses are being flooded in Louisiana, famine in Zimbabwe, typhoons in Japan, civil unrest in Turkey and wars and rumors of wars in several countries. So, I take great pleasure in my daily routines of greeting my neighbors, visiting the wellness center, playing golf with the Raintree Rascals, breakfast at the Tasty Shoppe Café, lunch with my Kiwanis brethren, and contributing to community development whether it's just sharing information, money, or time. I just love this place.

Some of the individuals I wrote about are happy because they are contributing to making Thomaston the remarkable place it is. Some people are already in on this secret to happiness. They are satisfied with just waking up each morning and making sure there isn't a tag on their big toe; I have a friend who has never been blind, but he wakes up every morning and shouts, "I can see! I can see!" He swears that it's a great way to start his day. My pastor's prayers always include the fact that not everyone woke up this morning, but we should be grateful that we still have warm blood flowing in our body and an opportunity to enjoy the bounty of Thomaston once again.

A professor once told me that a very large study was conducted with the goal of defining happiness. So, they interviewed a diverse group of rich and poor people from every part of the globe. After analyzing their data, they were able to define happiness with just two words, "Doing better." What does a patient want to hear? "Ms. Jones, you are doing better." An employee who is making $7.00 per hour can receive a raise and be happy and an employee making $100,000 will be unhappy with just a slight decrease. Whatever you define as important, (health, wealth, skills, knowledge, relationships) doing better makes you feel happy and doing worse will depress you. Are you doing better?

It is worth noting that your health is perhaps the most important ingredient in feeling joyful and content. It is also an important ingredient in creating wealth. If you are sick in bed, you are spending money and wasting time in waiting rooms. So, be sure to load up your diet with fruits and veggies, exercise often, get enough sleep and don't tolerate your aches and pains in silence. Get thee to a doctor.

The search for deep truth and meaning are positive contributors to your sense of peace and happiness. Take churchgoing, for instance. Many people, who believe in God, and feel that they are in conversation with God, still feel that church is "not for them;" that churchgoing people are somehow different from them, with fewer doubts and surer answers. But one of the great insights of churchgoing is the realization that you are joined together with your fellow flawed and weary pilgrims experiencing something larger than yourselves together.

Finally, our creator commands us to "prosper and multiply." It simply means to strive to better ourselves and improve our condition as well as nurture the next generation. These are pretty good reasons to be happy. It's not about 'what' we leave behind but 'who'.

27.

Human Propensities: Contemplating Human Nature in the Garden of Good and Evil

September 14, 2016

For the past few weeks, I have been exploring the meaning of life, why we are here and the true nature of human beings. Here is what I have to report: We are overwhelmingly complex organisms. We really don't know why we do what we do and what makes us human (thinking, feeling, and acting) and we will probably never know. We are the smartest and most creative of all of God's creatures. We are generally invested in preserving what is ours as well as acting in the best interest of those we love and oppose those who threaten us. We try to figure things out and improve our lot and accumulate possessions. We enjoy connecting with our fellow human beings especially with love and lovemaking with the expectation of thriving.

We play, dance, and seek entertainment. We evolve elaborate systems of rules, taboos and etiquette that assure us a sense of predictability and acceptance. And according to Sigmund Freud, what makes us happy is, "to love and to work." In Genesis 1: 28, our marching orders are to, "Be fruitful and multiply." "What you are is God's gift to you. What you can become is your gift to Him" (Henrietta Mears).

My wife and I were visiting Australia about 10 years ago and in a conversation with three Aborigine men, I asked about their goal in life and one of them said, "To us, whether it is the end of a job, a day or a life, we just want to sit down happy." On the other hand, Frederick Pearls (Founder of Gestalt Psychology) believes that human beings are completely selfish and never do anything for anyone else without a pay-off for themselves. Even when we appear to be charitable, we are only kind because it makes us feel good. Paul, writing in Romans 3, suggests that, "There is no one who does what is good—not even one. We all fall short of the glory of God."

Not necessarily in Thomaston, but whether gossiping, on our television screens, reading *The Beacon* or the internet, we are on a continuous diet of evil. We are also witnessing tremendous acts of charity, empathy, and kindness. Sometimes these contrasting behaviors occur on the same day by the same person. A person on his way to murder another human being can help a senior citizen cross the street or may drop money in a beggar's cup before continuing on his mission.

As I write this, a politician is arranging a secret deal that will benefit himself at the expense of those he or she is sworn to serve, someone is planning a robbery, raping a child, creating mischief and all manner of evil. Human beings, as it turns out, are capable of unspeakable evil as well as heroic acts of self-sacrifice and cooperation. Are we more likely to help our fellow travelers on the planet or are we selfish creatures? Is lying and cheating part of our make-up?

Can you imagine that there are human beings (ISIS) who can line up innocent people and cut off their heads? These people were children once and most likely had loving parents, grandparents, and teachers. Can you fathom the evil that has been committed in the name of "God?" As a psychologist, my orientation is that there are four schools of thought or attempts to explain how we become who we are. Human beings are:

1. Born good and learn some evil (Rousseau). We are highly rewarded to be cooperative and respectful of others and punished for selfishness and crime.

2. Born evil (like a mule) and has to be broken or evil will manifest itself (Hobbes). Are we just brutes living by our instincts and drives to increase our pleasure and minimize our pain?

3. Born with a blank slate (*tabula rasa*) with the propensity for either good or evil shaped by parents and our environment. (The apple does not stray too far from the tree.)

4. Infused with a dark side that makes us all capable of evil deeds under certain circumstances regardless of how we were raised and socialized.

Some people are born with a silver spoon in their mouths and grow up with all the comforts of a good home and then become paragons of virtue. However, those whose 'only' choice to survive is to commit heinous crimes just "to get their daily bread" and to survive. It is one thing to have supportive parents who willingly rescue their progeny from their misdeeds and quite another to have to suffer the slings and arrows without aid or succor from loved ones. It is one thing for a woman who anticipates being married and raising a family and another woman of lesser means who must sell her assets to support herself and her family.

According to C. S. Lewis, "Prostitutes are in no danger of finding their present life so satisfactory that they cannot turn to God. The proud, the avaricious, the self-righteous are in that danger." The point is that we should always attempt to be our best selves, unselfish, forgiving, kind and supportive of other seekers. According to Mahatma Gandhi, "Man's nature is not essentially evil. Brute nature has been known to yield to the influence of love. You must never despair of human nature."

28.

How Freud Thought of Human Nature

September 21, 2016

Last week, I wrote in general about human propensities. I am following up with one specific theory. According to Sigmund Freud, (Father of Psychiatry) while we may believe our behavior is rational and we know what we are doing, our actions are mostly governed by unconscious forces. Freud's great contribution was the discovery of the unconscious and its role in our decision making and actions.

A baby is all "Id." A baby has no ability to delay gratification or consider anyone else's needs, "I want what I want when I want it." "If I itch, I want it scratched." "He started it." Some of us never grow out of this immaturity." These are the bad-minded people who always want something for nothing and who want to prosper at someone else's expense. This childish conduct can be quickly recognized on the roads from reckless drivers who put others at risk by inappropriately passing others because only their needs matter.

Ordinarily, as one matures, we learn a reality principle, or the cause-and-effect rules of life which Freud calls the "ego." If I put my hand in a fire, it will burn. If I fall down, it will hurt. If I steal or otherwise break the law, the police will arrest and imprison me. A healthy fear of punishment takes hold. We learn to value the rights of others and respect boundaries. If I treat others special, they will be kind and helpful to me in my hour of need. If I work hard, develop meaningful skills, knowledge, and attitudes, I can find employment or own a business so I can support myself and take care of my family. If there is no family structure or if the rules of society are not predictably enforced, some people will not believe they will be punished for crimes and that they can get rich quickly and always get their way by intimidating others.

Finally, Freud believed that we also develop a superego or a conscience. Our family, our community, our schools, our religious institutions, and our culture impress ethics on us. If society is successful, we feel guilty when we don't do "the right thing."

We don't want to be disgraced. We are embarrassed if we violate a social code like going to a funeral wearing a bathing suit. Our conscience becomes our guide. If we have a conscience, we are motivated to be kind and generous to needy relatives, the sick and the elderly. We enjoy contributing to the development of our community, but we are also easily shamed. If you don't have a conscience, a criminal may even consider robbing the most vulnerable if they have something he or she wants. Let your conscience be your guide.

Ideally, we need a balance. We need the "Id" so we can have a good time. Sex, dancing, partying, playing games, competing, playing tricks on others, telling jokes, laughing and that whoopee feeling all come from the "Id." There is nothing wrong with fun, especially after the work is done, and you have actually accomplished something. We also need to know what is real (ego strength), as well as being responsible parents to restrain the less irresponsible among us from over-indulgence and to guide and nurture the next generation. While we don't need to be mastered by our physical needs, I don't believe we ever want to be so guilt stricken that we beat up ourselves every time we have a good time or make a mistake. However, we should also learn that moderation and balance are the keys to a truly successful life.

Imagine a little jockey (our developed ego and superego) riding a big, powerful horse (our Id). Even though the horse is ten times stronger than the jockey, the horse can be skillfully controlled by the jockey. If the horse is unbridled, however, the Id cannot be controlled, and we become undisciplined, unproductive, immoral, and completely selfish. These people are the knuckleheads that create havoc on society.

29.

Serving Two Years as the President of the Thomaston Kiwanis

September 28, 2016

The genesis of Kiwanis International was in Detroit, Michigan in 1915 when a group of businessmen thought it would be good for their individual businesses to meet weekly over lunch. Eventually, they were persuaded to adopt a higher purpose, so they changed the focus to service and particularly to advancing the interest of our youth. The idea caught on and Kiwanis now has a presence in just about every corner of the United States and in over 100 countries.

Our objectives are:

1. To encourage the daily living of the golden rule in all human relationships.
2. To promote the adoption of higher social, business, and professional standards.
3. To develop by precept and example, a more intelligent, aggressive, and serviceable citizenship.

Kiwanis came to Thomaston in 1924 and has been a staple in our community since then. I was invited to join the Thomaston Kiwanis by Hoppy Hopkins in 2012 and was elected to two terms in 2014 and 2015. In that capacity, I was honored to represent Thomaston and attend our centennial anniversary convention in Indianapolis, Indiana, in 2015 where I mingled with delegates from around the world. More importantly, I met all of our international leaders and officials and felt most welcomed at the Georgia Hospitality Suite. The nightly convention entertainment was spectacular, including a spirited performance by Sister Sledge and a plethora of inspirational speeches. I even felt like my vote counted for something.

I learned that Kiwanis touches the lives of a lot of people around the world. In some places, Kiwanis is the center of their social activities. They sponsor dances, outings and raise tremendous amounts of funds to help children. I think we take ourselves way too seriously in Thomaston. In some countries, they sing, share jokes, poke fun at each other and participate in a lot of rituals. Some even have secret handshakes. The one principle that defines us, however, is that we are all committed to serve children, and we take our mission seriously.

I then visited the New Kingston Kiwanis in Jamaica and was awed by their camaraderie and accomplishments. They have 150 members and over 40 projects. They meet for three hours on Wednesday evenings and even had a professional singer serenade them. They were just delightful.

After the convention, I returned energized with a great deal of zeal to do more and hopefully it was reflected in the activities that have occupied us since then. I am particularly proud of our support of the JOY program at Mount Moriah Baptist Church.

Every ending has a new beginning. I depart leaving the organization in good hands. Our new president, Mark Cotney, is not only a long-time member but a terrific leader. As a chiropractor, he has been helping us feel better and be more productive. I hold him in very high regard and his team will hopefully take the organization to new heights. I am at the ready to help whenever I can.

I would like to single out Mike Jones, our secretary for the past 15 years, for special commendation. I could always rely on him to keep me on the straight and narrow and as a man of tremendous integrity and commitment; I know that Mark will be able to rely on him for good counsel and direction.

When I was sworn in as president, I didn't realize how connected I would be to such a great community of leaders. I have been humbled by their many kindnesses and the fellowship of Kiwanians around the state and the world. I have been greatly enriched by the experience. It was a fantastic learning opportunity. I've learned how to take criticism, and even the occasional compliment. I have also learned to be more open-minded, to value other people's opinions and to consider other ideas along with mine. I've come to realize that being a part of a team is a lot more than just sharing credit. When you are on a team you have to lead, follow, and more often than not, meet in the middle.

My wish for everyone here is that you all continue to experience success and recommit to do even more for the children of this community and around the world. There is always an open invitation to people who want to join us in advancing the interest of our children. I encourage those interested to come and fellowship with us on Tuesday at noon at our Civic Center and enjoy a free lunch. As the Sufi mystic Rumi urges:

> Come, come, whoever you are: wanderer/worshipper/lover of leaving. It doesn't matter. Ours is no caravan of despair. Come even if you have broken your vows a thousand times. Come, yet again, come.

We are the friendliest people in town, and you may even learn something from the speakers that enlighten us each week.

I take fond memories of my term in office. And not to be overlooked, I particularly enjoyed ringing the bell to start and end our meetings.

30.
A Tribute to Grandparents

October 5, 2016

We recently celebrated Grandparents Day on Sept. 11. Having been raised by a grandmother and becoming a grandparent of six amazing children is a very special responsibility that I take seriously and enjoy enormously. Until you have held a grandchild in your arms, you cannot imagine the joy! If I had known how much fun they were going to be, I would have had them first and just skip the children. I firmly believe that If we are ever going to solve our social problems (juvenile delinquency, unwanted pregnancies, unruliness, and underachievement), we need the influence of grandparents.

Due to untimely death, incarceration, addictions, and irresponsibility, almost 20% of the children who receive care at our practice (ZÖe Pediatrics), are being raised by their grandparents and most likely their grandmothers. While it has been ordained those children should be raised by their parents, it may very well be a blessing to be raised by grandparents. My own grandmother was fond of saying, "Parents have no experience, children need grandparents." I am sentimental about grandparents because I spent my impressionable years in the care of my fabulous grandmother. She was one-of-a-kind and the library of my youth. So, I subscribe to the African proverb that when a grandparent dies, an entire library goes up in flames.

My grandmother prayed unceasingly. God was a part of every sentence ("Lord willing, I will see you tomorrow;" "God bless you;" "Isn't God good?" "What a friend we have in Jesus!"). I have very vivid memories waking up early in the morning and seeing my grandmother on her knees beside her bed. She sang hymns such as "A Mighty Fortress is our God," "Rock of Ages," "My company before is gone and I am left alone with God," "Brother, sister, let me serve you, let me be your servant too," "Amazing Grace" and her favorite, "Hark, the Voice of Jesus Calling." All day long while she cleaned the house and prepared our meals, the echo of her singing was ever-present.

The reason I so enjoy the hugs and kisses of friends, family, and even strangers is that I could not leave her presence without a hug and kiss. I could not return from school without a hug and kiss. She would end each day sitting in her rocking chair reading her Bible for all to hear.

Growing up with Granny was a blessing. She was so noble in sentiment and entertaining in conversation. She could strategically place the right Bible passage in a conversation citing chapter and verse to make the point. She was everyone's friend and the neighbors treated her with love, respect, and kindness.

My granny was forever frustrated with people who only cared about themselves. Her favorite quote from the Bible was Philippians 2(4), "Let each of you look out not only for his own interests, but also for the interest of others." She also quoted Romans 14 (7), "For none of us live to himself alone and none of us dies to himself alone." "We shall all stand before the judgment seat of God." She often said, "So for what profit is it to a man if he gains the whole world, and loses his soul? (Mathew 16:26). This was her reason for being, her sermon, her cause, and her message for all who would listen.

I was a very competitive boy. On numerous occasions, when I delighted in my own accomplishments, she was forever reminding me to never take pleasure only in my own success. When a learned aunt came home to visit for two weeks, she coached me about how to do my arithmetic every day and I got all my sums right on the test. Granny wanted to know why we didn't help others to also do well. With my competitive proclivities at the time, she tried in vain to help me understand that "If others succeed, you succeed; if they fail, you fail."

While not all grandparents are loving and caring, my experience leads me to believe that we are more likely than not to be a positive influence in every child's life. The love of grandparents is a great asset. I just wish they would hang around long enough to help nurture and spoil the next generation.

31.
The Americanization of the World

October 12, 2016

For those of you who know my wife (Dr. Stephanie Kong) you are likely to have been exposed to her wit. When we were dating, we were on a beach in California when I spotted a fallen branch from a nearby tree. I picked it up and wrote in the sand, "I love you." After she rewarded me with a kiss, she took the stick from me and scribbled something I could not possibly decipher. After I told her that I couldn't read it she said, "You don't know how to read Sanskrit?" I think I really fell in love with my future wife and the power of language especially when it endures the sands of time.

The joke does underscore another point about our culture. The play on words [Sanskrit = sand script] only works in English. At present, however, there are more people on earth who have enough facility with English that they could get my wife's humor. That's how dominant English has become.

According to the story shared by all Abrahamic religions, the history of language starts with the Tower of Babel when all human beings spoke the same language and were attempting to build a stairway to Heaven. As if to tell us that there is no shortcut to Heaven, God caused various groups of builders to speak different languages and migrated. That effectively put a stop to the building of the "tower", metaphorically, and also was the start of the loss of cooperation between nations. Eventually more than 50,000 languages emerged—8,500 in just one country (Papua New Guinea). This does not even include dialects and patois. I contend that the number of languages in the world will continue to dramatically decrease and predict that we are headed back to the pre-Babel period when we all spoke a common language. We are already down to about 6,000 languages in the world but a third of them have fewer than 1,000 speakers.

Back in the "Old World," the term for a common language, a lingua franca, literally referred to the language borrowed from and understood by the Franks, or Europeans. And right up until World War I, everyone from Istanbul to Buenos Aires would have agreed that all serious international negotiations were to be carried out in French. But how the mighty have fallen! Multinationals like Nissan, along with many others) recently made the decision that all company communications will now have to be in English. While the savings is tremendous, for a proud Japanese company to adopt English as their universal language is an interesting development.

UNESCO is concerned that almost one thousand languages spoken today will disappear in the next few years. While almost all Americans believe that English is the most popular language in the world, it currently ranks third with Chinese and Spanish leading the list. But the drift is to English. When we all end up speaking English in a few hundred years, will we be tempted again to find a way to heaven?

Last summer, I was visiting South Africa and as I was eating breakfast and reading the local newspaper, I came across an article that gave me pause. It turns out that when children leave their villages and go to the cities to study, get a job, get married and have children and the children's children go back to their village to visit, they are unable to communicate with their grandparents without a translator. All over the world, children do not speak the language of their grandparents. I find this very sad that the advocates of preserving their culture and language are the great losers. Anyone who cannot speak English will not be able to work for Nissan or even get a job as a dishwasher in advanced economies.

In Jamaica (where I was born), they have a word for those who leave our villages, travel to distant shores, accumulate wealth and return with cars and build great houses with plumbing and electricity. These are the "been to" people who went off to Canada, the United States and England while those who stayed behind envy their rich cousins and continue to struggle for their daily bread. Unfortunately, many Jamaicans now feel obligated to turn their backs on local language and culture and believe that their only salvation is to "go foreign" where those who can speak English are more economically advantaged than those who only speak patois. While Jamaicans bemoan the "brain drain," there is no doubt that Jamaicans who "go foreign" do well in comparison with their French and Spanish-speaking neighbors who are limited by their inability to communicate?

Each year, about a thousand languages are lost like Latin, Wukchumni in California, Norman in France and even Yiddish. Our high standard of living in the United States tempts people to want what we have, including our language, our movies, our music, and our freedoms. Except for the French, throughout the world, medicine, computers, engineering, and business are taught almost exclusively in English. We are ALL in the same enviable boat called America.

For Americans, our most important asset may be the one they picked up as a baby. Throughout the world, there is a huge demand for English teachers and the rich from other countries send their progeny to the United States, Canada, and England to become comfortable with English. So, whether it is a good thing or not, I am not sure if the march to Americanize the world can be halted.

32.

If You Love, You Are a Reflection of God

October 19, 2016

God is love. Even though we are all flawed, God loves us. He even sent His Son to sacrifice Himself for our sins. There is more joy in Heaven over one repentant sinner than ten who deem themselves righteous? Be patient, kind and forgiving with others. Do not be upset or take offense with those who hurt, revile and even despise you, which is the wisdom contained in His Word.

Sad to say, the Love of God has been lost in this election season which is turning into the worst in the political history of our country. The "Our" has been lost during this toxic election. Combined with instant and personal communications capability, we now know more about our candidates than we wanted to. The good, bad and ugly are in our faces. And ladies and gentlemen, it is in our faces—24/7.

Political intrigue and rancor are nothing new. The difference is that we now know how political sausages are made. We now have access to the backrooms, the words, strategies and private thoughts of each candidate and we can all individually get into the game by posting our opinions for all the world to see. The internet has given each of us a voice. We have become angry at each other and there is potential harm to our democracy. Every citizen is an American. Other than Native Americans, we all migrated from other countries. We came by boats, planes, and across borders on foot. Each ethnicity has contributed immensely to the building of the national fabric.

There is no America without diversity! Our diversity is the key to our progress. After election day, whether the candidates you favor win or lose, plenty of forgiveness and healing will be needed. Whatever the rifts may be, we have to forgive each other and support the new administration. After all, this is our country. You have a role in preserving it. As John Mellencamp reminds us:

Well, I can stand beside ideas
I think are right
And I can stand beside the idea
to stand and fight
I do believe there's a dream for everyone. This is our country.
There's room enough for science to live and there's room enough here
for religion to forgive
And try to understand other
people of this land
This is our country.
From the east coast to the west coast Down the Dixie Highway Back home
This is our country

In spite of the torments from members of the other party, it is important that after the election, we lay aside our quarrels and come together in familial harmony. If you have honor and are imbued with a sense of duty, resume your commitment to do what you can to build a truly great nation. It will be time to love your enemies and remember them in your prayers. Let us be reconciled even with those who reject, disgrace, or slander you. The future of our children, our country and the world are at stake.

33.
The Thomaston–Upson Senior Center: A Great Place to Hang-Out

October 26, 2016

Being a senior citizen is a special time in our lives. Being a senior citizen living in Thomaston is even more special. We are a happy and contented lot. I invite all seniors who live in cities teeming with ill-mannered people, traffic jams, high cost of living to move to Thomaston where the living is easy. If the life you are living does not suit you and you are exposed daily to meanness, ingratitude, cunning, envy and deceit and you have nothing to look forward to with hope—move. Give it up. I invite you to move to Thomaston where you can enjoy the rest of your days and cherish good memories.

For those of you who have been reading my weekly column, you know that I have been promoting Thomaston as a wonderful place to retire when the work is done. We are proud of our parks, roads, and recreational facilities. The cost of housing is about a third of what it is in Atlanta and property taxes are also low. There may be a connection, but crime is low, and churches are many. In my five years living here, I met, played golf, and worked with the wonderful folks who try to make Thomaston a really pleasant place to live.

Whether I need to go to the bank, the post office, the cleaners, the golf course, they are all only a few miles away where a parking space right in front is waiting for you. I find that I can trust local businesses and vendors and we have a state-of-the-art hospital and great doctors (especially pediatricians). We have no difficulty buying exotic fruits, meat, fresh fish, vegetables and as they say in New Orleans, "make groceries." In other words, a great place to live if you are over 60.

If you just want to hang-out with friends, consider the senior center a second home. From 8 a.m. until 5 p.m. each weekday, you can enjoy the many activities (Exercise Classes, Billiards, Arts & Crafts, Bingo, and Bridge) organized by the Thomaston-Upson Senior Center. It is actually a wonderful place to hang-out and here is a surprise, you can have a full lunch (including dessert, drink, and pleasant company) for a buck and a half. By comparison, that's how much it cost for a drink alone in most restaurants around town. See you there.

The Center is run by Ms. Donna Auth and can be found in what was R.E. Lee Military Building and Dining Hall as well as Memorial Hall commemorating the teacher and students who perished in the Winecoff Hotel fire in 1946. The address is:

302 South Bethel Street
Thomaston, GA 30286
Phone (706) 647-1607

34.

The Downside of Our Incredible Technological Innovations

November 2, 2016

I was a senior in college in 1970 when the book *Future Shock* by Alvin Toffler was first published and Simpson College in Iowa invited Mr. Toffler to speak at one of our assemblies. I was impressed by his prediction that in 50 years we would have personal computers, cell phones, social media, robots and e-mail. So, here we are with all the contraptions he predicted as indispensable parts of our lives. While he admitted that there will be a great deal of benefit, he also predicted that the ghost in these machines is that if they are not intelligently managed, will overwhelm us and may even put us in shock.

Future Shock is defined as too much change in too short a time than human beings can manage. We already know that after a fatal accident, if loved ones are immediately told that their loved one is dead, the trauma is much more damaging than if they are told that he is seriously injured, and the mind gets used to the idea that he might die and then told that he passed away. Consequently, it takes us time to adjust to changes and new technologies. If it is forced on us too quickly, we may become traumatized. Our minds need to ease into change. I often feel overloaded. We are all overwhelmed with a steady diet of information. When waiting to board a plane, we are bombarded with the TV and notices about the status of flights. We are trapped. We cannot turn off or even turn down this noise. One of the reasons I love golf is that I can actually experience silence on a golf course with just enough birds' songs and the wind rustling leaves and even butterflies attempting to commune with my ball.

Everything is changing so rapidly in how we live, work, and communicate that we run the risk of becoming disoriented and alienated from each other. Is the recent increase in hostility including cursing, addictions, assault and battery a result of our frustrations? Most of us cannot keep up but we have to try, and it is driving us crazy. Is this progress? Is chivalry dead? Fortunately, I am retired and don't have to be preoccupied with conquering the latest and best APPS and technology, but I do worry about those who are caught in its crosshairs.

Technology can make a positive contribution to every human endeavor. In fact, life has become more comfortable. We are all more productive. I am happy to know that I will never get lost as my GPS will save me time, fuel, and efficiency. I remember the days when we stopped people on sidewalks to ask, "Can you direct me to Washington Street?" or, "Do you know where the Johnsons live?" We live in a time when the private in the Army may know more about sophisticated weapons systems than the General.

Please be aware that 50 years ago, the U.S. Mail was in its heyday as we actually wrote letters, poems, and songs to each other. Birth control and the day-after-pill now give us reproductive freedom. We now have in-vitro fertilization and women can now buy sperm and become pregnant without intimacy. Some have decided that "I need a man like a fish needs a bicycle." We are undergoing a sea change in how we relate to each other.

So, here we are in 2016, obsessed with learning and keeping up with the newest computers, cell phones, and social media options, protecting our servers from being hacked and remembering the passwords that go with them. I pity the poor child who must respond immediately to postings by friends or be called to task with, "Why didn't you respond to my tweet? I am not special to you anymore?" When will homework get done if students must constantly monitor their phones? I was sitting in a restaurant with my wife and noticed that a young couple who must have been on a date never exchanged a word but spent the hour messaging. I attended a family gathering recently where several of us had not seen each other in several years. I tried to have a conversation with one of the teenagers and I still don't know what her voice sounds like. She never looked up from her phone or took out the earpieces. She had absolutely no curiosity about who I was or how we are related and resented my intrusion. Am I the only one who thinks this is downright rude? But why would a teenager care? She can always tweet to her friends that some old man, who said he is my grand uncle, is bothering her.

I am old school and have a lot of angst about where society is headed. I like the idea that things are more stable and traditional. I still enjoy county fairs, Buggy Days, church, parades, and the many options at the Rock Ranch. I am 73 years old and reluctantly adopt some technology. I love the convenience of e-mail but still value a hand-written letter. YouTube is fun and free. As I read constantly, my Kindle is very convenient. I also love that I can check on my bank balances but no social media for me. My son is pleased to receive happy birthday messages from 500 people he has never met and constantly sends messages and pictures about where he is and what he is doing. I don't happen to value these passions.

Ladies and gentlemen, it will get worse. Technology is rapidly taking over our lives. Some of it is great but I agonize over some of it. Does anyone read the newspaper anymore? Am I a voice in the wind?

35.

Brilliantly Educated and Exceptional Young Ladies

November 9, 2016

As you may have surmised from my previous columns, I am more than a little concerned about our youth. While I understand that the struggle between dependence and independence makes it the worst time of anyone's life, social media is making the teen years particularly challenging. The electronic divide makes it generally more unlikely that our kids are bonding with their parents and their extended family. Can we talk? Their biggest fans and advocates are often the bane of their existence and their greatest source of conflict. With all that is available to them on the internet, they are growing up fast and exposed to every manner of evil and debauchery known to man along with all the accumulated knowledge of the world—an amazing mixture of good and evil. What are they likely to gravitate to? It is difficult for teens to recognize that they and their parents are on the same side. Anyway, what's new? According to Socrates (450 BC) "Children today are tyrants. They contradict their parents, gobble their food, and tyrannize their teachers. "But then, on Tuesday, Nov. 2, my faith in youth was restored. Four Upson Lee High School students briefed the Kiwanis on "What High School Students are up to these days." It was like a breath of fresh air.

Laila, the daughter of Phillip and Lynn Fallin, is a junior. In addition to belonging to the National Honor Society, putting in 350 hours as a volunteer since starting high school, she is working as a Studio Assistant and dancer at Armstrong School of Dance. She is a Girls Scout and an intern at City Hall. Taking two honors classes and an AP class, she edits the yearbook, serves as President of the Key Club,

Junior class secretary, Student Secretary, Staff Writer for the school newspaper (Sword and Shield), member of the Homecoming and Prom Committee and active in her Youth Group at Grace Primitive Baptist Church.

Natalie Elizabeth is the progeny of Ben and Mandy Miller. Throughout her childhood, Ben has been known to pop a few buttons off his shirt from sticking out his chest. To start with, as Vice President of the National Honor Society, Knights of Academic Distinction and Outstanding student athlete, she has never brought home anything but A's. It's one of those situations where 99.5 wouldn't do. In addition, she is active in Chorus and GMEA Honor Choir, school drama shows, cheerleading, tennis, Art Club, Drama Club and Editor-in-Chief of the Sword and Shield. Outside of school, in 2015, she was the Georgia HOBY Northwest Ambassador and now the Northwest Junior Staff Member. Natalie and her parents attend First United Methodist Church.

Allie's parents are Matt and Bethany Norris. She has been a mainstay with TUAC for the past three years. You may have seen her in *Fiddler on the Roof, Beauty and the Beast* and *Willy Wonka*. She is an active senior who loves to sing and dance. She plans to pursue a career in mass media, so she spent last summer at a University of Georgia Journalism Camp. She has already been accepted to the University of Georgia with a 3.8 GPA. Having won the Susan B. Anthony and Frederick Douglass Award, she is Editor-in-Chief of the Sword and Shield, Student Council Secretary, Senior Class Secretary, and a volunteer in the library.

Alyssa's proud parents are Mickey and Heather Rawls. Over the past 11 years, as a member of the International Thespian Society, she has been a mainstay of TUAC participating in over 15 shows. She is Vice President of the Drama Club, plays the piano with the Youth Band at First United Methodist Church and enjoys her performances with the Glee Club. Her interests are not limited to the arts as she volunteers as the Swim Team manager, Yearbook Editor-in-Chief and newspaper staff and even works part time at the "Pie." As a member of the National Honor Society, she plans to attend Savannah College of Art and Design next year.

These young ladies give credence to the adage that, "If you want to get something done ask the busy person, others don't have time." When I inquired, "What about young people's obsession with social media?" They uniformly said, while they found phones useful, none of them are on Twitter. "We have more important things to do." Wow! Such wisdom! Such maturity!! Such ambition!!! If out of good healthcare, good parenting, and good education our youth find purpose, they will also find success and happiness.

Thanks to the four of you for restoring my faith. Thanks to your parents. Thomaston has been doing its job helping our children find a purpose for their lives and shielding them from becoming idle and fruitless. What a great place to raise healthy, wealthy, and wise citizens!

As our children go hither and yon, I would like to wish them this Irish prayer:

May the road rise up to meet you,

May the wind always be at your back.

May the sunshine warm upon your face

And rains fall soft upon your fields.

36.

The James Anthony Searcy Story: And Yet We Rise

November 16, 2016

I was inspired to write about Mr. Searcy this week after he was honored by the Upson Chamber of Commerce with The Lifetime Achievement Award at their annual awards banquet that I attended on behalf of the Kiwanis. His life mirrors that of someone else I admire.

Vivien T. Thomas was born in New Iberia, Louisiana, on August 29, 1910. His family later moved to Nashville, Tennessee. Having earned only a high school education, Mr. Thomas, an African-American, was initially hired at Vanderbilt University as a janitor. He happened to be cleaning Dr. Alfred Blalock's lab who observed how meticulously he cleaned. As he was told not to move anything in the lab, Dr. Blalock asked Mr. Thomas if he would like to learn how to take care of the lab. As the answer was in the affirmative, Dr. Blalock promoted him to a lab assistant.

He brilliantly followed all of Dr. Blalock's directions which further inspired Dr. Blalock to take time to teach him. He absorbed what he was taught like a sponge, especially how to operate on lab animals. When Dr. Blalock received the appointment as Chief of Surgery at Johns Hopkins University in 1941, he persuaded Thomas to join him in Baltimore. Together they developed the surgical procedures that cured the "blue baby" syndrome. Having worked out the procedure in the lab, he was able to guide Dr. Blalock through that first operation. Mr. Thomas was then promoted to the surgical faculty at Hopkins and went on to take part in the training of great cardiac surgeons like Dr. Denton Cooley and was awarded the honorary degree of Doctor of Laws in 1976. It was Dr. Cooley who first alerted me to the feats of this great man. A movie was made of his life titled, *Something the Lord Made*.

It turns out that we have our own Vivien Thomas in Thomaston, and his name is Mr. James Searcy. Born in 1947, he has spent his entire life in Thomaston. The son of Mr. Robert E. Lee Searcy and Mrs. Georgia Ann Walker Searcy, he attended Lincoln Park Elementary, Drake High School and Upson Tech where he excelled in sports as well as academics. He married Lonnie Akin in 1968 and fathered two children (James Anthony Searcy, Jr. and Cheryl Nicole Searcy, a counselor at Spalding High School).

Mr. Searcy started his career as an orderly at Upson Regional Medical Center in 1969. His genius was first observed by Dr. Mackenzie Dallas (Mac Dallas) who unsuccessfully tried to get him into medical school, but instead hired him as an orthopedic tech where he excelled. According to Dr. Dallas, "Mr. Searcy was so helpful to Dr. Oxford and me, we were referred to as the A Team. James greatly enhanced our surgical practice." Mr. Searcy went on to become a paramedic and then as an assistant in the pathology department with Dr. Mac Shaklee and then to the urology department. He was particularly skilled at putting patients in traction.

According to the citation at the Chamber of Commerce, "Mr. Searcy has always been known to show the utmost gentleness and compassion to his patients, calming them and putting them at ease. Each day, before James begins his 3-11 pm shift at URMC, he spends extra time going into the homes in the community to care for his patients. His first patient outside of the hospital was in 1970 caring for Mr. Julian Hightower. Since then, (47 years later) …many patients and their families frequently request his services…Mr. Searcy also provides care at Thomaston Hospice." We will continue to receive excellent care at URMC because Mr. Searcy has trained many of the employees there.

Among Mr. Searcy's many awards are: Dr. Frist Humanitarian Award (1983), First Recipient of the Make a Difference Award (2004) and the Hospital Hero Award for the State of Georgia (2012). The words that are often used to describe Mr. Searcy are brilliant, trustworthy, dependable, kind, considerate, thoughtful, influential, and compassionate.

In his personal life, he relishes the accomplishments of his grandson (Joshua) who is a football standout at Spalding High School and Morgan, who is in the sixth grade at Griffin Christian Academy. He also enjoys attending Mount Moriah Baptist Church where his nephew is the pastor (Rev. Ed Searcy).

My personal congratulations to Mr. James Searcy on his wonderful achievements as well as his most recent honor. You would have made Mr. Vivien Thomas proud.

37.
Promote Democracy

November 23, 2016

If you profess democracy, you accept the results after the ballots are counted. Those of us who promote democracy as the best form of government, when the people speak (never with one voice but a simple majority), whether we agree with the majority's choice or not, we give our support to the winners. We, however, continue to fight the good fight in the many avenues our democracy makes available to us but never violently. Enlightened self-interest makes this choice obligatory. We are invested in the survival of the world and love our country enough to support whoever is in power. At the same time, *"noblesse oblige"* obligates the winners to be magnanimous in victory without gloating. There is nothing admirable about only looking out for one segment of our society and being abusive in victory. This extends beyond their entitlements and requires people in power to fulfill their social and political responsibilities equitably.

It is worth noting that as the largest economy in the world, it is still sobering that the United States of America has less than 5% of the world's population. We need friends. Even if we own 50% of the world's resources, I do not believe in isolating ourselves. If we declare war on the rest of the world, as powerful as we are, it is not winnable and maybe a precursor of a dramatic decrease in the survival of our small planet, the only home we have.

The election of Mr. Trump as President was an extraordinary event in the history of the world. It will not be business as usual. Even people who were previously unsympathetic are enthusiastic over his almost single-handed victory. He now has the opportunity to be the greatest President of all time by being a President for all the people, forging a great country characterized by general prosperity, replacing hostility with kindness and a unity of interests. If this is his agenda, he will have a great legacy.

My image of the strength of the United States is in our diversity. In the parade of nations at the recent Olympic games in Brazil, Japanese people represented Japan, Chinese people represented China, Cuban people represented Cuba and Ghana was represented by Africans but the delegation from the United States was a rich cryoscopic rainbow representing all the nations and cultures of the world. We are great because of our commitment to diversity and inclusivity.

38.
My Relationship with the Great Architect of the Universe

November 30, 2016

At 73 years old, I have become an old man faster than I would have liked but enjoying my golden years after many fruitful, joyful years that were full of adventure. I have been blessed with good health, a loving and dedicated wife, successful children, and bright, beautiful grandchildren. As I undertake the final lap of my journey, I take the occasional liberty of imparting thoughts regarding my relationship with God and share the significant truths I have discovered. This is my testimony:

I have come this far by faith
leaning on the Lord
Trusting in His holy word
He never failed me yet.

My commitment in life is to live by Christian principles as taught to me by my grandmother. It is an issue of the heart that by its very definition is based on faith. Man without spirituality is just a torso. Life involves not only the satisfaction of physical and social needs, but also our mandate to have a relationship with the Great Architect of the Universe. This personal relationship with God requires an uncompromising commitment to human justice.

Religion without indignation for evil is intolerable. Religion cannot coexist with injustice. We must fight for what is good; we must fight for what is just; we must fight for what is decent and that fight should not be exercised by some, that fight should be exercised by all. We cannot worship God and abuse others—physically, financially, or emotionally. I believe in dignity, equality and respect for ALL human beings. You certainly can be better off but never better than anyone else. Divine likeness is something all human beings share. Because we are created in the image of God, each human being is a reminder of God's presence. Human life, therefore, is sacred and has intrinsic value. So, violence to any human being is an affront to God and a grave moral sin. Even the natural death of a loved one is traumatic enough, much less the senseless and brutal murders occurring in our country, particularly against children.

When anyone engages in acts of violence, he or she desecrates our likeness to the Almighty. On the other hand, he who loves his fellow travelers on the planet honors Him. When Christ was asked what the greatest commandment was, He answered, "To love the Lord with all your heart, mind and soul and the second was like unto the first, to love your neighbor as yourself." On these two commandments hang all the laws of the universe.

So, reach out to your fellow human beings, and beautify yourself with good deeds. It feels so good! These acts are the true essence of your beauty and strength. Your inner splendor can illuminate the world. The fear of offending or hurting another human being must be as sacred as your fear of God. To be arrogant towards God is blasphemy.

What does God want from us? I believe God wants us to serve Him with all our heart and soul; to keep His commandments and His statutes; to fear Him; to walk in His ways; as well as to practice honesty, stillness, humility, and obedience. We have eyes to see, but see not; we have ears to hear, but hear not. God is everywhere but many cannot find Him. We have His words, but we ignore them. I believe He is the way—the only way to a life of service.

39.

Forget Me Not, O Gentle Savior

December 7, 2016

I believe that human beings share a need to be a thought in God's mind and to be the object of His affection or his attention. The song, "Pass me not, O Gentle Savior" written by Fanny Crosby, in 1868, perfectly represent this sentiment:

> Pass me not, O gentle Savior,
> Hear my humble cry;
> While on others Thou art calling,
> Do not pass me by.
> Savior, Savior,
> Hear my humble cry;
> While on others Thou art calling,
> Do not pass me by.
> Let me at Thy throne of mercy
> Find a sweet relief,
> Kneeling there in deep contrition;
> Help my unbelief.
> Trusting only in Thy merit,
> Would I seek Thy face;
> Heal my wounded, broken spirit,
> Save me by Thy grace.
> Thou the Spring of all my comfort,
> More than life to me,
> Whom have I on earth beside Thee?
> Whom in Heav'n but Thee?

He may punish and discipline us, only let Him not forget me or abandon me. Sometimes He takes a two by four upside our heads, but in his testing and discipline, His sentence is never more than we can bear, and He does it out of His great love for us.

Repentance and redemption are important concepts in Christianity. As human beings, we are destined to sin, but a great renewal can be achieved by the miracle of repentance when we can start anew with a clean slate, a clean heart, clean hands, and a clean mind. However, repentance requires honesty, truthfulness, remorse, and responsibility. If it is coerced or done out of expected ritual or conformity, though not wasted, is not redemptive and does not carry the cleansing benefit and may even cause more conflict and misery. There is no return to peace without the readiness to examine ourselves for earnest—honest repentance before God. The harm we commit against others and ourselves is extinguished and transformed into salvation.

As we go through the cycle of sin, redemption, transformation, and rebirth, through forgiving guidance from God, we become better and better, more and more enlightened, holier, and holier with the goal of becoming one with God. Leviticus 19:2 "You shall be holy, for I the Lord your God am holy." Woe to us if we cease praying and God should forget us. We long for God. Emotional satisfaction and peace are impossible without Him. Shouldn't you want to talk with Him often if only to remind him that we are here? Put up your hand. You can count on him responding with mercy and love.

As the praises go up, the blessings come down.

40.

The Challenge of Making Each Hour Count

"Aspire to inspire, before you expire." —Eugene Bell Jr

December 14, 2016

Every hour is different from all other hours in which we are endowed with the opportunity to do something heroic. If you knew you were to die tomorrow, would you take the risk of unpopularity and change the world? If we recognize that providence rewards the bold, this is not the second, minute or hour to be timid and invisible. Each of us has the power to change things for good or evil. Every little bit you do helps or hurt a little. We must decide whether our life is to be about quick fixes, the avoidance of pain, and a pursuit of pleasure and material gain or in the service of mankind.

The need to "fit in" is swallowing us up. If we do not remain true to ourselves and our forefathers, we will drive ourselves into oblivion in our fancy cars. Our people need exaltation and justice, yet we remain consumed with the pursuit of material things. We may claim to be a success, but in the eyes of our heroes and sheroes, we are rightly regarded as failures. Our community is in spiritual distress suffering from a lack of commitment and most of us are paralyzed with fear. One can be a villain even though very cultured, learned and surrounded by luxuries. There are many among us whose entire existence is being taken up with the trappings of modern life. We have forgotten the value of human relationships.

The earth, our home, is a magnificent creation and generous gift from God. The glory of the creator is manifested in the spectacular beauty that surrounds us in Thomaston—our bountiful harvests, our mountains and rivers, our spectacular rainbows, and sunsets. But the greatest of all of God's creation are our neighbors— the very embodiment of His perfection.

We are interdependent with and partners with God. God needs us as much as we need Him. When we walk through storms, we never walk alone. We are not solitary in our toils or forsaken in our efforts. The smallest and weakest of us is a microcosm of the greatest one. A reciprocal relationship binds all of us with our creator.

When I study the Bible, God speaks to me. When I pray, I speak to God. Knowledge of the Bible is only a necessary first step to living the Bible and walking as a Christian. You cannot study philosophy through praying and cannot study prayer through philosophizing. Prayer fulfills a sacred function. When you pray, you talk to God, when we experience a flash of insight, a catharsis and understanding, God is talking to you. When God is betrayed and abandoned, we experience agony.

Holiness is not man's achievement. It is a gift from God that cannot be achieved without engaging others. It is not something that can be attained through merit.

Unlike Holy Rollers, we become holy not by who we are but by His grace and by how we treat our fellow travelers on our planet. Don't turn your backs on the world's most precious treasures. The light we shine to maintain our existence is the light that will transform the world and enrich others as well as ourselves. It is more than ever our duty to recover the relevance of our traditions to be engaged with each other.

Never doubt our capacity for generosity and forgiveness. We can teach the world a great deal about forgiveness and how to move forward. Organizing our lives for mere survival and getting by is an affront to our dignity. We should all strive to achieve a higher purpose. Our sense for meaning grows not by spectacular acts but how we treat the 24 hours we are given each day.

On one of my visits to Africa, several of us were taken to see Mt. Kilimanjaro. When the guide pointed in the direction of this great mountain, none of us could see it. The guide pointed out that we were not looking high enough and directed us to look above the clouds. There it was in its snow-covered splendor made popular by Ernest Hemingway. We are great people, great students, great bankers and business owners, great parents and great-grandparents whose only fault is that we do not aim high enough for ourselves and our children. We are guilty of low aim because we devalue ourselves. The ceiling of our aspirations is too low: a job, a house, car, flat screen TV and life insurance. We are capable of so much more. We have world changing ideals and power. We are only limited by our minds. What the mind can conceive and what we believe, we can achieve.

Our community's need for thought, understanding, and intellectual expansion is profound and urgent. If it is not satisfied, we will be bankrupt, squandering a great legacy and opportunity. Tagore's Confession:

> I slept and dreamt that life was joy.
> I woke and saw that life was duty.
> I acted and behold, duty was joy!!!

41.

The Lord Loves a Cheerful Giver

December 21, 2016

Just like it was against the law for lay people to read the Bible when it was first published, it was once against the law to celebrate Christmas. According to Dr. Al Simmons (a man who knows everything), "In 1659, Puritans in the Massachusetts Bay Colony put the following in the law books: Whosoever shall be found observing any day such as Christmas, whether by resting from labor, or by feasting, or in any other way...shall be fined five shillings. In Russia, there is still an official ban on celebrating Christmas because they believe Christmas never happened." Nevertheless, like it or not, Christmas is now widely celebrated throughout the world including countries where Christians are only 1.5% of the population (such as Japan).

That be as it may, we are free to celebrate and while our best sentiments are in play, the best way to celebrate the birth of our Lord and Savior is to be generous. I believe it does more for the giver than the receiver. I believe that so strongly that instead of someone saying thanks for a gift or a donation, we should thank the receiver of our gifts for the opportunity to be generous and even more importantly, creating an opportunity for us to earn a blessing. I view helping others as an opportunity to please God.

Whether we donate to the thrift shop, to the Empty Stocking Fund, Toys for Tots, Food for Thought and your neighbor. I also recommend that everyone drop some change in the Salvation Army pot and volunteer at a soup kitchen. "If silver and gold you have none," you can at the very least offer emotional support or pray for others. Studies show that giving helps us physically, mentally and spiritually. Helping others help you more. It feels good—and it is good. It may even amuse you to know that blood pressure and general health is better for people who demonstrate kindness.

Do you want a special treat this Christmas? The Accords (Bill Woodall, Larry Mitcham, Phil Leverett and John Cox) performed for the Kiwanis last week and they were fabulous! It was just what was needed to put me in the Christmas spirit. If you cannot see them in person, do buy their CD.

42.

Blessed Be the Tie That Binds: If My Brother Succeeds, I Succeed; If He Fails, I Fail

January 4, 2017

Wherever we may call home on this planet, for the New Year, let us recommit to the simple golden rule that we were taught in Sunday school, to treat others as we would have them treat us. This statement of egalitarianism is really the only rule we need to get along with each other and promote the common good. All our man-made laws, all our rules for living harmoniously, as well as our ten commandments are based on this inclusive principle requiring empathy and altruism with each other. These cultural and Christian norms to which we subscribe, requires that we respect all other human beings as brothers and sisters, common descendants of Adam and Eve. Love all of God's children!

In 1782, John Fawcett published this wonderful hymn:

Blest be the tie that binds
Our hearts in Christian love;
The fellowship of kindred minds
Is like to that above.
Before our Father's throne,
We pour our ardent prayers;
Our fears, our hopes, our aims are one,
Our comforts, and our cares.
We share our mutual woes,
Our mutual burdens bear;
And often for each other flows
The sympathizing tear.
When we asunder part,
It gives us inward pain;
But we shall still be joined in heart,
And hope to meet again.

In my study of the cultures and religions of the world, I believe we are bound together by the same teaching summarized by Jesus Christ:

> Do unto others as you would have them do unto you." Or "love your neighbor as yourself." These simple aspirational statements of morality are the ties that bind mankind, the "Golden Rule" or the "law of reciprocity" or the "maxim of altruism."

These teachings are found in some form in every culture and religion. It may be stated in many ways but imparts the same basic idea.

The Ancient Egyptians lived by the tried-and-true rule of brotherly love: "That which you hate to be done to you, do not do to another." Similarly, the citizens of Ancient Greece were obligated, "Do not do to others that angers you when they do it to you".

In China, Confucius advised his countrymen, "Never impose on others what you would not choose for yourself. What you do not wish for yourself, do not do to others."

The Great Buddha admonished his followers, "Hurt not others in ways that you yourself would find hurtful." Followers of the Baha'i Faith are guided by the statement, "And if thine eyes be turned towards justice, choose thou for thy neighbor that which thou choose for thyself."

Hindus are commanded to "make dharma (right conduct) your main focus, treat others as you treat yourself." Do what is right.

The Jews live by the principle, "That which is hateful to you, do not do to your fellow man." That is the whole Torah; the rest is the explanation. (Talmud, Shabbat 31a) In other words, everything else is commentary.

Muslims are supposed to anchor their conduct in the story about a Bedouin who visited the Prophet Mohammed and demanded to know the way to heaven to which the Prophet said, "As you would have people do to you, do to them; and what you dislike to be done to you, don't do to them…That which you want for yourself, seek for mankind."

While we all fall short of these ideals, in the coming year, we will be tested. We are being tested daily. If we just commit ourselves to live by the golden rule, you will be less self-absorbed and admired as a role model.

"Do to others what you want them to do to you. This is the meaning of the Law of Moses and the teaching of the prophets. (Mathew 7). This is further explained in Leviticus 19 which says, "Live generously towards the poor and alien…do not be partial to the poor or show favor to the great but judge honestly…Do not seek revenge or hold a grudge but extend forgiveness…You shall not take vengeance or bear a grudge against your kinsfolk…Love your neighbor as yourself: I am the LORD."

So, the Lord does not hate ugly and ask us not to impact others negatively. The Golden Rule is not only descriptive, it's prescriptive! "Many windows, one light; Many waters, one sea." (Kendyl Gibbons)

43.
A Tribute to Martin Luther King Jr.
(January 15, 1929 - April 4, 1968)

*"Darkness cannot drive out darkness; only light can do that.
Hate cannot drive out hate; only love can do that.*

January 18, 2017

I have no illusions about the strains in our relationships emanating from our recent national elections and change in government, but I hope we can all agree that Dr. Martin Luther King Jr. non-violently engineered a dramatic change in civil rights in this country and the World. He impacted every aspect of our lives. I join in honoring him in January each year for his extraordinary life and selfless service to mankind for which he sacrificed his life. What would be his message in these troubling times?

According to Colossians 3: 23-24: "Whatever you do, work heartily, as for the Lord and not for men, knowing that from the Lord you will receive an inheritance." My grandmother reminded me more than once that "good deeds are like planting seeds for which you will receive a rich harvest."

While most people will say that the "I Have a Dream" speech was the highlight of Dr. King's life, I much prefer his speech on "Service." Here is my abbreviated version:

No work is insignificant. All labor that uplifts humanity has dignity and importance and should be undertaken with painstaking excellence . . .

Everybody can be great . . . because anybody can serve. You don't have to have a college degree to serve. You don't have to make your subject and verb agree to serve. You only need a heart full of grace. A soul generated by love . . . If a man is called to be a street sweeper, he should sweep streets even as Michael Angelo painted, or Beethoven composed music or Shakespeare wrote poetry. He should sweep streets so well that all the hosts of heaven and earth will pause to say, ``Here lived a great street sweeper who did his job well.

As a member of Alpha Phi Alpha fraternity to which Martin Luther King Jr. also belonged, we pledge our love for all mankind with this oath: "First of All, Servants of all, We Shall Transcend All". I delight in joining with anyone to expand opportunities for service.

Live not just for yourself or for selfish gains. If you ever feel out of sorts and life has lost much of its meaning and value, reach out to someone less fortunate. True happiness and prosperity come from serving. We cannot believe in our Lord and Savior, attend a place of worship, and participate in any activity that is abhorrent to God. Service to mankind is service to God. You will be loved and blessed by God if you devote your life in the uplifting of our fellow travelers on this planet.

As for me and my house, we will serve the lord and serve humanity. It is a divine commitment.

44.

Is There Any Good in Goodbye? (Coping With Separation)

January 25, 2017

I am sure we have all used that old saying, "parting is such sweet sorrow." In fact, we never get tired of saying it because it captures our ambivalence exactly. Letting go and saying goodbye to someone we cherish is both sweet because we had the pleasure of their company mingled with the sorrow of our impending loss.

These thoughts came to me because two of my favorite people (Tom and Linda Hayward) are packing up and moving away. Thomaston has been fortunate to have had them making a positive contribution to our community for the past eight years. Linda served as president of the Kiwanis for two years with Tom serving as treasurer. They attended the Thomaston Presbyterian church and served on several community boards. As they will be moving to Mobile, Thomaston's loss is Mobile's gain. As I said to them, "You might be ready to say goodbye to us, but we're not ready to say goodbye to you. We will miss your many kindnesses."

Having lived in a dozen places over the past 73 years, I know a little something about saying goodbye. I was born in Kingston, Jamaica but got my *broughtupsy* in the Jamaican countryside. I then moved back to Kingston and migrated to New Jersey when I was 15 years old, in 1959. I went to Morristown High School in New Jersey, Simpson College in Indianola, Iowa, American University in Washington D.C., the University of Maryland for graduate school and Dickinson School of Law in Pennsylvania. In addition, I lived in Baltimore, Sacramento, Los Angeles, Miami, and Atlanta before finally moving to Thomaston five years ago. We have also visited over 100 countries. I don't have much difficulty making friends because I'm involved in church, business, golf and club-related activities.

Saying goodbye was always more difficult than meeting people. People grow on each other. We become attached. Thomaston is now home to me. I am a people person. I love the occasion when strangers become friends and hate the thought of friends becoming estranged or strangers. When you love someone, it is just hard to say goodbye.

Whether it is by death, divorce, moving away from home, or just friends and colleagues going separate ways, it takes about nine months to overcome the loss and move on. Sometimes the pain is almost unbearable. But as God doesn't give us more than we can handle and as time heals all, rest assured that the sorrow and pain will eventually go away. If it doesn't kill us, we emerge stronger and more resilient. If you never say goodbye, you will not know the joy of meeting again.

Last week, out of the blue, someone from my past (Dr. Noel Myricks) contacted me after a 30-year hiatus. He was the chairman of the department at the University of the District of Columbia when I was hired on as a professor. After a year, we were neighbors in Columbia, Maryland and I served as his campaign manager when he ran for the school board. But then, our paths bifurcated, and we lost touch with each other. He is now living in Raleigh, NC and came across my name because he contracted the Georgia Bar Association looking for a lawyer in Georgia to help him with a case. Ladies and gentlemen, it was an unexpected and happy reunion. We spent two hours on the phone sharing war stories and catching up.   When I least expected it, I was treated to this joyful moment. The reason people attend reunions is just that—to reconnect and catch-up. Do you have any idea how many hook-ups and marriages result from reunions?

As I explained to Dr. Myricks, in a way, we never say goodbye as long as we carry our memories. Don't cry because we have been away from each other or we are in the process of separating, smile because our paths crossed. Tom and Linda, we will miss you but wherever you may roam, may the road rise to meet you and may the wind be always at your back. We look forward to a future with you in it.

45.
Noblesse Oblige

February 1, 2017

Noblesse Oblige (Sometimes you have to be nice not because others are but because you are). I am writing about *noblesse oblige* this week because I was bragging about the honest and helpful people I met in Thomaston, our wonderful quality of life and the gracious hospitality we enjoy as I gave my friend from Atlanta a tour of our town. When we got back to my home, I showed him my column in *The Beacon* from last week which he liked, and he went on to read another column. He looked puzzled, so I asked him what was wrong, and he replied, "I want to believe you when you tell me that the people who live in Thomaston are gracious and hospitable, but this article is downright mean. I certainly appreciate and want people to express themselves and speak forthrightly but this column is downright hateful. How representative is this person's opinion? This is detestable!" He then read out loud some of what the columnist had to say about Democrats:

- "losers and I mean losers in every sense of the word…"
- "Democratic machine and the legends of misfit lunatic supporters"

- "the meanest, most corrupt, most dishonest and most vicious political machine in existence"
- "like the Flying monkeys in Oz, they blindly do their wicked best to wreak havoc...The only skill they possess is a will to destroy"
- "pathetic...riding the gravy train...vampires".

It sounded as if the columnist was saying that the only good Democrat is a dead Democrat. My response is that from my experience, this column is in no way representative of the people I know and who (I am proud to say), exemplify *noblesse oblige.*

According to Wikipedia, *noblesse oblige* literally means nobility obligates. It denotes that wealth, power, and prestige come with responsibilities. Being privileged extends beyond mere entitlements and requires the person who holds such status to fulfill their social responsibilities, particularly in their leadership roles. If you are a moral person who claims to serve God, you must act responsibly. Privilege endows responsibilities. Among them:

1. Don't gloat in victory or cower in defeat.
2. Don't show off or brag.
3. Don't take advantage of your position or power to abuse those who may be at your mercy.
4. Resist waste, extravagance, irresponsible spending, and self-indulgence.
5. Don't be a bully.

In other words, you should be considerate and decent to others—especially those less fortunate. Those who are privileged have a sacred and moral duty to the community. Privilege must be balanced by duty towards others. Andrew Carnegie was so imbued with this concept that he wrote in *The Gospel of Wealth* (1889) that people with great wealth should redistribute their surplus with those who are trying to help themselves.

Not only do I find the people of Thomaston similarly imbued with kindness, but this is also who we are as Americans. After World War II, we did not take advantage of the vanquished and demand reparations but immediately set about rebuilding their cities, their institutions, and their lives. We not only set up factories and opened our markets for their products, but we also provided aid and expertise that brought Japan and Europe back from the brink of disaster.

Speaking of disaster, we are going all out to help the people of Albany and if there is a hurricane, tsunami, volcano, or earthquake, anywhere in the world, the

United States of America is always the first to deliver supplies and lend a helping hand. We are a beacon to the world. We are good people who believe that everyone should have a chance at health, happiness, and prosperity.

Yes, with only 5% of the world's population, we are the most powerful and successful country on earth. The more generous and considerate we are of others, the more blessed and successful we become. According to Malachi 3:10, if we are generous, God "will open the windows of heaven for you and pour out all the blessings you need." Do we really want the rest of the world to start ganging up on us?

According to Mary Achor, "True *noblesse oblige* is a responsibility for all of us who have been given the benefits of living in a free land, founded on the highest principles. If we, as a country, miss the mark, it is not a reflection on the founding principles. It means we have a responsibility to use our energies and intelligence to return to basics and fix it."

I don't believe Americans and especially the people of Thomaston are bullies! Whether we are Republicans, Democrats, or Independents, we all want to serve our country, act with honor, and remain true to its high ideals.

46.
Doing the Right Thing

February 8, 2017

This week's column is about the moral decisions we face in our daily lives. We all know the right thing to do but sometimes our courage fails us. A few weeks ago, I wrote a column about treating others the way you want to be treated and concluded that if you do that, the rest of the *Ten Commandments* or any other set of rules and laws that purport to prescribe moral conduct (The right thing to do) is just commentary.

I find that when I do the right thing, I am happy and sleep soundly without a guilty conscience. I do not sleep like a baby who wakes up every two hours. And when I am happy, my relationships improve and I enjoy the company of family and friends, have fewer headaches, and smell the roses. Deep in our hearts, we always know when we have done wrong. Additionally, I succeed in my pursuits because of God's grace. According to Malachi, if we are generous and kind to others, God "will open the windows of Heaven for you and pour out all the blessings you need."

The Mayo Clinic reported that optimists enjoyed a 50% lower risk of early death than pessimists. Your attitude has a lot to do with how long you live.

Who would you rather do business with: a cheating lying SOB who cannot be trusted or a God-fearing person who is fair and square in his or her business and relationships? Unless you were desperate, would you date and marry a dishonest person? We crave relationships that we can count on through thick and thin. Ladies and gentlemen, honest people succeed in the long run. Dishonest people may succeed occasionally but never long-term. The word does get around. You get what you give. So, don't sabotage yourself by losing all claims to trust and respect.

While many moral questions are never simple and everyone does their best with what they are working with, Mark Twain is prone to believe that all human beings are dishonest from time to time. We often face conundrums when we have to choose between all bad options. Would you eat human flesh if you were stranded in a boat in the middle of the ocean and starving to death? Would you lie and not expose a fugitive from a criminal with a gun intending to kill the fugitive? Only when we act out of duty that our actions have moral worth but duty to who and what? Duty to loved ones, employers, and organizations we pledge to support is one thing, but would you sacrifice yourself for a cause or a religious mandate? I am reminded about the song, "If loving you is wrong, I don't want to be right." I get it, sometimes our passions will get the best of us.

My grandmother was fond of saying that good deeds are like planting seeds that predictably return a good harvest. She also quoted the words of Jesus, "As you did it to one of the least of these, my brethren, you did it to me." (Mathew 25:40) and "So for what profit is it to a man if he gains the whole world, and loses his soul?" (Mathew 16:26).

Winston Churchill said, "Americans will always do the right thing in the end." While he was frustrated that we didn't enter WWII sooner, he knew that we would eventually do the right thing.

The time is always right to do the right thing. Courage is being scared and doing the right thing anyway. Do you really want to be on the wrong side of history?

My own mother advised that one second on the lips, forever on the hips. The consequences of our actions live on in some form for a very long time. So, if you are motivated to live longer and enjoy a better quality of life—the most selfish thing you can do is to be kind to others and do the right thing.

47.

The Poor Do Not Have to be With Us Always?

February 15, 2017

I was amused to learn a few years ago that the winners of the U.S. $250,000,000 Powerball lottery were three millionaires (asset managers) in Connecticut. It started me thinking about how and why the rich get richer and the poor get poorer. I am also thinking of the gentleman who prayed fervently but futilely every day for God to bless him so he could win the lottery. Finally, God spoke directly to the gentleman, "If I am going to help you win the lottery you should at least buy a ticket. I can only help those who help themselves."

A year ago, a gentleman who could neither read or write told me that his father advised him that going to school was a waste of time and that as long as he could do manual labor, he would be fine. So, for 50 years, he has been laboring, never expecting to own his own home or an automobile. It's been a struggle. He will live his entire life without reading a book.

My fervent prayer is for the poor to become independent. But my wise friend and golfing buddy insists the rich have all the luck. I tell him that the harder I practice and work at my game, the luckier I get. While it is a common occurrence for rich children to turn out to be worthless and a few children from poor families become accomplished heroes and stars, in the absence of people with extraordinary talent and discipline, as a rule it doesn't happen. Babies of the rich are fed delicious and nutritious meals with silver spoons, exposed to the movers and shakers of society as they grow up, go to the best schools, have access to effective healthcare, get tutors to help them learn how to handle their lessons, play a musical instrument and excel in sports, travel, learn to speak eloquently, dress to impress, have their choice of employment from their extensive network of family connections and then they win the lottery. On the other hand, the poor child faces daily struggles, hustles to make a living and dies 10 years before his rich counterpart only because he was born at the wrong address.

Will the poor always be with us? Several countries including Singapore, Bermuda, Kuwait, and Oman have now wiped-out poverty. That's right—no poor people. Everyone has a floor they can comfortably live with.

Two Harvard professors (Acemoglu and Robinson) did an analysis of two cities and wrote:

> In Nogales, a city cut in half by the Mexican-American border fence, there is no difference in geography between the two halves of Nogales. The weather is the same. The winds are the same, as are the soils. The types of diseases prevalent in the area given its geography and climate are the same, as is the ethnic, cultural, and linguistic background of the residents. By logic, both sides of the city should be identical economically. And yet they are far from the same.
>
> On one side of the border fence, in Santa Cruz County, Arizona, the median household income is $30,000. A few feet away, it's $10,000. On one side, most of the teenagers are in public high school, and the majority of the adults are high school graduates. On the other side, few of the residents have gone to high school, let alone college. Those in Arizona enjoy relatively good health and have health insurance, not to mention an efficient road network, electricity, telephone service, and a dependable sewage and a public health system. None of those things are a given across the border. There, the roads are bad, the infant-mortality rate is high, electricity and phone service are expensive and spotty.
>
> The key difference is that those on the north side of the border enjoy law and order and dependable government services—they can go about their daily activities and jobs without fear for their life or safety or property rights. On the other side, the inhabitants have institutions that perpetuate crime, graft, and insecurity.

48.
Shakespeare Anonymous?

February 22, 2017

After paying good money and spending valuable time that could have been profitably spent doing something else, we regretfully saw the movie, *Anonymous* based on J. Thomas Looney's theories in his book, *Shakespeare Identified.* He was joined by Sherwood Silliman and George Batty—quite a credible crowd!

Here is my recommendation: Do not waste your time or your money. It is not even as good as the PBS Special (1996) that made similar claims. In fact, thousands of books and more coming suggest that not only were Shakespeare's parents' illiterate and signed their name with an X but the boy Shakespeare had minimal education. Some say he never read a book. So where and how did he gain the experience and culture to have written so knowledgeably and eloquently about the affairs of kings and the military, geography, law, the sea, and especially the human heart?

This film is boring rubbish based on someone's notion that Shakespeare from what we know was not wise enough, educated enough, worldly enough or sophisticated enough to have written the plays, sonnets, and poetry to be regarded as the "ultimate expression of the English language." So, based only on made up stuff (circumstantial evidence), the movie supposes that Edward de Vere, Seventh Earl of Oxford, and the Queen's consort, must have been the writer. In fact, the movie did not stop at claiming that de Vere was the ghost writer for Shakespeare, it depicted Shakespeare as an ignorant, illiterate blackmailer with no redeeming social value. The movie claims that Shakespeare could not even "form his letters."

As an aside, DeVere killed a servant in anger, but the court ruled that the servant ran into deVere's sword. Such were the injustices of the day.

How is it that not one of Shakespeare's contemporaries raised the question of his authorship? For that matter, no questions were raised for 200 years after his death that THE Shakespeare did not write Shakespeare. This question gained prominence in just the last hundred years.

I have a theory. I visited several of the Mayan Temples and Pyramids in Mexico 10 years ago and took great interest in the pyramids of Chichen Itza. These magnificent structures spoke loudly about the sophistication of the Mayan people of old, the inventors of astrology and the Mayan Calendar. So, what did Europeans devise as the explanation? Non-white people could not possibly have done this. Space travelers from other planets must have lived among these people and built these edifices. The rule is: If one's achievements are remarkable, they didn't do it and they will make up some preposterous explanations to explain it—most notably, foreign or inter-planetary influence. Tell that to Usain Bolt! How does little Jamaica produce the fastest runners (both men and women) that the world has ever known? Get ready for preposterous theories—anything but nurtured talent! Ordinary people do extraordinary things all the time. What's the difference between a day laborer who never went to school and a judge? Often, just one generation!

49.
We Need a Healthcare System that Promotes Health

March 1, 2017

It is difficult to imagine that with all the great weather, open spaces, and a sports tradition, more than 50% of our children are overweight.

Obesity has reached troubling proportions in Thomaston. Since 1980, we have seen a 50% increase in the incidence of obesity every decade. This dramatic rise in obesity is inevitably accompanied by an equally critical rise in diabetes, resulting in over 10% of adults suffering from this awful disease. Diabetes is particularly nasty as it impairs eyesight, causes impotence, and may result in the amputation of toes, feet, and legs. An unhealthy community is a community without a future.

The United States has taught the world that there isn't enough money to pay for all the diseases caused by obesity, lack of exercise, cholesterol, careless driving, unsafe sexual practices, smoking and diabetes. We spend 20% of our national budget on health care. While we have a so-called 'state-of-the-art' healthcare system, our average life expectancy is lower than 30 other countries and getting worse.

When a patient has a disease, treat the disease; similarly, when a large segment of a population has a disease, treat the community. If you want to reduce violence, crime, and unwanted pregnancies, give children grandparents. Grandparents are the key. Keep us around long enough to teach and nurture subsequent generations.

We need a system that promotes health and not an expensive "healthcare system" that only treats disease. A "System of Health" emphasizes prevention, while a "health care system" places emphasis on diagnosis and treatment when the cow is out of the barn. By being proactive instead of reactive, we can inspire people to take health promotion and disease prevention seriously.

Most of the diseases that plague us and cost so much are preventable. Just about all the heart attacks, heart failure, strokes, diabetes, kidney failure (diseases that kill 50% of us) can be prevented by making simple adjustments to our lifestyles. Being proactive in health can add 10 more years to enjoy the company of our grandchildren and guide them to happy, healthy, and productive lives.

An ounce of prevention is always going to be worth more than a pound of cure. We should all recognize that if we do not take time to exercise and eat well, we will prematurely succumb to disease. If we don't take health promotion and preventive health seriously, we will reap a bitter harvest.

50.

It Takes a Village

March 15, 2017

I am thrilled, excited, proud, elated and all the other superlatives that have been making the rounds in Thomaston since our very own Upson-Lee High School boys basketball team won the State Championship by beating St. Pius X 53-48 last Friday evening, ending a perfect season (32-0) —the only undefeated basketball team in Georgia. I have been playing Pharrell Williams "Happy" and dancing. I am a happy camper. What a team! (terrific) What a coach— (Darrell Lockhart) What loving supportive families! What a community! This is a victory for the ages indelibly occupying space in our brains. When the players reach 90, they will still be reliving their fabulous 2016-2017 season. It just feels so good.

I am also reflecting about what it takes to produce this amazing basketball team and ladies and gentlemen, it takes a village. We need the entire village to come together during the maturation of our youth so they can become successful. It takes good genes. The people of Thomaston have good stock. It takes good health care. Thomaston has excellent health care. Our hospital is one of the best community hospitals in the country complemented by amazing and caring community doctors. It takes good schools with state-of-the-art facilities, good leadership, good coaching, good equipment, and enthusiastic boosters.

I am happy to report that three quarters of the crowd was rooting for Upson-Lee. We have honest politicians, clean air and water, excellent parks and playgrounds, healthy food options, good roads and kind, generous, honest hard-working people. When it all comes together, we are awesome. No one and nowhere is perfect but when we all chip in to improve our community—it makes it more perfect! I am convinced that life outside the school yard is just as important as in the school. I found my village and never miss an opportunity to brag about what a great place to call home.

A famous politician was fond of saying," If you see a turtle on top of a fence post, he didn't get there by himself."

51.
Our Commitment to Diversity is a Commitment to Excellence

April 5, 2017

Last week, my golf playing partner for the day (Wayne Stone) at Raintree asked me if I am still happy about moving to Thomaston. I responded with an unqualified and enthusiastic yes. While the members of the Raintree Rascals call me "Waine with an I" to distinguish me from Wayne with a "Y", having read my book, Bad Boy from Jamaica, and knowing my heritage, Wayne greets me as "I man." He said, "I was born and grew up here and I have never even contemplated living anywhere else." I, on the other hand, lived in Jamaica; Morristown, NJ; Indianola, Iowa; Washington, D.C.; Baltimore, Maryland; York, Pennsylvania; Sacramento and Los Angeles, California; Miami, Florida; Atlanta and now Thomaston. I have also traveled to over 100 countries. So, for those who have spent their entire lives here as well as us newcomers who have seen a lot of places, the quality of life we enjoy is to be envied by anyone who does not call Thomaston home.

We were still in a celebratory state of mind as our high school basketball team had just won the state championship. So, I said, "Thomaston is a special place, isn't it?" And we proceeded to name a few of the things we both liked—our weather, hospitable people who delight in being civil, considerate and law abiding, affordable cost of living, honest politicians, clean streets, responsive city employees including police who actually serve and protect, good healthcare, no traffic, no paid parking, good schools, a variety of foods to please any palate, etc., etc. And then we looked around the golf course and found the most beautiful flowering trees—including a few "rain trees." Yes Wayne, it's almost paradise.

But I particularly want to share with you the one ingredient that makes Thomaston great—diversity! To start with, when we moved here, white patients had no resistance to receiving their healthcare from black physicians and black patients were treated well by white doctors practicing in Thomaston.

We continue to hear many expressions of gratitude to Dr. Stephanie Kong for establishing her practice (ZÖe Pediatrics) here. We continue to grow because parents have no problem with trusting the care of their children to us. Beyond that, when we try to motivate our patients to do well in school, we have no difficulty finding role models. In addition to the many black physicians, teachers, nurses, pharmacists, our fire chief, head of the City of Thomaston electric, principal of Upson Lee High School, principal of Upson Lee Elementary (South), president of Southern Crescent College, and my favorite: coach of our State Champions. Yes, our commitment to diversity is a commitment to excellence.

We did not become a great place to live by accident. Why do you think we have never had a lynching or KKK activity here? At a time when hate crimes and name-calling is on the rise throughout the country, why does everyone get along so well? Why does Rev. James Magill get so much support and cooperation for the Emancipation Day parade and celebrations? This celebration is probably the only continuous celebration marking the freedom of slaves.

When this city was a company town, I learned that the owners of the industry (Thomaston Mills) were leaders with scruples. I am not sure anywhere else in Georgia during the 60s had white men reporting to black supervisors and they did not tolerate racism and promoted diversity not only within the company but in the community as well. As role models, they promoted fairness and equality. I dare say that our wonderful basketball tradition goes back to the basketball team they sponsored that competed with other cities. If you were a racist and a troublemaker, you could never work at the mill. The owners gave generously to churches in both black and white communities. It is in that tradition that from the proceeds of a thrift store, Ms. Betty Goins gives over $100,000 per year to local churches and charities and the Kiwanis contributes generously to the JOY summer program at Mt. Moriah Baptist Church each year.

In my many conversations with children who aspire to do great things, I point out the difference between a day laborer and a Supreme Court Justice—one generation! Justice Sonia Sotomayor was born in New York City to immigrants from Puerto Rico and was raised by a single mother. Having been raised by my grandmother, when I was a thirteen-year-old barefoot boy in Jamaica, if you had placed my mother and father in a police line-up, I wouldn't have been able to identify either one of them. And yet we rise because some great people, a lawyer, a doctor, the owner of a very successful school for children with autism, and a businessman call me Dad.

Yes, I love living in Thomaston. I especially love that we value diversity. With great genes being nurtured in an appreciation of diversity, we will contribute more than our share of excellent basketball players and scholars to the world. Great things are in our future if we continue on this trajectory.

52.
Your Integrity Matters

April 12, 2017

This is not an article about politics or any individual. While integrity is defined as the avoidance of lying, deception, misrepresentation, and non-disclosure in interactions with others, this column is a statement of expectations about people we interact with. It's a statement about how you represent yourself to the world. It's about the fact that it takes a hundred years to grow a tree, but it can be destroyed in one act of careless indulgence—just one lie!

Integrity is a vital a part of our culture. Whether it is a spouse, a member of your extended family, friends and classmates, people we do business with and just about anybody. The question is, who would you rather have as a brother or sister, friend of those with whom you do business? Those who impulsively, conveniently, and recklessly follow their impulses or those with integrity and when they tell you something, you can take it to the bank. I believe that businesses and individuals succeed because they have a reputation for integrity. You cannot hustle your way to long-term happiness and success.

The cure for sleepless nights, stress and alienation is to be a person of integrity. While he advised young people to never tell the truth to the opposite sex, Mark Twain also advised, "If you tell the truth, you don't have to remember anything." You don't have to be confused about all the lies you have told if you always tell the truth. Is it really worth it if you lie and cheat to amass power, hurt enemies and shield ourselves and sacrifice your integrity in the process? "For what will it profit a man if he gains the whole world, and loses his own soul?" Mark 8:36.

I have written several times about my impressions of the people of Thomaston who demonstrate integrity in their interaction with others. A handshake is really all you need here. Whenever I have work to do at my house, I can rely on estimates. When I needed to replace my cooling/heating system at my house, the estimates I got from A&B Heating and Cooling were reasonable and the work was done in a timely and professional manner. I have confidence that the charges are reasonable, and the work is professionally done. Whether it's hanging pictures, painting, Billy Reliford is a great handyman who I can trust. I have come to rely on the services of Cody Adams Plumbing and appreciated his knowledge of the unique plumbing system in my house. The employees of Holloway Tire always come to the rescue when my wife's tire sensors tell her that the tires need air or replacement. They go the extra mile to advise her that she may need tires. I could go on and on.

Is verifiable truth merely a concept promoted by Sunday school teachers? I have become suspicious of all those who repeat falsehoods while insisting, against all evidence, that they are telling the truth. Are alternative facts valid alternatives that are available to used car salesmen, politicians, and lawyers? Are there segments of our society that are afforded more flexibility and don't have to be honorable men and women? Are our expectations different for ministers, judges, teachers, and doctors? I contend that truth telling should be the standard for everyone. But is that standard deteriorating?

While it takes courage, according to Barbara De Angelis, "Living with integrity means: Not settling for less than what you know you deserve in your relationships. Asking for what you want and need from others. Speak the truth, even though it might create conflict or tension. Behave in ways that are in harmony with your personal values. Make choices based on what you believe, not what others believe."

53.

Beauty is in the Eye of the Beholder

April 19, 2017

When a pastor was disgraced recently, I had a conversation with one of his friends about it and without skipping a beat, he quickly sprang into action defending his friend:

> Everyone makes mistakes, that is why we have a forgiving God. He really is a good man who has apologized for his misdeeds. If I wanted to make a highlight film about your life, depending on my agenda, I could choose really awful or complementary events to highlight. In my view, this man has done a lot of good things and he is revered by his congregation.

I then brought up the facts about a young fellow we both knew who was sentenced to three months in jail for not paying for breakfast at Piggly Wiggly. Well, that was something entirely different. "That was justified. We cannot tolerate stealing in our community." The point is: People who identify themselves with a particular social group are quick to defend members of their group and quick to denigrate those who do not belong. I am even amused by a recent TV commercial that said outright, "He is not one of us." Who is us?

Perhaps my most cathartic moment in college was the lecture I heard on "In-group/out-group," a concept that was developed by Henri Tajfel from Poland. I understood the world so much better after hearing that lecture. How did I come to love the things I do while my roommate felt just the opposite? It turns out that every one of us has prejudices based on who we identify with. The explanation is that our preferences and dislikes were largely based on our group—however we define it. We like sticking with other like-minded people. People who eat bacon, eggs and grits are inclined, for example, to feel hostile towards people in Portland who have a penchant for eating granola and yogurt and we even make fun of them. In fact, people not only have positive attitudes towards members of their own group and actively promote these values even when our actions conflict with our grandmother's admonition of fairness. She taught us that we should treat others as you would have them treat you. "Karen, you know better than to act like that!"

Even when you recognize that a member of our group is a dishonest crook, the very least you will say is "He may be a dishonest crook, but he is OUR dishonest crook gosh darn it."

We will find a reason, no matter how flimsy, to prove that our country, our race, our religion, our school, and members of our family are right and feel competitive and even aggressive with other groups. My team is better. And God help us if our group feels threatened. The challenged group will band together to war with any opposing groups. Other members of our group can do no wrong and outsiders can do no right.

I am always amused when I run across teenagers in love. This must be the epitome of happiness. Life is good, and as long as they can hold hands with the object of their affection all is well with the world. Food tastes great, they hear birds singing and music goes directly to their soul. They don't notice how much he or she yells at other drivers or how aggressive he is with others. They quickly forgive each other for everything. The only thing that matters is love—you complete me. When the rose-colored glasses come off, however, the same person is likely to wonder what she ever saw is this fool.

Just remember that when your emotions are engaged, you are not likely to see things objectively.

If you grow up in Thomaston, you are not only likely to root for the Knights but to be a Braves, Bulldog and Falcons fan as well. And even if we cuss at them when they let us down, we will defend them against all others. Just recognize that where you are born has a great deal to do with what you believe, how you dress, what you eat and drink and the music that delights you—just as your devotion to your group is determined.

An Iowa teacher, (Jane Elliot) used eye color to divide her third-grade class into groups and showed how easy it was to turn half the class into victims just by designating the blue-eyed kids "better." "Within minutes, the blue-eyed children sadistically ridiculed their unfortunate classmates, calling them "stupid" and shunning them in the playground during recess. Then she flipped the situation and showed that the brown-eyed children, when on top, exacted the same punishments onto their blue-eyed classmates." Just imagine how sad and afraid these children were when they were assigned to the out-group! Do you avoid people you don't know at social occasions? Do you make a point of making them feel welcome no matter what they look like?

Just recognize that we can belong to 100 groups: men, women, democrats, republicans, children, adults, old people, rich people, poor people, Methodists, bridge players, golfers, etc., etc., you can be part of an in-group one moment and an out-group the next. You can be assigned to, or you can assign yourself. Derogation of our groups and having an affinity towards "my people", "us and them" is as old as the hills and may be with us until parrots live at sea.

So, are we hapless victims destined to oppose others based on an infinite number of classifications? No. There is hope. Being a member of a group can (even at a football game) make us act like jerks sometimes. So, always remember that you do not have to follow the crowd. You are a responsible adult who respects diversity. It turns out that if you have concerns about being called out, you are less likely to go along with the craziness that can go on sometimes.

Even if your cronies are dining with you, would it really hurt you to try granola and yogurt for breakfast? Try it, you may like it.

54.

Invest Generously in Long-Term Genetic Success

April 26, 2017

First of all, is the sun rising or setting on Thomaston? Are our best days behind us? Will we regain the momentum of the years when Thomaston had full employment and produced a plethora of products the world needed? What will take the place of the Mill? We now have high unemployment and lower rates of upward mobility for our youth. So, children who move away now do better than those who stay in Thomaston. What are we doing to help our talented children to prosper at home? Are we raising them for export?

Thomaston parents are like all parents. We all want our progeny to do better—each generation exceeding the achievements of the previous generation. Enlightened self-interest should tell us that investing in our children is the best use of our time and resources. Wouldn't you like to have children like Tiger Woods and Serena Williams whose success was directly related to their parent's efforts? Even if they do not become world beaters, they and you will benefit from continuing to invest in your children. You have to go to war with the army you have.

Which is the better investment? Buying a big house, a fancy car, setting aside money for a rainy day and retirement or paying your children's college tuition? I contend that the best investment you can make is in your children's education. It appears that our children are either healthier, obtaining more formal education or earning more than their parents. So, it is going to require a little more concentrated effort and sacrifice to get them across. Just imagine how proud you are going to be when they graduate and become self-supporting to make sure your grandchildren prosper as well. Just one high achieving person in a family will change the upward mobility in your entire family.

Good health is still the foundation for children to achieve. While medical care and breakthroughs have advanced rapidly, we do not have a handle on obesity, diet and inactivity which are risk factors for a host of diseases—diabetes, heart disease, strokes and even cancer. Please remember that health and wealth go hand-in-hand.

Those who are sick are spending money they are not making and wasting time taking care of whatever ails them.

It is important that your children stay out of trouble. If they become parents as teenagers, get hooked on drugs, get arrested or drop out of school, it greatly reduces their chances of staying on track. Our country is a remarkably forgiving place but why make it difficult?

Are we providing the best education for our children? Our basketball team gave this city a wonderful gift by winning the State Championship and becoming the only team to go undefeated in the state. Now what? Will they build on this momentum to become stars for life or was this just a moment in the sun? There is no shortage of talented kids in Thomaston, how are we maximizing opportunities so they can and will become all they can be?

With all the advantages of growing up in a computer age, the current under 30 generation is perhaps the first time in American history when they are not doing as well as their grandparents were at the same age. This is probably due to the expectation that they should be loved, appreciated, and rewarded regardless of their effort. While previous generations would tough it out, they are much more likely to quit their jobs if they are not happy with the work as it is now all about me, me, me—still expecting participation ribbons even if they came in last in the rat race. Come what may, they expect to be taken care of by parents, employers, and the government.

A Harvard University study estimates that "only half the children born in the 1980s grew up to earn more than their parents did, after adjusting for inflation. That's a drop from 92% of children born in 1940." So much for the dream that with hard work the next generation will do better than their parents. Unfortunately, many of our young people bought houses, cars, and other big-ticket items just when the economy tanked with the housing bubble leaving some of them unemployed, in debt and a little shell shocked.

The old formula still works for the next generation. Investing in our progeny starts with nurturing parents and giving our kids the opportunity to grow up in good neighborhoods, good schools and exposed to a variety of pathways that will give them choices that will propel them to a higher income and a good life.

55.

Out of School Stories of Dr. Stephanie Kong, The Pediatrician

May 3, 2017

My wife does not know I am doing this, but I thought the kids of ZÖe Pediatrics might enjoy hearing about the humorous side of their doctor. I find it amusing that kids do not usually think that their parents and older people in general were ever young, made mistakes or even had sex—ooh yack! Take, for example, when Dr. Kong was 15 years old.

Her father owned a taxi company as well as being a deacon in their local Baptist Church and her older brother "Ko" played the church organ. At the base of their beliefs was strong objections to sex outside of marriage and dancing was a grave sin. So, 15-year-old Dr. Kong was a private dancer who spent a great deal of time secretly dancing in her room with the music turned way down. This was a source of great joy to her. She loved to snap her fingers and *cut a rug*. So, when she was invited to a dance, she told her father that she was spending the night with a girlfriend and went to the dance. To her surprise, just as she was "shining a boy's belt buckle," someone tapped her on the shoulder and told her that her taxi was waiting for her. She left the dance floor, got into the taxi and no one said a word to each other. The silence continued as she exited the car and made her way to her room. Nothing more was ever said about it.

Dr. Kong's father grew up in Macomb, Mississippi. After graduating from High School, he joined the Army and fought in World War 11, then served in the occupation force in Japan under General MacArthur for 10 years. While there, he married a beautiful Japanese woman and Dr. Kong was the third of their four children. When Dr. Kong was four years old, her family returned to the United States and settled in Milwaukee. Given that she quickly learned English, her mother decided she was a genius and exempted her from housework and cooking. Even when she volunteered to help, she was told to go study. So, when her mother and siblings were away and she was home with her father, she decided to make dinner. First of all, she saw that her mother added milk to the mashed potatoes and decided it would be OK to just boil the potatoes in milk. It wasn't long before the milk had boiled over onto the stove and the pot was burned. In fact, she broiled chuck steak that even the dog couldn't chew after the steak was rejected from the dinner table. Her father's only comment was, "Girl, it's a good thing you have book learning." But she justified her mother's confidence by graduating first in her class as well as being a cheerleader that gave her the opportunity to strut her stuff. Even today, if I get her in the right mood, she will occasionally delight her husband by dressing in a short skirt and doing one of her cheers, "Yea, yea Waine Kong!" A sixteen-year-old could not do better.

After we married, it was her turn to make Thanksgiving dinner, so she tried to be creative and stuffed the Turkey with spaghetti. When all the family gathered and the bird was carved open, to everyone's shock and dismay, it was full of what appeared to be worms. It's a good thing she has many other assets—she didn't win my heart with her cooking.

A Girl Scout came to the door to collect cookies, and I was searching Dr. Kong's purse to find some money to pay her when I came across a poorly written note folded up in her wallet from a seven-year-old (Johnathan) that merely said, "I love you." It meant a lot to her.

56.
The Self-Fulfilling Prophecy

May 10, 2017

On a recent trip to Jamaica, I came across a story of a gentleman who was told by an Obeahman (Black magic practitioner) that the victim would die within three months and the gentleman in fact died two months later—he literally worried and willed himself to death. I believe it was a simple case of the self-fulfilling prophecy. "The mind is the most powerful thing in the universe" (Mashable).

If you believe something will happen, you greatly increase the chances that it will come true because of your belief. When a segment of our population believed that slaves were not intelligent enough to learn sophisticated concepts and knowledge, the powers that be denied them teachers and schools. (Why waste money on something that will not yield any result?) Then they would pull the rabbit out of the hat by comparing their academic achievements to those of white children who went to school and proclaim, "See, I told you that Black children cannot learn." They then expected everyone to overlook the fact that they did not receive the same educational opportunities.

Dr. Robert Merton, a sociologist, came up with the "self-fulfilling prophecy" in 1948. He wrote:

> The self-fulfilling prophecy is, in the beginning, a false definition of the situation evoking a new behavior which makes the original false conception come true. This specious validity of the self-fulfilling prophecy perpetuates a reign of error. For the prophet will cite the actual course of events as proof that he was right from the very beginning.

Ergo, a strongly held belief, even if it is actually false, on many occasions, influenced by expectations, results in the fulfillment of a false prediction.

According to the Thomas Theorem, "If men define situations as real, they are real in their consequences." Our beliefs and behaviors are often determined by how we define our situation rather than how these situations really are. Even if ABC Bank is in fine shape, if someone falsely passed the word on social media that ABC Bank is in trouble and if people believe it, they will immediately withdraw their deposits while they can and cause a run on the bank and what do you have? Insolvency. The perpetrator then declares, "See I told you that ABC Bank was in the toilet!" Predictions often contribute to its accomplishment. If the rumor monger had spread the opposite statement, "ABC Bank" is a very stable bank, it will attract more customers and voilà! the bank succeeds mostly on reputation.

The same goes for the stock market. If the word goes out that company XYZ is in trouble, sufficient numbers of stockholders will immediately sell, causing a downward drift in their stock prices which then makes the stock price go down and add fuel to the fire and more and more people will yell, "sell!!!" which then leads to a dramatic depression of XYZ stock which was completely unwarranted. People who short stocks take advantage of this.

In our personal life, our expectations change our behavior in ways we may not notice. If a fortune teller tells you that you will meet the love of your life today and you believe it, you will likely go out looking for Prince Charming and pick up on a lot of unintended cues but since men are responders, a smile will attract some interaction and voilà! you have met your Prince Charming.

In a very memorable study, a teacher was told that previously labeled slow learning students were fast learners and the fast learners were the slow learners. At the end of the semester, the slow learners got better grades than the fast learners. Expectations are a very powerful part of performance. Don't judge a book by its cover! Keep your eyes wide open.

57.
Happy Mother's Day!

May 17, 2017

For this Mother's Day, I am sharing a part of my novel, *Bad Boy from Jamaica*. I am attempting here to describe the life of women in rural Jamaica:

The day begins early for women. From infancy to old age, from sunup to sundown, the women do most of the work. There is no job description or salary as they go about doing whatever needs to be done to promote the comfort and well-being of their families.

Ms. Minnet carved out an existence on "mi piece of *rockstone*" by digging, planting, weeding, harvesting, preparing the meals, getting down on her knees to scrub and polish the floors with a coconut brush and red beeswax with a rhythm that could serve as back-up for any reggae band. When they wash the clothes, the music they create from the simple act of squeezing soap and water from the rags invites voyeuristic fascination. Ironing, sewing on the buttons, darning the socks, mending the clothes, bearing children as well as carrying heavy burdens on her head on a *catta* of banana leaves were routine. It is sometimes a 10-gallon tin of water brought from the parish tank or a large basket full of vegetables to market. She is not required to work more than 16 hours per day except when her man wants her (which he does often).

As women are not allowed to wear pants, sleeveless or tight dresses, they wore their frocks with pride with the ever-present apron tied around her waist.

The women of Woodlands District are strong and waste no time fretting about the yoke on their backs even when they are bent over, ached, racked with pain and become bruised. They say, "A woman we name and we *trong*." They will not even take an aspirin. While she is often bare footed, unacquainted with even the basic necessities of daily life and unadorned with fancy clothes and jewelry, the love and dedication she feels for her family and community is genuine, earnest, sincere, and occasionally enthusiastic, providing the wind beneath their wings and an umbrella when it rains. They use every opportunity to elevate the members of the community physically, morally, and spiritually—no one goes hungry as they are perpetually gathering the ingredients for the next meal.

There is plenty of pain and suffering here, but it doesn't last. It just makes the joy of good times that much sweeter. Get to know any one of them, and you will find something to respect, something to admire and something to love. And when they reach the pearly gates of Heaven, the angels will welcome them with songs of praise and God will utter the familiar words, "Well done, good and faithful servant. Come in and claim your reward.

58.

The Hope of Sudden Salvation: Will He Ever Straighten Up and Fly Right?

May 24, 2017

Part and parcel of our Christian beliefs is that we believe in redemption. People can and do change—sometimes even suddenly. Like the conversion of Saul on the road to Damascus, who was converted by lightning or some other enlightenment, cathartic, purification, or liberation experience to become the wise and evangelistic advocate for the church—it does happen, but not often. One day, Saul was persecuting the new Christians, the next day he was a new man (Paul) who became the best, most articulate advocate for the fledgling church. We can only hope!

I can certainly testify that change is possible, but I can also testify that most of the time, it's not going to happen. For example, men marry women expecting their wives to stay the same but they inevitably change (especially when children become the priority). Similarly, women marry men expecting them to change but their husbands usually don't. Actually, trying to change others (except for your children) is a bad idea and often make them frustrated, resentful and even hateful. Can a leopard change his spots? No one is going to stop doing something even when it hurts them and others until they really commit to change. How many psychologists does it take to change a light bulb? One. But the light bulb must really want to change.

Some of us are early adopters. We know what's good for us and do it. In fact, some of us can just snap our fingers and immediately change our wicked ways or those ingrained patterns of behavior. Personally, I am not too fast or too slow to change, I am just half fast. At 73 years old, I am not a friend of technology and resist as much as I can. I wish I could buy a car without a computer and buy a TV with an on and off switch. Am I the only one who has difficulty operating a TV? And you won't find me on social media.

A long-suffering wife prays that her philandering husband will commit to his marriage vows. A lying businessman who makes a habit of cheating his customers. A criminal goes in and out of prison for the same reasons. A public servant (caught doing wrong) cries holding the Bible in his right hand and swears that he will change. Do you believe he will or is he just going to be more careful not to get caught next time? A teenager who doesn't read, skips school, shoplifts, gets into fights, drives recklessly and curses at his parents. Is there any hope?

And what about you and me? According to Michael Jackson, "I'm starting with the man in the mirror / I'm asking him to change his ways / And no message could have been any clearer / If you want to make the world a better place…" You have been trying to change some things about yourself for a long time. As much as you make a concerted effort to lose weight, stop smoking, be a better husband/wife/mother/father, you end up in the same place. How is that working out for you? Every year, you make the same New Year's resolutions, and you fall back into the same rut. So, just stop it already? We resist change even when the consequences are severe.

Changing habits that were ingrained since I was seven years old is hard. Mark Twain said it best, "Habit is habit, and not to be flung out of the window by any man, but coaxed downstairs a step at a time." When I stop denying and decide that something is not working for me and resolve to change, I have to own up to the habit and convince myself that change is possible. I can do this! Interestingly, I have discovered that when I change, people respond differently and now I have changed others as well.

I find that 99.5% won't do it! I have to be fully committed and make an oral pledge. In addition to supplicating ourselves to the Almighty, the great value of kneeling, holding hands and praying with my wife by the side of our bed each morning is that we get to tell each other what changes we want in our lives. So, with the help of our God and each other, we are more committed to live up to our promises. Sometimes it's baby steps and sometimes it's immediate. I recognize that people are always trying to break our oars as we paddle our way through life. So, I have to be careful that others will not talk me out of doing what I know is the right thing to do. If I hang around with alcoholics, they are certainly not going to help me stop drinking.

Instead of ordering someone to, "don't do that!" I share my feelings as follows: "When you do that, I feel betrayed." I tell them how I feel. I find that those who care about me are not likely to persist in doing something that will upset me.

Most importantly, if I fail to become the change I want, I will reset and start all over again. Even moderate change will make a difference. I find that successful changes in my behavior influence others (especially in my family) that greatly enrich my life.

According to Dale Carnegie, "Feeling sorry for yourself and your present condition is not only a waste of energy but the worst habit you could possibly have."

59.
Does Regular Church Attendance Reduce Crime?

June 7, 2017

Last week, I was engaged in a conversation, maybe it rose to the level of an argument, with one of my pastor friends. He claimed that "the crime rate is related to how many people go to church and accept Jesus Christ as their personal savior. Christian communities, (high participation in church) have less crime because we abide by Christian principles," he said with emphasis. As intuitive as this may be, after researching the issue, here is what I found when I compared the United States of America (especially the Bible Belt), a Christian country, with Japan, where few people belong to a religion and 75% of them are atheists, agnostics or adhere to no religion.

Even though Japan has 22% fewer law enforcement personnel per 100,000, the United States have four times more crime, 27 times more rapes, 148 times more violent crimes and 26 times more murders than Japan. It turns out that crime in Japan is the lowest of all industrialized countries. So, there doesn't seem to be a correlation. The Japanese claim that they can be moral, upstanding, considerate and know right from wrong without religion. Treating others, the way you want to be treated (brotherly love) is not just a Christian mandate, it is universal. It is just being human.

However, I will readily admit that the evidence would suggest that within Christian countries and communities, those who attend church are more likely to comply with the law and have more of a conscience, especially as it relates to petty crimes (traffic offenses, shoplifting, drugs, and juvenile delinquency). The correlation holds up even if only their mothers attend church. See, if you just pray for them, it will help.

Philip Hodges, the authors of this study, believe this is because, "religion not only teaches people about 'moral and behavioral norms', but also spending time with like-minded people makes it less likely they'll get mixed up with the 'wrong crowd.'"

But according to atheist Ricky Gervais, "I don't believe in God, but I live as if there is one."

60.
The Poisonwood Bible

June 14, 2017

My daughter (Jillian) read Barbara Kingsolver's novel, *The Poisonwood Bible* (published by HarperCollins in 1998), and excitedly recommended that I read it as well—which I enjoyed! I loved it so much, I am recommending it to the readers of *The Beacon*. It is a beautifully written novel and a fascinating story.

The story line is that a Baptist Preacher (Rev. Nathan Price) from Bethlehem, Georgia (Barrow County) sponsored by The Southern Baptist Mission League, sets out to take over a mission in a very poor remote village (Kalanga) in the Belgian Congo. In tow, were his wife and four teenage daughters. You can well imagine the culture shock they experience as, for example, while the village women wear long dresses to cover their legs, they wear nothing above their waist and all the children just go naked.

Rev. Price, a committed servant to the Lord, was anxious to be successful but he had several things going against him and his zeal to bring lost souls to Christ. First, he doesn't speak the language and needs a translator and has no idea what the translator is really telling the people. Second, he tries to increase his flock but since he is preaching the Christian principle of "one wife," he opposes the village chief who has six wives and this cannot be reconciled. Third, he tries to baptize the people, but no one is willing to put a foot into the river because it is infested with crocodiles. Fourth, he puts in a garden to provide food but doesn't recognize that they don't have bees to pollinate the pumpkins. In the meantime, they are either flooded out by the rains or become parched when the rains go away for six months at a time. Fifth, they are overrun with ants, the people are starving and infected with malaria. The final straw for Rev. Price is the great obstacle of the civil war that changed Congo into Zaire.

With the outbreak of the revolution, Rev. Price is ordered back home but the good reverend, believing that his work had only just begun, refuses to leave, and is cut off—penniless and without even passports. His wife and children cannot talk him into bringing them back to Georgia. This leads to a great deal of suffering and disruption of the family.

The Prices learn that the village chief is interested in marrying one of their daughters. Subsequently, they ask a man to pretend that she was already engaged to him, but the arrangement leads to a permanent relationship. Another daughter dies from a snake bite. The mother and one daughter abandon Rev. Price and return to Georgia where that daughter becomes a pediatrician, another daughter moves to South Africa and the fourth marries her father's translator and lives happily ever after with four children—kind of! Here is part of their narrative:

> ...by the time we were united last fall, I was unsure enough of God and too mad at everybody else to offer any kind of salvation. For sure, I'd had enough of poverty-chastity-obedience to trade it in on being Anatole's wife. A medical evacuation Jeep got me though disguised as a corpse all the way to Biloki, an

old rubber plantation settlement outside of Coquilhatville. My sweetheart, released from prison after three years without formal charges, was waiting here to raise the dead.

The novel is an excellent back-channel story of the revolution in the Congo, (known today as The Democratic Republic of Congo)

I hope I have shared enough to interest you.

61.

The Importance of Fathers

June 21, 2017

Happy Father's Day to all the wonderful fathers of Georgia. It's your day—celebrate and enjoy. You have done your part to bring a new life into the world, but your joy is far from over. And if you put your heart and soul into your responsibilities, your joy will be everlasting while your absence in their lives creates a void that cannot be replaced.

Maybe you heard that "if mama ain't happy, nobody is happy." What really make mamas happy are the support and kindness of fathers for them and your children. A father's influence is not only felt in his interaction with his children but in the kindness to his children's mother, and even their mother's mother. If you want emotionally healthy and mature children, be kind to mama. Studies show that:

> Parents who are in stable relationships are more responsive, affectionate and confident with infants; more self-controlled in dealing with defiant toddlers; and better confidants to teenagers seeking advice and emotional support.

And the most important ingredient is engaged fathers.

I hope you have heard about Dr. Elizabeth Kubler Ross. She interviewed thousands of patients who knew that they would die within 30 days and reported that not one of them ever said, "I wish I had spent more time at the office or at work." At the end of their lives, none of them took much pride in their accomplishments or the "things" they accumulated. However, one 100% of them talked about the quality of their relationships and wished they had spent more time with their children, family, and friends. At the end of the day, what do you leave behind?

My wife and I were visiting our friends (Dr. and Mrs. Malcolm Taylor in Jackson, MS) when their four children were sharing fond memories of their childhoods and the one memory, they all remembered, was that on Saturday mornings, their father would lovingly make bacon and individual pancakes with his special recipe.

"They were sooooooo good and made me smile just thinking about those pancakes."

"I would think about those pancakes all week and wake up to that wonderful aroma every Saturday morning."

Their mother (Gwen) could take it no more and yelled, "You ungrateful wretches'! I made almost every meal in this house for your entire lives and the only meals you remember fondly are those stupid pancakes your father made. And it wasn't even every Saturday morning either, it wasn't even once a month."

Gwen and Malcolm made a commitment to their extended family that they would never miss a birthday, anniversary, graduation, wedding, or funeral for any of their family. It is no wonder that they are truly happy people. One of the great life lessons Dr. Taylor taught me is, "If you have God, family and friends, you may stumble, but you will never hit the ground." I encourage all fathers to create happy memories with their children. Some day you may be surprised when one of your children becomes famous, they will wave at the camera and say, "Thank you Dad!"

Ladies and Gentlemen, family is important, and fathers are very important. I make a point of visiting with every father I see bringing their children to the doctor. I point out that only 10% of dads accompany their children to the pediatrician, so they are special, and I remind the mothers that they have a good man. Supporting your children and spending time with them will pay off in spades. We need you Dad!

62.

The Thomaston-Upson County Airport: An Important Asset

June 28, 2017

Believe it or not, an airfield (Reginald Grant Field) once operated where the county jail and Department of Transportation (DOT) is currently located. The idea of a modern airport was conceived in about 1980, but the petition to the FAA was rejected in 1986. Undaunted by the rejection, the founding board members (Dr. Dewey Jones, Mr. Lynn Bates, Mr. Foy Bentley, Mr. George Hightower, Jr., and Mr. Mike Lambert) praying as if all depended on God and working as if all depended on them, proceeded to buy land, re-petitioning the FAA as well as lobbying all the political connections at their disposal. Lo and behold, in 1991 the FAA not only approved the application but funded it as well. It was the first new airport approved by the FAA in Georgia in 20 years. So far, the FAA has spent approximately $20 million with Upson County and the City of Thomaston chipped in about 10%. And here is the important part, our airport is debt free. According to Mr. George Hightower, the success of the airport is a testament to "when people work together, (county and city governments) good things happen. For a town our size, a 6,350-foot, runway airport is an extraordinary facility."

The airport terminal was designed by local architect Mr. David Tyler, and built by Reddick Construction, and a great deal of credit goes to the enthusiastic support of Mayor Charles Kersey.

The current manager of the airport is Mr. Mitch Ellerbee and current Airport Authority Board of Directors include Mr. George Hightower, Jr., chairman, Mr. Jim Wagner, vice chairman, Mr. Henry Wilder, secretary/treasurer, Mr. Freddie Daniel, Dr. Wayne Dodgen and Mr. Bob Fletcher.

There are 97 based aircraft, including five business operations, 100 T-hangars and four corporate hangars. The joint city and county industrial development authority has successfully recruited several major businesses to whom airport access was an important ingredient. In addition to local pilots, our airport serves the needs of our important industrial partners: Standard Textile, Quad Graphics, Dart Container, Interfor, Jordan Lumber, Simms Bark, Caterpillar and Bandag. Our airport continues to be an important asset making a tremendous economic impact on our community.

When my wife and I visited Alaska, we were reminded about how important airports are to the local needs as with no roads or waterways, planes were the only way local villages (Eskimos) had any connection to the rest of the world. When we landed, the pilot had to first buzz the field to scare away the birds and beasts before landing.

Our airport is also fun! Each year, local pilots offer three opportunities for community residents to take 15-minute flights over Upson County: (1) as part of the Christmas Stocking Fund; (2) Wounded Veterans Spring Event and (3) ZÖe Pediatrics sponsors a "Come Fly with Me" picnic for all our children who complete their well child visits when over 150 excited children take to the sky and are exposed to the joy of flying. The pilots are the most gracious and hospitable people representing the best of Thomaston. Their dream is to introduce flying to every segment of our community.

"Skydive Atlanta " operates out of our airport and if you just crane your neck on weekends, you can see these brave souls falling from the sky. Have you ever told your children that if at first you don't succeed, you should try, try and try again? Please be aware that this does not apply to skydiving. After it was reported that President Bush had gone skydiving, I said, "If our President can do this, sign me up!" So, I went off to the blue yonder and actually jumped off a perfectly good airplane and not only survived to talk about it, it was amazing—the thrill lasted for two weeks. If you would like to try it, just call Trey Holliday 706/647-9701 and you too can have the thrill of a lifetime with certified jump masters.

According to Leonardo da Vinci, "Once you have tasted flight, you will forever walk the earth with your eyes turned skyward, for there you have been and there you will always long to return."

63.

Would You Place Your Party's Interests Above the Interests of Your Country?

July 5, 2017

There is something in us as Americans that is always itching for a fight. We like to stand our ground, and nobody is going to tell us what to say or do. This is often a good thing. It makes us the kind of people who would dump tea in the harbor or come to the aid of victims. There's a lot to be said for good old-fashioned American cantankerousness. This national trait is best when it makes us think critically, like in legal trials when two opposing sides make their best arguments to get at the truth or at least a decision. It does not serve us particularly well when picking fights with our friends and neighbors and that one uncle who exposed your family secrets. And, of course, it is a national disgrace when it leads to violence.

After James Hodgkinson opened fire on a group of Congressional Republicans at a baseball practice, injuring House Majority Whip Steve Scalise, there were renewed calls for "civility" in our national discourse. But that talk almost immediately devolves into calls for the other side to show civility. We have become a nation of people who can't—even with a congressman fighting for his life in the hospital—pause from posturing and jockeying long enough to examine whether, perhaps, we have been too coarse, too "scorched earth" in our rhetoric. Certainly, our leaders can't depart from their talking points long enough to show their humanity.

A reporter asked a politician, "Did the Democrats or the Republicans win?" A citizen standing on the sidelines asked, "What about us? Did the people win? What about the country? Isn't the duty of elected officials to be servants to all the people? Does loyalty to a chosen party trump all?" I then started thinking about individuals who would sell out or sacrifice their country for individual gain or the good of the party. Who cares if the country is doomed?

If an enemy of our country gave you millions of dollars to betray your country, would you deal? If you were a senator and your vote would be devastating for your party but great for the country, how would you vote? Does the party come first?

Who do elected officials represent, the people or the party? What if the elected representative must act against the party for the good of the country? This will most likely bring some of them in conflict with die-hard party loyalists but an absolutely necessary action for the good of the country.

The obligations of all elected representatives are to serve all citizens, promote the unity of the country, protect, and promote the interests of the people—justice for all! In other words, elected officials are required to serve the interest of all those who did not support them, who did not even vote or voted against them. Elected officials are responsible for the well-being of ALL the people, not just members of his friends, family, tribe, or party—friends AND foe alike. This is a tall order that requires wisdom and vision.

In some Third World countries, "to the victor go the spoils" and to take advantage of every opportunity to advance himself and his tribe. The ruling monarchy in Europe treated the country as a family enterprise. First and foremost, the interest of the King was paramount. The Magna Carta put a halt to that thinking. Maybe you haven't read The Constitution lately, but even the soundtrack to the musical, *Hamilton* will tell you that our Founding Fathers were very worried that the hard-fought unity of the states would be torn apart into factions. Mind you, that's when they weren't killing each other in duels. They were as stubborn and ferocious as any American before or since, but they believed in this little social experiment called America and they wanted it to succeed.

Can we just get along? In an era of aggressive partisan politics, there seems to be no interest in consensus, but it is being severely tested. War, war, war in every undertaking or initiative by hardcore party loyalists. How will the political drama play out? How does the country benefit?

According to Harvard Professor Laurence H. Tribe, it will require a serious commitment to constitutional principles and courageous willingness to put devotion to the national interest above self-interest and party loyalty. Where is the courage of caring patriots? Will someone stand up? Will you let the country go to hell because some personal advantage is being realized? Where is your patriotism?

Loyalty to self-interest and party politics ends when the best interest of the country is being compromised.

64.
How Is Your Compassion?

July 12, 2017

In a recent commencement speech, excerpted below, Chief Justice Roberts said:

> From time to time in the years to come, I hope you will be treated unfairly, so that you will come to know the value of justice. I hope that you will suffer betrayal because that will teach you the importance of loyalty. Sorry to say, but I hope you will be lonely from time to time so that you don't take friends for granted. I wish you bad luck, again, from time to time so that you will be conscious of the role of chance in life and understand that your success is not completely deserved, and that the failure of others is not completely deserved either...

This is one of the most amazing and inspirational commencement speeches I have ever heard. And I have nothing to add—my sentiments exactly.

John Glover Roberts Jr. (born January 27, 1955) has been on the Supreme Court since September 29, 2005, having been nominated by President George W. Bush after the death of Chief Justice William Rehnquist.

65.
Cultivating Successful Children: Raising Soaring Eagles in Your Household

July 19, 2017

Your children are talented, beautiful, born in the USA, living in the land of opportunity and Thomaston—a really nice place to grow. Given the gene pool in Georgia, some of them are geniuses. You don't just want them to stay out of trouble (unwanted pregnancy, drugs, and crime) when they have the potential to do remarkable things with their lives. So, become fanatical about their achievements. Devote yourself to their prosperity, success, and happiness. Your investment will pay off in spades!

While there is no ironclad set of rules or even set recommendations for cultivating successful children, here are seven suggestions for investing in your children's future.

1. **The most important gift you can give your children is good health**. Fortunately, with the growing sophistication of pediatric medicine and your access to good medical information, it is not difficult to learn that prevention is best. If you want happy exuberant kids, choose a good pediatrician. Take from the grocery store only what is good for your family. If you buy candy, doughnuts, sodas, hot dogs etc., someone in your family will eat it. Take sugar and animal fats out of your family's diet. Make food habits that are both mentally and physically healthy and the family that eats together nourish each other. Parents should be good role models with regard to healthy eating and have a positive attitude about food. Each day should include an hour of vigorous activity. Don't forget that health and wealth go together. If your children are sick, you are spending money and wasting time that should otherwise be used to make money.

2. **Education is key to prosperity.** Have high expectations for their achievement. Don't be guilty of low aim. You only have a few years to make sure they get a good education. This is the best guarantee that they will not be living with you until they are 40. Develop math skills early and read with them often.

3. **Ethics and respect for the law and other people are the ingredients for getting along with family, friends, and neighbors.** Raise socially competent children. Teach them good manners, cooperation, and social skills. Here are the rules of engagement with others. Smile, greet and inquire about their health as well as the well-being of their family members. Smile again. Those who are difficult, hard to get along with and who profess hate are destined to be unproductive and lonely. Enlightened self-interest should tell you that violence and hatred have no place in the life of successful people. They never miss an opportunity to help a damsel in distress or come to the aid of those less fortunate. By the way, criminals have a horrible quality of life, poor health, and a short life expectancy. If you value a good night's sleep, encourage your children to do the right thing.

4. **Money management**. Open a bank account for each of your children and teach them money management—specially to spend less than they earn. Money is not the root of all evil; it's the lack of money that tempts people to be dishonest and cunning.

5. **Create opportunities for your children to engage with teachers, preachers and other sophisticated successful people who travel.** Reach out to those who enjoy the respect of others—adopt mentors. Don't be too proud or too scared to ask for advice. Successful people are only too happy to share what they learned along the way including the secrets of how they got where they are. Have them read books about the lives of great people. If the people your kids hang around with are happy, it will infect them; if their company is sad, gloom will follow. Frustrated friends and family make kids frustrated and inclined to act out.

6. **Minimize distractions and embarrassing moments.** Family conflicts, divorce, crime create psychological pain and distress. Fight fair and teach them to compromise and get along. Teach them how to work things out when they disagree. Are your kids embarrassed or proud to bring a friend home?

7. **Keep them busy.** Have a dog or a pet to take care of. Give them chores (clean up the yard, put out the garbage). Teach them the value of work and responsibility. If they are lazy and shirk their responsibilities, it will invade all aspects of their life. Whether it's Tae Kwon Do, dancing, music, drama, or sports, they should all be taking lessons of one kind or another.

And to the extent you can, become passionate about the other children in your extended family and community. Don't hoard opportunities. If they succeed, you will also succeed; If they fail, we all fail.

66.
I Woke Up Not Dead Again in Thomaston

July 26, 2017

I was watching my favorite show "CBS Sunday Morning" last Sunday and one of my favorite people was being featured—Willie Nelson. Some years ago, a greatly exaggerated rumor circulated that he had died. So, he made lemonade out of lemons and wrote the hit song, "I woke up not dead again." It is on par with other great lines from country music, "If I told you, you had a beautiful body, would you hold it against me?" and "I am the only hell my mama ever raised." Country singers certainly have a way with words.

I woke up without an alarm clock about 6 a.m., not dead again in Thomaston (Sunday, July 16) checked my big toe and didn't find a tag tied to it. So, I got out of bed and found my wife already working on her computer. She is passionate about making sure our patients are receiving great care, so, as president and CEO of ZÖe Pediatrics, she reviews her patients' diagnosis and treatment plans and sends reminders to our wonderful doctors and nurse practitioners. So, she is always up and working early (seven days per week) —even when we are on vacation.

We greeted each other and I turned my back on her to get my morning back scratch (she does it just right and she always hits the spot). I take the cup of coffee she hands me, and I go outside to hear the cacophony of bird calls coming from the tall Georgia pines that guard our house. It really is an amazing concert each morning in Thomaston. I sit in a comfortable rocking chair and sip my coffee while I admire my domain and read. I get some reading and writing done each day. A former teacher advised me that if you love to read, you will never be bored. She was right.

I love the house we "inherited" (by purchase) from Ms. Sylvia Jorgensen and improved on by my wife as everywhere I cast my eyes, I find something pleasing. I smile a lot. As I take my morning walk, all my senses are alerted. It's a perfect 72 degrees and the sunrise is colorful. I celebrate my life, the wife I love, my accomplished children and my beautiful grandchildren. I am surrounded on all sides by elegance. My health and strength are not what it used to be, but I still play my daily round of golf, swim and workout at the Wellness Center at Upson Regional Medical Center. I find myself replaying the wonderful party for the Raintree Rascals at Al and Sybil Uphold's amazing house the evening before. What a wonderful group of human beings I am fortunate to associate with!

I go in to check my computer and see that Bob Gallman sent me another "funny" video which I appreciate, and I particularly enjoy the video my daughter sent me. She has a terrific voice and is the soloist in the choir at her church in Phoenix. So, thanks to the miracle of technology, I regularly see and hear her sing and she occasionally sends me sermons when she gets on her high horse. Other e-mail messages testify to the well-being and accomplishments of our children and grandchildren.

My reveries are interrupted by my wife calling me to our traditional Sunday breakfast (bagels, lox with pepper jelly, caviar, capers, red onions and cream cheese) fruits, berries, and cranberry juice. We then sit down to watch, *Sunday Morning*. It is wonderfully informative and entertaining and ends at 10:30 just in time to get ready for church. Unfortunately, since we opened our "After Hours Pediatric Care" Centers in Barnesville and Columbus, my wife works on Sundays and so, she cannot accompany me to church. Nevertheless, she faithfully studies her Bible, listens to Joyce Meyer and we pray together.

I get dressed for church. Due to my English upbringing, I am not comfortable going to church without wearing a suit but unlike other churches, the men who attend Greater Mount Zion Baptist Church (where I belong) most of the men are arrayed in sartorial splendor and the ladies are dressed in fine frocks and hats. It is Men's and Women's Day, and Rev. Reeves is in rare form. I particularly enjoy when he sings and today, we are treated to two of his renditions. He could be a professional entertainer if he wanted to, but he is seriously committed to serving the Lord. With Jimmy Harris on the organ, our music program is way and among the best in the county. So, with an inspirational sermon and well wishes from everyone, my spirits are lifted.

I have a wonderful brunch at Niecy's (I love her sweet potatoes) and make it to Raintree in time for our 2 pm tee time with Willie Bee, Randy, Calvin, and Curtis. We have been playing together now for over five years. As my driver was off-key and my putts were afraid of the dark, I paid everyone, but a good time was had by all. There was plenty of harassment and laughter.

Even though I know that none of us will get out of here alive, at 74 years old, I rejoice whenever I wake up, not dead. I marvel about how life is like a roll of toilet paper, the closer you get to the end the faster it rolls. It seems we only moved to Thomaston a little while ago, but it's been going on six years.

67.

Our Iceland Adventure: A Land of Wonder, Beauty and a Lot to Do

August 2, 2017

In 1833, Jonas Hallgrimsson, a nationalistic romantic poet, wrote about the country of Iceland, "Built from lava by divine creation; A fortress for a liberated nation." It is that and more. My wife and I just returned from our Icelandic vacation that will be the source of conversation for months. Our decision to visit Iceland was influenced by our search for wonder, beauty, and the variety of interesting things to do. Clearing customs in Iceland is a cakewalk. No interrogation, no searching of luggage or duty on anything. The country doesn't even have an army, navy or defense force. Coming out from customs, we easily found our luggage as well as the gentleman holding up a sign with our name. He greets us warmly and takes us to his car for a 45-minute drive to the Borge hotel in Reykjavík. En route, in perfect English, the driver gives us a general orientation: It is not as cold as one would suspect. In fact, thanks to the gulf stream, it's rather mild, given that it is close to the Arctic cycle/North Pole. Their ancestors were Vikings and because most of the land is uninhabitable, 80% of them live in Reykjavik.

Iceland has excellent universal health care—no private hospitals and no medical insurance companies. They emphasize prevention and have low rates of birth defects, infant, and maternal mortality. Iceland can boast that they are one of the healthiest people on earth and have a longer life expectancy than the United States. Their youth are particularly vigorous and spend a great deal of time hiking and climbing. They also party hard. The wonder of Iceland is that during the summer, there is hardly any darkness—so, no streetlights. I imagined that I could play seven rounds of golf in a day. In winter, the sun doesn't show itself for more than a few hours per day but is characterized by the colorful northern lights when the sun shoots off flares. The island is the size of Cuba but inhabited with only 330,000 citizens. On any day, there are more tourists than citizens.

There are 130 volcanoes causing continuous eruptions. It literally sits on a huge lava/magma bed that pushes up 1,000 geysers rich in sulfur and silica. This boiling steam is used to heat houses and swimming pools. It was really "cool" to immerse our bodies in the Blue Lagoon. They claim it will make you younger and more vigorous, but I could find no evidence for it. All I will claim is that it was warm and wet. They are really strict about taking complete showers before going out into the pool area. The reason the population is so diminished is that there have been several shocks to their system. In addition to devastating volcanoes and extended winters, there were two plague epidemics in 1402 and 1494 that killed off half their population leaving "babies suckling on the breast of their dead mothers".

Their language (Icelandic) is only spoken in Iceland but not to worry, everyone (and I mean everyone) speaks perfect English. The language is Norse in origin. Even though the English ruled Iceland for 30 years and we (USA) had a large base there for over 50 years, there are no English words in their language and take it from me, it is impossible to learn it if you were not raised on it. In addition to their language, naming babies is truly unique. The parent's first name becomes the child's last name. No last names!

They never say Mister, Madam, Doctor, Reverend. Everyone is treated as equal—grown-up and children alike. Most of the population is Lutheran. Can you imagine a country without even one Baptist Church? Where is their soul? In any case, my impression is that they are not regular churchgoers but use the church mostly for weddings, funerals, baptismal ceremonies. The Grand Church of Hallgrimur is the iconic symbol of Reykjavik. They have no mosquitoes, snakes, or dangerous animals. It is a country of mountains, glaciers, geysers, waterfalls, lava fields, crevices, pastures, and many rivers to cross. The landscape is just beautiful! The downside is that they have no fruit trees, and their tallest trees are about 20 feet tall. The joke is that if you are ever lost in an Iceland forest, just stand up.

In terms of things to do, if you stayed for a year, you would still have many mountains to climb. In addition to the guided tours of their museums, waterfalls, and concert hall, we rode horses, strapped on capons and climbed up Mt. Hekla (Gateway to Hell) and for about five hours, we toured the mountains, rivers and streams using four-wheel motorcycles. They are very versatile vehicles that can climb steep inclines and ford rivers even when the water came up to our knees. Their economy is almost entirely supported by tourism along with finance, biotechnology, fishing, and some manufacturing. As a result, everything connected to tourism is expensive. A glass of wine is $20 and be prepared to spend $50 for lunch. A hotdog is $10! Iceland has always had difficulty for one reason or another keeping their people home. Many of them migrate to Europe, Canada, and the United States. As a result, their population is not growing. They will only award citizenship to people who can speak their language. One lady was able to speak a little of it but told the panel testing her that she "washed Mr. Johansen" when she meant she washed his clothes. We are thankfully back in Thomaston. The real reason for traveling is the joy of returning home to our own bed. We have seen the lights of Paris and the lights of Rome but the lights we like best of all are the ones we turn off before snuggling in our own beds.

68.

Call Me Deacon

August 16, 2017

You may have heard the story of a Deacon Brown who was very enthusiastic about his role as a leader in his church and community. When it was prayer time, he was heard begging the Lord, "Use me Lord, use me." Back in the day when churches had wooden benches, the church ladies complained that the benches had splinters that were attacking them in the most inconvenient places and ruining their frocks. They begged the pastor to do something about this discomfort and the pastor immediately thought of Deacon Brown and assigned him the task of sanding out the splinters and varnishing the benches. But weeks passed and nothing was being done about the benches. The one thing that had changed however, was that during prayer time Deacon Brown was heard shouting, "Use me Lord, use me but use me in an advisory capacity."

While I hope to be more committed than Deacon Brown, you can now add "Deacon" to whatever you are used to addressing me. On Sunday, Aug. 5, the Leadership, and members of Greater Mount Zion Baptist Church voted me in to serve as one of 14 deacons presiding at our church. Rev. Charles Reeves and Chairman of the Deacon Board, Deacon Dwain Williams, were kind enough to invite me to stand before our church to be confirmed by the congregation. After an affirmative vote, I took my place among the other deacons.

In my acceptance, I merely relayed to the congregation that it didn't matter what was going on in my life, when I entered the welcoming doors of GMZBC, I felt uplifted and when I departed, I felt inspired and fed. I love Rev. Reeves and the warm embrace of the membership. I am proud to be a member of this incredible group of fellow servants of our Savior and as for me and my house, we will serve the Lord.

The other deacons I serve with include Dwain Williams, chairman; Terry Holt, vice chairman; Al Dailey, secretary, Andrew Walker, treasurer; Randy Williams, Edward Williams, Clifford Patrick, Charles Walker, Walter Walker, Paul Harper, JW Bentley and Jaheem Atwater—a dedicated lot!

As deacons, we are committed to a life of service to Pastor Reeves, the church, and our community. We provide oversight for the administrative and spiritual needs of the church. Working with various church committees, serving as God's witnesses to the poor, shut-ins and everyone who is in physical or spiritual distress, preside at the praise worship before the beginning of our weekly worship service as well as at baptism and communion services. We are also responsible for encouraging our members to support our programs, collect the funds, document its sources and the use of our funds.

During services, we see to the comfort of our members and guests and even make sure our church and grounds are clean, in good working order and presentable. We also provide counseling and emotional support. Whatever your needs may be, please talk to one of our deacons.

The word deacon actually means, "through the dust." Deacons are supposed to be so busy attending to the needs of the church that they raise dust in their wake. Actually, the tradition goes back to the selection of seven men by the apostles, among them Stephen, who paid the ultimate price when he was stoned to death on the orders of Saul before he became Paul. According to First Timothy 3:1, "We are required to be "blameless, the husband of one wife, vigilant, sober, of good behavior, given to hospitality, apt to teach."

In any case, if you enjoy good preaching, good teaching, good church music, warm hospitable Christian people, do plan to attend one of our services and if you are looking for a church home, look no further, the doors of our church are open to all seekers of truth and spiritual fulfillment. We have come this far by faith leaning on the Lord. Visit us at: 542 Parlor Street, Thomaston, GA 30286. 706.647-4819.

69.
The Consequences of Associating with Hateful People

August 23, 2017

Friends and family are near and dear to me. When it's good, it's a beautiful thing. But when you notice that some of the people who are near and dear to you lie, cheat, disrespect, and spew hate to those who are not in their favor, what to do? If you ever find yourself questioning whether they are worthy of your friendship, it might be time to re-evaluate and reset your relationships. Today, their venom may be directed to others, most predictably, however, it will eventually be directed at you. Maya Angelou is fond of saying that when people show you who they are, believe them.

If you associate with criminals, even if you obtain some short-term benefit, it will not only come back to bite you, but you will also spend a lifetime overcoming even a momentary lapse of judgment. If you take up with a violent person who abuses others, how long do you think it will take before you are being abused as well? If you associate with thieves, will you be their next victim? Are you prepared to compromise your life principles to corroborate and collaborate with your friend's schemes?

Lou Rawls sings a ballad about a young woman who, on returning from work, spots a snake freezing to death in the snow. She picks up the poor creature, brings him inside her house, wraps it in a blanket, feeds him warm milk and gradually nursed him back to health. On one fateful day, she returns from work and the snake reaches back, bites and fills her with his venom. Before dying, she asks, "How could you have killed me when I did so much for you?" He merely responded, "You knew I was a snake when you took me in." The message is, don't befriend snakes and rid yourself of the toxic relationships in your life.

It may be difficult if you are married to or otherwise related to the hateful person or persons in your life. Before it becomes ugly, distance yourself as much as you can from violent hateful racists as well as people who encourage you to make bad choices. Make a point of being kind and considerate to yourself and to others.

"Finally, all of you, have unity of mind, sympathy, brotherly love, a tender heart, and a humble mind." (1 Peter 3:8)

70.
How We Got Here

August 30, 2017

Before there was a Thomaston, inhabited by amazing people, lovely trees, flowers and birds, a lot of things had to have taken place to make it possible for us to be living in the greatest and best time in the history of the world. If you ever need reminding that God loves us, just look at all the things he placed at our disposal to see, hear, eat, drink, and feel happy about. We worship an awesome God who deserves our perpetual praise. And as our praises go up, the blessings continue to rain down.

Viewing the eclipse in Oregon filled me with wonder and had me contemplating the universe and our distant past. It was literally the shortest day. I watched the setting and the rising of the sun in less than two minutes.

While my grandmother taught me that only an apple tree can produce an apple and you need eggs if you want chickens, there was a time when only God existed and out of nothing, he created the universe some 14 billion years ago with a bang—a Big Bang. The Cambrian Explosion, which introduced a startling variety of animal life, occurred about 541 million years ago. The Ice Age was 2.4 million years ago and while dinosaurs roamed the earth 65 million years ago and departed because a meteor crashed into the earth, human beings appeared less than 300,000 years ago. So, let's get this straight, at no time did dinosaurs and humans live together. The oldest Chinese dynasty, the Xia, is only 4,000 years old, about the same time as Moses.

Jesus was born in a manger 2,000 years ago. Our beautifully written Bible was first compiled and published in English in 1611—a mere 400 years ago during Shakespeare's time under the tutelage of King James. Interestingly enough, the clock was invented about the same time. When the Bible was first published, the Pope forbade anyone but the clergy to read it. The Black Death greatly diminished the human population 661 years ago, but the Industrial Revolution grew the population to alarming numbers starting 257 years ago to our current 7.4 billion people. The United States is less than 250 years old and only has 5% of the world's population compared to China with 20%.

Of all the organisms that inhabited the earth, less than 1% is still around. In other words, 99% of all life forms became extinct. Thank God, human beings survived. As Einstein so eloquently pointed out, you cannot destroy matter. It just changes form. If you burn a piece of wood, it becomes ash and then rejoins the earth—dust to dust, ashes to ashes and then to atoms. Except for what we have sent out of the earth's atmosphere in rocket ships, all the elements on the earth (chemical chart) are essentially unchanged since the beginning of time.

While the warming of our planet over the last 50 years threatens our survival, it is worth noting that from the creation of the earth (14 billion years ago), the average temperature has not changed much. On any particular day, if it is warmer in Alaska, it's colder in Florida. The atoms that came into being when Mother Earth was created are the same atoms that make up who we are and everything under the sun. The atoms that you ate in your cereal this morning could very well have been the same atoms that made the first printing press, George Washington, or Genghis Khan's horse.

Aside from the eclipse, as the light is taken over by the darkness this evening and the light returns when morning breaks, do take a moment to contemplate the wonders of Mother Earth and recognize that we (all 7.4 billion of us) are His greatest creation. Let's take care of our home and treat everyone as you would like to be treated. I think that is called brotherly love.

71.
A Tribute to Heather Heyer

September 6, 2017

August 12, Heather Heyer was murdered by James Fields (a white supremacist) as he rammed his car at anti-racist protestors in Charlottesville, Virginia. She was only 32 years old. So, why do horrible things happen to nice people? While most of us avert our eyes and are skilled at not seeing or doing anything about the evil that is all around us, Ms. Heyer was standing up and resisting hatred and sacrificing herself—a soldier of the cross. She didn't deserve to die. Mr. Fields is guilty of an intentional act of cruelty and murder. It should be an assault on our morals. This was evil.

According to Ms. Heyer's mother, "She died doing what was right. My heart is broken, but I am forever proud of her." Mr. Alfred Wilson added that Ms. Heyer was often moved to tears by injustice and would not tolerate any type of discrimination. I can only hope that the Heyer family, friends and all who resist injustice find some comfort that she did not die in vain."

God did not intend for his people to be complacent and lazy. I believe He intended us to respond to the challenges of our time.

Heather's mother is joined by a descendant of Robert E. Lee to form the "Heather Heyer Foundation" whose purpose is to provide scholarships to activists from Charlottesville. According to her brother, "Heather never marched alone. She was always joined by people from every race and every background in this country."

Contributions can be mailed to: The Heather Heyer Foundation, c/o Stifel, 1759 Worth Park, Charlottesville, VA. 22919.

Evil exists in the world, even down the street from where we live and I dear say, may even exist in our homes and for that matter in ourselves. It is as robust as ever. With the passing of Heather Heyer, the world has one less compassionate soul. I invite all of us to become soldiers of the Cross.

72.
The Upson County Ministerial Association Celebrating 45 Years!

September 27, 2017

Have you ever heard someone say, "I am barely keeping the wolf from my door"? When the speaker is serious, things are really desperate, and calamity may be imminent. Fortunately, there is a place in Thomaston where the desperate can go to receive dignified emergency assistance.

The Upson County Ministerial Association (UCMA), in addition to encouraging moral uprightness in our community, has been keeping the wolf at bay since 1972. So, who are you going to call if you encounter someone in desperate straits? (706-647-3702) In fact, through the generosity of individuals like you, they give away over

$100,000 per year to help with housing, utilities, medications, food, transportation, clothes and whatever the need may be. Individuals can receive up to $300 every six months. No, they will not pay for cell phones!

In addition to their Community Assistance Fund, the UCMA sponsor:

1. Cancer Care Ministry for those who have been diagnosed with Cancer. For assistance, please call Mr. and Mrs. Pitts 706-656-8148.

2. The Empty Stocking Fund. For Christmas, needy families who are referred by churches or schools receive help with food, clothes and Christmas presents.

3. The Transient Ministry meets the needs of travelers who live outside of Upson County who become stranded while passing through Upson County. Help is provided so see them through to their destination.

4. The Community Thanksgiving Service. Each year, the UCMA sponsors a countywide, multi-denominational unity service. This year, they will gather at the Thomaston First Assembly of God Church at 205 W. County Road. All are welcome, so do plan to come together to thank the Lord for his goodness and generosity to our community. We have so much for which we should give thanks. As the praises go up, His blessing will rain down.

In addition, the UCMA sponsors the Upson County Baccalaureate the Sunday before the Upson-Lee High School graduation, the countywide "Back to School Prayer Service" to kick off the school year, and partner with the Heritage Pregnancy Center to provide parenting classes and free pregnancy tests.

If you would like to become involved and learn more about the work of the UCMA, they meet at the Tasty Shoppe on the first Tuesday of each month at 8:30 am. All ordained ministers of Upson County are welcome to join. While contributions are encouraged, there are no membership dues. Contributions should be sent to: The Upson County Ministerial Association; P.O. Box 375; Thomaston, GA 30286 Email: upsonministers@gmail.com

"The more we give, the more we reap the benefits of feeling good about helping others. We are all capable of giving as well as receiving from giving graciously. The blessing about giving is that it always comes back to us!" (Angie Karan) My grandmother probably said it just as well: "Giving is like seeds planted in fertile soil. It always returns a good harvest".

73.
The Impermanence of All Things

October 4, 2017

In view of the recent mega hurricanes, I had a golf course conversation with one of Thomaston finest regarding global warming. While he doesn't deny that planet earth has been warming up over the last 100 or so years, he believes it is a natural process and that there is no human involvement in global warming. It is just a result of the earth's natural rhythms producing periods of cooling and warming. There is nothing new under the sun.

He is not alone in this belief. The very person who is responsible for enforcing the nation's clean air and water, as well as numerous other environmental statutes, Mr. Scott Pruitt, head of the EPA, has been undermining international treaties and blocking legislation to reduce emissions and choosing instead to promote energy related jobs and profits. Last month, he accused scientists who link tropical storms to man-made climate change as trying to politicize the tragedy.

Over 99% of life forms (animals, birds, trees, fish, and insects) that have ever inhabited the earth are extinct. In the 14 billion years of the earth's existence, we have suffered five catastrophic events that wiped out all complex life requiring a reset. This included a spectacular collision with an asteroid, volcanoes that imprisoned the earth with carbon dioxide, dramatic shifts in tectonic plates, the Ice Age (a mile deep), pandemics, earthquakes and volcanoes.

Will future generations inherit a lifeless planet? What are the likely drivers of the next mass extinction? It took billions of years to bury fossil fuels (crude oil, coal, and natural gas) in the earth and since the industrial revolution 150 years ago, we are hell bent on extracting and burning all of it and injecting huge amounts of carbon dioxide into our atmosphere. The world economy is based on combustion and every time we double the carbon dioxide (greenhouse gas) in the atmosphere, we increase the atmospheric temperature. The result is predictably warming of our atmosphere. This will not end well. God gave us a resilient home, but it is not invincible.

There is no denying the signs:

1. Barrier reefs around the world are dying.
2. Ocean acidification is on the rise.
3. As the glaciers melt, ocean levels are rising.

4. Wind speeds of hurricanes are unprecedented.

5. Our oceans are getting warmer and warmer water holds less oxygen.

So, what is the fate of our civilization? While we have time, we should be vigilant and worry. We ignore the signs at our peril. As the levels of carbon dioxide rise in our atmosphere, I believe the earth is gradually becoming uninhabitable. We may need to try living in harmony with nature. Everything is fine until it's not—then everything goes to hell. It's the proverbial man falling from a tall building and after he passes each floor thinks everything is OKAY so far.

According to Trevor Nance (Geologist), several islands in the pacific (Kepidau en Pehleng, Nahlap, Laiap, Nahtik, Ros, the Carteret Islands and Bougainville) have all been swallowed up by the ocean over the last 50 years. Is Miami Beach and New Orleans next?

Should it concern us that a few thousand years ago all animals were wild? That is now down to less than 3%. Ninety-seven percent are now pets, grown in shoe boxes (chickens) and on farms. There were 50,000 lions 2,000 years ago. That number is down to 20,000. Over that same time, there were 5 billion passenger pigeons, they are now all gone.

As for me, I want to continue seeing a verdant world with cardinals, deer, and squirrels when I look out of my window each morning in Thomaston. I hope future generations will also enjoy this delightful privilege.

74.
Birthday Traditions

October 11, 2017

I suspect that children love lots of lighted candles on their birthday cakes and old people (both those who must light the candles and those who have to blow them out) hate them. So, I have come up with a solution. Why not start a kid off with 80 candles on his first birthday and subtract one each year? That way, as the candles get fewer and fewer, everyone will be reminded that the end is near. And when you run out of candles, you would know that it is time to go.

In addition to sweet 16, 18, 21, 65 (Maybe 75 is the new 65), since we have 10 fingers, the significant milestones we pay most attention to are usually those ending with a zero.

I grew up in rural Jamaica with outhouses and all, where people didn't worry themselves about birthdays because they were obsessed with the challenges of getting through each day. While people who lived in Kingston celebrated birthdays the same way we do here. Where I grew up, I never even knew how old I was and never had a birthday party. When I had to obtain a birth certificate, I finally learned the date of my birth but still had no party. So, when I migrated to the United States, my mother felt so bad about me growing up without a birthday party that she wanted to make it up to me. So, she said I could invite anyone I like, and she would do it up right for my 16th birthday. Yes, it was going to be grand.

Unfortunately, as I had only arrived, I had no friends and didn't know anyone to invite, so I told the entire school. On the fateful night, 200 of my fellow students showed up at my door asking about free food. As my mother only prepared for about a dozen people, she barred the door and asked quite seriously if I was stupid. My invited guests milled around outside our house for an hour before they dispersed, and a riot averted. Since my wedding, my darling wife has made it up to me—in spades. But I find that I am not as sentimental as I should be as I often forget the birthdays of my own children. Shouldn't they get a taste of what it was like to not have birthday parties or even birthday wishes?

Apparently, the reason we have birthdays in the first place is that it was believed that we are vulnerable as we transition from one age to the next. So, it was important to have family and friends around to protect us from whatever evil spirits may be lurking around us as well as light bonfires and candles so God would know where to find the person to be blessed. The smoke from the extinguished candles was sending up a prayer to the Almighty.

Obviously, the birthday that we celebrate around the world is that of our savior Jesus Christ who would have been 2017 years old this year if he had lived. Instead, he sacrificed himself so our sins could be forgiven.

According to Australianmedia.com, "The Happy Birthday song is more than one hundred years old. It was written in 1893 by two sisters, Patty and Mildred Hill, who were schoolteachers in Louisville, Kentucky. The tune was originally a morning greeting to their students entitled "Good Morning to All." The lyrics were copyrighted in 1935, 11 years before Patty's death, and the ownership has swapped hands in multi-million-dollar deals ever since. The current copyright is owned by Warner Communications. They purchased it in 1989 for more than $22 million dollars."

A hundred years ago in old England, birthday cards were sent out as letters of apology when an invited guest couldn't attend the party. Hallmark should thank them for their billion-dollar per year business.

I kind of like the "full year" system in old Japan that recognizes that babies are already a year old when they are born. So, life begins at conception—not birth. Unfortunately, this has since been Americanized. Whenever I pass a birthday, I announce that I am the next age up. On the other hand, my wife will stay with old age until the next one comes around. So, at any point in time, I am a year older, and she is a year younger.

If it is your birthday, may your life be filled with fond memories and happiness. Or as the Irish say:

May the road rise up to meet you.
May the wind be always at your back.
May the sunshine warm upon your face;
the rains fall soft upon your fields,
And may God hold you in the palm of His hand.

75.
The Joy of Exercise

October 18, 2017

I just returned from the Wellness Center and have a big toothy smile, enjoying my endorphin high and feeling like God is in his Heaven and all's right with the world. If you want to be one of the grumpy people, sit in your easy chair and watch TV for six or more hours per day. That is a formula for depression.

My routine is unique. I work out in the therapeutic (heated) pool. I grab my yellow paddles and move them back and forth in various directions (600 times) and then go for a swim. For those of you who don't want to get your hair wet, you can do a full work out without water touching your *chinny chin*.

After my swim, I then do 20 push-ups and some back straightening exercises. I am 74 years old and have no back pain or any aches and pains anywhere except when I get greedy and play two rounds of golf in the same day.

The great value of my exercise routine is that it helps my golf game. After my swim, I shower and change clothes, I stop by the gym for ten more minutes to do some flexibility exercises and that's it—all done in one hour and feeling fine. I am now in a good mood to take on whatever the world has in store for me.

I visit our wonderful and well-equipped Wellness Center about three times per week. The added benefit is that I sleep soundly. Notice that I didn't say I sleep like a baby because that would mean that I woke up every two hours.

If you want this happy feeling, find a routine, and stick to it. Choose something fun. Competition brings out the fight in most of us, so tennis or golf is natural. With the new tennis courts at The Greatest Generation Park, it is now an attractive place to play—free.

But you can work out in your bedroom or anywhere including a walk around the block. When my mother was alive, I was always encouraging her to take walks around the block and in response to my suggestion, on one of my visits, she announced that she was ready to take a walk around the block. My excitement turned to laughter when she took a child's one-inch square block out of her pocketbook and placed it on the ground. She bought the block at a fair and kept it an entire week waiting to spring it on me when I predictably nagged her about exercise. She was always telling me that she got enough exercise letting her fingers do the walking through the yellow pages.

Seriously though, there is nothing like exercise to reduce stress, boost self-esteem, lower blood pressure, improve sleep and improve muscle tone. After a work-out, instead of feeling tired, I actually feel energized and rather than feeling hungry, I feel full. I feel no pain after my workout but drink lots of water.

To be sure, my advice on exercise is not without detractors. According to Robert Hutchins, "Whenever I feel like exercising, I lie down until the feeling passes." Red Skelton also quipped, "I get plenty of exercise carrying the coffins of my friends who exercise." But the advantage of exercising every day is that you die healthier.

My favorite, however, is Ellen DeGeneres, "I got to work out. I keep saying I got to start working out. It's been about two months since I've worked out. And I just don't have the time. Which is odd because I have time to go out to dinner, watch TV, and get a bone density test and try to figure out what my phone number spells in words."

76.

The Embarrassment of Losing My Memory

October 25, 2017

I was prompted to write this when I saw my dear friend and playing partner picking trash from behind his ball on the golf course and in the process picked up his ball as if it was trash and tossed it aside. I also saw another gentleman leave his putter on the green and carry the flag stick back to his cart and then completely forget what he scored on the hole. When an old golfer proclaims "par" instead of a double boogie after completing a hole, it's not because they are trying to cheat, they just forgot the two shots they missed.

In my own case, I will be driving down the road and have to go back to the house because I forgot my glasses, my watch, my briefcase, or the list I made of things I must not forget to do. And sometimes when I go back, I forget what I went back for. While I will never forget my wife's birthday, I have forgotten our anniversary—more than once. So, there is an unwritten rule in our house that my wife cannot get pissed off at her husband because he forgot something. The other day she asked me if I was taking the omega 3 pills she prescribed for my memory loss and I responded, "What pills?"

At lodge meetings, they have stopped asking me to make long speeches that I had to memorize. There is no doubt that I have arrived at the point where my memory fails me even as I want to be the guy who remembers everyone's names, their telephone numbers as well as all my meetings and obligations without having to write them down.

My grandmother believed the myth that "If you pack up your brain with nonsense, you won't have room to learn the good stuff." What is true is that you will never exceed 10% of your brain's capacity. And the more you learn, the more you build on that foundation to learn and retain more and more. You have to use it or lose it. Within nature's design for human beings is that we make better what we seem to need and discard what we don't need. If you spend a month in a hospital bed, it will take some doing to walk again as your muscles will start to atrophy. A blacksmith's arms are always huge and strong. A learned professor can learn new things with not much effort because of his already amazing capacity while a fellow who doesn't know much cannot learn much. You need to keep learning and developing new skills at least to support your ability to learn new stuff.

My wife has worked out a plan for me. So, after eight hours of sleep, each morning, in addition to my physical work out that speeds oxygen to my brain, I give my brain a workout as well by calculating the square root of 13, reciting a poem I once knew or just multiplying numbers in my head. She also encourages me to have lots of conversations. So, it's therapeutic for me to spend 15 minutes talking with members of the Raintree Rascals before our tee time. Bob Gallman will tell me a joke and Doyle Allen always knows what is going on in the world.

One of her helpful ideas is to ALWAYS have something enjoyable and satisfying to look forward to. I am good at visualizing and anticipating upcoming events and replaying the highlights of past activities in my mind. So, next year's trip abroad is already planned, visiting with family and friends, playing in golf tournaments or even our weekly Kiwanis meeting. I wish I could remember to attend the breakfast club at our local café more often.

Human beings are social animals, so isolation and loneliness are cruel and damaging to our souls. Relationships nurture brain power. Lots of data support the idea that if you spend time with friends, the decline in memory as you get older will be slower. So, go to church, join clubs, volunteer, or even strike up conversations with neighbors and even strangers. You never know where it might lead. My favorite topic when I give talks is the value of regular church attendance. Dr. Robert Hummer at the University of Texas compared people who attend church to those who didn't and discovered that people who did not attend church live up to 14 years less. What a privilege we have carrying everything to God in prayer. In addition to God's grace, it turns out that just worshiping together (singing, praying, greeting, laughing, and holding hands) is a blessing!

In any case, I am learning to write things down. Otherwise, when I go out to get sandwiches at Subway, I could never remember what everyone wants. You know what, considering the alternative; I will take a little memory loss. I am still enjoying a full life living in Thomaston! Do you still say, "Hang up the phone?"

77.
We Are a Nation of Immigrants

November 1, 2017

At the summer Olympic games every four years, I marvel at the parade of nations that the Japanese contingent are all Japanese, the Chinese contingent, all Chinese, the Kenya contingent, all Kenyans, the Swedish contingent, all blue-eyed and blond but the contingent from the United States is a lovely plethora or a lovely kaleidoscope of people that hail from every corner of the world—no wonder we win! We continue to attract the world's most talented while also serving as a refuge for "huddled masses, yearning to breathe free." The United States is a magnet as a land of prosperity and upward mobility. We are what the world aspires to be.

I will immediately disclose that I am an immigrant from Jamaica who legally migrated to the United States when I was 15 years old and became a citizen when I was 22. Other than being arrested and thrown into the pokey for protesting in front of the South African Embassy in Washington, D.C. protesting against their apartheid policies, I have been a contributing member of society.

We have been welcomed to the City of Thomaston and feel right at home. With the guidance of the Almighty, my wife and I made our way to this amazing place where nice people, clean air and water and the opportunity to thrive prevails. Everywhere I travel, I am enthusiastic in my boasts about a city where people live in harmony and peace.

I am motivated to write this column because I believe we are about to make a huge mistake if we (in fact) deport our "Dreamers." While I am certain that there are a few rotten apples in the lot, almost all dreamers are either doing good in school or employed. The fates of almost 800,000 of them are now in the hands of Congress. I am hoping for responsible and compassionate immigration laws. These children were brought here and grew up as Americans. I am a strong law and order person and if we had immediately deported them after their arrival, I would have had no problem with that. But these children were allowed to remain, grew up like Americans and know nowhere else. I believe that deporting them would be unconscionable and will have adverse effects on our economy. Studies consistently have shown that immigrants are a net contributor to our economic output. Seventy-five percent of new patents and more than half of all American companies that are worth more than a billion dollars were founded by immigrants. The list includes Tesla, Google, Pfizer, DuPont, eBay, yahoo, Radio Shack, Colgate and Kraft. Would it surprise you that ALL the American Nobel prize winners this year were immigrants?

Immigrants bring a wonderful spirit of innovation and entrepreneurship when they migrate to our shores. Contrary to the perception that immigrants take away jobs and are a drain on our social services, health and educational systems, the brain drain to the United States has been a reality and a tremendous benefit to our country for three hundred years. Individuals who were educated and trained in other countries with scarce resources of their home countries end up migrating to the United States. For example, 90% of the nurses, doctors and pharmacists that are trained in Jamaica end up in the United States where the salaries and benefits are much higher. The nursing shortage in the United States is severe.

Let's not throw the baby out with the bathwater!

78.
Myths About the Common Cold

November 8, 2017

I am motivated to address the myths about the common cold. I accompanied my pastor on one of his speaking engagements and he expressed some trepidation about immediately going outside after his very passionate sermon as he suspected that he may get pneumonia or the dreaded common cold and a cough.

Many people harbor a great fear of catching a cold. Rain and changes in the weather are often believed to be culprits. Important events are cancelled because of rain, and it makes no sense to some why Freddie Astaire and Ginger Rogers would be singing and dancing in the rain. They must be stupid fools who probably caught a cold and could have died.

I am even told that over-exposure to "dampness" can give you not only a head cold but also precipitate sickness in the knees and back. I am puzzled when my very sophisticated golfing friends rush into the locker room to put on dry clothes after getting wet on a golf course. This started me thinking about the times I was encouraged to always wear a hat when outdoors; never get out of bed and immediately expose myself to water (shower); never go outside immediately after taking a bath; never wash your hair and go outside; stay warm with a jacket or sweater to avoid being chilled; and the many other myths about the common cold that is part of our belief system. There are three employees at ZÖe Pediatrics who must have a space heater at their desks even in the summer. These myths exist in all societies.

My grandmother thought the common cold was caused by "night air" and would call in the children as soon as it got dark. It turns out that she and others had noticed that during a malaria (dengue fever) epidemic, those who stayed out late at night, became sick and even died and so developed a healthy fear of the dark. The culprit were mosquitoes that bit malaria infected people and spread the parasite by biting new victims when the mosquitoes swarmed after dark and bit everyone in sight. A very important lesson is that a correlation does not a cause and effect make. That which is said to cause something, should exist when the cause is present and should be absent when the cause is absent.

The common cold, also known as a viral upper respiratory tract infection, is a contagious disease that can be caused by hundreds of different types of viruses. Because so many different viruses can cause a cold and because new cold viruses constantly evolve, the body never builds up resistance against all of them. For this reason, colds are a frequent and recurring problem. In fact, children can have up to 12 colds per year while adults typically have two. The common cold is the most frequently occurring illness in the world, a single infected passenger could infect an entire plane full of people who could in turn spread it to the entire population by sneezing on each other. As soon as the cold virus gets into our nose, it will rapidly reproduce and will not be relieved by frequent blowing of the nose or sneezing.

Cold viruses infect the victim's upper respiratory tract (nose, sinuses, eyes, and throat). Symptoms include a runny or stuffy nose, watery eyes, congestion, coughing and sneezing. You could have the virus and have no symptoms and you could have one or more of these symptoms but do not have the virus. These symptoms could be an allergy such as when you sneeze from cold feet or have runny eyes from pollen, dust, or smoke. What many of us call a "summer cold" is an allergy to tree pollen.

You can prevent getting a cold by disinfecting surfaces that are likely to be touched by an infected person (phones, doors, and doorknobs). So, wash your hands after touching potentially infected surfaces as well as after shaking hands. People touch their faces with their hands about three times per hour. Although difficult to remember, keeping your hand away from your eyes and nose works as well. This is one of the reasons people in India do not shake hands but will greet each other with Namaste accompanied by a slight bow made with hands pressed together, palms touching, and fingers pointed upwards in front of the chest. Officially, this may be a greeting of well wishes for your good health, but it could also mean, "You keep your germs, and I will keep mine."

While the common cold accounts for frequent visits to doctors, if you are infected with the cold virus and consult a doctor, it will last a week; if you don't, it will last seven days. You can make yourself more comfortable by drinking plenty of fluids and keeping up your nutrition to strengthen your immune system. Antibiotics work against bacteria, while most colds are viral. So, taking antibiotics, sucking on cough drops and drinking bottles of cough syrup may relieve symptoms but will not cure the common cold. Chicken soup or any soup, tea, coffee, or hot drink will help as the steam will help open the sinus passages and the warm liquid going down will sooth your dry, raspy throat. What is indisputably true is that water in any form, whether it is hot or cold, cannot make us sick except from drowning or hypothermia. You can shower ten times per day, stand out in the rain all day in wet clothes, swim in the ocean or a river, go from a hot steamy room into a cold, air-conditioned room, jump from a hot tub to an ice bath and you will not become sick with a cold.

Air conditioning does not infect you but will dry out your sinuses which are a cause of frequent sneezing. Though the common cold usually coincides with cold weather, it is not a direct cause. Rather, during inclement-weather, people spend more time indoors in close proximity to each other, making it easier to spread the virus.

So, the way to avoid the common cold is to exercise, eat a healthy diet and build a strong immune system as well as wash your hands frequently with a proper disinfectant soap. Rather than spread myths along with our cold germs, let's join together to spread scientific truths. A professor at The George Washington University Hospital made an offer to students that if they were able to "catch a cold" without a virus, he would pay each of them $1,000. No one has yet to collect, and these students tested every myth that was ever conceived by man. Are you courageous enough to put your myths to the test?

79.

Our Fourth Amendment Rights

November 15, 2017

Whenever I return from traveling overseas, I kiss the ground (not literally) and thank the powers that be that I am fortunate to live in these United States and more specifically in Thomaston.

Heading the list of things, I am most grateful for is our Fourth Amendment that guarantees that as long as I am not breaking a law or infringing on the rights of anyone else, I have a right to be left alone—free from engagement or harassment from law enforcement or anyone else representing the State. This is not the standard in most countries of the world.

While traveling abroad, we were stopped only because the officer needed lunch money, the police can walk into your house without permission, and I am randomly stopped in Jamaica just so they can search automobiles for contraband or guns without the consent of the driver. You see, only in the United States do we have a Fourth Amendment prohibiting unreasonable stops, searches, and seizures. Yes, without reasonable suspicion or probable cause, the police may be curious to find out what I am up to but restrained by the Fourth Amendment from even raising the question with me. So, when I heard about the case, I will describe it to you, I said, "This could never happen in Thomaston." So, to be sure, I spoke directly with our Police Chief Mike Richardson, posing the following hypothetical:

A poorly dressed black man was asked to stop by and pick up a package from the house of a gentleman who lived in an upscale neighborhood. On his way from the man's house, a lady called the Sheriff to report that a suspicious person was walking around the neighborhood. The Sheriff sent a deputy to investigate and located the man walking along the street and the following conversation ensued:

Deputy: "Good afternoon, can I ask what you are doing here sir?"

Carl: "You can ask but I am under no obligation to tell you."

Deputy: "We got a call that a suspicious person was walking around the neighborhood. Can I see your ID?"

Carl: "Am I under arrest or am I free to go?"

Deputy: "We can do this the easy way, or we can do it the hard way. Just show me your damn ID!

Carl: "Am I under arrest or am I free to go?"

Deputy: "One more time, show me your ID!!!"

Fearing where this could end up, Carl takes out his ID and shows it to the deputy and it is snatched away from him. The deputy then takes the ID back to his squad car to investigate. After a few minutes, he brought the ID back and told Carl that he was free to go with a question: "Why do you people always have to resist everything? Carl doesn't answer but is fuming but restrained as he retrieves his driver's license and walks away.

So, Chief Richardson: What is your take on this? "We don't ever stop anyone without reasonable suspicion or probable cause. Of course, my officers can engage anyone like any other citizen. We certainly say hello, hey or what's going on? I certainly encourage officers to engage citizens in consensual conversations like introducing themselves and asking the other person's name. But even if the person lies about who they are, it cannot be a basis for an arrest leading to charges of lying to an officer."

As a member of the Georgia Bar (a lawyer), I advise everyone who will listen to ALWAYS cooperate with law enforcement and do not place their freedom and their lives at risk. There is always the opportunity to file a complaint later when cooler heads can prevail. My Japanese roommate from college would remind me that "If the rock falls on the egg, too bad for the egg, if the egg falls on the rock, too bad for the egg." You can be dead right.

But thanks again for our good fortune that we live in a city where the Fourth Amendment is respected, and we have a really excellent police department.

80.
Freedom And Justice for All

November 22, 2017

In case you missed it, this is an abbreviated text of President George Bush's speech delivered in New York on October 19, 2017 entitled: "Spirit of Liberty: At Home, In the World." If you are a parent or teacher, I encourage you to have your children memorize it or at least read it to them. I found it enlightening and inspirational at a time when the divisions in our country are so exaggerated.

"...For more than 70 years, the presidents of both parties believed that American security and prosperity were directly tied to the success of freedom in the world. And they knew that the success depended, in large part, on U.S. leadership. This mission came naturally because it expressed the DNA of American idealism. We know, deep down, that repression is not the wave of the future. We know that the desire for freedom is not confined to or owned by any culture; it is the inborn hope of our humanity. We know that free governments are the only way to ensure that the strong are just and the weak are valued. And we know that when we lose sight of our ideals, it is not democracy that has failed. It is the failure of those charged with preserving and protecting democracy.

...We have seen our discourse degraded by casual cruelty. At times, it can seem like the forces pulling us apart are stronger than the forces binding us together. Argument turns too easily into animosity. Disagreement escalates into dehumanization. Too often, we judge other groups by their worst examples while judging ourselves by our best intentions – forgetting the image of God we should see in each other. We've seen nationalism distorted into nativism – forgotten the dynamism that immigration has always brought to America. We see a fading confidence in the value of free markets and international trade – forgetting that conflict, instability, and poverty follow in the wake of protectionism.

...We need to recall and recover our own identity. Americans have a great advantage: To renew our country, we only need to remember our values... The recommendations come in broad categories. Here they are: First, America must harden its own defenses. Our country must show resolve and resilience in the face of external attacks on our democracy. And that begins with confronting a new era of cyber threats.

...America is experiencing the sustained attempt by a hostile power to feed and exploit our country's divisions. According to our intelligence services, the Russian government has made a project of turning Americans against each other. This effort is broad, systematic, and stealthy, it's conducted across a range of social media platforms. Ultimately, this assault won't succeed. But foreign aggressions – including cyber-attacks, disinformation, and financial influence – should not be downplayed or tolerated. This is a clear case where the strength of our democracy begins at home. We must secure our electoral infrastructure and protect our electoral system from subversion.

...The second category of recommendations concerns the projection of American leadership—maintaining America's role in sustaining and defending an international order rooted in freedom and free markets. Our security and prosperity are only found in wise, sustained, global engagement: In the cultivation of new markets for American goods. In the confrontation of security challenges before they fully materialize and arrive on our shores. In the fostering of global health and development as alternatives to suffering and resentment. In the attraction of talent, energy, and enterprise from all over the world. In serving as a shining hope for refugees and a voice for dissidents, human rights defenders, and the oppressed...

...One strength of free societies is their ability to adapt to economic and social disruptions. And that should be our goal: to prepare American workers for new opportunities, to care in practical, empowering ways for those who may feel left behind. The first step should be to enact policies that encourage robust economic growth by unlocking the potential of the private sector. And for unleashing the creativity and the compassion of this country. The third focus of the document is strengthening Democratic citizenship. And here we must put particular emphasis on the values and views of the young. Being an American involves the embrace of high ideals and responsibility. We've become the heirs to Thomas Jefferson by accepting the ideal of dignity found in the Declaration of Independence. We've become the heirs of James Madison by understanding the genius and values of the U.S. Constitution. We've become the heirs of Martin Luther King Jr. by recognizing one another not as the colors of their skin but by the content of their character. This means that people of every race, religion, and ethnicity can be fully and equally American.

It means that bigotry or white supremacy in any form is blasphemy against the American creed. And it means the very identity of our nation depends on the passing of civic ideals to the next generation. We need a renewed emphasis on civil learning in schools, and our young people need positive role models. Bullying and prejudice in our public life sets a national tone. It provides permission for cruelty and bigotry and compromises the moral education of children. The only way to pass along civic values is to first live up to them.

Finally, the call-to-action calls to major institutions in our democracy, both public and private, to constantly and urgently attend to the problem of declining trust. For example, our democracy needs a media that is transparent, accurate and fair. Our democracy needs religious institutions that demonstrate integrity and champion civil discourse. Our democracy needs institutions of higher learning that are examples of truth and free expression. In short it is time for American institutions to step up and provide our cultural and moral leadership for this nation."

81.
A Godless Prophet: Jim Zeigler's Defense of Judge Moore

November 29, 2017

The law in Alabama considers it sexual abuse for anyone over 19 years old to have sexual contact with anyone less than 16 with or without consent, (even with the consent of the child's mother). The maximum penalty is 12 years in prison if the victim is less than 12-years-old and eight years if the victim is between 12 and 16. Unemancipated children under the age of 16 are legally incapable of consenting to sexual intercourse.

It is estimated that there are more than seven million cases of statutory rape each year resulting in a lifetime of psychological and emotional pain and suffering for the victims including post-traumatic stress disorder, depression, guilt, distrust of others, sleep and eating disorders, feelings of powerlessness and anger. Make no mistake about it, these are serious crimes. But those who defend Judge Moore do not seem to focus on his guilt or innocence but the cynical use of the Bible. So, according to Pastor Ed Stetzer (Billy Graham Center): "Bringing Joseph and Mary into a modern-day molestation accusation, where a 32-year-old prosecutor is accused of molesting a 14-year-old girl are simultaneously ridiculous and blasphemous."

State Auditor Jim Zeigler claims that the allegations against Judge Roy Moore are "much ado about very little...He's clean as a hound's tooth, Take Joseph and Mary. Mary was a teenager and Joseph was an adult carpenter. They became parents of Jesus...There's just nothing immoral or illegal, maybe just a little bit unusual."

When I heard Mr. Zeigler's attempted defense, I was appalled! The virgin birth is at the very heart of our Christian belief system. It is sacrilege to assert that Joseph was the father of our Lord and Savior. Having a biological father would completely annul Jesus' deity.

Mr. Jim Zeigler's using Biblical support to justify Judge Moore's dysfunctional conduct is mental gymnastics. How can anyone stoop so low as to regard attempted or sex with children as "much ado about very little?" Interestingly enough Judge Moore is quoted as saying, "The forces of evil are attempting to relegate our conservative Christian values to the dustbin of history." I believe he has it backwards.

Christians are aware that the law and civic "values" usually express the bare minimum of how we should behave toward each other. They tell us not to kill each other but not to open our hearts to each other. They tell us the age of consent but not the age of healthy decision-making. Christians rely on the Bible and our church leaders.

So, it is not unusual for a figure like Judge Moore to come to prominence making his reputation on "moral law" over secular (civil) law. Fresh from a battle to keep a "Ten Commandments" monument on state grounds, Judge Moore is running his campaign to replace Secretary Jeff Sessions as senator like a moral crusader against an encroaching tide of liberal nihilism. So, when faced with allegations of a pattern of inappropriate sexual conduct toward teen girls ranging from trolling a local shopping mall to physical contact, we would have expected Judge Moore to reconcile himself with his faith community the way any person of faith who committed a grievous sin: Confess and seek forgiveness. Our God is a forgiving God, and we are forgiving people who know that God often uses people who fail. As Christians, we believe that you may be a lost soul, but everyone can be redeemed. Instead, Judge Moore has dug in his heels. Some evangelicals, who cannot defend statutory rape, are tying themselves in knots trying to accommodate his sins. At most, they are attempting to denounce the behavior without renouncing Judge Moore.

It is heartbreaking to see religious leaders who made their reputations claiming to be moral vanguards trying so hard to pretend that they have ever picked up a Bible, let alone to live by it. Trying to use the Bible to justify the harm or abuse of children is disgraceful. I expect better from our religious leaders.

82.
Are you Curious About Cuba?

December 6, 2017

I have always been curious about Cuba, so, after Thanksgiving with my family in Orlando, accompanied by my wife, we made our way to Miami, boarded the Azamara Quest and set sail for Havana. For some reason that was never explained, it was indeed a slow boat that never exceeded nine knots. But, early one morning, just as the sun was rising, we saw the Cuban coastline as well as the Havana skyline come into view and after passing the forts on both sides, docked at the Sierra Maestra Terminal—almost in the middle to the city. Despite being less than a hundred miles from the United States, it seems isolated and shrouded in mystery and drama.

After a wonderful breakfast of English bacon, lox, bagels, papaya, almond croissants, tropical juices and Cuban coffee, we headed ashore through customs and the first things that delighted our eyes were the vintage 1950s Chevrolets, Fords, Thunderbirds, Cadillacs, Edsels, Oldsmobiles and Pontiacs that look brand new. This is a testament to the old adage: "When the world gives you lemons, make lemonade." As the United States outlawed the selling of American products to Cuba since 1959, keeping these cars running and looking colorful and glistening in the Caribbean sun with homemade paint became an industry. They even had to make their own parts. It was pure joy riding in my first car—a 1956 Ford Fairlane! Mine went to the junk yard in 1961 and the ones in Cuba are still going strong 60 years later.

The weather was a perfect 75 degrees, and the rain always seems to stop just before our engagements. So, while we brought umbrellas from our cruise ship on our many tours, they were unnecessary. We walked long distances on cobblestone streets meeting really friendly, engaging people, and feeling perfectly safe. They love to talk with strangers (especially Americans) and their English is actually very good.

Cuba has about 12 million people with about 2.5 million of them occupying Havana, the capital. Architecturally, it's a mix of modern and old Spanish colonial with their penchant for plazas and statues to heroes. Even with the mass migration to Miami after the Castro revolution, the city is over-crowded and plagued with infrastructure problems. Sporadic electricity, unpredictable bus schedules, sewer and water are daily issues. Thankfully, because of the cost of gasoline ($6.00 per gallon) and citizens not being able to afford cars, there is no traffic. The average family lives on less than $3 per day.

They make the best cigars in the world. The brands are familiar to all smokers (Partagas, Cohibas, Montecristo, Bolivar and Romeo and Julieta). Bacardi and Club Cuba rum are also internationally sought after. Tourism produces more foreign exchange than sugar.

They pride themselves on sports, dominoes, art, music and dancing, education, and healthcare. They are world beaters in baseball and boxing and everywhere you go in Cuba, there is music to be heard and people dancing. We attended a cabaret at the Tropicana where their amazing talent is on display—a really great show! All education and healthcare are free and excellent. There are no private doctors or hospitals. The entire healthcare system is government run. Their innovation is that each community is assigned doctors who are responsible for the overall health of the people who live in their neighborhood. They believe that people get sick because of the neglect of the healthcare system. If a patient suffers a heart attack it's because their blood pressure was not controlled. They maximize preventive care, and everyone gets a check-up every year. Even with the glaring poverty, Cuba has the same life expectancy as the United States.

The people are poor and suffer from the USA embargo which can only be lifted when there are no Castros in power and people who left after the revolution are compensated for their property. And since that is not going to happen, they will continue to suffer.

By the way, you cannot just buy an airline ticket or book a cabin on a ship headed for Cuba. Tourist travel to Cuba remains prohibited. Permission must be granted by the Treasury Department for tour groups for educational and cultural purposes so visiting museums, cathedrals and historic sites must be part of the itinerary—no hanging around at beaches and just having a good time. The USA also requires that we not spend money at any government owned businesses.

As part of our cultural tour, we spent a morning finding Ernest Hemingway: where he lived (Finca la Vigia), where he wrote his books (A Farewell to Arms, Old Man and The Sea, Death in the Afternoon, The Sun Also Rises, the Snows of Kilimanjaro, etc.), where he hung out, seeing his fishing boat, and learning that he loved big game hunting, fishing and drinking. But he obviously loved his adopted country and they loved him.

We also spent an afternoon learning about the spiritual life of the people and were treated to a Santeria ceremony that included vigorous drumming and dancing.

There is a great deal to admire about Cuba and its people and a great deal to criticize about government controls and the poor economy. While poverty is oppressive, the people carry themselves with pride and learn to live on less.

But it's always good to be back in Thomaston!

83.
Are We Witnessing the End of Morality?

December 13, 2017

I wish to thank Mr. Michael Mangum for his letter response to my column (12/1/17) about the "Godless Prophets" in Alabama who are twisting themselves into pretzels trying to justify Judge Roy Moore's conduct. Mr. Mangum makes a good point that in this country, regardless of how compelling the evidence, a man should be presumed innocent until proven guilty in a court of law. But he then accuses me of setting up myself as "judge, jury and executioner of Judge Roy Moore."

What I wrote was: "But those who defend Judge Moore do not seem to focus on his guilt or innocence but the cynical use of the Bible." So, according to Pastor Ed Stetzer (Billy Graham Center): "Bringing Joseph and Mary into a modern-day molestation accusation, where a 32-year-old prosecutor is accused of molesting a 14-year-old girl are simultaneously ridiculous and blasphemous." I did not judge Moore. My comments had everything to do with men of the cloth attempting to justify despicable conduct and nothing to do with Judge Moore's guilt or innocence and I do not harbor any desire to burn Judge Moore at the stake. As a lawyer, I am acutely aware of the rules of evidence and subscribe to them. I do not know if Judge Moore is guilty of these accusations.

I also wrote: "Mr. Jim Zeigler's using Biblical support to justify Judge Moore's dysfunctional conduct is mental gymnastics. How can anyone stoop so low as to regard attempted or sex with children as "much ado about very little?" Interestingly enough Judge Moore is quoted as saying: "The forces of evil are attempting to relegate our conservative Christian values to the dustbin of history." I believe he has it backwards." Again, I made no judgment about his guilt or innocence. I just take exception to men of the cloth who do not unequivocally stand up for Christian principles. Do we live at a time when moral Christian principles can be subjugated for political objectives?

As for me and my house, we accept human beings as they are. I believe all human beings do the best they can, 100% of the time. We are the sum of our pre-dispossessions and how we are programmed—products of our past. I promise that at the moment of your birth, I can predict 90% of what you will become if I know your parents. I will know what language you will speak, your party affiliation, your religion, your diet, your dress, your occupation, your recreational pursuits, your educational achievement, and your propensity to be law abiding, etc. etc. So, I do not judge anyone and accept them for who they are. I have a great capacity to accept people just as they are, but I will not cease from protecting myself and criticize hypocrisy.

As for your admonitions about forgiveness in which you quoted: Mathew 7:1-3 "Judge not that ye be not judged…Why do you stare from without at the very small particle that is in your brother's eye but do not become aware of and consider the beam of timber that is in your own eye." This happens to be one of my favorite passages and one that I contemplate daily. Make no mistake about it Mr. Mangum, I am flawed and make no claim that I am a model citizen. I am a mere seeker of truth and make every effort to live by Christian principles, but I know (as everyone does) the difference between good and evil.

I appreciate your letter to the editor Mr. Mangum and look forward to hearing from you again. I happen to believe that goodness, truth, and beauty are everlasting in the human soul. I also know that to be on the right side of history, we must be unselfish, respect our fellow travelers on the earth and strive to treat others the way we want to be treated. Right is right and wrong is wrong. Each person cannot be a law unto themselves.

84.
A Cure for Winter Blues

December 20, 2017

While I don't have a cure for the common cold or the flu, I believe I have the cure for the winter or holiday blues. Stick with me and you will be turning that frown upside down. You have no doubt heard of the 12 days of Christmas; these are the 12 steps to pick up your spirits.

1. **Be astonished at the universe, planet earth and all the richness of life.** These are the best things in life, and we can enjoy them free. Bask in the love of the Almighty. He really loves you. If you are feeling lost, look to Heaven for direction. He will be happy to take the wheel. If you never had a problem, how would you know that God could solve them? Tally up your blessings, pray and give thanks. Meditate. Get your fill of sunrises and sunsets and don't let a day pass without marveling at the sun, moon, and stars. The beauty around you (flowers, birds, rain, snow, and rainbows) isn't bad either. I get happy just seeing treetops swaying in the wind. Do you know that the earth is moving under your feet? But you have to be in love to really feel it!

2. **This too shall pass. In two days, tomorrow will be yesterday.** In a hundred years, no one will know your name. None of your mistakes will matter. Yesterday is gone and belongs to eternity. Tomorrow is only a promise. Today is all you have. That is why it is called a present. There is a silver lining in every cloud and there is a light at the end of every tunnel. Wander through antique stores and celebrate how much life has changed for the better. A sleepless night will not last forever. Joy comes in the morning. Life is hard by the yard but by the inch, it's a cinch. Take it one step at a time.

3. **Love conquers all.** Forgive your enemies and all who have done or said unkind things about you or to you. Laugh at their transgressions. Haters are saying more about themselves than about you.

4. **Give yourself something to look forward to.** Plant a seed. Buy a lottery ticket. Plan a party. Plan your next vacation. Plant a tree from which you will not enjoy either the shade or its fruit.

5. **Don't sweat the small stuff and everything is small stuff.** I have a deal with my wife, I will make the big decisions and she can decide everything else. I

will decide whether we go to war, increase inflation, who gets elected and when it will rain. Rather than being loggerheads with each other, "Yes dear" simplifies my life. Going with the flow is so much easier than swimming against the tide. Rejoice that thorn bushes have roses and stop fretting that roses have thorns.

6. **Live a healthy active life.** Be a doer. Get out of your house and into the world. Sing hymns and love songs and whistle while you work. Get in shape with vigorous exercise (dance), skip instead of just walking and kick up your heels ever so often.

7. **Hold a baby.** How can you not be happy holding a baby? Mark Twain tells the story of a man who lived like a hermit for 10 years panning gold and gave away his fortune to a lady who allowed him to hold her baby. Baby therapy.

8. **Accept change.** You cannot force or step into the same river twice. Let life happen. You were a different person yesterday. You are evolving into something great! On the golf course, everyday is different. One year, a professional shot a 64 on the first day at the Masters and an 84 the following day. What a difference a day makes!

9. **Have the courage to be imperfect and forgive yourself when you are disappointed.** A great baseball player only gets a hit three out of ten times. You are only human, and we are all prone to making lots of mistakes. And once you learn from your misfortunes, share what you have learned with others. Be patient with yourself. It takes nine months to recover from a traumatic loss.

10. **Read.** If you love to read, you will never be bored. Your home, the internet, the library, your doctor's office and everywhere we go has an abundance of great reading materials. While you are at it, listen to TED talks and marvel at the insights these scholars freely share with you.

11. **Pamper yourself.** Get a massage, your nails done and while you are at it, get a facial as well. Soak in a bubble bath with candles (champagne anyone?) Play with pets. Listen to music and dance at every opportunity. Ask your mother to make a recording of all the songs she sang to you when you were a child and listen to them as needed. Copy her recipes. Daydream and remember your first kiss and the first time you xxx, your first car, you're first "A" on a test and receiving an award. Test-drive an expensive car that you could never afford. It costs nothing. Keep your vows and tell the truth. Your honesty will pay off in

spades with a good night's sleep. Worrying accomplishes nothing. Building blocks, steppingstones and stumbling blocks are the same from a different perspective. When you stumble, pick yourself up and proceed with a renewed resolve. It's not how many times you fall, it's how many times you get up. Rejoice in the things you have and don't stress over what you don't have.

12. **Don't complain** about the pain in your leg; there are lots of people with no legs. Instead of focusing on yourself, turn your attention to others. But stay clear of negative, hostile, hateful people who are prone to violence. Fight for justice and fairness. Show gratitude. Do nice things for others and practice empathy. Become a good attentive listener. Look them in the eye and nod your head often. Put your mind to good use and think up ways to improve your community. Write down your ideas and share them with the mayor and city council. Make a gift basket (a greeting card, a rose, a Bible, a teddy bear, a cookie, a fruit) and give it to a total stranger. Spreading happiness is like planting a seed; it always returns a bountiful harvest. Congratulate someone. Genuinely celebrate the good fortune of other members of your family and friends minus the green monster (jealousy). Your problems pale compared to people living under dictators and in poverty, people in hospitals or living in refugee camps. There are many who would love changing places with you— even with all your challenges. Show compassion. Join a book club, chess, card game, play dominoes with friends and indulge in mindless activities. Tip generously and otherwise share your blessings with others. Take pride in your work and laugh at yourself at least once each day.

Finally, surround yourself with people who make you feel loved and connected. There are many of them in Thomaston. Isolation is a killer. A life shared is twice blessed. According to my friend, Dr. Malcolm Taylor, "If you have God, family and friends, you may stumble but you will never hit the ground."

85.

Be Lifted Up Rather Than Be Pulled Down

December 27, 2017

Imagine a playground seesaw. On one side are the positive things you can do to feel better, look better, have more energy, and live longer. On the other side are the things that pull you down, rob you of energy and compromise how long you will live. All of us have tasted the bitter fruit of someone close to us dying prematurely from a preventable condition. This is not one of those times when you want to be in balance. You literally need to fight to eliminate your unhealthy habits and increase your good habits. This is what it means to take care of you. The rewards are worth every sacrifice. While you are at it, pretend that you are a cowboy waving your hat above your head and successfully riding your pony into the sunset.

The negative list of bad habits is simply: (1) smoking; (2) alcohol consumption; (3) lying, being dishonest and not following the rules; (4) stress; (5) resisting going to the doctor for check-ups and preventive health care; (6) eating sugar and animal fats; (7) Excessive exposure to the sun.

1. **Smoking.** Is there any doubt about it? The catastrophic effects of smoking include lung cancer, emphysema, wrinkled skin, and discolored teeth. It constricts the arteries, increases carbon monoxide, lowers the good cholesterol, and makes a chimney of your nose, Children resist kissing grandparents who smoke. Yak!

2. **Alcohol.** While up to two drinks per day has been shown to improve cardiovascular function, more is detrimental. Alcohol destroys brain cells.

3. **Dishonesty:** Behave yourself. Criminals and other lying, dishonest, selfish, and hostile and violence prone people have the shortest life expectancy of any group as well as the worst quality of life. They don't sleep well. This is the epitome of "Living hard and dying young." Just hanging around these people will put your own life at risk as well. If you are a friend of a violent person, how long will it take before his violence will be directed at you?

4. **Stress.** A stressful lifestyle contributes to compromised performance, hypertension, heart disease, cancer and accelerated aging. There is actually

good stress and bad stress. Good stress wakes you up in the morning and gets you on your way to do the things that need to get done. Bad stress comes from struggling against the tide. The cure is simply living in harmony with others.

5. **Resisting the doctor.** Too many people have undiagnosed diseases. The earlier the diagnosis, the greater your odds of being cured. An ounce of prevention is still worth a pound of cure. You take your car in for a tune up so get an annual check-up for your body as well. All members of our society deserve respectful, culturally competent health care.

6. **Sugar and animal fats:** If you have sweet tea, sodas and dessert with every meal as well as a craving for hot dogs, hamburgers, sausages, bacon, ribs and steaks you are also likely to be overweight with bad cholesterol numbers. If so, diabetes and heart disease is in your future as well.

7. **UV rays.** While a little sunshine is good for the skin and the soul. Too much sun causes skin cancer and wrinkly skin. Use sunblock if you are going to be out in the sun for a long time.

The positive list includes: (1) an hour of exercise each day; (2) eating lots of fruits and vegetables; (3) drink plenty water; (4) Be spiritually active; (5) spend time with people who care about you; (6) get a good night's sleep (7) take medication as prescribed.

1. **Exercise:** We were meant to be strong and have a great deal of endurance. While not many of us will win a foot race at our age, we can all keep in shape. It feels wonderful.

2. **Fruits and vegetables:** In addition to being delicious and beautiful, they are nutritious. My wife just loves to have a bowl full of fruit on display.

3. **Water:** Up to 60% of the human adult body is water— the source of life! We need to keep it replenished. If the body becomes dehydrated, kidney disease as well as dry, skin follows. Drinking as much water as you can tolerate contributes to clean, smooth skin. On the other hand, if you are thirsty for a long time, toxins will build up in the body, causing cells to deteriorate and die. Are you losing your hair? Maybe you are not drinking enough water. It is so refreshing to drink a cool glass of water.

4. **Be spiritually active:** Dr. Robert Hummer from the University of Texas, compared people who go to church regularly to others who did not go to church and found that people who regularly attended a place of worship

lived up to 14 years longer than those who did not attend. Do you want to be welcomed with open arms, hugs, how have you been doing? Praying and meditating together is good for the soul. In addition, listen to inspirational songs and sermons.

5. **Quality time with good people.** We were not meant to live alone and apart from our fellow travelers on planet Earth. Let us break bread together often, forgive often and treat others as you would have them do unto us.

6. **Sleep:** Not enough or too much sleep makes you irritable, difficulty concentrating, forgetfulness and bad memory.

7. **Take medication as prescribed.** It does not help to get a check-up and get a diagnosis if you do not fill the prescription and do as it is prescribed.

The lifestyle choices that you make each day affect the way you feel whether you are a picture of health radiating warmth and goodwill. Healthy people are happy and prosperous. Unhealthy people spend too much time in the sick bed, and in the waiting rooms of doctors. You may even enjoy lingering in front of the mirror because you look so good. Your lifestyle can either enhance successful aging or send you to an early grave. It is entirely your choice.

My choice is to be "exceptionally healthy" — have no chronic disease and normotensive with normal cholesterol and less than 30% body fat. And if you are convinced that this is the way to go, share it and let's all become healthy specimens. Children should know their grandparents.

86.

People in Need Offers an Opportunity to Please God

January 3, 2018

I shared this idea with a friend who said:

> Before you get too carried away with that thought, let me tell you about a beggar we knew who lived on the side of the road and slept under a small tent. He gathered wood for a small fire that provided hot meals and coffee. As the neighbors got to know him, they would stop by his tent to give him money and food. One man gave $20 each Friday. But this generous gentleman's finances changed as he had to pay school fees for his three children and his business was not going well due to a downturn in the economy. As his finances got tighter and tighter, he explained to the beggar that he was forced to lower his weekly allowance to $10 per week to which the beggar asked, "Why are you asking me to supplement your children's education?"

As the CEO of a not-for-profit organization many years ago, I was a professional beggar (fundraiser). Some years, I raised $7 million for the Association of Black Cardiologists on our way to building a $10 million headquarters building. So, I was pleased to receive a promising lead from an acquaintance. I was warned, however, that this very wealthy lawyer was notorious for being stingy. But, being convinced that I could make a good case for a contribution from this scourge, I made an appointment for lunch which he agreed to pay for. So, I was encouraged that he was not so stingy after all. I made my best pitch about all the things we were doing to reduce the alarmingly high rate of cardiovascular disease among African-American men. I also told the lawyer that I was not able to find any evidence that he had ever contributed to any charitable cause and hoped he would find our mission worthy of support. The lawyer got a little testy and asked: "Did your research reveal that my mother needs a lot of help living in a nursing home? Did you know that my sister's husband died of a heart attack, and she is having a hard time supporting six children or that my church needs a new roof? Well, if I don't help them, why should I help your organization?" This lawyer knew nothing about the happiness and satisfaction we feel when we give.

One of the founders of Home Depot, Bernie Marcus, a man famous for his generosity, tells the story of being invited to tour the campus of a local university. But he understood all along that he was going to be hit up for a large contribution which he planned to make. On the tour, he encountered the "Arthur Johnson Arts and Science Building." So, out of curiosity, he asked who Arthur Johnson was and was told that he was a great writer. Bernie was even more puzzled and said: "You know, I am an avid reader and I have never encountered a writer by the name of "Arthur Johnson." What did he write?" To which the president of the university responded, "A check!" See, you can become great by just writing a check.

I don't remember the source of this story of the pastor who dressed in rags and begged alms with a tin cup at the gate to his church and was unrecognizable as the pastor. One by one and two by two the parishioners passed the beggar and offered no charity. When the church was full, the pastor showed up and took off his rags and the parishioners were rightly embarrassed. "I could have been God, testing our humanity. Aren't we all beggars before God—the sender of blessings? Don't we ask God to give us this day our daily bread, to heal us, protect us and give us traveling mercies?"

While we willingly give what is no longer useful, what doesn't fit anymore or desirable to us, the Japanese believe it is not a gift if you are not eager to have it yourself. They never give what they don't want but things they value themselves. The other approach they take seriously is they never give a gift in return for another gift or a favor. So, our idea of a gift exchange at Christmas is foreign to them. It is not a gift if you expect something in return. The true spirit of giving is when the receiver does not even say thank you. I must admit that I have difficulty with this. Due to my Western values, I do expect and get upset when I do not get a little recognition or something tangible in return—a plaque or something. I am always motivated to help someone along the way, but I lose interest and likely not do it again if there is no gratitude and I have even been known to become indignant about the "ungrateful wretches" who did not thank me appropriately. This is my confession, and I am praying about it. I have always admired the generous gentleman who gives $100 bills ($100,000 worth) to the police to give to needy families. I hope we can all be better givers in the future.

According to Rory Vaden (*The Mysterious Power of Giving*), "Giving makes you thankful." Now I can so clearly see in the lives of people around me that if you have a hard time giving it's almost always because you aren't thankful for what you have.

You think of yourself as a thankful person, but you're not. Until you learn to give, you keep score by money. And when you are keeping score by money and stuff, you spend more time thinking about how to get more than you do about being thankful for what you have now. At this stage, you might have heat in your house but like me, you will still have cold in your heart.

When you give money away you get to see how it fills a need in someone else's life and somehow in seeing how it makes their lives better, it makes you appreciate all the things you have in yours. There is something about giving to others that caused me to stop and ask myself, "How many of the things I have in my own life are truly entirely 100% in my possession because of only me and my work?" Very quickly, I realize the answer to that question is zero. And because nothing I have is through only my own work, it means that I'm 100% co-dependent on the world around me. Suddenly, in an all-consuming way, I become very thankful for each and everything in my life. Something I didn't see before. Giving creates an awareness of abundance."

My pastor once asked me what I owned and I naively answered, "My house, my car, etc." and then he followed up with, "What if I asked you the same question a hundred years from now?"

God's pleasure is hidden in our good deeds—not in the tangible rewards I receive from my generosity. He only asks that we be kind and generous with our fellow travelers on his planet.

87.
What's America to Me?

January 17, 2018

I am reflecting on the photograph of a Haitian soldier who graduated at the top of his class at West Point with tears streaming down his cheeks after his graduation. He was being hugged by a white classmate and an Asian classmate. All three will be leaders in our all-volunteer Army, ready to defend our country from all threats, both domestic and foreign; this is what being American means to me. A melting pot, an amalgam of personalities, religions and yes, colors. Unless you are a Native American, your forefathers arrived on these shores from other countries. They came because of the opportunity that these shores offered. Some came willingly and some came as slaves. Either way, they were transported to these shores from countries that did not offer the perceived opportunities that America had. No matter where they came from, our forefathers became the architects of what has made America great.

I don't think anyone can look at our history and call it anything but great. We have a democracy that allows all of us to speak our minds, dissent through peaceful protests and then to agree to disagree. Our courts are respected institutions. I am old enough to tell you how great it felt when John Glenn was put into space and then to find out a core group of black women helped to get him there. I am old enough to suffer through the pain of the Vietnam War when young men of all colors were drafted or volunteered to serve. I am old enough to suffer through the indignities of not being able to eat at some restaurants and then proud enough to admit as I was experiencing the transition with white brothers who believed in the brotherhood of mankind. This is why America is great and will continue to be great; Americans have a conscience.

Much has been made of the comments spoken by President Trump. Yes, I believed he said them and yes, they were hate-filled, vile and racist. Haiti is not a pleasant place to live because it has been purposefully underdeveloped and pillaged by the ruling class. The same could have been said of Ireland, Italy, China and Germany, the birthplace of Mr. Trump's grandfather. Those immigrants came to America because their birth countries did not afford them the opportunities of America.

The continent of Africa has many sophisticated countries. There are some countries on that continent that are still developing because of the slave trade and pillage by Europeans. I am proud that America stood up to the apartheid government of South Africa and helped in their liberation. I am personally proud that I was arrested and jailed for demonstrating in front of the South African Embassy in Washington D.C. America is great because we believe in justice, and we are always at the ready to come to the aid of victims. It does not matter how bad we individually may have it; we are always willing to help.

I was personally offended by the President's remarks regarding what he determined to be sh*thole countries. As an immigrant from one of the sh*thole countries (Jamaica), I understand firsthand because my mother left Jamaica as a young woman. She cleaned houses, waited tables, and worked the locker room at a country club. Her four boys benefited from the generosity of the people she worked for and the patrons of the country club. My first set of golf clubs came from a man I caddied for. At age 15 (1959), I was welcomed and afforded wonderful opportunities to obtain a solid education and achieved the American dream. Regardless of our flaws, America has been my home for the past 60 years and has received the best I have to offer because it is my duty. As for me and my house, we believe that diversity is the backbone of America's greatness, believe in the dignity of all human beings, respect our differences, and will defend your right to have opinions that are different from mine. This is America to me. We stand up and deliver.

I am aware that over 90% of the white population in Thomaston voted for President Trump. That has not prevented the people of this community from being respectful and considerate of others whether based on race, social or economic circumstances. These comments do not represent the wonderful people I have come to know. So, if I am not just being delusional, I invite the good citizens of this great city to speak up. People are hurting. I particularly respect Ambassador John Freely's decision to resign over these differences with President Trump. Whether we live in Thomaston or anywhere on our planet, we should never accept such characterizations. We are not a nation of hate. We are a nation of peace and committed to "one nation under God, indivisible, with liberty and justice for all."

According to Robin Wright, New Yorker Magazine, "Africa is home to 1.2 billion people and more than 50 countries. A whole continent can't simply be stereotyped or dismissed. A cursory glance of Africa's achievements includes Nobel Prizes in medicine, chemistry, physics, literature, and peace. Africa is home to some of the world's fastest-growing economies...roughly one out of every three women and one out of every five men in the U.S. military is African-American."

I have made the following points in previous columns:

1. The white population of the world is less than 20%.
2. Less than 5% of the world's population lives in the United States. Yes, our military might be beyond comparison, and we own more than 50% of the wealth of the world but we are a minority. When President Trump recognized Jerusalem, even with threats of the cutoff of funds from UN Ambassador Nicki Hailey, only eight countries (out of over 200) supported the United States (Guatemala, Honduras, Israel, Marshall Islands,

Micronesia, Nauru, Palau and Togo). I find the increasing ill will toward the United States is disturbing. We are being misrepresented to the world.

3. The United States is the beneficiary of people who were educated in sh*thole countries (nurses, doctors, pharmacists, and teachers) and migrate to the United States after their training which serves as a brain drain to the countries they came from.

4. Just because we are powerful does not mean that we should abuse others. *Noblesse oblige* requires those with power to treat others with kindness.

America was made great on the belief that "out of many, one." There is no you versus me. 'U' is half of us. We are all together on these shores. If North Korea attacks the U.S., they attack all of us. When China started making cloth at a fraction of the cost it took to make the same cloth in Thomaston, we lost an entire industry. Like it or not, we are part of a global village. Our strength is in our diversity

88.
Promises To Keep and No Time to Waste

January 24, 2018

While I have never met Mr. Bob Tribble, I certainly enjoy reading his positive faith-based columns each week. Here is a quote I particularly enjoyed from last week:

As we face the New Year, some of us know that our lives are a journey nearing the end of the road. Yet, we should take our handful of days and make good use of them and not have to look back sadly wishing we had used our time in a different way. When these handful of days have drifted through our fingers, let's be able to give a good account of our time and talents that God has given us.

I couldn't agree more. His sentiments remind me of that wonderful poem by Robert Frost, "Stopping by Woods on a Snowy Evening":

Whose woods these are I think I know.
His house is in the village though;
He will not see me stopping here
To watch his woods fill up with snow.
My little horse must think it queer
To stop without a farmhouse near
Between the woods and frozen lake
The darkest evening of the year.
He gives his harness bells a shake
To ask if there is some mistake.
The only other sound's the sweep
Of easy wind and downy flake.
The woods are lovely, dark and deep,
But I have promises to keep,
And miles to go before I sleep,
And miles to go before I sleep.

Dr. Benjamin E. Mays also wrote a little poem that should take a minute to read entitled, "Just A Minute":

I've only just a minute,
Only 60 seconds in it.
Forced upon me, can't refuse it,
Didn't seek it, didn't choose it,
But it's up to me to use it.
I must suffer if I lose it,
Give an account if I abuse it,
Just a tiny little minute,
But eternity is in it.

Make your moments count. Especially the ones spent getting hugged by your grandchildren. You have a contract with the Almighty to nurture those who come after you.

89.
The Business of Being Human

February 7, 2018

Whether I am trying to explain sexuality to preteens or what God had in mind when he created us and placed us on top of the heap in charge of everything that inhabit the Earth, I start my discussion with Genesis 9:7: "As for you, be fruitful and increase in number; multiply on the earth and increase upon it." In other words, we are programmed by God for self-preservation, to improve our condition and get together to reproduce ourselves. In this simple sentence are the great complications and unintended consequences of our lives. And it is complicated.

According to Howard Bloom, in *The Lucifer Principle*:

> From our best qualities come our worse. From our urge to pull together comes our tendency to tear each other apart. From our devotion to higher good comes our propensity to the foulest atrocities. From our commitment to ideals comes our excuse to hate. Since the beginning of history, we have been blinded by evil's ability to don a selfless disguise. We have failed to see that our finest qualities often lead us to the actions we most abhor—murder, torture, genocide, and war. For millennia, men and women have looked at the ruins of their lost homes and at the precious dead whom they will never see alive again, then have asked that spears be turned into pruning hooks and that mankind be granted the gift of peace; but prayers are not enough.

The enemy as well as our salvation is in us. We are saddled with great potential for good as well as evil—two sides of the same coin. A hitman can help a handicapped woman cross the street on his way to a contract murder. Human beings are ambitious and kind as much as we are destroyers. We are reaching out to the stars, exploring the great depths of our oceans, building skyscrapers and can, in an instant, communicate with every other human being on our planet. In our zeal to master everything, we are also bent on our own destruction. It is just a part of our will to survive but let us not be slaves to emotion. At a time in history when we are becoming increasingly polarized, we must find a way to get along.

Margaret Mead, the great anthropologist, who I loved when I was a college student, had an interesting idea about who make up our in-group (us) whose lives we cherish and who comprise those who should be treated with hostility (them)—

targets for murder. She started with classifying the most selfish among us who only had the capacity to think of themselves, others included blood relatives, members of one's tribe, one's country, one's race, religion and then the most mature, civilized and refined among us who consider all human beings as brothers—the universal brotherhood of man.

"Love the Lord your God with all your hearts and with all your soul and with all your mind and with all your strength." The second is this: "Love your neighbor as yourself. There is no commandment greater than these." (Mark 12: 30-31)

90.
Demographics of the World

February 14, 2018

I was giving a talk to a high school class and asked my audience, "What percent of the world's population live in the United States?" The estimates ranged from 20% to 50%. It's actually 4.3% (283 million) but the third most populated. While our economy and our military are (by far) the strongest in the world and we spend more on healthcare than any other country, the health status of our citizens doesn't make it to the top 30 in the world. We could be so much healthier.

Of the 7.6 billion people who inhabit the earth, 37% live in just two countries: China and India. The countries in Asia have 4.3 billion people. Europe has 12% of the world's population (733 million); the continent of Africa has one billion. South America and the Caribbean have 600 million (9%). The countries with the largest population are:

- China 1.27 billion
- India 1.05 billion
- United States 283 million
- Indonesia 212 million
- Brazil 176 million
- Pakistan 138 million
- Nigeria 123 million
- Bangladesh 131 million
- Russia 146 million
- Mexico 103 million

In terms of religion, there are an estimated 2.2 billion Christians and 6.9 million who identify as Islamic. Hinduism claims 900 million and Buddhism 376 million believers. The largest cities in the world are Tokyo with 33 million people followed by New York, São Paulo, Seoul, and Mexico City with about 17 million each.

Of the 6,909 languages spoken in the world, Chinese is number one, then Spanish and English third followed by Hindi and Arabic.

And just in case you wondered, the population of the world is projected to be 11.8 billion in less than five years. The number of people who ever walked the earth is about 100 billion. I want to be a real estate lawyer on judgment day when we will all emerge from our graves to reclaim our property.

91.
Human Achievements and Limitations

February 21, 2018

Like you, I have been watching a lot of the Winter Olympics. As I watch transfixed on the level of skill that human beings can master (twirling four times in one jump on ice skates, flying through the air on skis, traveling at breathtaking speed on bobsleds and fearlessly sliding higher and higher on snowboards) I marvel and even gasp on their achievements. Golfers, baseball, and football players get better and better with each passing year.

Among the most incredible achievements of human beings, I include:

1. Domesticated fire and learning how to cook.
2. Learning what to eat and drink.
3. The wheel.
4. Developed agriculture and animal husbandry.
5. Discovered electricity.

6. Mastered flight.

7. Invented language, writing, poetry, and music.

8. Traveling to the moon.

9. Created photography.

10. Einstein's theory of relativity and quantum mechanics

11. Split the atom.

12. Developed medicine, surgery, and vaccines.

13. Created the internet and electronic devices.

14. Identified all the elements in nature (periodic chart).

15. Mapped the human genome and DNA Instead of 15, the list could easily be 1,000! Human beings are also survivors. I marvel that a child in Haiti could be buried alive during an earthquake for more than two weeks without food or water, extricated from her grave and survive. I am impressed that human beings live in tall mountains, deep crevices, and caves, in the desert, in swamps, forests and at the North and South Poles.

The heaviest a human being can be is 1,400 pounds and the tallest is nine feet. The most a human being can lift is 1,000 pounds. We can go without sleep for 11 days; some people can hold their breath for over 11 minutes and the oldest we can live is 122 years. The most children a woman can have is 69 and for men, Genghis Khan fathered over 1,000 children but the potential for about any man who lives to be 60 years old is over one million.

Usain Bolt can run 100 yards in 9.58 seconds; Van Niekerk can run the 400 in 43.03 seconds; El Guerrouj can run a mile in 3.43 minutes. Javier Sotomayor can high jump eight feet and Mike Powell can long jump 29 ft. 4.5 inches. If we continue to break these records every four years, in a hundred years we will run the 100 in one second, the 400 in 10 seconds and somebody will be able to jump over a building on a single bound.

Over the past 2,000 years, human beings have grown stronger, faster, endured all kinds of punishing demands and we have become smarter. We are living longer and live in extreme temperatures and environments. Our world records are regularly broken but how much more progress can we make. Is this just the beginning of the end of human achievements or just the beginning? I am of the opinion that we haven't seen anything yet. Great things are in our future.

92.

A Brief Comparison of American and French Law

February 28, 2018

1. In 1804, France adopted the *Napoleonic Code* that ended not only the feudal system but replaced the very elusive, confusing, and contradictory "Customs of Paris" or wherever the case was being litigated. The new code was adopted as governing law throughout between the three.

2. While we have Criminal and Tort (civil) law in the United States, in France, they have "private" law and "public" law.

3. In the United States, there is a long tradition that we are only responsible for ourselves while the French recognize that each citizen has a responsibility to each other. In the United States, if you pass a car accident and people are bleeding and may perish, the law still recognizes that you don't have any responsibility to stop and render assistance. In the United States, if you are walking by a swimming pool and see a child in distress, you can leave the child to drown if you are not a lifeguard, police or a first responder. In the United States, you can see a horrible crime being committed and choose to ignore and not report it; in France, you are not only obligated to go to the aid of anyone in distress, but you are also even required to feed someone who is starving. In the United States, we believe it would be "nice", but you are not legally obligated.

4. Philosophically, in France, there is an acceptance of a stratification and class, if you were born poor, there is a consensus that your children and their children will also belong to the lowest rung of society and the laws tend to constrain individual initiative. Culturally, we are raised on the Horatio Alger "rags to riches" stories recognizing that each person should advance to the full extent of his talents and ambition and the role of government is the protection of these individual ambitions.

5. In the United States, we have an abundance of separatist organizations based on race, ethnicity, gender, etc. (ethnic separation). France does not allow any organization that excludes any French citizen. They vigorously

oppose any attempt to exclude or the appearance of excluding any citizen as going beyond the values and principles of the Republic. You would not even be allowed to have white and black churches.

6. Finally, here is joke #3 from the *Lawyer's Weekly:* One day in contract law class, the professor asked one of his better students, "Now if you were to give someone an orange, how would you go about it?" The student replied, "Here's an orange." The professor was livid. "No! No! Think like a lawyer!" The student then recited, "Okay, I'd tell him, 'I hereby give and convey to you all and singular, my estate and interests, rights, claim, title, claim and advantages of and in, said orange, together with all its rind, juice, pulp, and seeds, and all rights and advantages with full power to bite, cut, freeze and otherwise eat, the same, or give the same away with and without the pulp, juice, rind and seeds, anything herein before or hereinafter or in any deed, or deeds, instruments of whatever nature or kind whatsoever to the contrary in anywise notwithstanding..."

93.

How to Kill Your Husband

March 7, 2018

March Madness? For more reasons than one, March is the month when evil lurks in the hearts of even kindhearted women who would under normal circumstances never hurt a fly. If you are a woman who needs your husband's life insurance money, have had just enough of inconsiderate ways and cannot take his messing around one more day. Maybe he is not abusive but just selfish or maybe he just forgot your birthday and or anniversary one too many times, why kill him with an axe, a gun, a knife, push him over a cliff or even poison him? Why even leave him? You can accomplish the sinister deed and be praised for it. He will be pushing up daisies and your friends, family and the entire community will probably give you the "Wife of the Year" award accompanied with compliments like you have never heard. No police will call and there will be no embarrassing court trial. People who know your husband will tell you things like:

"Your husband was happy. You did everything to take care of that man."
"You were such a wonderful and devoted wife."
"There was nothing you wouldn't do for him."
"You loved that man to death."

Do I have your attention?

The average American wife can expect to continue living without her husband for about 15 years without her husband anyway. That's right! You are on track to inherit everything. That's because men usually marry younger women and then die about seven years earlier than their spouses. That is why American women are the wealthiest in the world. Here is the key to outlive your husbands and inherit practically everything. So, just leaving well enough alone, you will still have 15 years without having to wash his underwear, listen to his constant complaints as well as the lack of good judgment messing around for which some men are famous. But if you want to try for 25 or even 30 years without him along with the life insurance money, this advice is for you:

1. **Encourage him to smoke.** Tell him how masculine and cool it makes him look. Tell him not to let people tell him what to do. Because the anti-smoking message is so persistent from all the public health people, tell him that people have a right to smoke if they want to. That's just a scientific gobbledygook. Remind him how much it relaxes him, and he will never get tired of hearing how sexy he looks with a cigarette or cigar between his lips. Whenever you travel, buy him several cartons of tax-free cigarettes, or even arrange to buy it from the underground supplier that doesn't charge high taxes. Here is the kicker: "Baby, Uncle Charlie smoked a pack a day and lived to be 98!" Just be careful that after you light him up, you get away as far as possible from him. Passive smoking is dangerous for you and the kids. If you inhale enough of his smoke, you too could suffer from throat and lung cancer, heart disease and premature wrinkling of your skin.

2. **Encourage him to drink as much liquor and beer as possible.** As soon as he gets home, hand him a strong drink. A six pack of beer per day will do very nicely as well. That's what dutiful wives do! What is better to relax with and loosen him up? In fact, anytime is a good time to enjoy a beer or hard liquor. Let your husband know that a drinking man is a sophisticated,

glamorous, and sexy man. As a good host, whenever his friends come over, run out and buy a case of beer or a couple of bottles of their favorite liquor with a little branch water on the side. And insist that they drink it all up before they leave. Most likely, if you cannot stand your husband, you don't like his friends either so you can contribute to the demise of all of them. The other wives will thank you. So, go ahead, the life insurance policy will more than repay you. Each year, 200,000 premature deaths are attributed to alcohol in the form of accidents, liver disease, cancer, and violence. Caution: If he is driving drunk, don't just take the wheel, let him go on and get a ride with someone else. Riding shotgun with a drunk is very dangerous.

3. **Discourage him from exercising**, participating in sports and vigorous activities. You may enjoy your aerobic classes, swimming, morning walks and evening runs. Tennis anyone? But it is important to complain loudly about the pain you are in after you exercise. More importantly, remind him about Jim Fix and all the other joggers and athletes who died while running and exercising. Winston Churchill remarked that he got enough exercise going to the funerals of friends who do. What's the point of exercising when the amount of time you add to your life expectancy is the same amount of time you spend exercising? Why not spend the time doing what you enjoy." You can certainly be creative in coming up with lots of rationalizations and excuses for not following good health recommendations. In fact, have someone send him the following e-mail:

If walking is good for your health, the postman would be immortal.
A whale swims all day, only eats fish, drinks water, and is fat.
A rabbit runs and hops and only lives 15 years.
A tortoise doesn't run and does nothing, yet it lives for 450 years.

He will have fun repeating those messages back to you!

4. **Don't let him check his blood pressure.** Just explain that it may upset him to know that he has high blood pressure and cause the blood pressure to go up even more. If he sneaks around and gets it checked behind your back, be sure he doesn't see a doctor about it. This is not hard. Most men will not go to a doctor until they are in great pain or stopped in their tracks. Men are usually opposed to practicing prevention. If he has no symptoms, he will consider having someone take his blood pressure a waste of money a

sissy silly thing to do. So, it won't be hard to keep him away from the doctor's office. If he actually gets his blood pressure checked, follows up with a doctor and is prescribed medication, do two things:

(1) As men love to transfer responsibility for "everything" to their wives, tell him you will remind him to take his medication and then conveniently forget.

(2) After he takes his medication, make sure he gets upset. You do this by telling him about the bills that you cannot pay, the trouble the kids are getting into, the leaky faucet and all the things that need fixing then go to bed in granny pajamas, cold cream on your face and have a headache. Then invite him to be intimate and blame the blood pressure medicine for his inability to perform.

Note: Uncontrolled high blood pressure is the greatest contributor to heart attacks, heart failure, kidney failure and strokes. If he has a heart attack and dies quickly, all is well and good but if he suffers a stroke that is bad. Couples always stay together after a stroke. You may be heartless but not so heartless as to leave a man who needs his diapers changed. If you ever visit a home inhabited by a stroke victim, it is not a happy situation for anyone as the victim sometimes strikes out at the very people who must meet his every need.

5. **Church.** As 70% of the people who attend church services are women, it is not a hard sell to get your man to forget about church. While you are glowing in God's grace, an opportunity to serve your fellow travelers on our planet, have a reason to dress up and look good, getting lots of hugs from your sisters and brothers, inspirational sermons, singing that make you cry, bring a smile to your face, and otherwise make you stand up and shout, he would rather watch football. But when you get home from a truly inspirational service, be sure to complain about how two- faced and deceitful ministers are and how bored he would be. Tell him, "You would just fall asleep. It's more comfortable to sleep in your Lazy Boy than a church bench. That's no place for a macho man like you!" Advise him to sleep late, go for the big brunch they serve down at the local restaurants and come back to the football games with his friends. You love him so much you prepare hot dogs, ribs, hamburgers, chili with pork as well as lots of salty potato chips and other snacks to go with it. And don't forget the

beer! And for the piece de resistance. Buy him a 100-inch flat screen TV and put the fluffiest chair in front of it—one of those that stretch into a bed. Put a microwave oven to his right and a small refrigerator to his left. After a while, he will figure out that he never has to leave his spot. The only thing I haven't figured out is how he can take care of his bodily needs without getting up. Maybe you can help me out with some ideas.

6. **Feed him what he wants.** For breakfast, four eggs, sausages, bacon, coffee with plenty of sugar and cream. For lunch: nothing like hot dogs, hamburgers, fried chicken, bologna, pastrami, salami and ham sandwiches, pizza, potato chips, french fries, fruit pie and a large soda. For dinner: ribs, steaks, lobster with butter sauce, a blooming onion, more liquor and always cake and ice-cream for dessert. Who ever heard of having dinner without dessert? In fact, show him how much you love him by baking him a cake with lots of icing every week. He can help himself with a slice any time of day or night. You can get away with feeding him stuff like that forever. Just be sure that you are eating plenty of fruits, vegetables, grains, yogurt, chicken, and fish. Epidemiologic evidence clearly establishes that high cholesterol is one of the major modifiable risk factors for coronary heart disease.

Now that you have a start, you can be creative to your particular circumstance. Your husband will not know that you are loving him to death. The next time I see you and your husband in a restaurant, if you are eating fish and vegetables and he is enjoying a steak with a blooming onion, a drink in one hand and a cigarette in the other, I will wink at you. If he is living like that he will not be living long. You, on the other hand, can smile a devilish smile. It won't be long before his family, neighbors and friends will be assuring you about how much you did for that man.

94.
And Yet We Rise

March 21, 2018

I recently completed the reading of, *Educated: A Memoir* by Tara Westover (Random House, 2018). I was inspired to read it because I heard the interview on NPR where she discussed her life. I am not overstating the case; it really is a remarkable story. Ms. Westover grew up on a mountain in Idaho in an unlearned Mormon family that were extremely suspicious (paranoid would be more accurate) about the government and determined to be self-sufficient. So, they avoided contact with the outside world as much as possible. Ms. Westover was delivered by a neighbor (midwife) who had no medical training:

1. Did not have a birth certificate until she needed one to apply for college.
2. Never attended elementary or high school.
3. Never saw a pediatrician or a dentist in her childhood.
4. Worked on the family enterprise (a junk yard) from four years old and was deprived of playmates.
5. On several occasions she was seriously injured but was never treated by a doctor and was never taken to an emergency room.
6. Was physically abused by her brother.
7. As her family believed that an attack by the government was imminent (Armageddon), they prepared for war and survival by storing away weapons, food, water, and fuel.

On the other hand, when she decided to go to college, she taught herself to read, studied for the SATs, passed, and was accepted to the University of Idaho and went on to study at Cambridge University in London and finally obtaining a Ph.D. from Harvard, traveled the world and became a famous author. How was this possible? It happens all the time. It happens to have the ring of truth and a reflection of my own life.

I was born in a small mountain village in Jamaica and obtained a very fractured education, did not have a birth certificate until I needed one to migrate to the United States, so I never knew my date of birth and never had a birthday party growing up. When I was 14 years old, if you had placed my biological parents in a police line-up,

I could not have identified either one of them. I read my first book when I was 13 but nevertheless became a lawyer and obtained a Ph.D. in psychology; AND with the grace of the Almighty and a great wife, produced four brilliant and accomplished children. The message is: never give up on your children. Even when it looks like they are headed in the wrong direction and the odds are they will become good for nothing bums, lightning strikes and they become great men and women to nurture the next generation—and yet we rise!

The other side of the story of children who hail from humble beginnings and achieve great things (Horatio Alger Stories) is that they predictably become alienated from their biological family. Ms. Westover has not been on talking terms with her parents for 10 years and she is forbidden to even visit.

Recognizing this phenomenon, the Amish persuaded Congress to pass a special law allowing them to limit their children's education at eight grades. Once children become educated or have visited Paris, it is almost impossible to keep them down on the farm.

Several other religions discourage higher education because they lose their young people. There are many stories of children who become educated, get good jobs, move away and never return. They will even cite examples of these children who would not even bring their intended spouses to meet their parents, and some will even confess that they have never met their grandchildren because their high and mighty progeny don't think their parents are good enough to be around the children. Education changes perspective and values. Are you willing to let them soar or keep them close to home?

When this rift occurs, everyone loses. Cutting children from their grandparents is a mortal sin and not being invited to your children's wedding is hurtful.

The twist on Ms. Westover's story is who becomes rich. No, it's her parents. Like the theme of the book, *Rich Dad, Poor Dad*, where the professor of nuclear physics dies with debt and his brother who drops out of high school invests in real estate and becomes rich. It so happens that one day, the father sets himself on fire trying to remove a fuel tank from a junked car with a setline torch. He was severely burned all over his body. Did they take him to the hospital? Of course not! His wife wrapped him in a homemade poultice and took care of him at home. When he recovered, she became famous for her ointments and there was great demand for her home remedies. They could not make enough of it, set up a factory hiring a lot of people— and they were delighted to disinherit her!

95.

The Free State of the Isthmus

March 28, 2018

A few weeks ago, I traveled to Panama City, Panama to attend an international meeting with the research team at Merck and Co. (a pharmaceutical company), with representatives from Canada, the United States, Central and South America. Most of the meeting was conducted in Spanish so it was a good time to be bilingual. Since I am not, I had to strap on headphones and listen to the English translation. Fortunately, mathematics and statistics are universal.

In my distant past, long, long ago, I took two years of Spanish in high school and four more years in college and still don't speak it. Oh, I can ask your name and which country you are from and even ask for a glass of water in a restaurant, but I have never had a conversation in Spanish. I was amused when Father Carlucci (Saturday Night Live) promised that he could teach me four years of Spanish in one easy lesson. Impossible you say? Well, he asked those who took four years of Spanish what they retained, and it turned out to be a half dozen sentences. "Oh hell, I could have taught you that in one easy lesson." If you don't use it, you will lose it.

We, (ZÖe Pediatrics), are participating in a clinical trial for Merck for a new treatment for diabetes. While the drug Sitagliptin is now available by prescription for type two diabetes in adults, it is being tested in children for safety and efficacy before it can be made available to kids. We have been one of the centers of excellence recruiting patients between the ages of 10 and 18 years old with hemoglobin A1C higher than 6.5%. Hopefully, we can help get this approved and available for kids who suffer from diabetes around the world.

Unfortunately, type two diabetes is a menace to young people because of the obesity epidemic. If it is not adequately treated, blindness, fatigue, amputations, heart disease, impotence and premature death are the predictable outcomes. So, it's an awesome feeling knowing that we are doing something about it. The new treatment, (if it pans out), will be available in about five years.

Arriving in Panama City is a little bit of an adventure. Unlike Hartsfield-Jackson Airport in Atlanta, when we disembark, I wasn't immediately directed to customs but to a regular gate. I eventually made my way to customs and then picked up my luggage. I searched unsuccessfully for the driver who is supposed to meet me and out of frustration decided to take a taxi to the Marriott.

On our way, my guide (the taxi driver) informs me that Spain once owned Panama and then it was part of Peru, then Venezuela, then Columbia, then Ecuador, and then Colombia again. In 1846, the U.S. signed the Mallarino–Bidlack Treaty to protect them from foreign interference in return for granting the U.S. right of way across the Isthmus. In 1912, President Theodore Roosevelt had to pay Colombia $10 million to stop interfering in the affairs of Panama and the United States finally granted Panama their independence—kind of! The two countries then agreed for the United States to build, operate, and maintain the canal forever. The capital, Panama City, is inhabited by about a million people.

After checking in to the hotel, I went for (what Australians would say) a walk-about—a stroll. It is an understatement to say that the Panama people are of mixed heritage. As people came from near and far to get jobs building the canal, many stayed on and intermingled producing beautiful people of every hue, tall and short, a variety of eye colors and hair textures. It's a blend of about 20 cultures.

After our scientific sessions on the second day, a group of us piled into a tour bus to visit the Canal—and what a wonder it is! While there, we saw a 30-minute film about the building of the Canal and the widening that was recently completed. We also saw three huge ships pass through.

Before the canal, a railroad transported goods across the Isthmus from 1855. We learned that the first effort to build the canal was undertaken by Spain and then the French in 1880. After spending huge sums of money and losing many lives to yellow fever, both countries abandoned the project. But with Yankee ingenuity and financial backing, the U.S. Army Corps of Engineers completed the project in 1914. It is considered one of the world's great engineering triumphs. The United States ran it until December 31, 1999, when it was turned over to Panama (lock, stock, and barrel) by President Jimmy Carter. Panama assumed full operation and control from that time forward, but the United States retained the right to intervene militarily, if needed. Wasn't that generous of us?

You may recall that after an attack on the United States Embassy, President Reagan arrested President Manuel Noriega in the 1980's for his involvement in drug trafficking and froze all of Panama's assets. Noriega died in a United States prison and the country seems to have stabilized since then.

When I visited the Patagonia two years ago, I learned that in the old days when ships going from the Atlantic to the Pacific had to traverse the dangerous journey around the tip of Argentina and Peru, as ships had to be repaired, refitted, refueled, supplies taken on, etc., that part of the world was wealthy. Well, it all went bust when the Panama Canal opened its locks.

My vision of how ships move from the pacific to the Atlantic or vice versa was just a waterway that they sailed through, but no. Ships must go through three sets of locks with the ships being lifted and lowered.

The Canal is not without unintended consequences. Tons of fish and other sea life perished as they went from salt water to the freshwater lakes and vice versa. Contrary to my expectations, it is not all salt water. The biggest surprise, however, was the toll for ships passing through. Would you believe an average cost of USD $300,000! There is gold in them der locks. Personally, I would rather have a canal than oil wells or even gold mines. I am not really sure why the country is not better off. I am certainly not saying that they do not have modern cities, there just seem to be too many poor people on the streets. And yes, renowned professional boxer, Roberto Duran and Major League Baseball's Rod Carew were both from Panama.

96.

The Arc of Time Bends Toward Progress: Better Must Come!

April 11, 2018

Before I proceed with my message this week, I must tell you that something phenomenal happened to me last Monday (April 2). Playing with the Rascals at the Raintree Golf Club, I shot a 72—three less than my age (75) and 12 less than my handicap—that included an eagle and three birdies. I am a happy man! Nothing like golf to either frustrate poor souls when we are playing out of the woods or to elevate our spirits when the putts drop. So, I am in the mood to write about the goodness of life and our blessings.

Contrary to what you may have been told that our best years were in our past rather than the future, I am here to proclaim that as time passes, the human condition improves for everyone in the world but particularly for us who are fortunate enough to live in the United States. Whether you are highly educated or not educated, rich or poor, EVERYONE is better off than at any time in our past. Wonderful things are happening. Opportunities abound and an even better world is coming. So, don't worry, be happy. Unfortunately, however, as quality of life gets better people generally feel worse and want even more.

I find it interesting that during wars and famine when everyone is suffering and has nothing, we are thrilled just to get hold of a loaf of bread. But during times of prosperity, when all our needs are being met but some have more, jealousy raises its ugly head and we become envious and unhappy—"I should be doing better," and, "How come the Johnsons have so much more than we?"

While there are still too many people living in poverty and pain, at every stage in the past, life expectancy was shorter, disease was more common, discrimination and pollution were worse, and liberty was more imperiled. Now, excellent health care has never been more accessible, living conditions have never been better. Our military is stronger than the rest of the world combined and most of the money in the world resides in the United States. In 1900, our life expectancy was 47; now it is 79. By 2500, it will be 100 when our children can realistically expect to be centenarians.

Worldwide, in 1900, 80% of humanity could not read or write, illiteracy is now down to 15% and will soon be eradicated. In 1900, 90% lived in abject poverty and 10% lived well and by 2015 only 10% of all the people of the world lived in poverty.

From all indications, this is the golden age for Americans as well as the world. All our children have access to their daily bread, to health care and free from disease to a good education, breathe clean air, drink unpolluted water and protected by highly respected law enforcement. In Thomaston, we live in an almost crime free community where people are kind and civil to each other. Whether I need a tank of gas, apples in winter or any household convenience, I can get it at a reasonable price within five miles. I can work out at any number of places with great equipment and pools. I can sleep soundly at night without fear of a home invasion. Unemployment is low. I can trust the people I do business with to do the right thing and I am free to say what I want and worship my God anytime and anywhere I like. The list of our many blessings is endless. So, why are some of us so angry and frustrated?

Throughout the world, every generation has done better than the one before. Our children were born in the best time and the best place in the history of mankind. These are good times. Celebrate!

97.

Being Married

April 18, 2018

I recently saw a cartoon depicting a couple exchanging marriage vows that concluded with, "Let the harassment begin! No more pretending. Now we can be as miserable as we want to be." There may be something to that.

My wife and I celebrated our 30th anniversary. If you are bold enough, you can ask us how we celebrated. Suffice to say, we celebrated and celebrated and thanked the Lord for these many years of bliss. Through it all, we have learned to forgive each other and stay engaged.

I married a good woman! One of the high points of our union occurred when she was the keynote speaker at an AΦA Scholarship Banquet attended by 1,000 people and I was asked to introduce her. So, after telling everyone what a highly educated and erudite soldier she is, I serenaded her with the Alpha love song: "Sweetheart of A Phi A, from you I'll never stray. I will always be in love with you." She started to cry, and tears of pure joy overflowed their banks and ran freely down her cheeks. She finally got it together to thunderous applause.

Let's go back to when I proposed, and she accepted. We drove overnight from Baltimore to her parents' home in Milwaukee ostensibly to ask for her parents' blessings. She said she would take the first shift driving so I went to sleep. She woke me up 12 hours later and asked if I wanted breakfast. I asked if she wanted me to drive and she informed me that we had arrived. She could have been an amazing truck driver. She loves to drive, and I don't, so she does the driving.

Her father was sanguine and only had two questions: "Son, do you have a job? Do you go to church?" Her mother was sympathetic and worried about me. She asked, "She makes you happy?" The laughter that followed gave me pause. You know she is controlling and has a temper. I told her that I loved my feisty wife-to-be just as she is. She said, "It's your funeral. Just don't forget that you had fair warning." There have been fleeting moments when I wished I had heeded her warning, but it doesn't last long because she is the most giving person I have ever met. She does so much for me that I could not ever deny her anything she requests of me.

But we have opposite personalities. She wants to change the world. Our house is a forever evolving project. In our old age, she is still working 12 hours per day trying to slay dragons and build empires. I play golf every chance I get. I am laid back and tend not to fix things that are not broken. I am gregarious and love to meet and spend time with family, friends as well as strangers. She would be happy spending all her down time with just family and a very few friends. She loves kids but has reservations about adults. She is constantly counting her chickens and making sure everyone in her circle is OK. "Call me when you get home!" I will wait for them to ask if they need something. She is a helicopter parent and I like them to test their wings. When they get hurt, she is more likely to say, "Don't do that again." I encourage them to learn from it and do it again. You will survive and do it better next time. But we accepted each other's differences and decided early in our relationship that we would complete each other, and "U" is half of "US". If I ever have to go to war, I cannot think of anyone else I would rather have at my side.

This is the "Waine and Stephanie Way." We actually developed and adopted these seven strategies:

1. **We take turns solving conflicts.** When it is her turn, I will remind her, "This one is bad, I am glad it is your turn to fix it." While we have gone to bed mad as hell with each other and not talking, we find a way to come back from the precipice. Disagreeing is a good thing. Get the other person's perspective and then walk a mile in their shoes. If you love your partner, you will want to make it good for them.

2. **Cut out Criticizing.** We recognize that if you criticize your mate and insist on winning every argument, what does that make your partner? You may win the argument, but you are now married to a loser. Will you respect him or her in the morning?

3. **No one and nobody is perfect.** As I get older, as much as I try to write reminders, my memory is not what it used to be, so I do forget birthdays and anniversaries. We are kind and forgiving because we recognize that everyone does the best, he or she can—100% of the time. Keep wearing your rose-colored glasses and interpret everything in its most favorable light.

4. **Maintain Balance.** While men only have three requirements for their partners, (sex, food and just leave me alone), women have at least 150 requirements including a good provider, good memory, protector, passionate, considerate, kind, gentle, helpful, forgiving, etc., etc.

5. **Don't try to change each other.** Women enter marriage expecting their husbands to change and they don't. Men get married expecting their women to stay the same and they change. At least their priorities change. "You used to love my sports car and now you want to spend everything we make fixing up the house and on the kids!"

6. **Leave your crown at the door.** At work, you may be the great Godzilla who strikes terror in the hearts of all. Don't bring it home. At home, kindness prevails, and we are Nana/Pop-Pop, wife/husband, mother/father, daughter/son, and daughter-in-law/son-in-law.

7. **It is always a good time to be kind.** I happen to believe that kindness is more important than love, and don't betray the trust you have in each other.

One of the endearing things my wife does is to document our memories. I am the photographer but, on the many trips we have taken to other countries, we have diaries where she carefully documents our trips. What great memories!

After all is said and done, half of all marriages end in divorce. Japanese men are turning their backs on marriage in droves (40%) because they don't want someone else spending their money and have to put up with in-laws. I happen to believe that marriage is sanctified by God and is really awesome. Being married is a great way to live. I just don't understand why so many people choose to remain single.

How awesome is it to be married?

1. Who are you going to call if you become sick in the wee hours of the morning? I have a partner who I can count on and doesn't mind waking up if the need arises.

2. Who are you going to call when you cannot figure out how the remote or computer software works?
3. Who is going to scratch your back and bring you coffee?
4. Who are you going to call when the kids get on your last nerve or stump you with a question? I refuse to believe one person can raise children. It's just not possible!
5. Studies show that married people have twice as much sex as single people. Spouses know each other's likes and dislikes. And snuggling with your best friend is big fun. Spouses make great teddy bears.
6. When the labor is done, who will listen to how it all went down—the good, the bad, and the ugly? We take turns listening and we don't judge each other.
7. Give each other some space and independence! I have never heard: "Where are you going? When are you coming back? Who are you going to be with? What did you do with all the money you had?"

Not everyone is happy in their marriage, but the potential is there. Marriage requires work and a lot of kindness. You have it in your power to make your spouse, your superhero—he or she is not the enemy!

98.
Blowing Smoke and Other Arcane Medical Practices: Sometimes Facts Don't Matter

April 25, 2018

Recently, a friend of mine (Dr. Glen Laman) was on vacation at Jewel Resorts (Runaway Bay, Jamaica) with his family and was walking back to his suite when he suddenly collapsed. The hotel nurse was immediately summoned and successfully administered CPR. Once a regular pulse resumed, he was taken by helicopter to the University of the West Indies Hospital in Kingston where he was diagnosed with a cardiac arrest and two stents were inserted. So far, so good. He received what could very well be described as state-of-the-art medical care and he is now living normally with no limitations and considers himself lucky.

Then he did a little research and low and behold, he found that stents are not helpful, and they should not have been inserted. Several controlled studies (Courage, Rita-2, Ban2D and Orbital) show that stents are NOT beneficial. And yet, every day and in practically every major hospital in the world, stents are being inserted at tremendous cost and risk to patients. Sometimes, what seems obvious and logical is just not true. A correlation does not a cause and effect make. While I am sympathetic to the cardiac surgeons for dedicating their lives honing and practicing their skills, it is just time to stop this practice if it is not justified.

Have you ever wondered where the term "Blowing smoke up your a..." came from? What it means figuratively is that someone is just lying, conning, and flattering someone else. In the 1700s, some doctors actually became famous for devising the "CPR" of his day by literally blowing smoke up the rectum of a drowning victim or someone who had passed out. The practice was so popular that smoke stations were established all along the Thames River in London like the defibrillators we have installed at airports and public buildings today. Smoke stations persisted for 100 years with the logic that nicotine helped to resuscitate victims until an even smarter physician did the clinical trial and proved once and for all that it was of no value and was even dangerous. These smoke kits (with hose attached) are still available as antiques.

As late as the 1940s it was common practice in medicine to extract blood from patients to reduce high blood pressure. In addition, "bloodletting" or "cupping "was in common practice for 2,000 years and harmed every patient who received it, but the practice persisted because (I was told by good authority) medical myths die hard. Maybe all myths die hard. So, what are the myths we continue to believe? Does the sun revolve around the earth? Are men smarter than women? Will you get sick if you go out in the cold without a coat? Do vaccines cause autism? Do you still believe that even really smart people only use 10% of the brain's capacity? Swallowing chewing gum will stay in your stomach for years? Reading in the dark will hurt your eyes? Fingernails and hair continue to grow after death? Eating turkey will make you drowsy? Ulcers are caused by stress. You lose most of your bodily heat through the top of your head? There are more suicides during the holidays especially Christmas? Crazy people act up during full moons? Really?"

I am certain that many of you who read this column remember when cigarette smoking was the healthy choice. Doctors recommended "Camel cigarettes." Doctor Penguin says, "menthol is good for you." "Don't be foolish, take your doctor's advice and smoke a fresh cigarette." And "more doctors smoke Camel than any other brand." Hopefully, we at least don't believe that anymore.

Wouldn't we all be better off if we just give up the myths we live with? Like Jack Webb from *Dragnet* used to say, "Just the facts, Ma'am."

99.

About People Who Hate

May 2, 2018

Proverbs 10:12 says, "Hatred stirs up conflict, but love covers over all wrongs." On workday mornings, my wife is usually gone when I back out of my garage. Unbeknownst to me, she had gone to the Wellness Center, returned, parked behind me, and planned to go to work late. So, when I backed out without looking, my car dented her car. The first lesson is that you should ALWAYS look before you leap and the second lesson is that you cannot hurt someone without hurting yourself. Both cars were dented and had to be repaired. The two dents cost $2,000—a very expensive mistake on my part. Of course, there was no love lost nor any hatred stirred.

I am never impressed with anyone who attempts to scandalize someone else. It always says more about the gossip monger than it does about the person targeted for slander. Their attempt at self-aggrandizement does not create a favorable impression. You see, at the core of all haters is self-hatred. Blowing out someone else's candle will not make their candle brighter but maybe it's worth a try. You are busy commenting on the speck in someone's eye completely disregarding the boulder in your own.

Would you believe that there are people in the world who hate other people because of their race, religion, country of origin, sexual preference and age? As illogical as it may seem, there are people who harbor these prejudices.

A hater is someone who cannot be happy when someone else is happy and takes the opportunity to pour cold water on happy occasions or the success of others. They are inclined to point out the flaws in everyone else. If I am convinced that I am not worthy, my job is to bring everyone down to my level. The job of haters is to make everyone as miserable as they are. Haters just love sentences like: "Just because (they are successful doesn't give them the right to…)"

Hateful people are really good people to avoid. They are not even good company for themselves. Who would you prefer to work with and have as friends? People who accept others as they are (warts and all) or haters? As an employer, we never hire people who have a history of hate, and they are the first to go when this trait is demonstrated in the workplace. If you give in to the temptation to love a hater, it will only be a matter of time before you will also be hated and abused as well.

Hatred of people with different beliefs is destructive to those who are hated but twice as destructive to the hater. No one can be healthy, wealthy, and wise with hatred in their hearts. It's debilitating!

Hatred is corrosive of a person's wisdom and conscience;
The mentality of enmity can poison a nation's spirit;
instigate brutal life and death struggles; destroys a society's tolerance and humanity;
And block a nation's progress to freedom and democracy. (Lin Xiaobo)

100.
We Are Held Together by Integrity: Do You Walk the Walk?

May 9, 2018

I worry about our children. Have we normalized lying? How can we accept lying and continue to admonish lying for kids? Yes, I worry that as we normalize lying, we are encouraging them to go ahead and lie. It is certainly easier to lie and perhaps there will be no consequences. But there are always consequences. Are you concerned about our daily diet of hypocrisy? Will you be proud of your children if they grow up to be financially successful through some fraudulent and illegal activity?

How do you feel about people who lie? Wouldn't you prefer to have friends who are honest? While it is absolutely true that everyone lies, you know what I am talking about. I am talking about people who have a great deal of difficulty facing up to the truth and cannot be believed—con men who paint a different reality than you can verify. They always have a different version of the facts. How many times are you willing to believe the boy who cries wolf and then laughs at you for coming to his rescue? When someone attempts to convince you that a tomato is an apple, do you go with the flow and accept your friend's version because you like him, or do you trust your own experience and try to convince your adversary that a tomato is a tomato? I guess we expect lawyers, used car salesmen, politicians, and advertisers to lie and hold ministers, teachers, doctors, and pharmacists to a higher standard even though we know that many lawyers, car salesmen and politicians tell the truth, and many ministers, teachers, and doctors lie.

It is a common human experience that if you like someone you are likely to believe what they say and never believe anything your enemies spout. This is known as "in-group, out-group theory." If you love someone, they can do no wrong; if you hate someone, they can do no right. After people pick teams, they are quick to denigrate others who don't belong.

My mother believed that lawyers could not go to heaven because they have to lie to win cases and represent their clients. So, it gave me pause when I was graduating from law school and she reminded me. I had a feeling that she actually wanted me to not accept my degree.

What is integrity? According to Rev. John MacArthur: "It is the quality of being undivided.... It is being true to one's standard. It is, I guess, honesty. It is sincere. It is incorruptible. It is the opposite of hypocrisy…It's something that has to mark a leader." If we claim to be Christians trying to persuade sinners to be more righteous, we must have personal integrity. While we are all sinners and fall short of the glory of God, and while God is a forgiving God, do we persist in telling lies? Are we who we claim to be? Do we deceive and claim that we don't? Do we live a life of honesty and sincerity, or do we go with the flow and believe whatever we are told even though in our hearts we know it is false? Reverence for the Lord should motivate us to live a life with integrity compelled by the love of the Almighty. Integrity matters. Do we walk the walk and talk the talk?

> *Mathew 16: 26: "For what will it profit a man if he gains the whole world and forfeits his soul? Or what shall a man give in return for his soul?"*

101.
Teachers: Arsonists of the Mind
(Speech to the Retired Teachers Association)

May 23, 2018

While this forum is much too brief to recount both the trauma and victories of adjusting to life in the United States, I can tell you that engaging in athletics, specifically running, saved me. As a Jamaican, I am a natural runner. In fact, I must tell you that my grandmother had a boyfriend and as we lived in a very small house, whenever he visited, he would give us money and send us off on a five-mile journey to New Market to buy something for him. We ran all the way there and back thinking that we would please him by getting back quickly. So, with a smile on his face, whatever we bought was a present to my grandmother, and we got some small change for our efforts. Everyone got what they wanted.

This translated into me setting a track record in the 440 yards (now called the 400 meters) at Madison High School in New Jersey. With that, I earned a scholarship to college, obtained a master's degree, a Ph.D., and a law degree. In the meantime, I married well and raised four children who are all doing well and gifted us with six beautiful grandchildren. And, if you will allow me to brag just a little, our youngest son (who is a physician) retired at 35 years old because he has accumulated incredible wealth by writing science fiction books. The publisher obtained 40,000 preorders for his seventh book and he is now one of the 100 most popular authors in the country. You too may enjoy his books. Look him up—Aleron Kong. In addition to the teaching, he got from his parents, he had great teachers who lit fires …. instead of just filling buckets.

As amazing as you may believe my story is, I recently read the book, *Educated* by Tara Westover that chronicles her journey that included being born at home, never went to elementary or high school, never saw a dentist or a doctor, abused by her older brother, and had no playmates and yet obtained a Ph.D. from Harvard. It is truly an amazing story.

I have a friend whose daughter is a gifted musician who spent her life receiving great tutoring, practicing daily and even graduated from Julliard. She went on to play for the New York Philharmonic making about $50,000 per year. Fat Joe, who you may not have heard of, dropped out of high school, and never studied music, wrote a song with two words and repeated "Lean back, lean back" for about 50 times and when it became number one on the charts, he earned more than a million dollars.

My point is, never give up on young people. They may seem hopeless, but these knuckleheads often surprise us. In the words of Maya Angelou: "And Still We Rise."

As I never had a father figure in my life, I adopted my English teacher in high school, and I visited him after school just about every day. I would write and rewrite a paragraph after he corrected my errors. That is where I learned to write. When I tried to obtain an educational loan in college and found out that I didn't qualify because I was not a citizen, one of my professors drove me to Omaha (150 miles) at his own expense to obtain my citizenship papers so I could qualify for the educational loan. I salute great teachers.

We moved to Thomaston going on seven years ago to start up ZÖe Pediatrics. We expanded to Barnesville and Columbus and now see 200 patients per day with seven pediatricians and 55 employees. We believe so much in the gospel of prevention that our mission states: "Children do not have to be sick to get better." When they reach 90 years old, they will blow out their candles and hopefully thank ZÖe Pediatrics for setting them on a road to good health.

After a life of wondering, my wife and I ended up in Thomaston, a great place among really amazing people where we dropped anchor. I am a deacon at Greater Mt. Zion Baptist Church where we love God, love our pastor (Rev. Charles Reeves) and love each other. Please plan to visit. I think you will enjoy our hospitality. I also served as president of the Thomaston Kiwanis, and I write a weekly column for *The Beacon* about the bounty of Middle Georgia. I also get to play golf almost every day. Last week, I had the most phenomenal luck with an eagle and three birdies in the same round. It doesn't get any better than that.

I would like to end with the story told of two smart-ass teenage boys who caught a bird and were determined to play a trick on their know-it-all teacher. Their plan was that the biggest boy would hold the bird behind him and ask Ms. Johnson, "Is the bird in my hand dead or alive?" If she said it was dead, they would present a live bird; and if she said it was alive, he would squeeze the bird to death and present a dead bird. So, they were all giggly when they asked Ms. Johnson the question. But Ms. Johnson merely said: "Boys, it is in your hands." My message to all teachers, "The future is in your hands. Set their minds on fire!"

102.

What's the Meaning of Southern Hospitality?

May 30, 2018

I do worry about what we are teaching our youth. Is it now OK to mock the impending death of Senator John McCain? What are we normalizing?

When I moved to Thomaston almost seven years ago now, I was puzzled when I was pulled over on Hwy 36 by a state trooper when a funeral procession was headed north, and I was headed south. I understood that I should have pulled over if I was headed in the same direction out of respect to the family, but even though the officer didn't write a ticket, I was lectured about the legal requirement to pull over and stop on both sides of the road for a funeral procession. I find that (in the South) we take our pleasantries and consideration for each other's feelings seriously.

As I never heard of this rule, I learned something. I learn about the great respect and the sensitivity we show for each other. So, I cannot believe that saying Dr. McCain is dying anyway so we don't need to pay him no mind comports with anyone's values in Thomaston. But I find it interesting that there is no outrage. I hope I am not alone in finding this comment reprehensible. I don't believe there is any place for these comments—regardless of who the victim happens to be. Even if we love someone, we should always take the opportunity to correct people and let them know that these comments are out of line.

Our youth should know that correct spelling is important, correct grammar is important, common decency is important, truth telling is important, kindness is important and respect for each other is important. Regardless of how much we admire and support people who violate these values, we should be nudging them to act more nobly and not accept these outrageous comments as normal. *Noblesse Oblige* requires all of us to act with respect and kindness towards each other regardless of status differences.

I love southern hospitality especially when it is more than sipping on sweet tea, gently swaying on a bench swing on our front porch and a gathering of our extended families at Big Mammas on Sundays after church. We extend ourselves to strangers to make them feel at home and always extend a helping hand to the less fortunate without an expectation of them returning the favor. "There are no strangers, just friends we haven't met yet." A right hand of fellowship is extended to everyone because we take our pleasantries seriously.

According to Michelle Darrisaw in her essay: "These are the six qualities that really Define Southern Hospitality": Southern hospitality is not a choice; it's more than an institution that has six elements: politeness, good food, kindness, helpfulness, charm, and charity.

I, for one, admire the amazing life of Senator John McCain and I am enjoying reading his book, *The Restless Wave*. I recommend it to everyone. But even if I hated him, (I don't hate anyone) is it never appropriate to hit a man when he is down and particularly when he is dying? A little respect please!

103.
Small Towns are the Happiest Places to Live

June 6, 2018

If you are wondering why you are so happy, it's because you live in a small town! Yes, a recent study confirmed that the quality of life is better in places like Thomaston and confirmed that large cities are miserable places. According to the authors, "Life is significantly less happy in urban areas." It turns out that wealth and formal education has very little to do with the quality of life and personal happiness, regardless of where you live.

When I read *The Beacon* each week, I marvel that so many kids get their pictures in the paper, especially if they are athletes. Birthdays and anniversaries of ordinary folks are published and celebrated. If they lived in the city, there would be no chance! You even get folksy columns.

According to Christopher Ingraham, people who live in small cities spend less time in traffic, enjoy affordable housing, low crime, are less transient, more likely to attend church and feel a "sense of belonging" to their communities. It feels like home with good neighbors. This describes Thomaston to a tee. Having a strong social network is key to your sense of well-being. The farther away people live from the madness of cities, the happier their life is likely to be. Living here helps me accomplish more because I thrive in solitude when I want it. The downsides are not having access to specialists if you have a difficult medical problem, lack of upscale restaurants, theaters, and stores. But all that is only an hour away.

But here is the worst thing about living in a small town: if you break up with your spouse or friend, you cannot avoid them. If you commit a crime or do something embarrassing, somebody is going to tell your mamma, and everybody will be pointing a finger at you. People will talk. Maybe that's why we are so nice to each other. But if you are an outlaw, it will probably be a good time to try living in the city and away from decent folks.

In addition to our great weather and the absence of environmental threats (hurricanes, droughts and floods, earthquakes, tsunamis, volcanoes, etc.), I am surrounded by green leaves and things are growing all around me. I know the history of the fruits and veggies I buy from local farmers. Now that we have Walmart, internet, cell phones, Netflix, music, and great books to read and listen to at my heart's content, I have not been bored since I moved to Thomaston. What a good decision we made!

So, it appears that the ideal situation is to be far enough away and close enough—the goldilocks place or the sweet spot. Guess what? That is where Thomaston is located—an hour from Atlanta, Macon, or Columbus! You also made a good decision to live here. Heaven is wide open spaces and always finding a parking space.

104.

A Leaning Tree is Not Always the First to Fall

June 13, 2018

According to Win Tomkins, "The leaning tree is not always the first to fall It doesn't matter the age when you are called. While you're young and strong, God may call you home. Oh, the leaning tree is not always the first to fall."

I am coming upon my 75th birthday in July and reflecting on my blessings. I am particularly grateful for those close calls when I would have been history and pushing up daisies. While death will eventually have its day, I have had a number of near-death experiences that served to strengthen my resolve that I am one of God's anointed.

Imagine a bright sunny day at the beach, the first day of a greatly anticipated vacation with my family. My youngest daughter (who was about 10 years old at the time) and I ran into the waves at Ocean City, Maryland with glee. Our joy turned to panic when I looked back and realized we were about a mile from the shore. Unknown to us, the undertow from a riptide had pushed us out to sea and our efforts to swim back yielded no progress. Resigned to my fate, I prayed for help and advised my daughter to swim to shore and don't look back. Just then I heard someone yell: "Grab the ring and swim parallel to shore. Don't try to swim directly to shore." A lifeguard (AKA an angel) saw that we were in distress and saved our lives. Hallelujah.

A riptide or rip current forcefully flows from shore to sea at up to eight miles per hour creating a danger to swimmers. Over 1,000 people lose their lives per year from getting caught in a riptide compared to only 38 from shark attacks. My daughter and I were indeed lucky, blessed and highly favored.

I am one of those people who live under the guiding hand of our Heavenly Father. Throughout my lifetime and daily, I can point to divine intervention in my personal life.

Once, having lost an important document on my desk, in total frustration, I called my wife and explained that I had deliberately put it on my desk, and someone must have moved it because I had searched high and low—all to no avail. She calmly said, "Darling, just stop and let's pray about it. As I put my head down in supplication, there was the piece of paper under my desk. I hollered: "Thank you Jesus!"

These are examples in my life that the direct hand of God has steered me or a family member out of harm's way into a blessing. The blessings come in all shapes and sizes and are only limited to my faith which I hope is a little bigger than a mustard seed. Whenever I find myself on the ropes, in trouble, confused, desperate or otherwise in need of divine intervention, I smile and put myself into the hands of the Almighty.

I have come this far by faith.
As my praises go up, showers of blessings come down.
"I have seen miracles after miracles performed in my life.

You kept having mercy on me.
I didn't even deserve to be alive. When you saw danger that I couldn't see.
You kept your angels all around me.
And I want to take time out
And say, I thank you Lord I'm still alive…I am a living testimony
I could have been dead and gone." (Williams Brothers)

105.

Yes, I am a Bleeding Heart for Children

June 27, 2018

In Matthew 19: 14, Jesus said, "Suffer little children and forbid them not, to come unto me: for such is the kingdom of heaven."

I am the Lieutenant Governor for District 2 for the Kiwanis in Georgia. We are a global organization of volunteers dedicated to being a positive influence in communities worldwide—so that one day, all children will wake up in communities that believe in them, nurture them and provide the support they need to thrive. And at the Kiwanis Children's Fund, our mission is to develop resources that transform the goodwill and vision of Kiwanians into programs that serve the children of the world. We have spent over a billion dollars fighting childhood diseases. Our children, wherever they may be, are our future.

My wife became a pediatrician and founded ZÖe Pediatrics dedicated to the proposition that children do not have to be sick to get better. Her passion is to care for children. She receives a great deal of satisfaction from seeing sick children become healthy. She and her team would love for all children to be healthy and strong. She works 12 hours per day—practically every day, to advance this cause.

Personally, I will willingly sacrifice my life to save a child. I am the father of four amazing children and six even more amazing grandchildren and there is nothing I will not do to advance their cause. What I want for my own children is also what I want for children everywhere. I want a world where all the children of the world are happy and nurtured by their parents and their "village" to achieve their dreams. Why?

Jesus loves the little children
All the children of the world
Red and Yellow, Black and White
They are all precious in his sight
Jesus loves the children of the world!

What we are seeing playing across the news cycles is not reflective of our Christian values. God embodies grace and mercy and has a heart for children. As a reflection of God, we should do everything in our power to protect the little ones that are left in our charge REGARDLESS of how they got there. In our practice we take care of children being raised by loving grandparents because the parent or parents are in jail or strung out on drugs. We take care of children who are being raised by foster parents because of the same reasons and these kids are not lucky enough to have grandparents willing to raise them. In each case, we see that the children bonding with their adult caretakers soothe and reassure them. Children need that anchor, and the best anchor are their parents. They suffer irreparable damage when they are abandoned or forcibly separated from their parents.

As a prosperous nation, most of the world looks to us as we do become our brother's keeper. The scriptures also say, "To whom much is given, much is expected." The Irish came to escape famine, the Jews came to escape Nazi Germany and the Cubans came to escape Castro. As President Ronald Reagan reminded us in his inaugural speech: "We shall be a city upon a hill. The eyes of all people are upon us, so that if we shall deal falsely with our God in this work we have undertaken and so cause Him to withdraw his present help from us, we shall be made a story and a byword through the world." Those are not words to be taken lightly. Everyone wants to come to America because of our prosperity, safety, and opportunity. There is obviously a right way and a wrong way to do that. However, having said that, we don't put the children in the crosshairs for their parent's mistakes and medicate them to make them manageable.

Jesus loves me this I know   *Yes, Jesus loves me*
For the Bible tells me so   *Yes, Jesus loves me*
Little one to Him belong   *Yes, Jesus loves me*
They are weak but He is strong.   *The Bible tells me so.*

106.

Being Devoted Doesn't Mean I think Our Country is Perfect— Just That I Love It

July 4, 2018

As with most things in life, my grandmother reminded me that when you eat fish, as much as you may enjoy it; you have to spit out some bones. If you are the type of person who believes the glass is half full, you focus on the wonderful meal; if you are someone who believes the glass is half empty, you complain about the bones. I don't complain that roses have thorns, I celebrate that thorn bushes have roses. My mother also told me that "nobody is perfect." There are always bulges here and there, little imperfections that detract from what would be an admirable body. But I bet you thought I was talking about your habits and personality—well that too. Corey Kent White's "She isn't Perfect" sums it up perfectly:

> She puts holes in the living room wall when she hangs a picture
> She nearly burned the house down last week, just cooking dinner
> She's got a smile that lights up the room She's got a short-fused temp too
> She's everything that drives a man insane, But I can't help but love her
> She's strong like whiskey, smooth like summer wine
> Got a red-hot touch, burn me up when the moon shines
> She's mine all mine 'til the day I die
> And it ain't hard to see she ain't perfect but she's perfect for me
> We fight like hell sometimes, make up til the sun rise
> I go crazy when she calls me baby I can't get enough
> She's strong like whiskey, smooth like summer wine
> Got a red-hot touch, burn me up when the moon shines
> She's mine all mine til the day I die
> And it ain't hard to see she ain't perfect but she's perfect for me
> I'm a mess at my best I know Lovin' me isn't easy
> If I were her I'd be gone by now But she never leaves me
> She's strong like whiskey, smooth like summer wine
> Got a red hot touch, burn me up when the moon shines

She's mine all mine til the day I die
And it ain't hard to see she ain't perfect but she's perfect for me
She ain't perfect but she's perfect for me

Whether we are talking about our spouse or our country, I can be mindful of their imperfections as well as having great love and pride for them. Happy Fourth of July!

107.

High Falls State Park: A Wonderful Place to Visit

July 11, 2018

I was on my way to visit friends in Jackson (Rev. Harry and Dr. Toni Clark) when I was pleasantly surprised by the beauty of High Falls State Park. It was right there on my left in Monroe County—a 600-foot-wide waterfall! I followed the signs, passed the kiosk and pulled into the parking lot. The view of the dam was breathtaking. I called my friends and told them that I would be late as I could not resist seeing this amazing place.

In addition to the dam and the falls, they have lakeside camping, they have boating, they have miniature golf, they have fishing, they have areas set aside for picnics, they have walking, biking and hiking trails, they have paddle boats, they have a large swimming pool, and they have lovely large, well-equipped playgrounds. But mostly what they have is beautiful scenery. The place was so special to me, I sat on a bench, took a piece of paper out of my wallet and wrote:

As the water departs High Falls Lake
And makes its way down the Towaliga River
Cascading over rocky cliffs and dam
I find the beauty of the falling waters
Most pleasing to both eyes and ears

I stopped in the "office/country store" and the rangers were entirely accommodating. What I wanted to know is why is this place a secret? It is only a 30-minute drive from Thomaston, (close to Exit 198 from Interstate 75). Why don't more people spend recreational time there? If camping is too rustic for you, several hotels with restaurants are close by. According to the park ranger I spoke with, Creek Indians were the original inhabitants and after a prosperous period in the early 1800s with a shoe factory, cotton mill and sawmill, and about a hundred years of prosperity with hydroelectric power, the area was abandoned when the railroad bypassed the area and people followed the action out of town. It became a state park in 1966.

Try it. I think you will like it. The Park is restful and the wildflowers will inspire you with wonderful memories.

The Clarks forgave me for my tardy arrival and were pleased that I enjoyed the journey.

108.

Failure is a Prerequisite to Victory

July 18, 2018

"But those who hope in the Lord will renew their strength;
they will soar on wings like eagles; they will run and not grow weary;
they will walk and not be faint." Isaiah 40:31

You may know that one of our greatest presidents (Abraham Lincoln) grew up in a log cabin, but did you also know:

1. His parents could not read or write and worked as day laborers.
2. His family was homeless when he was five years old.
3. His mother died when he was nine.
4. Without a formal education, he had the audacity to apply to law school but was rejected. So, he borrowed some law books and taught the law to himself, passed the Bar exam and became a fabulous lawyer.
5. As a young man, he fell in love and got engaged only to have the love of his life die prematurely. He took it hard and had a nervous breakdown. For a

year he was so depressed he could barely drag himself out of bed.

6. He ran for public office and failed seven times before being elected to the Senate and then lost the next time around.

7. So, he ran for president and the rest is history.

The story of Joseph in our Bible has always inspired me. You may recall that out of 12 boys and one girl, he was his father's favorite and the recipient of the multicolored dream coat from his father, which incurred jealous rage in his siblings. So, what did they do? When Joseph was 17 years old, his brothers banded together to sell him into slavery for 20 pieces of silver, soaked the famous coat in animal blood and reported to their father that Joseph was killed by wild animals.

While in slavery in Egypt, Potiphar's wife found Joseph irresistible and tried to seduce him. When he didn't accommodate her advances, she charged him with rape, for which he was unjustifiable sentenced to prison. When the Pharaoh needed his services as an interpreter of dreams, he was summoned to court and asked what it meant that the Pharaoh dreamt about "seven lean cows rose out of the river and devoured seven fat cows." Having predicted correctly that Egypt would have seven years of abundance and seven years of famine, he was put in charge of storing grain during the good years.

As predicted, the famine came and people from around the known world came to Egypt to buy grain including his brothers. When they confessed that they left their youngest brother (Benjamin) at home, Joseph concocted a way to get the entire family to join him in Egypt. Eventually, the Jews rise to fame and fortune was resented by the Egyptians and they were enslaved giving rise to the Exodus to the Promised Land led by Moses. The 12 brothers then became the genesis of the 12 tribes of Israel.

You must know that my favorite stories have to do with rags to riches and people who pull themselves up with their bootstraps. Lincoln had a face only a mother could love, so he said: "My face, I don't mind it because I am behind it."

If you are floundering and getting nowhere, God is getting you ready to succeed. No one could be more of a failure than Abraham Lincoln and Joseph. If Lincoln could become President of the United States and Joseph the head of the Jewish nation with their record of personal failure, there is hope for all of us. You are never too old to give it your best shot. Colonel Sanders was 65 living on social security when he started his fried chicken business.

So, I believe that failure is a prerequisite for success and joy comes in the morning. Oprah Winfrey was not only poor and abused as a child, but she was also fired as a television news reporter because they thought she didn't have any talent. Bill Gates was kicked out of college. Great baseball players only get a hit three out of ten times. Whether it's tennis, golf or any sport for that matter, the failure rate is high. You do not have to be perfect to succeed. You just have to be better than your competition.

Maya Angelou said it best in her poem, "And Still I Rise"

You may shoot me with your words,
You may cut me with your eyes,
You may kill me with your hatefulness,
But still, like air, I'll rise.

109.
A Family is Not a Sprint!

July 25, 2018

As I write this, I am celebrating my 75th birthday in Costa Rica with my wife, my four children, their spouses and six grandchildren. It is grand! Watching the setting sun each evening with a celebratory drink in hand has become the metaphor of my life. As I mingle with my children and grandchildren, my legacy, the proof that I walked this earth, it occurred to me that a family is not a sprint. Whoever you may be, from birth until death, from the womb to the tomb, from the sperm to the worm, you will have family. While families can be difficult from time to time, in my case, I am a proud papa. Now that I am the patriarch or Pater, I glow in the happiness that emanates from our children, their spouses, and their children. They all love each other and like their life's work. While the road has sometimes been rocky, they have come past their anger and frustrations, and we have arrived at this moment with unprecedented love and caring for each other. So, we celebrate!!!

My children have been generous with their praise for my role in their lives.

The most important ingredient is that I have an amazing spouse. I get so much credit for her initiatives. We are a team—partners to the end. We have learned many lessons along this wonderful journey called life—particularly knowing when to hand off things to each other.

The other important lesson is that you can only be as happy as your saddest child. Parents wear their hearts outside of their body. In the process of protecting and instilling them with the skills, values, and the discipline to succeed in life, as parents, we tend to be overprotective. At some point, however, we recognize that each must leave the nest and find their own way. Still, with every bump that they take in the road, we bleed. Worries and sleepless nights are not uncommon. The truth is, life brings both triumphs and tragedies, so you just have to keep hitting the ball from where it is, not from where you want it to be, and being mindful that you have to go to war with the army you have. Hopefully, there will be enough occasions where you can be proud of their achievements.

Elisabeth Kübler-Ross spent 10 years of her life going around the world interviewing people who had less than a month to live and not one of them ever said: "You know, I wish I had spent more time at the office." One-hundred percent of them talked about family. They particularly wished they had been more attentive, supportive, and especially forgiving of their children.

The greatest privilege we have is to be parents, grandparents and, God willing, to also be great, great, great-grandparents. All I feel in my heart is love and appreciation. Through them, I have true meaning in my life.

110.

If Lincoln's Mother Came Back as a Ghost

August 1, 2018

In trying to make the point that failure is a precursor to victory and success, several weeks ago, I wrote about how Abraham Lincoln rose from humble beginnings and a miserable life to become the Greatest American President. I showed my daughter (Jillian) the column and she immediately sang this beautiful song about Mrs. Nancy Hanks Lincoln coming back as a ghost and wondering what became of her son. You may recall that Lincoln's mother died when he was nine years old. As a ghost, she wanted to know: Did he learn how to read? Did he get on?

> If Nancy Hanks
> Came back as a ghost,
> Seeking news
> Of what she loved most;
> she'd ask first "Where's my son?
> What's happened to Abe?
> What's he done?"
> "Poor little Abe,
> Left all alone
> Except for Tom,
> Who's a rolling stone;
> He was only nine the year I died.
> I remember still
> How hard he cried."
> "Scraping along
> In a little shack,
> With hardly a shirt
> To cover his back,

> And a prairie wind
> To blow him down,
> Or pinching times
> If he went to town."
> "You wouldn't know
> About my son?
> Did he grow tall?
> Did he have fun?
> Did he learn to read?
> Did he get to town?
> Do you know his name?
> Did he get on?"
> He made you and all of us proud,
> Mrs. Lincoln.
> Your pitiful son became a giant and
> changed the world for good.
> God uses ordinary people to do
> amazing things.

According to the late Dinsmore, *Ten Surprising Case Studies of Ordinary People Doing the Impossible:* Everyone starts out as ordinary. They do things that everyone does. But then at some point, they decide they are going to stand and do things a little (or a lot) differently. It is a decision that turns the ordinary into a living legend. Then they go to do things that most people tell them are impossible—the things most only dream of. And it's that transition that embodies the work we do at Live Your Legend and the community we have created here.

It may be as simple as deciding to walk from Thomaston to Atlanta. Has anyone done it?

The "Nancy Hanks" poem was published by Rosemary Benet (1933) entitled *A Book of Americans.*

111.

Where Would You Prefer to Retire?

August 15, 2018

If money was not an issue, where would you prefer to retire? As it turns out, in a national survey, given the choice between retirement communities, where the sun shines all year, close to the ocean, the big city and small town/country, the number one choice (40%) was the small town/country option. Does that surprise you? It turns out that you are already living in paradise. Tell your friends and family who live elsewhere, their best option is to live well is a move to Thomaston. It reminds me of the interview with a famous professional golfer who when asked when he planned to retire, replied: "What am I going to do, retire and play golf?" I already live in Thomaston.

> *Green Acres is the place to be.*
> *Farm livin' is the life for me.*
> *Land spreadin' out so far and wide,*
> *Keep Manhattan, just give me that countryside.*
> *You are my wife. Goodbye, city life.*
> *Green Acres we are there.* (Green Acres TV Show)

No dream location fits everyone's retirement needs, of course. There are plenty of options around the world if you can afford them. Most wallets, however, can afford Thomaston. Affordable housing and reasonable property taxes help. You can live in a house with a garage and a yard. A $200,000 house here would cost $20 million in New York City. You can do whatever is on your list as to what you want and don't want (pros and cons); Thomaston should be an attractive option for many—though not for everybody!

For non-residents, come retire in a place where no one cares about expensive cars and brand names. A Ford pick-up truck is good enough. When you walk your dog, neighbors appreciate the fertilizer, so no pooper scooper is necessary. Spending two hours per day in traffic, crowded trains and buses with no elbow room and sweaty, smelly people standing over you is not my idea of a good time. So, move to

Thomaston and drive yourself anywhere in town and park free. The cost of parking in big cities is $10 per hour.

On the other hand, it takes longer to take care of business in Thomaston because you are always going to run into friendly neighbors who genuinely want to know how your mama is getting along as well as the rest of the family, and don't try to just talk business without exchanging pleasantries and catching up with how the kids are doing. So, we usually allow enough time for small talk. It is expected and makes us feel like we are part of a community.

Museums and galleries, we have none, but the Hightower library is first class and easily accessible. TUAC does a good job bringing us live entertainment and art exhibits. Our movie theater is a vintage building showing us the best Hollywood has to offer. And while we have no restaurants with tablecloths, you can enjoy a wonderful meal at Chili's, Aviano's, La Fiesta, Peachtree Café, Country Cupboard, Georgia Avenue Café, Justin's Place and plenty of burgers, ribs, fish and sandwich shops.

Whatever we don't have in Thomaston is available an hour away in Atlanta, Columbus, and Macon. We also have access to wonderful State Parks and I love the Rock Ranch. What a wonderful resource for families!

After all is said and done, we have access to everything we need or want as a social center, and our churches make up for whatever is lacking socially. What I don't miss is crime, pollution, traffic, and noise. I love living in a place where locking your door is an option and neighbors look out for each other.

In Thomaston, I enjoy looking at blue skies, sunsets, stars, and planets (without the obstruction of skyscrapers), green grass, birds, and flowers are everywhere adorned. I can play golf 12 months per year because of our mild weather and most important of all, we are not prone to any environmental disasters. When was the last time we had a volcano, earthquake, flood, hurricane, forest fire, insect infestation and tsunami?

We should never cease to count our blessings that include being able to live and retire in an amazing town. I really love this place.

112.
Kindness May Be More Important Than Love

August 22, 2018

No one disagrees that kindness is a good thing. We are kind to our mothers, children, extended family, and friends. Is that where kindness should end? For me, I extend acts of kindness even to my adversaries. When I am playing in a golf tournament, I root for my opponents and help them look for their wayward balls. I wish everyone well. If they beat me, I congratulate them. If I win, I always find something positive to encourage and help them feel better. I learned a great lesson some time ago, whatever the outcome, those who love me are still going to love me. That is not on the line.

This morning, I received a call from a mother and daughter who had a flat tire on their way to work and I immediately went to their rescue. I like opportunities to serve others—especially if they are damsels in distress. How can that not make me feel like a hero?

As we note the anniversary of ugly demonstrations of hatred in Charlottesville, I have a special and urgent request. Please, please, please make a special effort to show acts of kindness to everyone you meet. I actually have not lived in a place where people were more kind. But I am asking you to be extra kind with a cherry on top. We are all hurting and need kindness. Meanness abounds and haters are on the loose. I bear witness that no act of kindness, no matter how small, is ever wasted. If Thomaston had the reputation of being the kindest town in the United States, I would be pleased as punch. It starts with a simple greeting.

I once talked to a friend who had just returned from a visit to Bainbridge, and he excitedly told me how friendly everyone was down there. He said wherever he went everyone waved at him. As it turns out they were just shushing gnats from their faces. As the gnats are migrating north, we may soon be perfecting the hand wave.

In Thomaston, our culture defines our expressions of goodwill to each other. When my wife and I first moved here, going on seven years ago, I would call someone and if someone else answered, I would say, "Can I speak to George?" And the person who answered would say, "Good morning to you, too." It wasn't long before I learned that the protocol is that you greet the person answering the phone or the receptionist first before asking a question or asking to speak to someone else. See, I learned a little southern hospitality.

It is not possible to encounter someone in Thomaston or on the road of life without saying "How are you?" "Hi!" "Hey!" "How's your mama and 'dem?" "Hi y'all doing?" "Good morning" "Good afternoon" "Good evening", and in parting, we never just walk away, we say "Bye" or "Have a good day" "Enjoy your evening" "Traveling mercies" "Safe travels" or any polite expression of your desire for someone else's welfare. My friend Billy Reliford always says, "I will see you when I look at you." These gestures of respect are important. Unlike city folks who just walk on by without even tipping their hats or a nod of the head, in Thomaston, we NEVER ignore each other. We can stand rejection more than being ignored. "Savior don't forsake me." The worst punishment for children is to give them the cold shoulder or the silent treatment. "Please Mom, beat me all you want, just talk to me." I am not sure spouses handle it any better but strangers on the street are just as vulnerable to hurt if they are ignored or if you look past them.

It probably doesn't matter what the question or greeting is around here, but "I'm good," is the most typical answer. Can I get you another iced tea? "I'm good." How are you? "I'm good." I have never heard, "I am not good." And, let me just slip this little Jamaican saying into the conversation, it's "Walk good." In Costa Rica, it's "Pura Vida" (To the good life); and in Brazil, it's "Tudor bein" (All's well). In marriages or any relationship, while love and passion are great for a time, only partners who show each other kindness will last. Enlightened self-interest should tell haters that it is self-defeating. If you are going to be a hater, I hope you are independently wealthy because it makes you unemployable. I hope you don't need friends because who wants to hang-out with a hater. The thing is, haters are losers with so much self-hatred that they are determined and focused on defining others as worse than they are. They will always find something to criticize. You know you are doing something right or becoming successful if you attract the attention of haters. Even haters hate haters and haters never succeed. It really is a terrible affliction. I find that every time you hate on someone else, they will wait their turn to someday take great pleasure in saying, "Now I got you, you SOB!" Or even better, to see God turn that hatred away.

By the way, do you know why people in New Zealand and Australia call each other mates? Historically, England decided to empty their prisons and send all their criminals off to populate these protectorates. So, the English built prisons in the new lands and sent their most undesirable citizens to these new prisons. A "ball and chain" was also tethered to each prisoner. Each morning, the prisoners would greet each other with, "Good morning cellmate." After a while that got abbreviated to "mate," or "'Good on you mate" or "Ow ya doin mate?"

In addition to a pleasant greeting, go the extra mile and extend the conversation: invite someone to sit a spell and have a conversation, visit a different church, invite someone to join your breakfast club. Reach out and touch someone. The bottom line is: Treat everybody with brotherly love. Isn't that the right thing to do? Please step up your game. You may just make a lifelong friend.

113.
The Lord Moves in Mysterious Ways

August 29, 2018

The background of this story is that when western missionaries first went to Nigeria (Africa), while they were treated with hostility by most of the native people, the Igbos, a small tribal group, welcomed them. As early adopters, the Igbos welcomed change. For the most part, they became Christians, learned English, adopted Biblical (Christian) names and were educated in missionary schools. Students who showed promise were sent off to Europe to earn University degrees and became professionals. Gradually, the Igbos became large and in charge.

They also became conspicuous consumers and bragged about their education, skills, and wealth. This was greatly resented not only by the majority Houses as well as most other groups—the same scenario that played out in Egypt when the newly arriving Jews flaunted their wealth and the Egyptians prosecuted and enslaved them leading to the exodus and the crossing of the Red Sea with Moses as their leader.

Starting in about 1965, under daily threats and violence against them, the Igbos retreated to an area called Biafra intending to be an independent country. And while the Federal strategy was to cut off the Igbos and starve them, there was also an active attempt at genocide. As heroically as they fought, the losing strategy for the Igbos was that they had isolated themselves and became easy targets.

According to Wikipedia: In August 1967, federal troops invaded Biafra first entering a town called Asaba around Oct. 5 and began ransacking houses, burning crops, and killing civilians. The townspeople were ordered to assemble on the morning of Oct. 7. They complied hoping to end the violence. Hundreds of men, women, and children, many wearing the ceremonial *akwa ocha* (white) paraded along the main street chanting "One Nigeria." The men and boys were separated in an open square. The soldiers then produced machine guns, and on orders by Maj. Ibrahim Taiwo, opened fire resulting in the death of roughly 700 men and boys, in addition to those killed in the preceding days.

The interesting story that emerged out of this sad episode was that Maj Taiwo, in the process of rounding up the remaining residents of Asaba, broke down the doors of a church where he found a woman with her two daughters praying at the altar. He shouted at her, "Do you believe that praying to your God is going to save you and give you food?" The young woman answered: "Yes Sir, my Lord has never failed me." "Stupid woman, if you want food, I am the only one who can give it to you. Your life is in my hands. You should pray to me." "No Sir, I only pray to my Lord and Savior, the provider." 'Okay, you stupid woman, I am going to sit here and see how your God is going to send manna from heaven to feed your children."

So, for the next hour, while she and her daughters loudly prayed, the major and his soldiers mocked them. Then suddenly, convicted by her faith, he started to cry, walked up and got on his knees beside the woman and her daughters and prayed with them. Several soldiers followed suit. He then ordered his soldiers to bring food and water, left the church, got in his jeep and departed Asaba.

In all your ups and downs, just remember who is in charge. What we don't know now, we will know later. The arch of the universe always bends toward justice and truth.

> *God moves in mysterious ways*
> *His wonders to perform;*
> *He plants His footsteps in the sea*
> *And rides upon the storm.*
> William Cowper (1974)

114.

The Fluidity of Truth: For Every Truth the Opposite May Also Be True

September 5, 2018

I was amused when Rudy Giuliani recently said, "Truth is not truth." I also recalled that Kelly Anne Conway assured us that our president was not lying but was using alternative facts. So, what is the truth? Can we approximate truth by using synonyms like veracity, authenticity, honesty, consistency, candor, and sincerity? Are facts different from truth? After studying this quite a bit, I find that the concept of "truth" may actually be difficult. That being said, having Mr. Trump in the White House has certainly made Americans think daily on this concept of truth in the context of facts and hyperboles.

Here is a perspective when we tell our children, "Don't lie to me. Just tell the truth." From whose perspective would we like the "truth" to be defined? Do our children hear the real question, or do they hear us asking for a version of the truth parents can accept, rationalize, and deal with? Jack Nicholson once said in a movie, "You can't handle the truth." Perhaps that's why we are hearing pundits talk about "alternative facts" and truth is not truth.

For a long time, I believed that "the early bird gets the worm." Why? Because I heard it from a reliable source (my grandmother) who NEVER lied to me and it made sense. Ms. Rosie, my grandmother, was trying to inspire me to take initiative and to work hard. In general, her advice has held me in good stead. I have talked to others who believe that the "early bird" sometimes takes the brunt of inexperience and often it's the second person on the scene that can take advantage of the experience of the first person. Regardless of your perspective, Ms. Rosie's truth worked for her and since her opinions and truths hurt no one and helped many, it was TRUE for her and didn't affect anyone negatively.

On the other hand, when I was in college, I read Plato's, Allegory of the Cave. In this story Plato wrote about a society where everyone spent their entire lives in a cave and came to believe that the shadows on the walls were reality. One day, someone escapes and after hitting his head on a tree and stubbing his toe on a rock came to realize that the people he left behind were believing in shadows and not the real world. So, he hurried back to educate them about the "truth." But they stoned him, called him crazy and killed him. "How dare you say something that stupid?" Again, perspective matters especially if you are introducing new "truths" to people who perhaps are happy to be in the "cave." Facts for the people in the cave were defined by shadows; facts for the person who stumbled out of the cave was defined by the tangible world he had discovered. Prior to Christopher Columbus, everyone's truth was that the earth was flat. He discovered an alternative truth which reflected that the earth was round. The fact that he returned from his travels did not convince everyone that the earth was not flat. The powers that be tried to discredit him and kill the infidel.

His truth was gradually accepted as time went on and more and more people found it more advantageous to accept Christopher's "truth." But every so often I will run into someone who still believes the earth is flat and that the sun revolves around the earth.

In my 75 years on earth, I have come to believe and accept that there is truth and also that being truthful matters. I have learned the difference between integrity and expediency. I have also learned that just because someone does not share my perspective, that doesn't make them a bad person. It makes them a person who doesn't share my reality or perspective. It doesn't make my truth less real for me and unlike the people in Plato's cave, I have people in my circle who accept my truth because they know I have integrity.

My wife (Stephanie) is a Biblical scholar that accepts the Bible as the inspired Word of God. She believes the Bible literally and when we get into debates about whether the men delivering God's words were using metaphors or was speaking literally, she responds: "I take God at His word as written in the Bible and when I don't quite understand all the ramifications, I take comfort in my acceptance that I need not understand completely but I do have to follow faithfully." She is a firm believer that the truth is always revealed to all those who seek the truth and therefore does not get caught up in the tweets or the Facebook posting of the day. Her truth is that God is a God of truth and mercy and cannot exist in the same space as confusion, so when she sees confusion, she knows that it is not of God and moves right along. My wife lives by the motto expressed in Matthew 6:25-27: Therefore, I tell you, do not worry about your life, what you will eat or drink; or about your body, what you will wear. Is not life more than food, and the body more than clothes? Look at the birds of the air; they do not sow or reap or store away in barns, and yet your heavenly Father feeds them. Are you not much more valuable than they are? Can any one of you by worrying add a single hour to your life? "Therefore, do not worry about tomorrow, for tomorrow will worry about itself. Each day has enough trouble of its own."

You see, good things come to those who wait, especially if they wait on the Lord.

My synthesis of the "truth" is that one's perspective will define the truth to that person. Most of us can make a truth claim regardless of what we believe. Our beliefs notwithstanding, I feel it is important to be truthful and if your truth is going to affect the lives of others, then the facts should be weighed for the greater good. While we all know the truth, I will claim that no one knows what the truth is. Is an apple red? We often use our shared agreement about "reality" in which to form our community's concept of the truth. Is it true that no one can predict the future? Yes and no. I know the sun will come up tomorrow, except the sun doesn't move and it's the earth that is revolving.

Many people believe man never went to the moon and what we saw was a movie made in Hollywood. Do juries get it right? Who and what do you really believe? Do you have to play to win? But 99.99999% of people who play the lottery are in the same boat as those who don't play. In fact, they are worse off, they are losers. If it is true that we should always look our best, it may mean that we should always wear our best suit.

"Everyone's experience of the world is a bit different—we all have different life experiences, background beliefs, personalities, and dispositions, and even genetics that shape our view of the world. This makes it impossible… to declare an "absolute truth" about much of anything since our view of the world is a product of our individual perspective. Some say that our worldview makes up a set of lenses or a veil through which we interpret everything, and we can't remove those lenses. Interpretation and perspective are key ideas in postmodern thought and are contrasted with "simple seeing" or a purely objective view of reality…this is how things tend to work. A scientist discovers something she takes to be true and writes a paper explaining why she thinks it's true. Other scientists read her paper, run their own experiments and either validate her claims or are unable to invalidate her claims. These scientists then declare the theory "valid" or "significant" or give it some other stamp of approval. In most cases, this does not mean the theory is immune from falsification or to being disproved—it's not absolute. It just means that the majority of the scientific community that have studied the theory agree that it's true given what they currently understand. This shared agreement creates a communal "truth" for those scientists. This is what led Richard Rorty to state the oft-quoted phrase, "Truth is what my colleagues will let me get away with." (Paul Pardi, "What is truth?")

115.
Redemption: What a Concept!

September 12, 2018

When my wife and I traveled to Greece several years ago, we specifically toured Corinth. We also took the opportunity to study the Apostle Paul and his travels. Books were readily available. Saul, who became Paul, had me contemplating the concept of redemption. It brought home to me that God knows our weaknesses and provides redemption to atone for our sins, guilt, and shame so we can be reunited with Him with clean hands and open arms—fully reconciled.

We are then afforded the opportunity to live by His grace and mercy, the twin towers of His love for His ultimate creation. He did all this by suffering and dying on a cross at Calvary. In 1 Peter 1:18–19, we are assured that if we are in Christ, we have been ransomed from our futile ways with his precious blood. He sets our captive souls free. Salvation is free to us because He paid the price. This is a genuine comfort to me that I do not have to bear my shame alone and Saul represents one of the most striking examples of redemption that comes to mind.

The dictionary defines redemption as the action of saving or being saved from sin, error or evil. It comes from "redimere" which is a combination of the words "back" and "buy." Technically, we are delivered from sin, hate and corruption through the DEBT that was paid by our Lord and Savior.

In the case of Saul, I was tempted to place him beyond redemption but now know that God never abandons anyone, and His love is sufficient and knows no boundaries. He may take a two by four upside our heads every so often but no one and I mean no one is ever beyond redemption. As you may have read and remember, as a Roman citizen, Saul was on a murderous rampage of the Jews (that included the stoning of Stephen) when he (Saul) met God on the road to Damascus.

As you may recall, Acts 9 tells the story of the conversion of Saul. As Saul neared Damascus, suddenly a light from heaven flashed around him. He fell to the ground and heard a voice say to him, "Saul, Saul, why do you persecute me?" "I am Jesus, whom you are persecuting." Saul was blinded but found his way to the street called "Straight" and there Ananias spit in his eyes and lifted the scales so he could see again. When the early Christians found out that this despicable man was in the neighborhood, they tried desperately to kill him. So, Paul humbled himself to be carried in a basket so he could be let down over the walls of the city to safety. With his epiphany and soul redeemed, he became the greatest advocate for brotherly love and mercy the world has ever known. Instead of Peter, I believe the foundation of the Christian church was Paul—even though he never met Jesus. Unlike Peter, whose main focus was spreading the Gospel to Jews, Paul was able to spread the good news to Gentiles as well.

You may have thought Paul was a disciple, but he was not one of the 12. Having accepted Jesus Christ as his personal savior, he traveled thousands of miles to win souls for Christ under very unpleasant circumstances and wrote the most beautiful letters. My favorite is First Corinthians 13.

Do you know the backstory of "Amazing Grace"? The author (John Newton) was the captain of a slave ship, probably the most in-human profession one could practice, but God used him to write THE most beautiful hymn of all time.

"Amazing grace, how sweet the sound
That saved a wretch like me! I once was lost but now I am found,
Was blind but now I see"

With surprising frequency, we commit shameful acts of disobedience to God's commandments. We do things that we should not do and leave undone things we should have done. Instead of brotherly love and kindness, we hurt, harm, and neglect our fellow human beings.

Jerry Givens was an executioner for the government who put 62 inmates to death but became a great opponent to the death penalty. Joshua Milton Blahyl recruited child soldiers and personally killed 20,000 people sometimes disemboweling mothers and eating human hearts but today he is a minister of God who has confessed his sins and asked God and the survivors of his victims for forgiveness. You thought you knew wicked?

In any case, why be mired and paralyzed with sin, shame, guilt, and emotional pain when immediate relief is readily available to you? Just like he did for Jacob, God provides a ladder through Christ, so we can climb out of our personal pits of hell. Jesus the Christ died for us while we were yet in sin. He forgives and washes away, not some, but all our sins. What an amazing God we serve. It is His Amazing Grace that is available to us on this side of Jordan. Don't cross that River before making it right with Him!

116.
Improving the Health of All Our Citizens

September 19, 2018

Improving the Health of All Our Citizens: Dr. Carlisha Gentles on *The Front Line* asks, "Wouldn't it be nice if everyone achieved a high level of health and longevity?" In terms of life expectancy, citizens of the United States rank 31 when compared to the rest of the world. The Japanese are the longest-lived and the healthiest people on earth with an average life expectancy of 84. Even though we spend twice as much on healthcare (per person), our life expectancy is 79. Even Costa Ricans live longer. Therefore, there is room for improvement all around. So much more could be done to enhance the quality and the quantity of our lives. Contributing to the lower life expectancy for African Americans are higher rates of obesity, heart disease, stroke, cancer, asthma, pneumonia, diabetes, HIV/AIDS, and homicide. It is important to recognize the impact that social status has on health outcomes. The stated goal of "Healthy People 2020" (U.S. Government publication) and our local health department is to achieve health equity, eliminate disparities, and improve the health of all groups.

The absence of disease does not result in optimal health. That is why our mission statement at ZÖe Pediatrics is: "Your child does not have to be sick to get better."

Good doctors cure disease, really great doctors also prevent disease. These determinants of health reliably predict whether you will enjoy a good long life. The more education and the higher your household income the better. You are what you eat, so good nutrition is important. Is your home environment safe, peaceful, and pleasant? Do you have access to reliable transportation? Are your healthcare providers culturally sensitive? Do you have health insurance, clean air to breath and pure water to drink? We have it all in Thomaston, but we do not all have equal access.

Across the board, African Americans live five years less than white Americans and suffer a disproportionate burden of disease. Diabetes is twice as prevalent for African Americans and is a particularly troublesome disease leading to blindness, amputations, impotence, and early death. So, who is doing something about this?

If you meet Dr. Gentles, you will be impressed by her boundless energy and passion for giving back to her community. She is the daughter of Fire Chief, Renee Harris and Jimmy Harris (musician and businessman), is married to a fellow officer, Dr. Andrew Gentles, and they have a beautiful and spirited 2-year-old daughter, Drew. When asked why she's been doing this, she shared with me that her background as a pharmacist, diabetes educator and board-certified clinician exposed her to a lot of challenges that she just could not ignore. Having served on the largest Native American Navajo reservation in Arizona and working with a medical team that included physicians, nurses, pharmacists, psychiatrists, native medicine healers revealed to her that collaborative care is the best way to make a meaningful difference in our communities. A lot more should be done to educate and motivate the people of Thomaston. There are a lot of health myths that plague our community and more should be done to improve nutrition. Why does breakfast have to be eggs and bacon? When asked what drives her volunteer spirit, she says "It's about values and beliefs. As Christians, we are taught that to those who much is given, much is required. I am about simply being a contributing member of society volunteering and sharing an encouraging word."

Dissipating Disparities, Inc., spearheaded by Dr. Gentles, to engage communities through community service events and collaborative efforts with health care providers, educators, financial advisors, and community leaders to uplift and enhance opportunities that may not be self-evident. There is much work to be done with churches, barbershops, beauty salons and wherever people gather. In order for DDI to continue and expand their programs, they are always in search of volunteers, community partners and additional funding.

Achieving health equity should be a priority for all of us in Thomaston. Please support Dr. Gentles in her work. Their website: www.ddi-ga.org or on Facebook at www.facebook.com/dissipatingdis-parities. Let us all start down the road to a healthier community by focusing on the person in your mirror. Are you as healthy as you could be?

117.

Crime Does Not Pay

September 26, 2018

Crime Does Not Pay: Particularly if you are not the sharpest knife in the drawer. In the front-page story in *The Beacon* (09/12/18), a woman locked the keys in her car and called the sheriff's office for help. They dutifully obliged, but after Deputy C. J. Kirschmann successfully opened the car door and smelled a certain odor, what do you think he found? How about 2.5 pounds of marijuana and other drug paraphernalia? The lady was arrested, and our deputy did not stop at go before locking her up. Really? This story reminds me of other "dumb criminal stories."

Do you remember the one about the gentleman who waited until a heavy snowfall to rob the appliance store? The police merely followed his tracks in the snow from the store to his house and recovered the stolen refrigerator. Or how about the bank robber who forgot to put gas in the getaway car and after successfully holding up a bank ran out of gas a block from the scene of the crime? I think sometimes the job of law enforcement officers is too easy. Some criminals are not playing with a full deck. I particularly liked the one about a criminal who broke into a house and thought he had scored a jar full of coke but after snorting some, discovered that it was the cremated ashes of the lady's husband. May he rest in peace in the robber's lungs.

Here is another one: With guns drawn, two criminals wearing masks jumped the line of patrons paying their bills at a restaurant to rob the cashier without noticing that two of the people waiting to pay their tab were police officers who immediately arrested them. Do they understand that if they do the crime, they will have to do the time? Do they understand that criminals don't sleep well and have a short life expectancy? It's a horrible life but criminals disproportionately suffer from "optimism bias" which assumes that in disasters, they will be the one left standing. Even if they take great risks, they will get away with it. They may have been caught and punished several times, but they will get away with it this time. They are short on taking proper precautions and planning. They would rather pay more for something from a questionable source than buy in the normal course of business.

So, are criminals less intelligent than the rest of the population? With a lot of exceptions, generally yes. Only less intelligent people would attempt these high-risk practices. People with low intelligence may be more likely to resort to quick fixes and shortcuts without understanding the consequences of their behavior. They choose to rape rather than develop relationships, steal instead of working for the funds to buy the goods and services they want. They may also believe that the only way to get what they want is not through the sweat of their brow but at the expense of someone else. Others have suggested that criminal-minded people lack socialization, are emotionally disconnected, and did not learn the rules of society. The rules are very simple—follow the Ten Commandments.

I suspect the real issue is impulse control—I want what I want when I want it. Are criminal-minded people more likely to fidget, unable to resist temptation, react aggressively to provocations, drive recklessly, prone to promiscuity, quick to anger, get into fights, and take what they want without permission? You would be amazed at what misery 30 minutes of thoughtless crime will get them—for the rest of their lives! Maybe the real reason children who attend Sunday school and go to church are less likely to participate in criminal conduct is that they learned impulse control—how to sit, pay attention and be quiet while the minister's sermon went on and on and on.

But I am amused that in the movies anyway, the detectives are always smarter than the criminals. Elementary my dear Watson!

118.

The Bystander Effect: Birds of a Feather Flock Together

October 3, 2018

What would you do if you looked out your window and saw a 10-pound bird perched on a tree? You would obviously get excited and invite everyone within earshot to come see the phenomenon. But what if no one else saw what you saw? Do you need confirmation? Does it matter what the group thinks? Apparently, it does. To paraphrase Richard Pryor: Who are you going to believe? The group or your lying eyes?

Individuals in a group will monitor the beliefs and behaviors of others around them before deciding what to believe and how to act—particularly if they have a relationship (family and friends). The more cohesive the group, the harder it is to escape their grip and do something we perceive to be contrary to the group's wishes. Do you stand up when everyone else stands up in church? We may not even realize we are doing it. This is more specifically called the "bystander apathy effect."

Closely related is the diffusion of responsibility that comes with a group. This is harmless enough in household chores, where siblings will "cooperate" in creating a mess, yet all seem to have been struck blind when it comes to seeing the mess that needs to be cleaned. It is much worse that we tend to think "somebody else will clean up the mess" – somebody with more authority, skills, or insight into the situation -- even when we are witnessing a brutal act.

While movies love to create this drama like Romeo and Juliet, it usually takes a lot to break from your tribe. Yes, their opinion of you and what you do is oppressive. We need their approval and fear rejection—even when we are angry at them. At the moment of birth, I can make reliable predictions of what a child will become as an adult. I can predict speech patterns, what they will like to eat, their music and movie preferences, what clothes they will wear, how much formal education they will achieve, the occupation they will pursue, whether they will be a Democrat or Republican, a nice guy or an SOB or even whether they like to wear hats or not, etc. just by knowing a little something about their parents.

Your group wants to count on you, and you want to be known as someone who can be depended on to think like the group thinks and support what your tribe is supporting. Collective consciousness requires that we suppress our individuality to act as we perceive the group would want us to act. What would grandpa think? While our wish to be noble is a powerful motivation, we mostly end up going alone with our group. As any teenager will tell you, we wish to be individuals, in exactly the same way as our friends.

Why is it dangerous when several teenagers are in a car? After all, their vision and hearing are sharper, instincts faster than they will be later in life, the instructions from their driver test are probably still fresh in their minds. The answer is peer pressure: The driver may otherwise be a careful driver but with the group egging him on, he will likely go along and speed up and pass in unsafe zones.

We are more likely to help a person in need even when we have to inconvenience ourselves, especially if the person in need is relatable to us. Sometimes, it's because something about that person signals that we are part of the same group (either explicitly; flashes a fraternal sign, wears a jersey of our team, has a tattoo or uniform; or in more subconscious ways; gestures, talks, dresses in a way that looks expected and standard to us). The internet is full of examples of those kinds of culture clashes, where a person may seem suspicious simply because we are not seeing these indicators that signal, they are "one of us."

The charter of human rights and freedoms that is accepted in most countries states that "every person must come to the aid of anyone whose life is in peril, either personally or calling for aid, unless it involves danger to himself or a third person, or he has another reason." In the United States, there is no legal obligation to come to the aid of anyone to whom you are not related in some fashion.

In 1964, Kitty Genovese was stabbed to death outside of her apartment in Queens, NY. Up to 38 people heard or saw the attack, but no one intervened. Although the real story is more complicated, Ms. Genovese's case became a touchstone for people to talk about the responsibility of bystanders.

Because it feels good to be "accepted" by the group and really awful to be rejected, human beings are prone to "go along and get along." In other words, we have a need to act in a socially acceptable manner as we deem to be correct by the standards of our reference group. While your morals may want you to do something out of sync with your group, are you willing to buck the tide and go against the grain? There may be consequences. Not many people are willing to risk rejection and the loss of important relationships.

If you live or socialize with obese people, you are likely to just go along with the program of overeating and not exercising rather than doing what is "good" for you. Are you really going to ask for different food and portions? If all the other wives are complaining about their husbands, you had better find something about yours to complain about or you may find yourself excluded from future conversations.

If you live and work around racists, are you willing to stand out and proclaim that this is just wrong? If a teenager is smart and earns excellent grades, is he likely to keep up his grades if the group he now hangs around with thinks studying and earning good grades are stupid?

If you see someone from a hated group in an emergency and you are with friends who say, "Let him die!" Will you go along with that sentiment and take no action? Well, studies show that the sentiments of the group go a long way in determining your course of action, particularly if it is a large group. The bystander effect can clearly have a powerful impact on your behavior.

During chaotic situations, people often look to others in the group to determine what is right. When people look at the crowd and see that no one else is reacting, it sends a signal that maybe they don't need to do anything either. Could you stand by and not object if the crowd was lynching someone? Psychologists recommend that if you need help from a bystander, look directly at one person, make eye contact, and make your plea to that individual. By personalizing your request, it becomes easier for the targeted person to act against the perceived wishes of the group.

119.

Snowmen Fall from Heaven Unassembled

October 10, 2018

The City of Thomaston and Upson County are in great shape: Why Don't We Have a Municipal Golf Course?

I wish more of the citizens of Upson County/Thomaston could have joined me for the annual state of the city and county breakfast meeting organized by the Upson County Chamber of Commerce. On Wednesday, (Oct. 3, 2018) our mayor (J. Stallings) had wonderful surprises for us. I was pleased to know that:

1. Our sewer infrastructure is being improved with a $7.65 million grant which will cover half of the total cost. The work should be completed in four years. It will include the construction of a new clarifier, system joint repairs, reconstruction of lift stations, as well as a bypass pipeline.
2. The city has demolished 28 nuisance and dilapidated structures and the clean-up/spruce up is evident wherever you go.
3. We doubled the number of police officers per shift and improved our insurance rating.
4. The employment picture has drastically improved as industry is finding Thomaston a good place to do business.
5. While there is much more to be done, the downtown area is being redeveloped with the launching of "Main Street" the Downtown Development Authority and the sponsorship of festivals and parades. (personally, I look forward to crowded sidewalks)
6. The city and county are cooperating on several initiatives.

Norm Allen then reported that the county now has more than $8 million in our emergency fund and all county departments are fully funded. Did you know that a new fire truck was ordered with high ladders that can handle any fire in the county? We will also have to build a new firehouse to handle this longer/higher vehicle. Most notably, our school system is fully funded. No wonder that our children are excelling in all their endeavors. With our amazing school superintendent, the educational experience we are offering is getting better and better. We live in a well-run city/county that is governed by honest well-meaning folks (politicians and civil servants).

Having said that, there is a photograph on page 5 of The Upson Beacon (10/3/18) with the following caption: "What once was a luxurious country club clubhouse on the south side of town is now just a memory to those who dined there. Demolition of Raintree Golf's clubhouse began Sept. 26 by Thomaston Land and Grading Company." Is it the beginning of the end of a golf course in Thomaston? Mr. Caldwell (owner) is not saying what his long-term plans are.

From the mountains to the prairies, from the deserts to the swamps, golf courses contribute to the local economy and quality of life. We are not just talking about jobs and taxes, it's about property values, green space and the attractiveness of business and individuals who may locate here. Norm Allen particularly believes that there are not enough golfers in Thomaston to make this investment worthwhile and sustainable. I would like to engage and convince our political leaders that a municipal golf course in Thomaston is an important asset. But we need active community engagement. Wouldn't you hate to NOT have a Raintree Golf Course?

While Norm sees the value of the golf course to our county, he would prefer that the golf course be privately owned and operated. Can we get 100 investors? Can we find someone with deep enough pockets to take it over and improve the condition of the course?

The game is played by young and old, blind, one handed and just about anyone can discover the marvel of this game. We invest in city parks, tennis, and pickle ball courts, why not invest in a golf course? It would certainly help with the marketing of our city to industry and always have a positive impact on property values.

I happen to play our Raintree course three to four times per week, and it would create a serious dent in the quality of my life and the 200 golfers who enjoy playing there. No golf course, no high school golf team and most of the golfers who now enjoy the game will probably just give it up and die sooner than later.

120.
Courage Over Adversity: In Defense of Bullies

October 17, 2018

Well, Hurricane Michael passed through and no harm was done in Thomaston. With all the disastrous predictions, we weathered the storm. If you never had a problem, how would you know that working like all depended on you and praying as if all depended on God could overcome them?

I am thinking about the story of the Great Buddha. He was born a prince and his father (the king) ordered that his son would never experience any adversity, disappointment, or sadness in his life. Whenever anyone was in his presence, they had to smile and only talk about loving, complementary and pleasant subjects. It was a capital offense to say anything that could potentially make the prince sad, angry, or even upset. He ate the best food, wore expensive robes, listened to the best music, literature, and philosophy. He had an army of handmaids to take care of his every need. His life was sweetness and light. So, what did he do the first chance he got? He said, "Let me get the hell out of here" and escaped to live a minimalist existence exposed to all the cruelties of life. In the process, he discovered that the lack of want is the road to happiness and fulfillment. This is the opposite of our western ideals of buying everything.

Would you rather be a great general with a million men to do your bidding? A trillionaire who can buy anything or someone who has no lust for power, control, or wealth? Mother Teresa turned her back on the world of wealth and power and moved mountains with her work among the poor in Calcutta, India.

I believe that life in these United States has taken a turn for the worse. Rewarding kids who come in last is just wrong and this current campaign against bullies is worse. So, am I a champion for bullies? Actually, I am. I learned a lot from the bullies I have encountered in my life. While my childhood would have been easier and more pleasant, I would not have had the confidence to manage my adulthood if I had not encountered and successfully dealt with the bullies of my childhood. The truth about bullies is that they are victims. They are hardly ever successful or happy as adults. They grow up believing that they can get what they want the easy way and at someone else's expense while those who were bullied had to develop creative ways to handle them and, in the process, developed important life skills.

Just about every state now has anti-bullying laws and more and more mothers will fight all their children's battles for them. It is a set up for failure. Would you have been better off if all the people you know as a child were nice and respectful? Without adverse experiences in childhood, would you be prepared to handle the really difficult ones in adulthood? The next time you encounter a bully, thank him for teaching you one of life's important lessons—how to deal with bullies. There is an endless supply of them in the world. Get used to it.

School policies now define bullying in the widest possible terms. Do we really want to take away all the challenges of life from our children? The zeal of helicopter parents pushes them to protect their children from any harm or bad experiences. They have formalized the following rules.

- My children will not be exposed to sex and violence on television and in movies,
- No bullies, no football, no germs, no guns, no cussing, no bad words, always tell the truth and respect your elders, never lose your temper, and they must always be supervised and be told what to do.

You insist on raising dependent kids when your focus should be on raising adults.

It really concerns me that modern children NEVER have an opportunity to be by themselves for even an hour. When I was a child, I roamed the woods with my childhood friends hunting birds, harvesting fruit, and playing all the games of childhood where I learned the importance of rules. My grandmother believed that kids should be a little bad. She was never delighted in goody-goody kids. Courage is not the absence of fear, but the triumph over your fears—and the harder the struggle the more glorious the triumph. The only way to prepare for future challenges is to experience them in childhood. Challenges, adversaries and strife strengthen and develop the mind the same way exercise does for muscles

121.

Our Future Depends on What We Do in the Next Minute

October 24, 2018

"I have only just a minute, only 60 seconds in it. Forced upon me, can't refuse it. Didn't seek it, didn't choose it. But it's up to me to use it. I must suffer if I lose it. Give an account if I abuse it. Just a tiny little minute, but eternity is in it."
(Benjamin Mays)

I have a hard time believing that this actually happened in Thomaston, but recently a man was leaving his house with his wife and infant daughter to attend a family gathering. Suspecting that he might have a confrontation with an adversary, he decided to pack his gun. Sure enough, the feared altercation ensued, and he shot his adversary in a crowded room that included his wife and infant child. What kind of decision-making was that?

I also know of a man who is serving a 50-year sentence without the possibility of parole because upon taking a walk on an unfamiliar path, he saw a house and chose to break in. In a moment of curiosity and mischief, he thought he could get away with stealing something. Instead, he saw a young lady coming out of her shower and in a split-second decision, attempted to rape her.

I also know of a man who decided not to pay for a hot dog at Piggly Wiggly and was arrested and sentenced to 12 months in prison. As soon as his neighbors found out that he was sent away, they took his clothes, appliances, and everything else he owned. He returned home from jail devastated and penniless.

Sometimes we make mistakes and get an outcome that we didn't want. It's not the end of the world. Should we have learned something that will help us make better decisions going forward? Making good decisions is always the better option. In golf, we say you have to hit the ball from where it is.

When confronted with a major decision, I consider IRAC (Issue, Rule, Application, Conclusion). One of the enduring lessons I carried away from law school is the legal process for making decisions, the acronym is IRAC.

Issue:	What is the question that when answered leads you to a course of action?
Rule:	What is customary, what do people usually do?
Analysis:	Apply the rule to the facts.
Conclusion:	What is the final answer?

IRAC functions as a method for legal analysis on law school exams all the way to Supreme Court decisions. I find thinking like a lawyer is a useful approach for everyday decisions as well.

Let's say that someone proposes that the Thomaston City Council install speed bumps on streets where motorists tend to speed which places pedestrians (especially children) at risk.

1. What's the Issue: Should the city council approve the installation of speed bumps on busy residential streets?
2. What's the Rule: We currently do not have speed bumps.
3. What's the Analysis: What are the pros and cons? (Maybe yes, maybe no) On the one hand it's an effective device to slow down traffic and makes it safer for pedestrians—especially children. On the other hand, it will also slow down emergency vehicles and damage the cars of unsuspecting drivers who are also annoyed.
4. Conclusion: Depending on how you feel about the analysis, you are now prepared to vote to abandon the speed bump plan.

In my next example, a student who is graduating from high school in May, (2019) is trying to decide whether to attend college or start working in his father's business.

1. Should I go to college or start working in my father's construction company after high school?
2. My advisors unanimously say I should go to college.
3. If I work in my father's business, I would earn four years of income instead of four years of debt. If I go to college, I would be better equipped to make a bigger contribution to the success of my father's business. On the other hand, I will have four years of experience instead of four years of studying a lot of irrelevant subjects that have very little to do with running my father's business.
4. Conclusion: Go to college.

Every choice we make has consequences. Some of those consequences are minor and some are catastrophic. If we make better decisions, we'll get better outcomes. Bad decisions likely lead to more bad decisions. We become the sum of the choices we have made.

122.

Winning The Lottery Mostly Makes People Big Losers

October 31, 2018

It was announced recently that a 20-year-old gentleman in South Carolina won the billion-dollar lottery and I am happy it wasn't you. Almost unanimously, lottery winners proclaim, "I wish I had torn up that damn ticket when I found out I won." The life of lottery winners can be a hellish existence.

I once interviewed one of the Atlanta airport taxi drivers who had pooled their funds to buy weekly tickets and won $200 million. The first thing that happened was a member of the group who was on vacation the week when the winning ticket was purchased and didn't contribute his $5 sued for his share, believing that they were a defined group with a defined purpose. After squandering a large sum on legal fees, the court ruled that the plaintiff was not entitled to any of the winnings because he did not contribute to the pool the week when the lucky ticket was purchased. But maybe he was the lucky one. The others went on to live a life of misery.

In my interview with one of the winners, he confessed to me that since he won, he had not had one conversation with anyone that was not about his money—including my conversation. This included his wife and children. He had to literally divorce his extended family and friends and cut himself off from just about everyone because no matter how generous he was it was never enough. "So, how can I be happy without family and friends? I wasn't even able to attend my church without being bombarded and harassed. There was never any shortage of needs and my money was the answer to all prayers."

What he regretted most was that it took ambition away from his children who now thought they lived on "Easy Street" and didn't have to go to school or engage in any worthwhile endeavors. In fact, his children were being harassed, seduced, and blackmailed as people attempted to use them to get to his money. To be honest "I wish I never won. It is nice not to worry about bills and to have all the luxuries I ever wanted, but it turned out to be just stuff. Caring for family and friends is the stuff of happiness and a good life, but they just cannot help themselves. Whenever they see me coming, they start thinking about how my money can solve their problems."

Lottery winners are the target for lawsuits, robberies, blackmail, death threats and the anger of everyone who is denied. Someone in Mr. Urooj Kahn's family poisoned him even before he got his first check. Mr. Abraham Shakespeare was murdered by his girlfriend and Ibi Roncarjoli was poisoned by her husband after she gave away $200,000 without his permission. Many become divorced, die of drug overdose, alone and unhappy.

A minister, "Billy Bob Harrell," won but ended up committing suicide five years later. In fact, I believe his church had sued him for their 10% (tithe). Mr. Gerald Muswagon also hanged himself after winning $10 million. But mostly, lottery winners like Andrew Whitaker blow through their money and end up broke and those they helped when the money was running were not sympathetic. When he was now down on his luck, he couldn't even get his old job back and became homeless. 70% of lottery winners are broke 10 years after their windfall.

Ms. Sharon Tirabasi, a welfare mother of four children, after winning $10 million couldn't say no to any of the million requests for money until it ran out. She is back to her old job and taking the bus to work. While $73.5 billion per year is spent on lottery tickets, I have to confess that I NEVER buy. First of all, the odds are better for being hit by lightning, but I am afraid I might win. I would rather have my family and friends than all the money in the world. Money cannot buy you happiness.

123.

When The Parent-Child Roles Are Reversed

November 7, 2018

I have had to ask a few of our parents, "Who is the adult?" I see children using operant conditioning to control the relationship with their parents and reversed roles. The formula is simple: What is followed by something pleasant is likely to be repeated and that which is followed by something adverse and unpleasant is likely not to be repeated. All animals and humans are vulnerable to this rule. It's the rule that animal trainers use and the rule that children use sometimes to get control of the relationship with their parents. In other words, some children figure out that parents' love living with happy nice kids and hate when children act up, throw temper tantrums, become mean and disagreeable. So, there you have it, children quickly learn how to reward you with hugs when you give in to them and peace prevails. They also know that parents will do anything to prevent drama. So, rather than parents offering the reward and punishment to shape their children's behavior so they can get along with others, the relationship is reversed, and the children end up telling the parents what to do, become bossy and threaten their parents with:

- "If you don't give me what I want, I will make your life hell."
- "I want pizza for dinner. I don't want this stupid dinner you fixed."
- "I will use my phone to tweet anytime I want to."
- "I will stay up as long as I want. You cannot make me go to sleep."
- "I am in love with Will, and we can have sex if we want."
- "You cannot make me…"
- "I will hold my breath until you give me what I want."
- Parent: "You are not leaving the table until you finish eating your vegetables". Child: "Ok, then we are going to sleep here."

A parent's relationship with their children is not equal. Parents are not supposed to be friends and buddies. Parents must be in charge. Children need limits and good firm parenting. Children flounder and feel insecure when anything goes wrong and will actively try to fill the vacuum. Just because children are bossy doesn't mean they know best and have the ability to make decisions. Bossiness actually comes from insecurity, and it is absolutely inappropriate for children to be giving orders to adults. Parents and teachers should learn that changing behavior is accelerated by consequence. If you find yourself in this situation, here are the do's and don'ts to regain control:

1. Don't yell or scream back and take things away.
2. Don't ask your children's permission and indulge them too much in arriving at a consensus about what to do—what they want for dinner, movies to watch, when you go shopping. Making decisions for your children is part of how you take care of them.
3. Threatening ("If you don't do xxx, I am going to beat you to an inch of your life") only communicates that you may not know what you are doing. There is a natural authority between parents and children. Children want to please their parents. Never doubt that you are in charge.
4. Don't make caring for them conditional. Children are entitled to nourishment, hugs, kisses, and assurance of your unconditional love. "I will only love and take care of you if you behave" is inappropriate and harmful.
5. Don't be a pushover. Maintain your authority.
6. Don't make decisions based on what your children want, think of what they need.
7. Take the lead and give directions with confidence. Act like you know what you are doing as a parent. Children will then trust your instincts and follow your lead.

Loving parents become frustrated because they are invested in their children's happiness and are inclined to give in to their children's demands. Obviously, children have the ability to "hurt" their parents because it is wonderful when they are loving and kind and feel awful when they say and do hateful things—especially when they withdraw their affections. Your smile and attentiveness are a powerful tool. Smile when they meet your expectations and look away when they act inappropriately. If you want to go a step further, give them the silent treatment and always carry "M&M" in your pocket and pop one in their mouths when you observe them being good. Just be careful that your children are not the ones carrying the candy.

124.

Disappearing Islands Are No Myth

November 14, 2018

I read an article recently that reported that Esanbe Hanakita Kojima, an uninhabited island off the coast of Japan, had disappeared. It was right there, and it magically disappeared. In the same article, they also reported that East Island (Hawaii) disappeared after a severe hurricane.

I was born on an island in the sun (Jamaica) and when I visit, I see evidence of rising ocean water washing up on hotels in Negril at high tide that came no closer than 20 yards down the beach 50 years ago. The owners of the hotel futilely use sandbags to keep the ocean at bay.

With rising sea levels from the melting of the polar ice caps, coastal soil erosion and extreme weather, it is predicted that several of the most breathtaking, beautiful but low-lying islands will be covered with sea water within the next hundred years—you will be able to pick coconuts under the sea as many islands around the world are running out of time.

Five islands have already disappeared from the Solomon Islands and five more are at risk. The Maldives, Palau (one of the Philippine Islands), Seychelles, Cook Islands, San Blas, Torres Straight Island, Tegue, Marshal islands, Tuvalu, Carteret Island, the World Islands and French Polynesia are likely to be greatly compromised or gone in less than 100 years. Sea walls will not keep out the invading ocean.

The United Nations has adopted the concept of "ex-situ Nationhood" to accommodate island nations that have no land. The proposal is that these countries would continue their status as a country even if they live in another country.

In our own backyard, before 1900, the water level of the Chesapeake Bay (Maryland) rose at the rate of three feet every thousand years. The water level is now rising one foot per 100 years. As a result, several islands in the bay are disappearing. A highly developed resort (Tangier Islands in Virginia) is on the critical list as well. If you have a boat visiting "Disappearing Island" (just west of Ponce Inlet in Florida), this could be fun. It disappears during high tide and appears again during low tide. So, bring your own food and water and enjoy it while you can.

Greenland and Iceland are losing miles of glacial ice each year that flows into the ocean! This was readily observable when we visited two years ago. Interestingly enough, some parts of Europe are rising after being weighed down by ice in the last Ice Age. So, countries close to the poles will gain more land and those low-lying countries around the equator will lose their homes.

I feel sad. Don't you?

125.

The Harder the Conflict, the More Glorious the Triumph

November 21, 2018

The difficulties we face in life are inevitable, so when life gives you lemons, make lemonade. In the Chinese language, opportunity and adversity are different sides of the SAME coin. The Chinese believe that within every adverse situation is the opportunity for achievement. David would never have been a hero without the presence of Goliath. In a world where everyone is at peace and everyone's needs are met, there is no opportunity to excel. It turns out that we need adversity to be successful. In every adverse situation I encounter, rather than focus on "woe is me," I embrace the struggle and look for solutions. In times of drought, how can I bring water to the thirsty?

A few weeks ago, I wrote an article defending bullies and heard from several people agreeing and disagreeing. I was making the point that there is too much effort in our schools to "ban the bully," leaving those who are being bullied no opportunity to face their adversaries. Would the world really be better off without bullies? How will kids learn how to cope? Christmas is around the corner and all of us will watch our favorite Christmas movie, *A Christmas Story.* The best part of the movie for me was when the victim found his courage, gave the bully some of his own medicine and went home victorious. Everyone felt the joy when he conquered his fears. Do we really intend to take away all obstacles from our children's lives and rob them of these moments of joy?

One of the themes that I find fascinating is how often ordinary people overcome amazing adversity. When I am faced with these challenges, I ask God, "Is it supposed to be this hard?" But then I draw inspiration from the Apostle Paul, who continued his mission to expand Christianity even though he was repeatedly beaten, stoned, shipwrecked, prosecuted, suffered from sleep deprivation, hunger, and exhaustion. This was no bed of roses—especially his physical attacks and imprisonment in Philippi. Few people ever experienced these torments. But these adversities did not impede Paul's progress and served only to strengthen his faith and resolve. Life is not so much what happens to us, but how we respond to life's challenges.

There is no such thing as an old coward. If you lived long enough to be old, you have triumphed over many adversities. Let us celebrate the struggle. It gives us drive and purpose. A strong support network of people who care for us is essential for dealing with life's problems but that does not mean that we should be dependent on others. If we start defining ourselves negatively, we will not have a foundation of values to help us get through setbacks and challenges going forward.

You will have your own opportunities to stand and deliver. When the opportunity presents itself, don't back down, cave-in, or sit on the sidelines. When you see integrity being undermined and truthfulness vanishing like the morning dew, when you are in the minority position but know in your heart that you are right, become someone who is willing to swim upstream when everyone else is swimming downstream. While it is harder, it is so much more satisfying. Walk in a manner worthy of God. I believe the last words He uttered from the cross was, "It is finished." Christ was not talking about His death; He was talking about His victory over death. He took on our sins and His death meant we would not have to live a life apart from God because He defeated sin through His physical death. By His sacrifice, Christ was able to release the power of God's Grace and Mercy.

The Scriptures teach us that God and sin cannot exist in the same space. We are separated from God because of sin. Christ's sacrifice gave man the ability to be in God's presence because when God sees us, He sees Christ and therefore strength, power and success become ours. The Bible teaches that we are the children of the King. Our horizons are always bright. If that is not the vision you hold, if like Elijah you are living afraid in a cave, then ask God's forgiveness, take His nourishment, and face your fears through the power of Christ.

"For every achievement there is a price; For every goal there is an opponent. For every victory, there is a problem; for every triumph there is a sacrifice."
(William Henry Ward)

126.

You Are Wealthier Than You Think

November 28, 2018

The 2018 Global Wealth Report (Credit Suisse Research Institute) reports that we are wealthier than we ever imagined. Your net worth is the value of all your assets minus your debts and obligations. The average income worldwide (200 countries) is less than $5,000 per year. If your net worth is more than $100,000 that will put you among the highest 10% of the world's population and if your assets are worth about $1 million, you are in the 1%. That's right; you are worth more than 99% of the people on earth. Did you not complain recently that you didn't know how you were going to make it?

Worry no more. You are better off than you think. The poverty line for Americans is actually middle income globally. So, don't worry, be happy. In terms of military might, the United States rank first by a large margin followed by Russia, China, India, France, United Kingdom, Japan, Turkey, Germany, and Italy. Might makes right. Have you heard of the golden rule? "He who has the gold makes the rules." Again, the United States has more gold, followed by China, United Kingdom, Germany, France, Italy, and Canada.

According to *Forbes Magazine*, based on the average annual income of individuals living in a country, the 12 richest countries of the world (per capita) are:

1. Qatar ($124,930)
2. Luxembourg ($109,190)
3. Singapore ($90,530)
4. Brunei ($76,740)
5. Ireland ($72,630)
6. Norway ($70,590)
7. Kuwait ($69,670)
8. United Arab Emirates ($68,250)
9. Switzerland ($61,360)
10. San Marino ($60,360)
11. United States ($59,500)
12. Saudi Arabia ($55,260)

There is a great deal of inequality in the world. For instance, did you know that the richest 10% of the world owns 85% of everything, and the bottom half collectively own just 1%?

About half of all the millionaires in the world live in the United States where the average citizen earns about $60,000 per year with a net worth of $400,000. By world standards, 88% of Americans are either upper or middle income. There are 123 billion acres of land in the world and if everyone got their fair share, it would be about four acres per person. I want my four acres in the heart of NYC. See, we still have enough land to double the population of the earth, which is currently about 7.5 billion.

No matter how you look at it, we are fortunate to live in the United States and Thomaston is an amazing place to call home. Consider yourself blessed.

Having said that:

"Before you speak, listen. Before you write, think. Before you spend, earn.
Before you invest, investigate. Before you criticize, wait. Before you pray, forgive.
Before you quit, try. Before you retire, save. Before you die, give." (William A. Ward)

127.
Sometimes the Apple Falls Far from the Tree

December 12, 2018

Undoubtedly, your values and personality are born from your early experiences to whom we are closely related. But this is not always the case. In my column last week, I was making the point that "Apples do not fall far from the tree," and I was taken to task by a mother who said she did everything right and one of her sons ended up with life in prison and the second son is a model citizen. No one else can imagine the pain of a mother whose child must spend a lifetime in prison.

She made sure that both her sons went to Sunday school, helped them with their homework, attended teacher conferences, gave them piano lessons and most of all, taught them to respect their elders and obey the law. They had both parents in the home. The result is more common than you would think. While California made it a crime for parents to fail to "exercise reasonable care, supervision, protection, and control" over their kids as a rule, the law recognizes that parents are not always responsible for the sins of their children.

The rule came from an old case in which a teacher was visiting, and the child pulled out the chair as the teacher attempted to sit down and was severely hurt. The court ruled that parents were not legally responsible for their children's behavior. We often apply the "Apple tree" quote to someone with obvious failings and to describe families that generation after generation produce criminals—"Like father, like son" or the chip off the old block. While children take after their parents for the most part, religious institutions, schools, neighbors, siblings, peer groups, television, movies, drugs, and alcohol, as well as other influences, have an impact. How do you explain children who become superstars in sports and no one in their previous extended family showed any interest in sports, or someone who becomes a popular singer when there were no performers in the entire history of their family?

Straight parents produce gay offspring, the pastor's daughter is seduced by sex and drugs, children with autism are born to healthy achieving families, criminals produce law abiding citizens and law-abiding citizens produce criminals. Who can really tell what's the right formula for producing children who are healthy, wealthy and wise?

Social research predictably makes correlations that bear out the "apple tree analogy." For example, Ann Duffy and Julianne Momirov (2000) wrote about "intergenerational transmission" when children grow up in violent families, they tend to inherit patterns of managing emotion and predictably express it violently. But sometimes, children are turned off by the anti-social behavior that is all around them and become saints. Some of the worst criminals in history were raised by "normal families." One never knows. Obviously, wealthy families have the wherewithal to counter bad influences by hiring good lawyers, engaging therapists, paying for damages and a host of other strategies to help their progeny to straighten up and act right. While poor families are at the mercy of the legal system. There are a lot of bad apples in the world—even with the best parenting.

This week, I want to speak up for all the parents who feel guilty and wonder what they did wrong. Maybe you didn't. Life is very unpredictable and sometimes sh## happens. Like in golf, sometimes a perfectly executed putt does not fall and sometimes a bad putt will find its way to the bottom of the cup. One never knows, do one?

128.

Christmas Comes
But Once Per Year...

December 19, 2018

Am I dreaming or does the Christmas season start earlier now than in my youth? Oh well, all the better. I know most of it is driven by merchants who just want to put us in the mood to spend, spend, and spend some more. But the truth is (for me anyway), I do get into the mood and that is a good thing. Actually, there are those who keep their Christmas lights up all year in an attempt to extend the mood and I don't blame them.

I thought it was strange traveling in Ghana a few years ago and I was greeted with "Merry Christmas" through January. We are more likely to move on, so, for most of us: out with the Christmas tree and no more Christmas greetings the day after Christmas. In Jamaica (where I spent my first 15 years before migrating), on Dec. 1, we talked about "Christmas breeze a come." You would then be tempted to prematurely wish your neighbors a Merry Christmas only to hear, "When it comes."

Year after year, Thomaston goes all out to create wonderful joyful memories and it is not wasted. Personally, I look forward to the festivities and the extra special music performed where I am a deacon (Greater Mount Zion Baptist Church) but the majesty of the cantata presented to Mountain View and First Baptist is not to be missed. I took the family to Callaway Gardens and to Christmas Lane and they really enjoyed it. But don't forget about the Rock Ranch, they also do a great job.

Two thousand and eighteen years ago in Bethlehem, so the good book says, our savior was born to us. Can you think of a better reason to celebrate? So, enjoy your family suppers, the company of returning relatives, ravishing Christmas dinner at Mama's, exchanging presents and Christmas cards, singing Christmas carols, viewing your neighbor's Christmas decorations, and being kissed under a mistletoe. But do remember that in this glorious time of the year, you can help those who are not as blessed as you by putting a little pep in everybody's step. To those who much is given, much is required.

As the festive season kicks into high gear, so too does the appeal of the various charitable organizations. It really is the season for giving; I encourage you to spread the Christmas cheer with the Salvation Army, The Ministerial Alliance, the Christmas stocking and your church. Do something for needy families as well.

I wish you much happiness this Christmas. I hope you will be blessed with merriment as you enjoy the festivities with those you love most. Happy Christmas and a most prosperous new year.

O come, all ye faithful
Joyful and triumphant
O come ye, o come ye to Bethlehem Come and behold Him
Born the King
of Angels!
O come, let us adore Him
O come, let us adore Him
O come, let us adore Him
Christ the Lord.

129.

Go Easy on The Pie This Holiday Season

December 26, 2018

In the 1970s, medical schools routinely taught that heart disease was a function of aging. We came to this conclusion because the autopsies performed on WWII GIs between the ages of 18-25 years did not show any coronary artery disease. Fast forward to the Vietnam War and autopsies on those 18-25 years old GIs all showed coronary artery plaque. What was the difference? Diet, diet, diet, and lifestyle. Most Americans moved off farms and hard labor to the cities and less manual labor. On farms, the biggest meal was at noon which gave workers the entire afternoon to burn calories and not at 6-7 p.m. after work. We are now eating fewer home-cooked meals and more fast foods and less fruits and vegetables. What you eat does have consequences on your health as well as your ability to live a quality life without disabilities.

If you believe the Norman Rockwell depictions of the holidays, large meals were reserved for major holidays like Christmas, New Year's, Fourth of July, Easter, anniversaries, and birthday celebrations. Some may remember when dessert was only served on Sundays. We are now able to binge almost every day. Food is relatively cheap and readily available. You have snacks and candy in your car, purse, office and everywhere just in case you feel a little peckish. We now graze throughout the day.

If you have a photograph from a family gathering, look at it carefully. Predictably, what you will find is that those older than 70 will be normal weight and those less than 20 will be obese. According to the CDC, in 1976, only 15%of American adults were obese and now its 40%. We have gone from selling bath towels to bath sheets. Look at the members of your church. There is not likely to be any obese members over 80 years. If they were obese, they would have suffered from sleep apnea, back, hip and knee pain before succumbing to diabetes, heart disease, stroke, and cancer.

Why are our bodies changing so much and what do we have to look forward to in the future? If a teenager is obese at 16 years old, the expectation is that they will have diabetes by 40. Will they then develop the discipline to change their eating and exercise habits to prevent premature death and disability? It will be difficult, so why not adopt healthy lifestyles now, today—the first day of the rest of your life?

While experts point to cheap fast foods being supersized and our food industry is incredibly effective at making snacks and products that are high in calories with an addictive taste—you cannot have just one. Yes, they do a lot of research to cater to our taste preferences. We seem to love whatever is salty, sweet, and greasy. When most of us did back-breaking work on our family farms, we could eat whatever was available and worked it off. We ate big because we did physical labor. We could consume 4,000 calories per day because we burned up 4,000 calories per day. Now we continue to eat 4,000 calories per day but only burn 2,000 because we mostly work in offices and buildings where our physical exertions are few. What do you think happens to the 2,000 excess calories?

The weight loss industry is huge ladies and gentlemen. All the before and after photographs you see are fake. None of these diets keep off the weight. It's a lifetime of gaining, losing, and gaining it back. It's a frustrating cycle. No diet will overcome the basic formula. Don't eat more than you burn. At some point you will have a catharsis and recognize that the problem is your lifestyle. So, set your mind and focus on your family's lifestyle—eat less and exercise more. I have further simplified the strategy: One hour of vigorous exercise per day, a healthy breakfast, no snacking, and avoid animal fats and sugar. What could be simpler and more straightforward than that? No doughnuts, cakes, candies and sugar treats and no ribs, steaks, bacon, sausages, hamburgers, and hotdogs. This, in essence, is a healthy lifestyle.

No, you cannot do it alone. If only one person in a family decides to change, they will be quickly drawn back into the fold by the other members of the family. So, the only way this will work is to make it a family project. Dr. Jules Hirsch (Rockefeller University) recruited obese people to stay at the hospital on a 600 calorie-a-day until they reached a normal weight. On average, they lost 100 pounds. But regained it as soon as they returned to their families and their old lifestyle. Even those who participated in the *Biggest Loser* TV show quickly regained their weight. Adopted children adopt the lifestyle and weight of their adopted home.

You have a lot to look forward to! Children should know their grandparents so they can become great-grandparents. Today is the first day of the rest of your life. It is the day the Lord has made, let us not only be glad and rejoice in it but make a commitment to be healthy—even during the holiday season.

130.

Sound the Alarm: Our Life Expectancy is Now Decreasing

January 2, 2019

After 100 years of progress living longer, healthier lives, we have been regressing since 2014. That's right, our life expectancy doubled over the previous 100 years, but primarily due to the obesity epidemic, we are becoming increasingly unhealthy. Your great-grand uncle looked like he was 90 when he died, but he just looked like that because life was hard. He was actually in his 40s. Can you imagine life on the farm with a lot of farm accidents, incurable infectious diseases, no air conditioning and practically no access to hospitals and health care?

According to Betsy McKay, *Wall Street Journal*:

> Global comparisons often focus on economic factors, like gross domestic product, unemployment or income. I think it's time we paid more attention to the most fundamental measure of living standards: how long we live. By that measure, the United States is an outlier in the worst possible way. The U.S. has lost three-tenths of a year in life expectancy since 2014, a stunning reversal for a "developed nation.

Three out of four of us will die from heart-related diseases and cancer, which together killed 1,229,000 Americans last year. We also lost 40,000 to gun violence and led the western world in traffic fatalities, opiate related deaths, and infant mortality. The CDC reported that 186,000 people now die from obesity-related causes each year. We take a great deal of pride knowing that we are the largest economy in the world with extremely low unemployment, and with only 5% of the world's population we own 50% of the world's wealth. But is that all? Shouldn't we take as much pride in public health and protecting the lives of our citizens? If we are so well-off, why do we lead in diseases of despair—overdoses, alcoholism, and suicide?

Drug overdose was the cause of death for 63,632 of our citizens last year—a dramatic increase from previous years. Fentanyl, heroin, along with prescription narcotics were the preferred choices. There are effective strategies to combat this epidemic, we just don't seem to have the will to make it widely available.

Don't get me wrong, we have made tremendous progress making health care accessible to all our citizens, conquering infectious diseases, and lowering the rate of cigarette smoking, lung cancer as well as heart disease related deaths. But the important point is that most of these maladies are preventable. If we commit to doing something meaningful about it, before you know it, on average, we will be living to be 100!

This is not the second, minute, hour, or day for us to make bad choices. If we allow this to continue, we will reap a bitter harvest.

131.

Paying Back China
for Its Contributions to
Our Quality of Life

Jamuary 9, 2019

There are four zoos in America where one can see China's giant pandas, but we are fortunate to live near the only zoo that has panda twins. So, when counting our blessings in Georgia, it would be only right to count our pandas twice. And to what do we owe this made-in-China dose of cuteness? A history of "panda diplomacy" dating back before President Nixon's breakthrough visit in 1978.

Well, it has been a while since our relations were that warm and fuzzy. We have lately been ramping up our charges against China, ranging from the folk wisdom that Chinese "sweatshops" produce cheap and cheaply made trinkets to international intrigue that would make even James Bond spill his martini. Forget trade war, this is beginning to look like The Cold War. The Chinese are dogged by accusations. We estimate the value of theft of our intellectual property to be $500 billion. We are amazing when it comes to developing technology, but they are amazing at manufacturing. When we set up factories in China to make cell phones, computers, and microwave ovens, we are also revealing our innovations.

Our minimum wage here in Georgia is about $7.25 per hour; theirs is less than a dollar. This difference has just about wiped out our textile industry as they can make a tablecloth and ship it here for 50% cheaper even accounting for the mark-ups by a dozen middlemen. They can buy our trees, ship them to China, make furniture, and ship them back and sell them for 50% less than our homemade furniture. I bought a microwave oven from Walmart for less than $50. I had expected to pay $200. It has been an incredible boost to American consumers.

Granted, we are trying to be paperless, but where would we have been without paper? It turns out that some smart people in China invented paper and paper money 200 years before the birth of our Christ. In contrast, the art of producing paper was not brought to Europe and the United States until a thousand years later. When the printing press caused a revolution in our theology and politics by making books accessible to the common people instead of only priests; every man, woman, and child in China had already been using books for 20 generations.

China gave us some of our earliest calendars and astronomy, including some of the earliest known uses of the magnetic compass, the rudder for ships, iron smelting, metallurgy, pottery, the clock, crop farming and of course, some of the earliest known distillation of alcohol. As indispensable as it is in everyday life, maybe we would have been better off without alcohol. In 1290, Marco Polo took a 24-year trip from Venice (Italy) along the Silk Road to China and brought back ice cream, noodles, tea, the umbrella, gun powder, fireworks and the toothbrush. Americans only started brushing their teeth two hundred years ago, about a thousand years after the Chinese. Our first president had wooden teeth, but I never understood why the toothbrush is not called a "teeth-brush". Maybe it was invented by someone who only had one tooth.

I am particularly grateful for ice cream and enjoy this creamy indulgence almost daily. When I was traveling in China eight years ago, I stopped to buy some ice cream from a street vendor. It was delicious. As he spoke English, I asked him where he thought ice cream was invented. He said, "America." We get unearned credit for many things.

For the two weeks we spent traveling around China, what do you think we ate every day?

132.
We Have So Much More in Common Than What is Different

January 23, 2019

Biologically, attesting to our common parents (Adam and Eve), while we are all different, human beings, regardless of where we hail from, are more than 99% alike. What is the difference between a black cat and a white cat? Color. What is the difference between a long hair and a short hair horse? Hair texture. I sometimes wonder what all the fuss is about when it comes to color and hair in humans. It turns out that these are all just variations like eye color, height, blood type and personality.

In addition, these are a few things I have observed that most people share.

- Desiring approval from others.
- Having misconceptions about people who do not look like them.
- Lack of tolerance and understanding.
- Pride and ego.
- Craving for love and a partner.
- Repeating the same errors.
- Lack of ability to accept one's own faults.

Words matter. "In the beginning was the word." "Let there be light and there was light." If you were standing in front of a firing squad and the commander says, "Fire," it would mean your demise. Words comfort and words hurt. Just don't give in to hate speech. We use words to communicate important matters spurring people to action or inaction. The words you use and when you use them matters. It makes a big difference if you say a simple "hello" when you pass them on the street and when you walk ahead without acknowledging the person we just dissed. According to Proverbs 17:27, "The one who has knowledge uses words with restraint, and whoever has understanding is even-tempered."

It is moral and wise to have rules of engagement to get along in a pluralistic society that start with brotherly love and compassion.

133.
Child Naming Conventions Around the World

February 6, 2019

There are more than 200 countries in the world and most have unique conventions regarding the naming of newborns. I am partial to the scene in *"Lion King"* where big Samba takes little Simba to the sacred rock and proclaims, "Behold, the only thing greater than thou."

Traveling around Iceland, I learned that they have no last or family names—only first names. Jill is daughter of Bob and Christine and Jill and her husband Fred's child is Jeff, son of Jill and Fred—very confusing!

In Ghana, most children are given the first name of the day of the week when they were born and a middle name by their birth order. For male children, Sunday: Akwasi, Kwasi, Kwesi, Akwesi, Sisi, Kacely, Kosi Monday: Kojo, Kwadwo, Jojo, Joojo, Kujoe; Tuesday: Kwabena, Kobe, Kobi, Ebo, Kabelah, Komla, Kwabela, Kobby; Wednesday: Kwaku, Abeiku, Kuuku, Kweku; Thursday: Yaw, Ekow, Yao; Friday: Kofi, Fifi, Fiifi, Yoofi; Saturday: Kwame, Kwamena, Kwamina. For females, Sunday: Akosua, Akasi, Akos, Esi, Awesi; Monday: Adwoa, Adjoa, Adzoa, Adwoma; Tuesday: Abena, Araba, Abenayo; Wednesday: Akua, Aku, Kukua, Akuma; Thursday: Aba, Yaa, Yawa, Baaba, Awo; Friday: Afua, Afia, Afi; and Saturday: Ama.

For most Asian countries, the family name comes before the given name—just the opposite of the United States.

According to Wikipedia: "Russian names have three parts: a given name, a patronymic (a middle name based on the father's first name), and the father's surname. If Viktor Aleksandrovich Rakhmaninov has two children, his daughter's name would be Svetlana Viktorevna Rakhmaninova. (The "a" at the end of all three names shows that she is female.) Her brother would be Mikhail Viktorevich Rakhmaninov.

For some Spanish-speaking countries, in addition to a given name, children are given two surnames: The father's family name followed by the mothers.
I was playing golf in South Africa and learned that my caddie's name was Daniel. When he became a Christian, he was required to not only give up three of his wives so he could be monogamous; he also gave up his traditional name in favor of a "Christian" name from the Bible.

Hindu names are often determined by the position of the planets at the date and time of birth. But what is a good name? In India, while they would never ask your "bad" name, people you meet often ask: "What is your good name?

I often make the point when I speak to students that their good name is better than gold. It may take a hundred years to grow a tree, but a chain saw can cut it down in one minute. You can spend your entire lifetime building a good name and one moment of mischief can destroy it. According to Benjamin Franklin: "Glass, china, and reputations are easily cracked, and never mended well." But I also believe that Saul was redeemed in his conversion to Paul. According to John Wooden: "Worry more about your character than your reputation. Character is what you are, reputation is merely what others think you are."

A good reputation (or a good name) will engender trust in others and therefore good in every aspect of life and therefore should be a priority for which we should strive. This is all well and good except, you will most often attribute good qualities to those we love and bad qualities to those we are suspicious about. In other words, if you love someone, they can do no wrong, and if you hate someone, they can do no right.

While our parents did not ask our opinion on what you will be called, Proverbs 22:1 says: "A good name is to be chosen rather than great riches, loving favor rather than silver and gold." Seeking self-worth over Godly worth will lead us to a state of moral and/or spiritual poverty— a good name is not enough without the character to accompany it. Is your goal to have a good name with a fervent desire to extend brotherly love to your neighbor?

134.
What I Stand For

February 20, 2019

In these polarized times, we invest so much time counter-arguing the other guy that we don't take time to articulate what we stand for. Well, in celebrating the 90th birthday of Martin Luther King, we would do well to contemplate his vision.

It's a good one. You don't need me to tell you that people should be judged not by the color of the skin but by the content of their character. This concept will surely stand the test of time. It is not my aim to defend his great intellect and his body of work. Rather, my aim is to place his achievements among that great library of highfalutin and grandiose mission statements that so characterize the American spirit and have given shape to our lives. His message contains all the chicken soup a soul can possibly thirst for. I wrote in a previous column that genetically and biologically; all human beings are more than 99% alike, attesting to the fact that we all came from the same parents. Human beings only appeared on earth 300,000 years ago and just like most animals, developed unique characteristics (eye and skin color, blood type, hair texture, height, body shape, fingerprints etc.) depending on our migration patterns. These are just variations on a theme. What is the difference between a white horse and a black horse? What is the difference between a long-haired cat and a short haired cat? We are all brothers and sisters that deserve respect and fairness from each other. As religions evolved, they all end up subscribing to the universal principle: "Do unto others as you would have them do unto you."

Thoreau exhorted us to "Go confidently in the direction of your dreams." Well, then, hadn't we better set to work figuring out what that would look like?

A vision can be as prosaic as Bart Simpson seeing the bright side of a shipwreck, "It'll be just like the *Swiss Family Robinson*, only with more cursing!" If you prefer dreamier fare, consider Alanis Morrissette's barely rhyming and strangely metered yearning for a utopia, where "We would stay and respond and expand and include and allow and forgive and enjoy and evolve and discern and inquire and accept and admit and divulge and open and reach out and speak up. We would open our arms. This is my utopia; this is my nirvana."

For me, I'll start with Reinhold Niebuhr's serenity prayer. God, give us grace to accept with serenity the things that cannot be changed, Courage to change the things which should be changed, and the Wisdom to distinguish the one from the other. Living one day at a time, enjoying one moment at a time, accepting hardship as a pathway to peace, Taking, as Jesus did, this sinful world as it is, Not as I would have it, trusting that You will make all things right,

If I surrender to Your will, so that I may be reasonably happy in this life, And supremely happy with You forever in the next. Amen.

135.
Truth Decay

February 27, 2019

There is no one living in Middle Georgia who is not an advocate for truthfulness and 100% of our parents tell their children: "Don't lie. Just tell the truth." We used to hate liars. But we now live in an age when cynicism, fear and weariness make us vulnerable to rejecting truth and scientific facts in favor of conspiracy theories and fake news. Is there no decency or universal truths left? It turns out that the photo of presidential candidate Gary Hart with a woman who was not his wife sitting on his lap on a yacht was a set-up staged by "friends" who were determined to sabotage him.

Ignorance is now fashionable. Of the 30 people interviewed by Professor Asheley Landrum at a Flat Earth International Conference in 2018, twenty-nine of them said they were now convinced that the world is flat after watching conspiracy videos. One in ten Americans apparently still believes that the sun revolves around the earth—everyone can see that from the rising and setting of the sun. Despite numerous credible studies showing no correlation between autism and vaccines, many parents are still refusing to inoculate their children because Dr. Andrew Wakefiled (a discredited English doctor) who published a made-up study in *The Lancet* suggesting that the measles, mumps, rubella (MMR) vaccine caused autism. Jussie Smollett reported that he was attacked by racist thugs and even received treatment at a hospital that turned out to be a hoax because the fake threatening letter he wrote to himself and circulated did not get enough attention. So, he decided to turn up the volume by paying two Nigerian acquaintances to attack him and make it look like a hate crime. It turns out that some people will believe almost anything if it is uttered by someone they admire and trust and it fits into their own prejudices.

We seem to be cherry picking facts that support our emotional beliefs and whatever feels right. In the age of the internet, we are more and more comfortable with blurring the lines between truth and outright lies. In our highly polarized society, once we are locked into our like-minded windowless silos, we tend to believe everything other birds of a feather represent and not only reject what others have to say but refuse to even listen or in any way feel like they contradict our newfound reality. We now read and listen to reinforce what we already believe—the wisdom of our tribe and loyalty to them is more important than truth. Your friends will have a problem if they merely find out that you listen to CNN rather than FOX or vice versa. This toxic polarization has overtaken our community. We now limit our political discourse with those who agree with our point of view. Because there is no longer a shared reality (truth), we are all vulnerable to political manipulation making us more inclined to emotions rather than reason. And the reality is that once we become emotional, reason, reality and logic become distorted.

I heartily recommend that everyone see the Japanese movie *Rashomon*. The point of the movie reflects the concept that your reality depends on one's point of view. Four people seeing the same crime come up with four different versions tempered with exaggerations and conspiratorial fantasy. Even though there were four perspectives concerning the crime, no one disputed that the crime took place. I will support anyone's right to express their opinion, however, I will not support anyone's attempt to make up facts.

While both can lead to your demise, truth decay is worse than tooth decay. There are no harmless lies. There will be consequences. While you are entitled to your opinions, you are not entitled to your own facts. Even though we can all agree that truth is the cornerstone of our democracy, we are witnessing an assault on everything we hold sacred. The demise of objective, empirical and evidenced based facts in favor of conspiracy theories and outright lies is the flavor of the day. We cannot just look the other way and pretend it doesn't matter. What are we teaching our youth? More importantly, what are we risking? The death of truth does not relieve responsible citizens of the obligation to make decisions based on truth and reason. In a world suffering from information overload, we have a moral obligation to pursue objective truth.

136.
The Divine Symmetry and the Christian Story

March 6, 2019

Have you heard of Tesla? No. I don't mean that eccentric genius behind electric self-driving cars (Elon Musk), but the eccentric genius Nikola Tesla, who had a photographic memory and pioneered electricity, electric motors, and cell phones among 300 other patents. He was also a noted poet and philosopher who once graced the cover of *Time Magazine*.

Nikola was obsessed with "threes." He organized his entire life with the suspicion that three and its derivatives had magical powers. He once said, "If you know the magnificence of three, six and nine, you would have a key to the universe." He would only stay in hotel rooms with numbers divisible by three and thought it was more than coincidence that the circle is 360 degrees, and a minute was divided into 60 seconds. There are 12 months in a year, 12 hours of the clock, 12 inches to the foot, 12 disciples, 12 tribes of Israel and 12 knights of the round table. I am curious about why we live in a three-dimensional world and why there are three pyramids of Giza rather than two or four? So why was six afraid of seven? Because seven ate nine.

As we approach Easter, it is worth noting that over the last 2,000 years, the number "3" has also been highly respected by Christians as symbolic.

The number "3" occurs hundreds of times in our Bible:

The Trinity (Father, Son and Holy Spirit); The Patriarchs (Abraham, Isaac and Jacob); Lazarus was dead three days before Jesus resurrected him; Judas was given 30 pieces of silver to betray Jesus; Peter denied Jesus three times; Noah had three sons and Job had three daughters; David bowed down to Jonathan three times; Jonah lived in the belly of a whale for three days; there were three archangels (Michael, Gabriel and Raphael) Daniel prayed three times per day; Satan tempted our Lord three times; Paul had three shipwrecks; spent three months in Ephesus, three months in Greece, three months in Malta and then three years in Arabia. Sampson stumped the men of Tinmah with a riddle for three days; The Lord told Amos that he would stop the rain when the harvest was three months away. And Jesus said he could destroy the Temple and rebuild it in three days and Absalom fled to Greshur for three months.

Now I come to "In three days he rose." According to Corinthians 15: Christ died for our sins, was buried, raised on the third day, and bodily appeared to the disciples. When I learned to add as a boy, it didn't add up to me that we celebrate Good Friday and then celebrate Easter two days later on Sunday. My wife tried to convince me that Friday, Saturday, and Sunday are three separate days. When we rent a car, they charge us for each day—not 24-hour days. I am not convinced.

My favorite Easter story is that the Great Buddha lived, made significant contributions, died, and was buried. Period. Gandhi lived, made significant contributions, died, and was buried. Period. Muhammad lived, made significant contributions, died, and was buried. Period. Confucius lived, made significant contributions, died, and was buried. Period. Our Lord and Savior Jesus Christ lived, made significant contributions, died, and was buried. Comma. And he rose again.

But I am not blinded by various levels of evidence that "maybe" the body of Jesus went missing because Mary Magdalene went to the wrong tomb; Jesus had survived the crucifixion and walked away to appear before the disciples. Was His body stolen by grave robbers, some of the disciples or enemies? The official version of the Jewish religion is that the body of Jesus was stolen by the disciples to be buried elsewhere.

Some speculate that the sighting of Jesus was an aberration as physiologists report that family members often see and encounter their loved ones after they were buried. Or maybe it was an imposter dressed up like Jesus who appeared to the disciples. Speculation all. The resurrection was one of many cases of divine intervention into the natural order of things. If you want a miracle in your life, try praying. Because as our prayers go up, miracles occur in our lives—especially broken hearts.

What a mighty God we serve! But is it two days between Friday and Sunday or three?

137.
Wedding Traditions

March 13, 2019

I attended a traditional Nigerian (Igbo) wedding recently and left jealous. Yes, it was a grand affair attended by beautiful people of all hues dressed in colorful flowing robes and fancy dresses congratulating, dancing and yes, lots of laughing and hugging. We all enjoyed the rituals, entertainment, music, food and libation—a feast for the eyes, ears, and palate. No, I was not jealous about that, weddings are happy extravagant affairs around the world, but I looked with envy as the bride and groom kneeled before the father of the bride to receive their blessings from the big man and then they kneeled in front of the groom's father. It was a brief investment on the part of the bride and groom, but it meant a great deal to the parents—a memory for a lifetime.

For both my own daughters, I proudly walked them down the aisle and "gave" them to their husbands. Ladies and gentlemen, it is not enough! As much as I got them to agree every year since they appeared on the earth that when a man proposed to them, they would kneel before my throne and make their case. I would listen and then give them the thumbs up or thumbs down and they would dutifully abide by my wishes. To my disappointment, they forgot about our deal and how much I had invested in bringing them to this point in their lives and merely announced that they were getting married. My only duty was to pay for it. I didn't realize how deprived I was as the father of the bride until I witnessed the bride and groom on their knees before their parents. And this was not just a brief moment, they bowed their heads in front of him for a two-minute prayer and lecture. Can you tell I loved that! I would like to be an advocate for fathers everywhere, this tradition should be part of every wedding. Don't fathers everywhere deserve this?

Thanks Dr. and Mrs. Chemente Nwosu for the invitation to your daughter's wedding. While you may be in great debt after this wedding, I know that you are a happy man and a proud papa. I wish the new Mrs. Nneka and Mr. Adam Rector a lifetime of happiness and prosperity. They are off to a great start. Best wishes.

138.
His Eye Is on The Sparrow... And I Know He Watches Me!

March 20, 2019

These words have a very new meaning for me. No way did I think I would be writing this column from a hospital bed at Emory University Hospital-Midtown. The only thing I was looking forward to on Wednesday, March 13 was coming home to Thomaston to see my wife after being away for eight days on a golf trip. What was not on my mind was that I would end up in the emergency room being evaluated for chest pain and now, here I am waiting for my scheduled three vessel coronary artery bypass graft (CABG) surgery which will take place on March 18. I am anticipating that all will go well and will update everyone with my column in the ensuing weeks. Joy comes in the morning! I am looking forward to continuing this amazing journey and to living the amazing life I enjoy.

Let's take a step back. I left for Jamaica for a week of golf with friends on Wednesday March 5. Each day, I would head for the pool or the ocean for my morning work-out. The afternoons were filled with 18 holes of competitive golf with my caddie. In retrospect, I was laboring when I had to trudge up hills, but at 75 years of age who wouldn't? Up till now, other than high cholesterol, I thought I was doing well for my age. Annual exams inclusive of EKGs were always normal.

I enjoyed the Jamaican sun each day and the camaraderie of my friends. The three losers each day would pay for a magnificent meal where the winners stick it to the losers. I only paid once as I was playing well. In fact, I almost got a hole-in-one on the 17th hole "White Witch" course in Montego Bay. My ball hit the flagstick and ended up a few inches from the hole. It would have been my first. When later I was experiencing chest pain, I actually had the thought that I might die without achieving this goal.

In any case, on my last day (3/13), I went down for a last dip in the pool before leaving for the airport. Just about a third of the way through my routine, I got severe bilateral pain in my arms, shortness of breath and cramping in my chest. I stopped and rested, and the discomfort ceased. I then got dressed, packed my suitcase, and made my way to the airport. The pain and shortness of breath returned as I walked to my gate. However, as soon as I took my seat on my Delta flight from Kingston, the pain went away and I enjoyed my meal, watched a movie; read a book and landed on time.

It is a long walk from the international concourse (F) through immigration and customs and with increasing shortness of breath, chest pain and sweating, I barely made it to the curbside where my Lyft driver was waiting for me. I immediately called my wife and asked for her advice. Should I come home or go to an emergency room? She did not hesitate, "Go to the closest emergency room that partners with Kaiser Permanente" (my insurance carrier). So, that is how I ended up at Emory University Hospital where I am receiving a very high level of care from the moment I entered the emergency room. After several tests showed nothing out of the ordinary, we finally solved the mystery with a coronary catheter.

We truly live in a great country!

Now to the meaning of my title. As it turns out, my coronaries have been in trouble for a while. We know this because one of my occluded coronary arteries had developed its own system of collateral branches feeding the cardiac muscle for the blocked artery. As I never had chest pain and had normal EKGs and echocardiograms, there was no way my doctors or I would suspect that my heart was in trouble. The God of this universe not only had His eye on the sparrow, but He was also watching out for me.

By the time you read this, I will have either had successful surgery or have been called home. Thank you for your prayers.

139.
His Eye is on the Sparrow…
My Hospitalization (Part 2)

March 27, 2019

Apparently last week was not to be my final column. After an eventful week, I am home again and enjoying the sunshine on my face—just delightful after 11 days in Emory Hospital - Midtown. You really cannot imagine how nourishing it is to be outside smelling fresh air after having your chest cracked open, your heart beating outside of your chest cavity, and not only your life but your fate in the hand of a great cardiac surgeon. Dr. Omar Latoutf replaced three of my three blocked heart vessels with three from my leg, gently replaced my heart back in my chest cavity, ran tubes from my lungs to drain excess fluids, closed my chest with wires and sent me to post-op where I was walking just four hours after surgery. Amazing.

I will spare you the details of the following five days of pain, nausea, lack of appetite, weakness, boredom, awful hospital food and post anesthesia hallucinations and nightmares. However, my wish is that no one should have to endure this operation and its aftermath. The post-operative care was wonderful. The nurses and med-techs were attentive and encouraging. If you took a lap around the unit you were applauded. No effort went unnoticed. Although obviously understaffed, I felt that special care and attention was afforded me, especially by my special nurse, Ms. Brandy Perry.

I ended my column last week telling you that I had developed chest pains in Jamaica that increased to crushing chest pains as I made my way through Atlanta airport, so I immediately went to the emergency room at Emory Hospital. Having then been diagnosed with almost total occlusion in three vessels, one daughter came in from Portland another flew in from Phoenix, Freddie came up from Columbus with his family and we were joined by Aleron (who lives in Atlanta) and my wife who has been by my side night and day for 11 straight days—that was a lot of togetherness! In case of my imminent demise, I wanted to have this time with them to share the family stories and verbal expression of the love and commitment we have for each other. I felt remarkably at peace as they all became happy and successful. None of them would miss me for any financial support but they made me understand that they would miss ME and more importantly, the bond we share. My wife is hardly emotional. However, she was teary at the thought of this journey I would have to make without her. She was also consumed with the love that our children, friends, and extended family demonstrated by coming to visit us in the hospital, calling, texting and otherwise praying. We enjoyed each other's company as a family until I had to go under the knife. Now I am back home and appreciate them more than ever.

So, the point is, please reduce your cardiovascular risk. If this had happened on a golf course or some remote part of the world, I would have been in my heavenly home. Maynard Jackson died from this very problem at Reagan International Airport in Washington DC. In fact, more than a half a million people die from coronary heart disease in the United States each year. We all can and should commit to healthy lifestyles going forward? As my columns and healing go forward, I will share my new lifestyle tips with you. We live in a country where in the span of 10 days I can go from three blocked coronary arteries to a life of 30 more years with my beloved, our children and grandchildren.

It is good to be back. I am taking each day as it comes and am confident that with each day will come new strength and new challenges. I can't drive for three weeks, no golf for THREE months and six months or cardiac rehab! It really doesn't matter though because at the end of the day I have my health restored, the love of a good woman, our wonderful children, and grandchildren and yes, my Association of Black Cardiologists family, my Greater Mount Zion Baptist Church family, my Alpha Phi Alpha family, my lodge family, my ZÖe Pediatrics family, my Kiwanis family and my golfing friends at Raintree, Constant Spring and Green Island.

Thank you for your prayers and well wishes. Thank God that His eye is on the sparrow and He watches me.

140.
American Aviation: Look How Far We Have Come in Less Than 100 Years

April 3, 2019

As you are aware, I got home from Emory Hospital last week after cardiac surgery (CABAG) and recuperating. While I am not back to my old self, I am in no pain and able to walk a mile twice a day, I must wait for my follow-up visit with my surgeon as to what I can and cannot do going forward. I am advised to take it easy, but that makes no sense to me, so today, I had a friend (Dannie) take me to Raintree where I putted for ten minutes in the sunshine—just lovely. By the way, the golf course looks great! Apparently, it will be three months before I can play again. It is going to be a long three months. In the meantime, I will concentrate on being a good putter.

I actually feel very fortunate. On the heels of the death of 20-year-old "Ms. Teen Universe" recently from coronary heart disease. Apparently, this is no longer a disease of the old. I also learned that 80% of people who develop chest pain, sweating, nausea, and arm pain do not survive. I am just glad to be part of the 20% who got the care I needed and can look forward to a longer life.

With all my restrictions, I spend a lot of time reading. As you may guess, the selection of my reading material has to do with philosophy. But I am also reading Bill Bryson's, *One Summer: America, 1927*. I have read and enjoyed several of his other books (*Notes from a Small Island, African Diary, In a Sunburned Country and Shakespeare* but *A Short History of Nearly Everything* is his best work). I enjoy his attention to detail and his humorous perspectives.

He points out that the summer when Lindbergh made his fateful trip across the pond, there was a lot going on in America. (Read all about it) Because of our fascination with flying, we named our youngest son Aileron (spelled Aleron). He has become a wonderful wind beneath our wings. You see, the reason a plane is able to fly is that "nature abhors a vacuum." When the wings of a plane slices through the air, a vacuum is created on top of the wings and in nature's attempt to fill the vacuum, a lift is created and sustained. Here is some of the information I picked up from the book.

1. While the life expectancy for pilots (before 1917) was described in days. (Fifty percent of planes that took off came down the hard way) but there was no shortage of brave men who wanted to fly. These Barnstormers were heroes.

2. By 1927, Europe had already had commercial airlines that ferried thousands of passengers per year while the United States only used planes for the U.S. Mail.

3. There were two other aviation groups making preparations for the flight across the Atlantic outspending the Lindbergh crew ten to one, but they got bogged down in politics and dissension while the Lindbergh crew was a lean, mean machine.

4. Charles Lindbergh, (Lucky Lindy) the first man to fly solo on *The Spirit of St. Louis* from New York to Paris, was an extraordinary human being who deserved all the credit he received. He seemed to have enjoyed a "curious immortality."

5. When he took off from Lambert Field in New York, he was so concerned about weight that he did not pack a radio, toothbrush and he had cut the white margins from his maps. He ended up with "5,000 pounds on a blast of air."

6. In order to estimate the distance between New York and Paris, he went to the public library and used a tape measure on a globe of the earth.

7. After Lindbergh became famous, the dance "Lindy hop" became the rage even though he had never danced or been on a date.

8. He took off around 8 a.m. narrowly missing some cable and landed in Paris about 10:30 (34 hours later) on May 21, 1927--staying awake for the entire trip. He had been without sleep for 60 hours.

9. He did all this making his calculations on his lap and flying a very unstable plane.

On his arrival, exuberant pandemonium broke out throughout the world. People went wild with the news. And it changed the direction of history.

141.
Thinking Like a Lawyer

April 10, 2019

First of all, after my CABAG operation, I had a little setback on my road to recovery that ended in my having to access the wonderful services of the emergency room at Upson Regional Medical Center just before midnight on Monday. Swelling developed on my right leg where my cardiac surgeon had harvested the veins to do the bypass. It was now bleeding into my inner thigh. Dr. Johnny Bonner was absolutely spot on in his grasp of my situation, ordered the tests that made sense, especially the echo on my leg that showed that while there was bleeding, he found nothing out of the ordinary following my procedure but more importantly—no clots!

Deep Vein Thrombosis (DVT) is a major killer. This is a clot that forms in a leg, breaks loose, travels through your bloodstream and lodges in your lungs and/or heart creating havoc. I was sensitive to it because my cousin (Carlen McDonald) died from DVT following a long trip on an airplane five years ago. When you travel, either by car or plane, you are advised to get out of your seat and stretch your legs every two hours to make sure blood is not pooling in your lower extremities.

My topic for this week is thinking like a lawyer. Like most people, when I started law school, I was under the mistaken assumption that laws were written like the Ten Commandments or a statute that sets the speed limit. "Thou shall not... and if you do, this is the punishment." I found out that lawyers must "find" the law. I learned about the doctrine of *stare decisis* used in legal proceedings, meaning that courts must look to past rulings on similar cases to make judgments on the case before them. This creates some predictability in the law.

One of the unsung heroes of American law is Mable Walker Willebrandt, who was appointed assistant attorney general by President Harding with the income tax portfolio. Immediately she noticed the lavish lifestyle of known crooks, mobsters and mafia leaders and decided that it was because they didn't pay income taxes. So, she decided to go after organized crime. You recognize of course that everyone, including notorious crooks are still entitled to legal representation. Having indicted Manley Sullivan on tax evasion, his lawyers made the following creative arguments:

1. Criminals could not pay or file tax returns without incriminating themselves.

2. It would be a breach of their Fifth Amendment rights against self-incrimination.
3. In claiming a portion of ill-begotten gain, the government would become an accessory to crime—a breach of their fiduciary duties.

Judge Martin Thomas initially ruled with the criminals claiming that "It is hard to conceive of Congress ever having in mind that the government be paid a part of the income, gains or profits derived from successfully carrying on this crime." The case had to go all the way to the Supreme Court (United States v. Sullivan, 274 U. S. 259) and in May 1927, the court decided in favor of Mrs. Willebrandt and the IRS establishing that all financial gains, whether legal or illegally obtained, are taxable.

It was later determined that Judge Martin Thomas was bribed ($186,000) and he served 17 months in prison along with the criminals he tried to protect.

The point is that you don't have to attend law school to enhance your own logic and critical thinking skills. You just have to be creative and think like a lawyer.

142.
Preventing Cardiovascular Disease

April 17, 2019

I am now 76 years old and just returned home from a triple bypass operation at Emory University (03/14/19). It seems ironic that after investing a lifetime attempting to reduce the high rate of heart disease and living by these recommendations, I would be a victim. I never smoked, wasn't overweight, my blood pressure and cholesterol were a little high and I exercised daily. I have been preaching, cajoling, pleading, and begging everyone with whom I come in contact that "prevention" is the real key to a long life. The most important lesson we have learned over the past 20 years is that cardiovascular disease is preventable for 90% of our citizens. But the lives of too many Americans (especially men) continue to be cut short by this preventable condition.

What I recently learned was that 80% of us who develop chest pain die before reaching a source of care. So, I am fortunate to have developed chest pain, sweating, nausea, shortness of breath and weakness after a brisk walk from the international terminal in Atlanta to the curb and went directly to Emory University Hospital where I received state-of-the-art care and a CABAG. It now appears that I can look forward to many more years enjoying my grandchildren. People like Marlon Brando, George Carlin, James Brown, Christopher Reeves, Presidents Eisenhower, Theodore Roosevelt and Gerald Ford, Mayors Maynard Jackson and Harold Washington, Henry Fonda, Christopher Reeves, John Ritter and Willie Kendall, to name a few, did not survive. I dare say that all families have tasted the bitter fruit of a close relative succumbing to coronary artery disease.

The cost of my procedure and 11-day hospital stay was about $200,000. This is a very expensive disease to treat. However, if we implement preventive measures in our daily lives, we will be able to reduce this tremendous cost multiplied by 500,000 per year. It is never too early or too late to adopt a healthy lifestyle. The earlier that children adopt these steps, the greater will be their chances of living to 100 years old. That is now a realistic goal!

1. **Be spiritually active.** Humans are spiritual beings. Meditation, prayers, joking and laughing, holding a grandchild, being in love, spending time with family and friends are uplifting and important for our spiritual development. We are almost required to continually feed our six senses—seeing, hearing, tasting, smelling, feeling, as well as our penchant to appreciate the beauty (our sixth sense) that is all around us including a sunrise or sunset, waterfalls and all the art and beauty of man and nature. Traveling, having adventures, visiting museums, star gazing, creating, listening to music or even the rustle of leaves should be a part of every child's experience. In addition, an important study from the University of Texas tells us that people who attend church regularly live more than seven-fourteen years longer than those who do not go to church. Apparently, the fellowship, goodwill, meditation, inspirational words and singing together increase our ability to cope. According to Dr. Malcolm Taylor: "If you have God, family and friends, you may stumble, but you will never hit the ground."

2. **Take charge of your blood pressure.** Despite steady progress over the past 33 years, uncontrolled high blood pressure is projected to increase by

60%over the next 20 years. Tell your doctor you want to keep your blood pressure as close to goal (120/80 mm Hg) as possible.

3. **Control your cholesterol.** Keep your HDL high and your LDL low and total cholesterol low. High cholesterol leads to plaque, which restricts the flow of blood. Diet, exercise, and statin therapy are the keys to maintaining healthy cholesterol levels.

4. **Track your blood sugar and maintain ideal weight.** Obesity and diabetes track each other. As the rate of obesity goes up, so does diabetes. If you are overweight, you run a high risk of developing diabetes which increases your risk of heart attacks, strokes, blindness, amputations, and impotence. Why must sugar and fats accompany every expression of love and every celebration? Is it possible to have a birthday party, a wedding, or an anniversary party without a cake? By reducing obesity, we are taking a swing at diabetes. Three out of four diabetics will die from heart disease and stroke. If you experience fatigue, blurred vision, excessive thirst, frequent urination, unexplained weight loss and non-healing wounds and sores, consult a doctor immediately.

5. **Enjoy regular exercise** (60 minutes per day-every day), follow a sensible diet, and get a good night's sleep! Move those muscles. Increase your intake of fruits and vegetables, reduce fats and sugars, but most of all, eat less. Every little bit you do can either help or hurt your health a little bit. Don't be a fat maker by insisting that your kids "eat up" what they don't need and resist being a victim of a fat maker. Let's be more creative about demonstrating love for each other than to force feed the ones you most care about. If you don't sleep well, get a sleep study, and then follow your doctor's advice.

6. **Don't smoke.** Smoking is our most preventable cause of premature death. Nobody argues with this anymore, not even smokers. Smoking constricts the arteries, increases carbon monoxide, lowers the good cholesterol, and is the primary cause of lung cancer. According to Benjamin Waterhouse (1754-1846): "Tobacco is a filthy weed that from the devil does proceed, it drains your purse, it burns your clothes, and makes a chimney of your nose."

7. **Access better health care**, get a check-up and faithfully take your medication as prescribed. It is no longer acceptable for the most vulnerable among us to receive the worst care. Just because some of us are poor does not mean that

we should be relegated to poor care. All members of society deserve to receive effective and respectful health care. More importantly, it does no good for you to be evaluated by a physician, have your condition diagnosed and medication prescribed if you do not then fill the prescription and take it as directed.

Good doctors treat disease; really great doctors also prevent disease.

143.

You Don't Have to Be Perfect to Be a Champion

April 29, 2019

Along with the rest of the world, I was mesmerized by Tiger Woods this past weekend when he won the Masters Golf Tournament for the fifth time. This win, coming 22 years from the last time he won it is truly remarkable! At that point in his life every pundit predicted that he would be the greatest golfer of all time and would overtake the record held by Jack Nicklaus for the most majors in a career. Then came his fall from "grace," his physical limitations, back surgery and wondering if he would ever play golf at a high level again. He not only came back last weekend—he roared back. He won even though he missed a lot of little putts, made plenty of bogies and played several shots out of the woods. I loved every minute of it. This is a redemption song!

I have pointed out in previous columns how individuals can turn things around after being down and out. Joseph, in the Old Testament, was sold into slavery and imprisoned for something for which he was unjustly convicted only to become a pivotal leader in the salvation of Egypt and the building of the Jewish nation. Sampson had his greatest victory when chained and blind. David was just a shepherd when chosen by Samuel to be king, won many battles, committed adultery with Bathsheba and had her husband killed, but God still called David a man after His own heart. Great baseball hitters only get a hit three times out of ten times at bat.

The difficulties we face in life are inevitable so when life gives you lemons, make lemonade. In the Chinese language, opportunity and adversity are different sides of the SAME coin. The Chinese believe that within every adverse situation is the opportunity for achievement. David would never have been a hero without the presence of Goliath. In a world where everyone is at peace and everyone's needs are met, there is no opportunity to excel. It turns out that we need adversity to be successful. In every adverse situation I encounter, rather than focus on "woe is me," I embrace the struggle and look for solutions. In times of drought, I think about how I can bring water to the thirsty.

I draw inspiration from Paul, who continued his mission spreading the gospel even though he was repeatedly beaten, stoned, shipwrecked, prosecuted, and suffered from sleep deprivation, hunger, and exhaustion. Few people ever experienced these torments. But these adversities only served to strengthen his faith and resolve. Life is not so much what happens to us but how we respond to life's challenges.

I would like to encourage everyone who is feeling down and out and at a low point in their lives to be of good courage; great things are in store for you. Joy comes in the morning. Step out on faith, great glory is in your future, if you have the courage to be imperfect, anything is possible. Last week was Easter Sunday week. Without Good Friday, there would be no Resurrection Sunday!

All of us will experience our "Good Friday." The point is to remember no situation can hold you for long if you believe in the resurrection story. Life is about ebbs that then gives us the flow of new opportunities. Each day you are able to get up and breathe will bring both challenges and opportunities to shine.

My wife reminds me daily that although I was shaken after experiencing my heart surgery, I emerged stronger and better. I went through the fire a little singed and came out smoking and with a better heart. You can be a champion each day that you live a life that celebrates the good in all and not the minor things that make us different. The choice is yours and mine to make daily.

144.
Something Wonderful is Going on at Gordon State College

May 1, 2019

Even when we have our doubts, the arch of the universe bends toward progress and justice. In just the last hundred years, infectious disease deaths are way down, life expectancy is way up, we have almost wiped-out illiteracy, and we produce enough food to feed the 7.5 billion people on our planet. The arch also bends toward progress at Gordon State College.

It started out as a one room high school in Barnesville in 1832 so children could learn the classics. Twenty years later it became "The Barnesville Male and Female High School," "The Gordon Institute" in 1872 in honor of General John Gordon who, in addition to an illustrious career, was serving as governor of Georgia. In 1890 it became the "Georgia Institute" noted for training soldiers.

In 1933 the name changed again to the "Gordon High School and Junior College." In 1960 it was commissioned as a junior college by Governor Carl Sanders, becoming an official part of the University system of Georgia when it was desegregated. Designated "Gordon State College" in 2006, offering degrees in a wide range of subjects including a nursing school, they have been serving approximately 4,000 students. Ladies and gentlemen, this is progress. Gordon State College has become a gem of an institution—such a beautiful and well-appointed campus!

So, with an invitation from Dr. Kirk A. Nooks, I attended both the investiture (April 26, 2019) and the banquet that preceded it on Wednesday evening. The investiture was awesome, featuring the Georgia Highway Patrol presenting the colors; National Anthem by Ms. Dijonai Gentle, invocation by Dr. Benny Tate, and remarks by the provost (Dr. Jeffery Knighton), State Senator Marty Harbin, Representative Robert Dickey, Barnesville Mayor Peter Banks, representing the University System of Georgia presidents (Dr. David Bridges); representing the alumni (Ms. Kathryn Claxton); representing the faculty (Mr. Tony Pearson); the staff (Ms. Gratasha Banks) and the student body (Ms. Riley Fuller). While they were all eloquent and witty, the most heartfelt testimonial came from Dr. and Dr. Nooks' daughter (Ms. Anniston Nooks) who spoke about integrity and love for all mankind that exudes from the man she calls her father.

Dr. Nooks became the fourth president of Gordon State College and a highly qualified individual to take the college forward. Having earned a B.A. and MBA from Mercer College and a Ph.D. from George Washington University, Dr. Nooks previously served as campus dean, dean of student services and "brings a blended set of skills reflected from over 20 years of education, business and engineering experience."

Sing Praises to Gordon State College
Our Gateway into knowledge
Our path from base uncertainty
To honor, courage, loyalty

Gordon State College attracts students from around the country and certainly the place for a great educational experience. They do need people of goodwill to contribute to their scholarship fund so eligible students will have a shot at a good education.

Their nursing school is first class and let me say this about nursing: Not only is there a 30% shortage of nurses in this country, but I regard nursing as a special profession not only because of its humanitarian pursuits but any nurse can travel the world and work as a nurse without having to become further credentialed. Just about every country in the world has a shortage of nurses and would welcome you. Doctors, lawyers, dentists, and pharmacists do not have this privilege.

145.

Moral Development: Our Conscience is the Glue that Binds Us

May 8, 2019

Some believe that moral development starts at birth because when a baby hears the crying of another baby, they also cry (global empathy).

Children develop a sense of self (individual entity) apart from everyone else by age two when they realize that they have to take their own shower. Shame and guilt, right and wrong is evident by age five. Children are programmed to fall in line and adhere to the routines, rhythms, processes and moral codes of their families. In essence, we develop a conscience with the attendant guilt when they are out of sync and enjoy a clear conscience when one's behavior reflects the community's values and expectations which are different from community to community—country to country. But like it or not, all human beings care what others think—more or less. How does it feel when the Pastor calls you out in church; your family and friends forget your birthday; you do what you think is something fabulous and no one applauds you. Do you become shame-faced if you are caught stealing something or show up inappropriately attired for the occasion? Moral codes help to make our transactions with each other predictable and smooth out edges. We also invented "forgiveness" to assuage our guilt. While some of us like to live on the edge, some also would never, and I mean never, never violate a social code—Mother Hawkins at your church whose vocabulary is full of shoulds and advice for everyone is the epitome of an enforcer. She produces feelings of guilt just seeing her approaching.

When I first moved to Thomaston, I was traveling through Zebulon when I was pulled over by the local police. As I believed I was not speeding or in violation of any laws I was anxious to know why?

The officer said: "Did you see the funeral procession going by on the other side?"

I answered, "yes but what is the violation?"

"Down here, everybody must pull over on both sides when a funeral procession goes by."

"I never heard of that rule officer."

"Yes, that's how we roll down here. Now you know the rule, be more considerate next time."

But what is morality really? A sense of fairness, sympathy, sharing and cooperation, appropriateness, treating others the way you want to be treated. It also involves loyalty to one's group. In other words, kids just grow up knowing not to talk back to Mama, to tell the truth, that it is not appropriate to wear a bathing suit to a church service or a funeral and you are supposed to help out family members in need even when it involves sacrifice. Deciding when to laugh or hit another is a difficult lesson to learn. More importantly, learning that it is taboo to have sexual relations with blood relatives—and whatever else we decide is our "moral duty."

Our human feelings (remorse, embarrassment, guilt, shame, the feeling we get in our gut that something is not right) carries the possibility that a philanderer could be killed by a jealous husband, admonished, or ostracized by others for lesser offenses but the real value of a conscience is that we get to punish ourselves with worry, sleepless nights, lack of focus, headaches, depression or just feeling bad. Oh, we are so much happier and relaxed doing the right thing than when we allow our fickle passions to have their sway—those awful secrets can be worrisome.

In terms of our loyalties, children are naturally self-centered. Teenagers are focused on their peer group and out to establish alliances and hooking up; Parents are focused on their offspring and building a better world so their DNA can thrive. And with maturity comes a concern about the well-being of our planet and its people. My wish is that more people would evolve to this stage.

If we are going to get along, we need moral codes. We would be a chaotic society without them. But I will let your conscience be your guide.

146.
Casual Relationships Nourishes the Soul: Why Exchanging Pleasantries is Important

May 15, 2019

A recent study confirms what I suspected for a long time. Apparently, these simple hello/ goodbye transactions that we engage in are good for our sense of belongingness to our community and looking away from someone is like paper cuts.

Staying socially engaged is vital to our mental health. This is especially true as people get older and close friends and family die off as well as when people relocate and live long distances from those primary relationships. A little time with others who care about you makes life nice and adds a little more texture to our daily grind. Whatever brings a smile to your face is good.

I take you back to Eric Berne, who wrote the book, *I am OK; You are OK* (1967). Dr. Berne determined that every human being needs at least 20 strokes per day to maintain good health. A stroke is someone just speaking your name, smiling at you, a tip of a hat, a wave, a shout out, saying good morning, a handshake, a wink, a hug, someone saying verbally or nonverbally that they like you. And, according to Dr. Berne, this is good for both the person who initiates the transaction as well as the person who is the target of the transaction. AND, most importantly, you cannot meet your need for daily strokes from one of just a few people. The wider the circle of acquaintances the better. It pays dividends to exchange pleasantries with as many people as possible. If we all practice this simple truth in Thomaston, we could become the friendliest (and healthiest) city in Georgia.

So, "low stakes" relationships such as a bartender who knows your name and the drink you like; knitting and quilting circles, church groups, Kiwanis members who only see each other on Tuesdays for lunch; senior citizens who meet to do crafts and have lunch together, the people you meet walking the dog; or when you take your kids to the playground and spend a moment with the other mothers; the barber and hairdresser; the manicurist; the grocer and butcher shop who knows how you like your cut of meat; the greetings at church, PTA meetings; classrooms, the softball team, and the bridge club members you only see on Thursday evenings— all keys to your sense of well-being.

Southern hospitality is particularly good about greetings and handshakes. In New York, it would be weird to greet a stranger but down here, we speak to strangers all the time without exception. But, as we become more politically divided, we are having fewer of these transactions and more ill will and bad feelings. But we have a lot to learn from people other than "family and friends." When was the last time you struck up a conversation with a stranger?

So, you can readily see that isolation is deadly. Do you realize how quickly death comes for a surviving spouse? Human beings were not programmed to be alone. I recall a Mark Twain story about a man who panned gold in the hills of Colorado and accumulated a huge fortune. After he returned to civilization and converted his gold into cash, he saw a woman with a baby. He was so hungry for human contact he gave the woman all his wealth to just hold her baby. They apparently went on to have a good life together as a family. But let us not underestimate "baby therapy" except people are so fussy these days about who can hold their babies. They don't belong to you. Those precious little angels are God's gift to mankind—share the joy!

Personally, I do not participate in social media. There are so many downsides that I just resist the pressures from members of my family to just give in and join the rest of mankind. My son bragged to me that on his birthday he received over 500 "happy birthday" wishes from strangers and I didn't get why that was important to him. But I know people who got jobs and important "hook-ups" from social media. Yes, it has its value, but I continue to resist. I like my strokes the old-fashioned way through human, face-to-face interactions.

I learned my social skills from my grandmother who sat on her veranda (porch) each morning with a big pot of coffee and invited every-one who happened to be walking by to sit a spell and enjoy a cup of coffee and a little conversation. She quickly and predictably got her 20 strokes each day AND people often brought small gifts to repay her for her kindness. Now, get out there and say hello to somebody!

147.
A Sense of Purpose
is Essential for Happiness

May 29, 2019

I made the point last week that we are happy when we do happy things and especially when you are doing good things for others. I then pointed out how we can feed our five senses each day. I was brought to task by a reader of my column that the piling on of good experiences (good food, seeing the beauty of the world, music to my ears, feeling wonderful, smelling sweet perfumes) does not get us to happiness. "True happiness" he said, "comes from having a purpose in life." It was one of those moments that made me go hmmm. I responded: "You know, you have a point there." I immediately thought about my youngest son (Aleron Kong) who found happiness when he found his calling. He was a successful physician with Kaiser Permanente in Atlanta, and we had invested a great deal in assisting him to that point in his life. I am also certain that he was indulging all his senses, but he felt unsettled and started to write science fiction books which has taken him in another direction and allowed him to launch himself as a happier human being. He resigned his position with Kaiser and is now a highly acclaimed writer and literally cannot wipe the smile off his face. He is living the dream and glowing with happiness. So, yes, I agree. It is as important to find your calling in life.

I am also thinking of my grandson (Brooks Kong-Sivert) who is only 17 years old. I am writing this column from Phoenix, Arizona where he is graduating from high school. But I have never known anyone who feels so accomplished and happy. He was a chubby, awkward nine-year-old when his parents signed him up for Taekwondo and he took to it like a fish takes to water. When he was up for his black belt, he was told that if he could not run an eight-minute mile that was the end of the road for him in achieving a Black Belt in Taekwondo. At the time he could only run the mile in over 10 minutes. In the ensuing three months, he woke up early each morning by his own volition and ran and ran and ran and low and behold, he achieved his objective to run the mile in less than eight minutes. He has since continued to hone his skills, passionately preparing, and competing at every opportunity. In addition to excellent grades, last spring, he competed in Portugal in the Taekwondo International Tournament and won four first place medals! His next stop is Arizona State University where he wants to major in business so he can manage a chain of Taekwondo studios around the country. He is dedicated to helping other kids achieve their dreams.

I believe there is a longing in all of us to have purpose and feel like our life matters. So, while I still believe you can be happy by feeding your five senses each day and achieving the multitude of successes (getting an A, completing a task, getting a date to the prom, winning a race, being part of a winning basketball team, graduation, admission to college, finding a job, getting a promotion, making a friend), I now include a continuing quest to find your life purpose. I also advocate that your purpose may change as you mature and find meaning in life. That's ok as well.

I will continue to advocate that finding something to which we can dedicate our lives, is the true path to satisfaction and happiness. My belief is that all of us have the promise of finding that purpose of uplifting each other and improving society as a whole. Finding your "true passion" in tearing down others is not what I think the reader was alluding to. If you have pivoted your life toward "purpose," you can be making a positive difference in the world. If you believe that a rising tide lifts all boats, as they say in Australia, "Good on you mate!"

148.

There is Such a Thing as Too Much Information

June 5, 2019

We get it from 900 channels, plus social media, radio and newspapers, family, and friends. When was the last time someone said, "You won't believe what happened?" If they did, you would have replied, "I already heard about that this morning." So, do we really need 24/7/365 news? It is just too much and feels like a tsunami that just keeps on coming. The sad thing is I cannot turn it off. Have you tried turning off your phone, computer, and television for just one day?

Our fears are being way overblown. As a result of all the news from around the world, little problems loom large as well as feel intimate. The odds of a shark attack are over a million to one even when you are swimming in an ocean, but with news and movie depictions of shark attacks beating down on us, some of us avoid the joy of ocean swimming. My friend, Dr. Linda Gordon, has a long list of things that will not end her life because she will never participate (mountain climbing, skydiving, deep sea diving, horseback riding, car racing…) Dr. Gordon, you are missing out!

Our fears are fueled by the need for eyeballs to sell us stuff. Every earthquake, forest fire, flood, volcano, twister, hurricane, snowstorm, and mass shooting are the worst, biggest, most devastating in history—all in the name of grabbing our eyeballs and higher ratings.

Two years ago, they predicted a monster snowstorm in New York, they got five inches. It feels like the world is falling apart with the intimate exaggerated reporting of disasters.

The myth of a creepy stranger is way overblown —especially in Thomaston. Are you aware that most children are no longer allowed to walk home from school for fear of encountering a pedophile or bully? So, we never let them out of our sight and tell our children never to talk to strangers. Are you also aware that most American children live their entire childhood being supervised? If you were born before 1990, you enjoyed the luxury of just running off to play. Our modern children have no autonomy or independence to even decide anything about their comings and goings. All children's activities are now supervised and organized by adults. We accompany them everywhere or make sure they are accompanied by trusted adults. There is no longer a thing we used to call a "pickup game" or riding their bikes around the neighborhood. Halloween is almost a thing of the past and those brave parents who venture out, hold their child's hand up to the neighbor's door and if the neighbor chose "trick," kids have no idea what that means, and all candy and fruit must be inspected before being consumed. But the precaution is based on a myth and too much information. There has never been a case of contaminated candy or a razor blade in an apple in Thomaston—it happened once (long ago) in a place called California and is renewed every year and reported as if it occurred down the block, so we pull our children closer and closer to us. Do you even allow them to cross the street?

Stranger abductions are not even based on fact but on a movie (Adam, 1981) but there are thousands of false claims of child abductions that make it seem commonplace. The disappearance of a child anywhere in the world will now put us into a frenzy as your phone is captured to report it—even when the phone is turned off. Our nation is now safer than ever before. Crime is way down and our children are safer now than in the "good old days" when they could run around without a care in the world. The danger comes from being overfed on bad news and catastrophes. FBI statistics show that the number of missing persons of all ages went down 31% between 1997 and 2011. All crimes against children continue to go down. In fact, 80% of crimes are committed between people who know each other, and kids are 20 times more likely to be killed by a family member than a stranger. Ninety-nine percent of strangers are good people. The obesity epidemic is partly a result of parents no longer allowing their kids to play outside. I think it would be best if we don't frighten our children to death about all the bad things that can happen to them. They are bewildered and lost because they are not allowed to try their wings. For one thing, we must turn down the volume on these fear mongering safety vigilantes who will call the law on you for leaving your kid in the car or the playground and otherwise scanning for unsupervised children. Terrible things happen in the world, but it is safer now than ever. Ease up and give your kids some breathing room and allow yourself to take some risks.

149.

When Your Children Graduate from High School?

June 12, 2019

I think it is a miracle when immature little boys and girls stop messing around and grow up to be responsible adults, earn a living, and live meaningful lives. Were you the same kid that used to be so awkward and silly, and look at you now with a wife, children, and a mortgage! They mostly turn the corner and become engaged as citizens. They had better; the future belongs to them. According to Dr. Julie Lythcott-Haims (*How to Raise an Adult*), St. Martin's Griffin Edition, August 2016), in addition to their academic preparation, high school graduates preparing to live away from home will need to know how to:

1. Make regular doctor and dentist appointments and follow-up on recommended care.
2. Manage his/her bank account, balance a checkbook, pay bills, and use a credit card responsibly. Do they know how to spend less than they earn?
3. Understand basic contracts, like renting an apartment, a car lease, or loans.
4. Find out about job openings, apply for jobs, and make a good impression at a job interview; and then of course, show up on time and ready to perform at said work regularly and reliably.
5. Perform or at least schedule oil changes and other basic car maintenance, change a tire and fill up with the proper grade of gas and oil. Do they know what a dipstick is for?
6. Perform basic plumbing and electrical around the house. Can they change a faucet washer and wire a lamp?
7. Produce food from a vegetable garden and cook basic recipes from scratch.
8. Maintain good health (choosing nourishing foods, committing to an exercise regimen and having thoroughly rehearsed before-hand how to handle any engagement with sex, drugs and alcohol).
9. Know how to propose, plan, and execute an outing, such as a date. They should know when and how to apologize and make peace.
10. They should know how and when to seek help and how to thank people for their help.

11. Take the lead in situations where public speaking is called for, such as blessing a table or stating a position at a forum.
12. Dressing appropriately or maybe even to impress.

The formulary for all these skills is: First we do it for you, then we do it together, then we watch you do it and then you do it by yourself. According to Dr. Haims, our kids fall short because: (1) We shield them from experiences like hothouse flowers; (2). We over direct them like robots; (3). We entertain them and make excuses for them like petty tyrants.

It turns out those children who were not allowed to be bored, had to walk, or bike where they wanted to go, had chores and responsibilities at home, and had jobs as teenagers are phenomenally more successful and happier as adults. Go figure.

Thinking about ourselves, according to *"Psychology Today,"* there are six major aspects that distinguish children from adults.

1. Rationality: Adults make rational decisions instead of responding emotionally.
2. Formulating and implementing goals: Adults formulate goals and take the appropriate actions to achieve them rather than giving in to temptations, the influence of friends and advertising.
3. Mutuality in relationships: Adults seek peer relationships whereas those who operate from a child's perspective often assume the role of either the parent or the child.
4. Active versus passive: Adults don't feel victimized by life or complain or dump their problems onto other people; instead, they face their problems or challenges directly and work out solutions rather than depending on others for direction.
5. Adults do not have defensive or angry reactions and are willing to explore new ideas.
6. Personal power: While no one has control over what they think and feel, adults exercise a great deal of control over their behavior and take responsibility for their actions.

The ability to think for ourselves is probably the most important. According to the Foundation for Critical Thinking: "In a world of accelerating change, intensifying complexity, and increasing interdependence, critical thinking is now a requirement for economic and social survival."

150.

Do We All Lie?

June 19, 2019

The story goes that as a child, George Washington confessed that he had indeed cut down the cherry tree because he could not tell a lie. Honest Abe said: You can fool some of the people some of the time, but you cannot fool all the people all the time. In an era of hyperbole, fake news, and alternative facts, do you wish all our Presidents have the same moral compass?

We live at a time when it is difficult to tell fact from fiction. It is now possible to implant your face on someone else's comments and present this false representation to the world or substitute someone else's words. I am concerned about what this is doing to our humanity and our concept of truth. But my question is: Are lies always bad and truth telling always good?

Mark Twain argued that everyone lies and that, on occasion, lying can be more virtuous than telling the truth. He used the example of a potential victim that breaks into your house to escape a criminal with a gun who was trying to end his life. The criminal then knocks and when you answer the door, there is a man with a gun who inquires, "I saw the man I have been chasing come toward your house, is he here?" I hope you would lie and say that you have not seen him. Or do you tell the truth: "Yes, he broke into my house and is hiding under my bed." Yes. I believe lies are justified if they save lives and the worst lies are the ones that hurt others. I still want my friends and business associates to be truthful in our transactions but clearly understand that some occasions require a lie.

Remember the lie Rahab the prostitute told to protect the Israelite spies in the Bible. (Joshua 2:4-6) Without exception, we all tell numerous little lies daily. It's the oil that keeps our relationships engaged. How many times others ask you: "How are you" and your response is "fine" when you feel like hell or saying: "It's nice to meet you" when you cannot stand to be in his company. It's not quite as bad as when a used car salesman sells you a cream puff and the engine falls to the pavement after just five miles from his lot or a movie being promoted as the greatest comedy of all time that doesn't trigger a chuckle or the politician who promises to cut taxes, provide free healthcare, and cut college tuition at the same time.

Sometimes, lying is not only advisable but virtuous and in the spirit of Christianity. I actually know someone who never lies. In fact, he has made the statement that he would rather die than tell a lie. He regularly suffers severe consequences but sticks to his guns. He is not an easy person to love. When a woman asks, "Am I pretty?" He says, "compared to what?" And don't push the question if you don't want your feelings hurt.

If you recall the movie: *"The Crucible"*, the wife would never tell a lie and the husband could never tell the truth but when faced with a life and death decision, the wife lied and the husband told the truth.

It's the lies (both of commission and omission) that hurt others that I personally abhor. Did you just happen to not give someone the information they needed or purposely steered them wrong? Do you invent stuff? My thought is that if you are making up stuff, it will not be long before no one will believe anything you say. Consider the boy who cried wolf, he could fool others repeatedly until the day when he really needed others to believe him, they didn't, to everyone's detriment.

So, do you still tell your children, "Just tell the truth?"

151.
Celebrating the Emancipation Proclamation

June 26, 2019

According to Wikipedia, Georgia under Governor James Oglethorpe was the only colony of the original 13 British colonies to have banned slavery in 1735 but reinstated it in 1751 by Royal British Decree. And with the invention of the cotton gin and fertile lands, the economy in Georgia became prosperous due to high demand and free labor provided by slaves for the next hundred years.

Upson County was founded in 1824. The City of Thomaston (a large producer of moonshine, cotton, wheat, corn, cows, and pigs) came into being in 1825 as the seat of Upson County and by 1886, became (according to Penny Cliff) one of the

100 Best Small Towns in America offering slow-paced southern charm and hospitality. That charm and hospitality lingers today.

On January 1, 1863, the Emancipation Proclamation was signed by President Lincoln, freeing all slaves in the land. In Georgia, however, there was a conspiracy to keep the information from the slaves and continue business as usual. The Union Army was ordered into Georgia to enforce the Emancipation Proclamation. "Wilson's Raiders" burned crops and related properties from Columbus to Thomaston.

On April 18, 1865, the Union Army occupied Georgia and invited all slaves to the courthouse in Thomaston and proclaimed that they had been freed since 1863. General Lee surrendered on May 10,1865 and on July 13, 1865, Governor James Johnson made a public proclamation that "slavery is extinct, and involuntary servitude no longer exists" in Georgia. In Texas, the news of the Emancipation Proclamation did not get to the slaves until June 19, 1865. In Texas, June 19, became known as Freedom Day and thus the celebrations of "Juneteenth Day" became an annual ritual.

According to Rev. James McGill, in 1866 the emancipated slaves in Thomaston commemorated the occasion with much dancing and singing and started the tradition of an "Emancipation Celebration" that has continued unbroken for 154 years. Ex-slave, Mr. William Guilford, is honored as the visionary who organized the first Emancipation Celebration on May 29, 1866. With the generous support of the city fathers each year, Thomaston distinguishes itself by having the largest and longest running Emancipation Day Celebrations in the United States.

Emancipation Day is celebrated each year on the Saturday before Memorial Day, and it is spectacular! It's a day of great celebration and family reunions when past residents are expected back to Thomaston. Tents are pitched on lawns, fans are hooked up to keep everyone cool, horseshoe stakes are hammered into the ground 10 paces apart, card games are organized, the grill is lit and keeps going all day burning hot dogs, hamburgers, sausages, ribs, chicken, and steaks. Coolers are put out and everyone who stops by is offered libation and food of one sort or another. Everyone is in such high spirits and generous, it feels like Christmas in May!

The big parade starts on Bethel Street and ends at Abraham Lincoln Park and includes "floats, horses, show cars, recreational vehicles and marching bands from Upson Lee High School, Greenville High School and E.D. Evans of Macon."

Festivities are organized at churches making May 25-27 a weekend of music, prayers, speeches as well as the reading of the Emancipation Proclamation.

The current officers are Brenda Hobbs (president); Deneane Jones (vice president); Shirlene Jordan (secretary); Mattie King (asst. secretary); Patricia Strickland (treasurer) and Patricia Reeves (asst. treasurer). Other members of the organizing committee are Doris Walden, Sheila Colbert, Jimmy Gray, Jennifer Sullivan, James McGill, Lankston Johnson, Greta King, George Carriker, Daphne Drake, Mr. and Mrs. Bennie Barnes and Jarreau Walker.

Any member of the committee can assist if you wish to support this annual historic event. Chief Richardson and the entire police department were extremely supportive.

152.
I am Sorry,
It Is Just Evil to Abuse Children

July 10, 2019

My favorite song at Sunday school was always:

> *Jesus loves the little children*
> *All the children of the world"*
> *"Red and yellow, black and white*
> *They are all precious in his sight*
> *Jesus loves the little children of the world.*

Surely of all the songs, this one is pure and captures a simple truth. So, my heart bleeds whenever I witness or hear about children being injured through neglect, physical, sexual, and emotional abuse. I find that there is no justification, particularly when I hear "They brought it on themselves." As if children choose the circumstances in which they find themselves. And really, in the cold light of day, it would be a stretch to say their parents "chose" their circumstances either.

It is easy to harden our hearts, to argue ourselves into abstraction. Like the legal nitpicker in Luke 10:28, when presented with the pure, true absolute of "Love thy neighbor," keeps straining for that loophole, Yeah, but, when you say "neighbor," you mean like, neighbor, though? That guy's intellectual heirs are among us still arguing, "What part of 'illegal' don't you understand?"

What do you suppose is the right course of action when people cross our borders without our permission? Shoot them? Leave them in the river to drown or in the desert to die of dehydration? Inhumanely imprison them so they have to sleep in overcrowded conditions and spend endless days of idle tension without soap or toothbrush? Separate newborns from the women who birthed them and children of tender years from their parents? How is the treatment of these families reflective of our Christian values?

Yes, our country is a nation of laws. But what we have difficulty grappling with is that it is legal to enter a country to ask for asylum. Part of the problem is that we don't understand or accept the concept of "asylum." We are losing the generation that remembers when we turned back the "St. Louis" only 80 years ago. This was a ship carrying Jewish refugees from Germany with good visas in their hands from Cuba, but whom Cuba rejected once they arrived. Slow to appreciate that we were sending them to their deaths, we insisted that it was impossible to tolerate their "jumping the line." We were very insistent on what was absolutely not possible back then. World War II taught us a lot about what was possible.

You no doubt enjoyed the *"Sound of Music"* story of the Von Trapp family who out of desperation and war, climbed mountains and crossed rivers to resettle in another country. You should also support the Valdez family from Guatemala escaping terrible circumstances.

I understand that the news of desperate children illegally crossing our borders is troublesome, but it does not justify our abuse. In the name of God, do not hurt little children and allow this abuse to be continued in our name. The Irish came to escape famine; the Jews came to escape Nazi Germany; the Cubans came to escape Castro. The Puritans came to escape politicized religion.

President Ronald Reagan reminded us of our Puritan foundations when he quoted John Winthrop's admonishment:

> We shall be a city on a hill. The eyes of all people are upon us so that if we shall deal falsely with our God in this work, we have undertaken to cause Him to withdraw His present help from us, we shall be made a story and a by word through the world.

All these separated and imprisoned children know is pain and desperation with no relief in sight from their overwhelming loneliness and isolation. Their existence tells them that they are nothing but nuisance to the country of their birth and they find no welcome mat anywhere. They (no doubt) will suffer irreparable damage for the rest of their lives for what we are doing to them.

I am a father to four amazing children and six even more amazing grandchildren. What I want for them I want for all children throughout the world. Jesus loves all the children of the world.

Now that you're aware of the problem, you cannot pretend you don't care. For Jesus said in Mathew 19: "Suffer the little children and forbid them not to come unto me for such is the Kingdom of heaven." In the movie, *"Sophie's Choice,"* the Nazi guard dispenses life and death and, when made aware that Sophie and her family are Christians, uses this passage against them, forcing her to make the famous choice. When we allow legal technicalities and sophistry to make an abstraction of real children before us, are we not like that guard, quoting Bible verse while doing evil? Let us insist on something better.

153.
Euphoric Moments

July 17, 2019

Euphoria is described as the experience of intense feelings of well-being and happiness.

During this past week (July 3–10, 2019) I had several occasions to suddenly jump from my seat, feet and arms extended, shirt buttons popping, with wide eyes and a shout that ordinarily would embarrass everyone—let's call it a yell, yes even a rebel yell. These were happy moments that I thoroughly enjoyed and made life exciting.

First and foremost, our lady's soccer team made us proud by winning our fourth world cup. Yes, we are the best in the world. And why are they not being paid the same as the men? On the field, the offense was potent, setting the record for the most goals scored, and the defense tough, setting the record for the least number of goals scored by their opponents. They were physical and aggressive and throughout the series their style seemed to overwhelm their opponents. The 2-0 score in the final against the Dutch reflected the hard work, dedication, and determination of each player. Nevertheless, it was a thrilling match and an hour after the game was over, the stadium was still full. Fans could not get enough and wanted to prolong the euphoria. So, they looked on while the team received their hugs, trophies and medals and generally expressed their exuberance. It was a proud, euphoric moment.

Another proud moment for Americans was the brash ninth grader from Atlanta who won three matches at Wimbledon, our own Cori (Coco) Gauff was not only the youngest player to qualify to play at Wimbledon but beat her idol Venus Williams as well as Magdalena Rybarikova and an amazing come-from-behind victory over Polona Hercog before losing to Semona Halep. A 15-year-old beat Venus, the 39-year-old. Coco wants to be the greatest tennis professional of all time. I am a believer. She is a focused and determined young lady from Georgia.

Then on Sunday, Golfer Matthew Wolff, a 20-year-old college champion who recently turned pro and has a strange swing, sank a long and winding eagle putt on the last hole to win the 3M Open with 21-under par and said: "I just proved to myself I can be out here." He hails from Blaine, Minnesota. Watch out for him at the Master's next year.

Finally, on Saturday, I started my round of golf with two birdies and made 35 points (Stableford system). My son tells me that if you are going to birdie all 18 holes, you have to birdie the first two. Although I wouldn't recommend a heart attack to anyone, to the regret of my friends I compete against, I am playing better after my triple bypass surgery than before. Credit that to a smoother and slower swing. I am enjoying myself.

And the best euphoric time of the day, week, month, or year, is going to bed with my wife of 32 years! Happy Birthday Darling.

154.
My Visit to Portugal

July 24, 2019

I am writing this column sitting beside a swimming pool in Lisbon, Portugal. During July for the past 25 years, my wife and I have joined a group of 60 fellow travelers from ten states for a 10-day trip to exotic locations arranged through "Admiral Travel" out of Sarasota, Fla. While we have not run out of places to visit, this is our second go-round to Portugal, and it has been well worth it. It has taken 16 hours to get here from Atlanta, stopping in New York, and by God we are determined to enjoy every moment of it.

We travel because it always ignites passions—discovery, joy and a little romance. Our group is mostly physicians and we always arrange to have a medical symposium with local physicians when we visit. There is a mix of ages, but most are on the older side. We believe in travel and have visited over 100 countries. Each year we head off, expecting surprises as well as reconnecting with old friends and meeting new people from diverse cultures—always learning and appreciating. We are explorers of planet earth. We sometimes experience this planet as big and sometimes as a small village.

Portugal is part of the European Union on the Iberian Peninsula and so, only the Euro is legal tender. It borders and is in the same land mass of Spain. I find it odd that if you look at a world map, why it is not just a state within Spain—in fact, the entire peninsula was Spain at some point then Portugal broke off again and took the coast on the Atlantic Ocean. Unlike the United States, buildings and houses are mostly "wall to wall" or built in the Seismic style of architecture. In other words, the buildings have no space between them as they believe it shores up the buildings against their frequent earthquakes. They were once a powerful maritime empire with established bases in Japan, China, Brazil, Angola and Kenya. When it became a dictatorship, the economy suffered. But following democratic rule in 1974 and joining the European Union in 1986, they are enjoying prosperity. Tourism is their primary income earner. While golf courses were abundant, this was a family vacation, so no golf was planned. The sacrifices one has to make.

We toured São Jorge Castle, the Tagus Estuary, the beautiful gardens on the waterfront, the carriage museum, the Geronimo Monastery, the Belem Tower and enjoyed various wine and food tasting. I believe the entire population is Catholic. However, there is a Muslim influence in Portugal as the Moors from northern Africa occupied this territory and southern Spain for more than 700 years from 711 AD to 1411 AD. There is a saying here that "when Columbus sailed the ocean blue in 1492, Portugal became a country too."

It was a pleasure meeting with the local physicians and exchanging medical information. The Portuguese are fighting all the chronic illnesses faced by Western cultures, such as heart disease, diabetes, high blood pressure and strokes. They spend a fraction of their GDP on healthcare costs and enjoy a life span that is longer than the average American. All the citizens of Portugal are provided healthcare at no cost to them but those who want to can buy private health insurance and seek care from private physicians and hospitals—a dual system.

So, while we are here, about 150 miles away they are using helicopters and planes to fight three blazes which started in the central region. Over 700 firefighters are on the scene and several of them were trapped because of the accelerating winds.

On one of our lazy mornings, my wife and I walk hand-in-hand over hilly cobblestone streets observing people and enjoying the warm sunshine and cool breeze feeling a little sorry for the hot temperatures we heard about in Georgia. The hot front in the U.S. made international news for several days.

Tomorrow, we sail for Tangiers, Morocco, Gibraltar, Port Banu and finally to Malaga, Spain. Stay tuned!

155.
Traveling Makes You Richer and Wiser

July 31, 2019

My wife and I have invested a lot of time and money traveling and it has returned dividends. When we were raising children, we would trek the world with them to ensure they understood the meaning of being part of a global community. We now travel with our grandchildren whenever possible to impart the same sense of community. On this venture it was just me and my BFF traveling with a group of like-minded "Gulliver's."

We have found that the world reveals itself to us when we travel. We rub shoulders with strangers who are eager to share the beauty of their culture. Do you want business ideas? Travel to distant shores and see how other people do things and make a living. Maybe one of these ideas can be adopted in Thomaston. Maybe something we do well in Thomaston can be adopted in another country. We have experienced a great deal discovering how other people live: how they pair up to establish families (many young people around the world are more than happy to have their parents choose their spouses); how they treat their elderly (do they honor and respect them or leave them behind so the bears will eat them); the rituals of giving birth (some feast on the after-birth); how they handle the last moments of death and disposing of the body; how they dispose of waste; how they take care of their sick. (Can you imagine having a toothache and having no access to aspirins, antibiotics, or dentists); what are their beliefs, values, and morals? How do they educate their children? What they eat and drink, the music and dancing they enjoy, their sleeping arrangements, the sports, games, and activities. (Did you know that England won the cricket world cup?) For the past 25 years, we have been cruising with the same group. Last week I wrote about our first stop in Portugal and hope you enjoyed my description, as we certainly enjoyed the experience. From Portugal, we set sail for Tangier, Morocco—the land of spices. If you wanted to, you could arrange to get a shipment of spices wholesale and sell retail from a spice shop. I am sure it would go over well anywhere. Who doesn't want a little spice in their life? We encountered stores with up to 50 large bags of herbs and spices—a cure for every ailment that also tastes good, baked, cooked or fried. We were so enchanted; we took a cooking class as my wife was excited about how to spice up her dishes. The secret? Cardamom. We even learned to bake bread and enjoyed the meal the class prepared.

From Tangiers, our next stop was Puerto Banu, Spain. This is one of the most luxurious places we have ever visited. There were over 100 yachts docked, fantastic restaurants and condominiums with a starting price of $2 million per unit and as we walked along the streets, Rolls Royce's, Lamborghinis, and other cars we have never heard of were parked. We thought we were traveling in luxury but when we got back on board our own ship, it was no comparison to the yachts in the harbor.

From Puerto Banu, we sailed to Gibraltar (Rock of Gibraltar) where we visited the monkeys as well as deep caves (where they put on concerts), tunnels with English propaganda) and the view from the top of the rock was breathtaking. We noted with interest that they have so little land; a major highway crossed the runway at the airport. That's right, when a plane approaches, traffic must be stopped like a railway crossing to give right of way to the approaching aircraft. Geographically, Gibraltar is a part of Spain, but it is governed by England. When Brexit happens and England is separated from the European Union, it is a potential problem for the residents of Gibraltar. It is worthy of note that when we contracted with our local tour guide, he asked us to pay him in English pounds. But at the end of the tour that we enjoyed, we went to the bank to exchange dollars into pounds but when we returned to pay him, he had already left with another group. Fortunately, we had his card, and we were able to track him down to give him his money. He said he just forgot. From Gibraltar, we set sail again for Malaga, Spain where we extended our trip by a few days. I went to use the swimming pool and noticed that several women were sunning themselves topless—no big deal.

On our various walking tours to visit the Picasso Museum, (Malaga is his birthplace) cathedrals and find good restaurants, as street signs were in Spanish and most people couldn't be bothered giving tourists directions, we were forever getting lost—but that is also part of the fun. We were always running into interesting sights that we had not planned on. We came, we saw, experienced, and embraced the experience. The food was delicious, and the wine was cheaper than water. You should know that the style in Europe is that a great brunch is included in the hotel charges, and you would not believe all the breakfast options. You could actually spend the entire morning trying unfamiliar fruits, vegies, hams, bacon, eggs as you like it, breads, salmon, herring, caviar, juices and jellies. They even had a tray of honeycombs—straight from the hive.

We went to see a Flamingo performance and it was just grand. These women exude a lot of power. I invite you to check our flamingo dancing on YouTube. While I was inspired to join the dancers on stage, my wife grabbed my shirt and held me back from making a fool of myself.

We have returned safely with the clear recognition that there is so much to be gained by traveling the world. While most people cannot travel due to visa restrictions, as Americans, we have the privilege of traveling to anywhere in the world. If there ever was a time to travel it is now. I have been enriched by traveling. Our memories will last a lifetime. You want to see the pictures?

According to Brooke Saward (World of Wanderlust): "Think of travel as an investment. The more we travel, the more we see. The more we see, the more we grow. The more we grow, the more we change and evolve as a human being. Traveling the world would have to be one of the most direct ways to go out and understand other cultures, other places, other people, and other understandings of life. This is something you will then take home with you to change your life and the people around you for the better."

156.

Does the Politics of Hate Jive with Southern Hospitality?

August 7, 2019

Writing for *Southern Living*, Ms. Michelle Darrisaw beautifully describes the six qualities that define southern hospitality. She believes it is a way of life for those of us who live south of the Mason-Dixon line. She makes the point that southern hospitality is not just a catchphrase, but a way of life. According to Ms. Darrisaw, the characteristics of southern hospitality are:

1. Politeness
2. Good home cooking
3. Kindness
4. Charm, and
5. Charity

I do not need to explain what these qualities are as we all live them, and they are as natural to us as breathing. On the other hand, you will not find these qualities in northern cities like New York City or other large cities like Los Angeles or Chicago. If you were brave enough to say "hey" to someone on a street in Los Angeles, do you think you would get a pleasant response?

I have told this story before, when my wife and I first moved to Thomaston and opened our practice (ZÖe Pediatrics) I went door-to-door introducing myself and to let our neighbors know that we were open for business. I knocked on the door of a house and the voice on the other side yelled: "Come on in!". While it caught me off guard, I opened the door and the kind lady of the house said: "And who are you?" So, having explained myself, she invited me to join her and her husband to share some sweet tea by their pool. So, we spent the next two hours getting to know each other and them telling me all about Thomaston. When we had our official grand opening, she sent us a large variety of flowers from her garden. Shelby is no longer with us, but I will always remember her kindness. We have a wonderful culture that should be celebrated and retained.

As we live in the Bible Belt, we also believe in God and what the good book has to say about how we treat each other. We also believe in regularly attending services where we stand for prayer and when the Bible is read. We enthusiastically shake hands, hug on each other and catch-up on what is going on with the members of each other's family. Ernest Hamlin Abbott wrote in 1902, "Hospitality in the South is an integral part of church services." When someone you know dies, are you inclined to bring a covered dish and do what you can to comfort the family? In Matthew 25:40, Christ said "Truly I tell you, whatever you did for one of the least of these brothers and sisters of mine, you did for me."

In this season of mass shootings, I was dismayed yesterday to find out that the politics of hate took its toll in El Paso, Texas. Yet again, young people who should be looking forward to a productive life, instead, with hate in their hearts, decided to take the lives of others. What are we buying into? What exactly are we doing? This is not who we are!

The legacy of slavery that all of us deal with in the South is difficult enough without the added challenge fostered by the fear mongers spewing their rhetoric of hate and division that is completely at odds with our culture. Does this politics of hate, division, and confrontation jive with how we should treat each other? As a naturalized immigrant, should I go back to Jamaica? Do we no longer believe in being kind to strangers and being respectful to those who are different and may disagree with our points of view? Do we no longer believe in the parable of the Good Samaritan?

Jesus taught us how we are to treat each other every day He walked the earth. He continues to live in our hearts. Whether defending the prostitute Mary, or ordering His disciples to "suffer the children," or when He embraced the "lepers," Christ showed by example that we are our brothers' keepers. In Luke 10:25–37:25, Just then a lawyer stood up to test Jesus' "Teacher," he said, "what must I do to inherit eternal life?"

26 He said to him, "What is written in the law? What do you read there?"

27 He answered, "You shall love the Lord your God with all your heart, and with all your soul, and with all your strength, and with all your mind; and your neighbor as yourself."

28 And He (Christ) said to him, "You have given the right answer; do this, and you will live."

29 But wanting to justify himself, he asked Jesus, "And who is my neighbor?"

30 Jesus replied, "A man was going down from Jerusalem to Jericho, and fell into the hands of robbers, who stripped him, beat him, and went away, leaving him half dead.

31 Now by chance a priest was going down that road; and when he saw him, he passed by on the other side.

32 So likewise a Levite, when he came to the place and saw him, passed by on the other side.

33 But a Samaritan while traveling came near him; and when he saw him, he was moved with pity.

34 He went to him and bandaged his wounds, having poured oil and wine on them. Then he put him on his own animal, brought him to an inn, and took care of him.

35 The next day he took out two denarii, gave them to the innkeeper, and said, 'Take care of him; and when I come back, I will repay you whatever more you spend.'

36 Which of these three, do you think, was a neighbor to the man who fell into the hands of the robbers?"

37 He said, "The one who showed him mercy." Jesus said to him, "Go and do likewise."

Jealousy and hate got Lucifer kicked out of the presence of God. There are only two forces in this life, the forces of good and evil. Christ always invites us to choose wisely the path we will follow. I don't worry about those that spew this rhetoric of hate. God will take care of them in due time, as He always does. That being said, those of us that profess the salvation offered through Christ should give some thought as to whether we are the "Priest" or "Levi" in the parable of the Good Samaritan. We will all face God on that good morning. How will you answer when asked, "Did you show mercy," "Did you suffer the children?" There will be no black or white on that morning. Some will spend eternity with Christ, and some will not. We can't choose then, but we certainly can choose now.

157.

Becoming a Successful Leader

August 14, 2019

As one of the trustees at Gordon State College in Barnesville, we participated in an "Evening with The Trustees" for the 150 students who were identified as potential leaders on campus. They were invited to return to school a week early to hone their leadership skills. This is just one of the many innovations that President Kirk Nooks has brought to this beautiful campus. It was a unique opportunity for students to have direct access to accomplished members of the community —a rich experience for students and trustees alike. We were all very candid and forthright in our advice as light bulbs went off to an appreciative audience.

Here are some of my comments:

1. Health and wealth go hand-in-hand. Nothing will more effectively compromise your leadership and success in life than illness. People who are "not well" are terminated from jobs and account for business failures because they cannot be depended on to show up and show off. If you are sick, you are spending money on doctors, hospitals, medicines and wasting precious time when you should be honing your skills and forging ahead with your life's work. It so happens that most things that will compromise your health can be prevented. Using condoms will prevent venereal disease. Living an active lifestyle and making good food and beverage choices will prevent diabetes, heart disease, cancer and stroke, the major health challenges in these United States. The obesity epidemic is so out of control that children may not outlive their parents.

2. Have the courage to stand up for yourself as well as the courage to be imperfect. You don't have to know the answer to every question or have the solution to every problem. Know your weaknesses as well as your strengths and accept both. Try to do things right, not just your way.

3. Failure is just getting you ready for success. Do you remember Joseph from the Bible? His father gave him a colorful dream coat that made his brothers jealous, so they sold him into slavery and told his father that he was killed by wild animals. While a servant in Egypt, when he refused the advances of Potiphar's wife, she accused him of trying to rape her for which he was sent

to prison. And after all that, he became one of the greatest leaders of his time.

4. Courage is a two-edged sword. I think all the trustees would agree that having the courage of your convictions is an important characteristic of leadership but speaking up when you should be quiet or not going off half-cocked are also important traits. When my own daughter graduated from law school, she prided herself in being a women's libber and took every opportunity to call out members of her firm when they were being sexist or racist. Three times, she was fired. I finally advised her to start her own practice and she excelled.

5. In this amazing country we call the United States of America, there are millions of paths to success and opportunities for leadership. You never have to walk in anyone's shadow or footsteps. We have family friends whose daughter very early showed great promise in music, so they nurtured her talents and gave her the best instruction and experience and she excelled. She graduated from Julliard School of Music and got her dream job as a violinist with the NY Philharmonic making $50,000 per year. Maybe you have heard of "Fat Joe," who dropped out of high school and never took a music lesson in his life but made up a song with two words, "Lean Back," which he repeated 50 times and made a hit song for which he earned $2 million. While there are guidelines, this country is so amazing that there is no formula for success or leadership. You just have to find your own way and sometimes history makes the hero as much as the hero makes history.

6. A good leader has thirsty ears. In other words, you have one mouth and two ears, listen twice as much as you speak.

7. For every truth you heard this evening, you will find that the opposite is also true. The most obvious example is your grandmother implying to you that "The early bird gets the worm" and found no contradiction when she also said: "Good things come to those that wait." So, just wait on the Lord and be of good courage but the Lord only helps those that help themselves. You heard several of the trustees say that integrity, kindness, and truth telling are vital ingredients of leadership, but you must know at least one person who lies often, has no empathy or integrity, spews hatred but is still regarded as an effective leader. It's complicated. But I hope you have all been inspired and enriched by what you heard this evening.

158.

Mr. Rogers on Making Goodness Attractive

August 21, 2019

Fred McFeely Rogers, host of *"Mr. Rogers' Neighborhood"* (a PBS TV show for preschoolers), died in 2003 at the ripe old age of 79. I loved watching this gentle soul walking down the stairs, putting on a cardigan sweater and assuring his audience that they were special, and inviting young and old to be his neighbor. The program was a wonderful respite for my children and me in the 70s. The show ran for 900 episodes before finally ending in 2001. According to Wikipedia:

> The program emphasized the child's developing psyche, feelings, sense of moral and ethical reasoning, civility, tolerance, sharing, and self-worth. Difficult topics such as the death of a family pet, sibling rivalry, the addition of a newborn into families, moving and enrolling in a new school, and divorce were also addressed.

Do you recall the opening song, *"I have always wanted to have a neighbor just like you? I've always wanted to live in a neighborhood with you. So, let's make the most of this beautiful day; since we're together, we might as well say: Would you be mine? Could you be mine? Won't you be my neighbor?"*

I purposely tried to position my temperament between Mark Twain and Mr. Rogers—brothers from another mother! I may have mentioned that Mark Twain wrote 100,000 pages in his lifetime but most of his books were embargoed until 100 years after his death to avoid embarrassing anyone. So, when his entire "works' ' were released in 2008, my wife bought the collection for Christmas and it took me a year to read it all, but it was well worth it. I have been enriched. While Mr. Rogers lacked Mark Twain's bite and sarcasm, his kind and gentle manner left a lasting impression. These are some of his important messages:

1. Think of the children first! Anyone who does anything to help a child is a hero. We should raise our children so that they can take pleasure in both their own heritage and the diversity of others. Invest in the welfare of the next generation.

2. Have an empathetic ear. Be attentive and listen keenly to others—especially children. "I have always called talking about feelings important. Knowing that our feelings are natural and normal can make it easier for us to share them."

3. The people we love the most make us feel the gladdest and the maddest! Love and anger are intricately related because of our high expectations from those we love. So, it is quite natural to have angry feelings toward members of our family and friends but since we have a permanent bond, they are also the easiest people to forgive. To err is human. Even good people sometimes offend each other. But just because someone you love is angry doesn't mean that it will be permanent. It may require corrections, apologies, forgiveness, repairs, and interventions but you will love again. According to Elizabeth Kubler Ross: When human beings contemplate their mortality, no one will say I wished I had spent more time working and accumulating wealth, we will all regret not spending more time with family.

4. Have the courage to be imperfect and accept who you are. While some will think of you as a sissy, it is OK to be sensitive.

5. Collect laughs and good memories. Music helps me to understand that several people playing different instruments can produce a magnificent symphony and individuals with different talents can sing together with one voice.

6. The people with disabilities are the "people who cannot find fulfillment in their lives, or those who have lost hope, who live in disappointment and bitterness and find in life no joy, no love." We are impoverished without each other.

7. Tradition is to human beings what instinct is to animals. Imagine the chaos if animals lost their instincts. That's how it would be if human beings were to lose all their traditions. We can learn from the successes and failures of our ancestors and fashion our responses to enhance attributes like generosity, altruism, compassion, sympathy, and empathy. "Civilization is a stream with banks. The stream is sometimes filled with human blood, stealing, shouting, and doing things historians usually record—while on the bank, unnoticed, people build homes, make love, raise children, sing songs, write poetry, and whittle statues. The story of civilization is the story of what happens on the banks."

According to his wife (Mrs. Joanne Rogers), While Fred was as human as the rest of us, he strived constantly to live up to this inspirational statement by Bessie Anderson Stanley:

> He has achieved success who has lived well, laughed often, and loved much, who has enjoyed the trust of pure women, the respect of intelligent men, and the love of little children, who has filled his niche and accomplished his task, who has left the world better than he found it, whether by an improved poppy, a perfect poem, or a rescued soul, who has never lacked appreciation of Earth's beauty or failed to express it, who has always looked for the best in others and given them the best he had, whose life was an inspiration, whose memory, a benediction.

We have only one life to live and will all leave the same way. We can choose to use our time on earth encouraging others or we can be hateful. Life is so much better for givers as well as receivers when we cherish our time together. Love will always conquer hate; peace will triumph over war and justice will prove to be more powerful than greed and avarice. As for Mr. Rogers, he liked me just the way I am.

159.
Nobody Blames Themselves

August 28, 2019

I was having lunch today with a friend and he made the observation that "Nobody blames themselves" when things go wrong. I responded that I think it is mostly true that we commonly blame others for our mistakes and bad outcomes, but I have also known people who love to take all the blame? In fact, there are people who cannot wait for something to go wrong so they can take the blame. "It's all my fault. I never do anything right." Maybe they also live with manipulators who are skillful at shifting the blame for their own misdeeds.

"Projection" is probably the most common defense mechanism—when someone attributes their failures to someone else because they don't have the ability to find fault with themselves or anything they do. I am OK but you are not so hot—you, on the other hand, screw up all the time. However, if you insist on winning all your arguments, just be aware that you are living with a bunch of losers. Is this the way to build self-confidence and ego strength in the members of your family? Whenever you win an argument with your husband or wife, you belittle them. Isn't your job to build them up?

On the other hand, we have people who see the good in others and play the victim—self-hatred. It's my fault that the kids are such a mess. It's my fault we missed the bus… we lost the game…our marriage didn't work out…the business failed…I lost my job…I lost our money on the stock market…we don't have enough money… the deal fell apart…we missed the sale… I was robbed. Do you remember Linus?

With the goal of soothing our ruffled feathers and disgust with unpleasant outcomes we make up excuses, rationalize and justify. I was hungry. I was sick. I was tired. I was drunk. I was high. The Devil made me do it. It was just not my day. The stars are aligned against me. I am only human. I am not perfect. I am bi-polar. He hit me first. I got it from my mother. It was way beyond my control. It was an act of God.

There are also those who blame their misfortunes on inanimate objects. It's a damn computer. I just cannot cook with these pots and the flame is very inconsistent. Whenever I watch tennis or golf, inevitably when the player misses a shot, he looks at the racket or club and sometimes they even smash one, two or all of them. Ladies and gentlemen, "It's the Indian, it's not the arrow."

Even though I am always tempted to blame others when s--t happens and hog the credit when I win, (Its only human) I do try to take responsibility and the consequences for whatever happens without making excuses and blaming others. That does not mean I don't try not to get fired from a job I want or talk the officer who pulled me over out of writing a ticket. I've always put myself in a position to solve problems and refuse to be the victim of circumstances. We have power over what happens to us and there are at least 12 solutions to every problem. You are the solution. I should not have been speeding in the first place or did a better job with my job. Just maybe, if we ate less of the wrong foods and exercised more often, we wouldn't have to come up with excuses for our obesity and the inevitable illness that follows. We would have less need to justify and make up excuses if we practiced "preventive strategies" in all our endeavors. We can exercise more and have the outcomes we want. Finally, practice makes perfect. We tend to do best at what we do most.

160.
Can Change in a Moment (Man Proposes but God Disposes)

September 5, 2019

My wife and I watched the movie, "The Backup Plan" with Jennifer Lopez the other night and it brought to mind something Woody Allen once said: "If you want to make God laugh, tell him about your plans." Ms. Lopez's character was about 36 years old and had no prospect of a boyfriend, husband, or anyone willing to father the children she desperately wanted. So, she went to a fertility clinic and paid to be inseminated with the sperm from an anonymous donor. As soon as she became pregnant, she met the man of her dreams and I mean the perfect guy who wanted to marry her and father her children except that she was already pregnant. Without revealing too much of the plot, it gets complicated, but they do end up married and lived happily ever after. Did I happen to mention that this was a Hollywood movie? In any case, my own life can attest to the fact that God does have a sense of humor and He is still in charge.

My grandmother clearly recognized who was in control by punctuating every plan with: "God willing." What are we going to do tomorrow Granny? "God willing and the creek don't rise, we will..." The Jewish way to express this is, "I'm yirtza hashem," fully recognizing that if God does not will it, it will not happen.

Is this an assault on our free will? This is an endless debate about whether God is in control or whether we make our own decisions or at least He gave us free will. There is no end to this conversation. How do you react when a six-year child tells you that she is going to be an astronaut when she grows up? We laugh. Why? We recognize how naive it is. As adults, we are just as naive about our plans. Did anyone plan to travel to Florida or the Bahamas last week? While the Lord helps those who help themselves and rewards the bold, when will we recognize that almost everything is beyond our control? Some call it serendipity, fate, good luck, or bad luck, but our Father in Heaven still holds the keys to our future—tomorrow and forever.

James 4:13-16:

> 13 Come, now, you who say: "Today or tomorrow we will travel to this city and will spend a year there, and we will do business and make some profit,"

14 whereas you do not know what your life will be like tomorrow. For you are a mist that appears for a little while and then disappears.

15 Instead, you should say: "If Jehovah wills, we will live and do this or that."

16 But now you take pride in your arrogant boasting. All such boasting is wicked."

I was amused by the story of a wealthy gentleman who worked up to 20 hours per day doing his business and making a fortune while his chauffeur and the rich man's wife were having an affair. So, eventually the rich man had a heart attack and died. The wife and the chauffeur married and when the chauffeur was interviewed, he said: "All this time I thought I was working for my master and came to find out he was working for me."

Proverbs 27:1:

Do not boast about tomorrow, for you do not know what a day will bring.

Life never turns out the way we plan it.
Plan all you want but God will always have the final say.

161.

Our Fractured Politics: Let's not Buy into the Binary

September 12, 2019

Almost no one is untouched by the rupture in our politics these days. At the extremes, we all know about disaffected young men who are lashing out violently against their fellow citizens. In addition to the tragedy of killing people, they destroyed their own lives and left a lifetime of pain for their friends and relatives as well as the friends and relatives of their victims. Young men who should be romancing lady friends, preparing for a career, getting married and raising a family will be rotting in prison or executed, leaving a nightmare of suffering in their wake. There have always been disaffected young men. In a different, more civil time, there would have been institutions that could have brought many of these men back into the fold.

I wrote before about the fact that male elephants that grow up without role models become rogue, unruly and create havoc. They throw their weight around and kill everything in their path, but when alpha males are around, they get it that they have to keep their rage in check. The larger males spar with them, help them to expend some of their youthful energy and give them time for their raging hormones to settle down.

I know, of course, that people are not elephants but there is a lesson here in the importance of intergenerational influences that prepare our youth to take their place in a civilized society. Teaching and modeling hate is always a disaster. Love and respect for all humanity will assure everyone a future.

Politics is also contributing to fractured relationships and divorces. People who have been close friends almost all their lives are now not on speaking terms. Family members no longer talk and are alienated from each other. This isn't only about Kelly Ann Conway and husband George, and Steve Miller's family has disowned him—even his own mother! Your family will probably not escape this acrimony either. Have we all gone mad? As I am writing this, I just learned that a young man in Alabama killed his entire family. I have no idea (at this point) what that was about.

Is it helpful to make a rule that no politics will be discussed at the dinner table? If so, then expect family members to become angry and spoil Thanksgiving and Christmas this year because everything is now political, and it cannot be avoided. Simply advocating for respect for humanity, truth and integrity, human rights, and cooperation with other nations has a tinge of politics.

In response to my column on how the South is abandoning "Southern hospitality" for New York City in-your-face bluntness, a friend told me:

> Yes. I don't like Trump's morals or how he does things, but the opposite is Jimmy Carter who exuded Southern charm and hospitality and he was our worst President. Everybody took advantage of us because he was so obsessed with being nice. I cannot believe he gave away the Panama Canal. I don't want my president to be nice. I like Trump because he just takes all the attack they can heap on him, and he keeps on ticking.

So, yes, there has to be a difference between being civil and being a doormat. As James Baldwin famously puts it, "We can disagree and still love each other, unless..." And of course, the whole argument is in the "unless." "Unless," he said, "your disagreement is rooted in my oppression and denial of my humanity and right to exist."

I think that goes for the dinner table too. Let's not have "no politics" at the dinner table. After all, everything is political and maybe that's ok. It is good for children to see their elders hashing out the issues of the day, really digging deep and coming to mutual understanding. So long as that conversation happens on a bedrock of love and shared values. Just treat everyone nice. If your Mama raised you right, it comes naturally.

We may disagree on whether kneeling during the anthem is an effective strategy for making a point, but I'm pretty sure we don't disagree that police have to be accountable to the communities they serve. We may disagree on whether a border wall would be an effective immigration strategy, but I'm pretty sure we don't disagree that whatever we do at the border should observe some minimal standards of humanity, and so on. Can you love someone and be angry at them at the same time? Definitely. It is called unconditional love.

We seem to have abandoned the diversity of ideas we once found acceptable. I disagree with you, but I will defend your right to say what you want. You may have a point there! According to Alan Landers, nothing short of the total elimination of Democrats will do. He may also believe Trump is our savior and the Chosen One. On the other hand, I saw a sign in someone's house: "If you voted for Trump, get the hell out of my house." I do not share these impulses. I don't buy into the binary. There is much that divides us, but these characterizations are not helpful. Before we become so hardened in our corners, shouldn't we be thinking about what is best for our country?

Can we get back to a civil discourse? Let's not do it your way or my way but the right way. If not, can we at least compromise? We used to find a way to do that.

162.

You Don't Need a Weatherman to Know Which Way the Wind Blows

September 19, 2019

First and foremost, we welcome two new family physicians to Thomaston. Drs. Corey and Meagan Fussell will be opening their office soon.

In 1969, Prosenjit Podder was being seen by a psychiatrist (Dr. Lawrence Moore) and in one of their sessions, he revealed plans to murder his girlfriend (Tatiana Tarasoff). At the time, Dr. Moore believed that he had an obligation to keep everything his patient divulged confidential. So, he tried to talk his patient out of carrying out his plans but did nothing else. When Mr. Podder did the wicked deed and killed Ms. Tarasoff with a knife (as promised), her family sued the psychiatrist and the court ruled and legislation followed that physicians have a duty to warn potential victims of serious danger to others, even without the perpetrator's permission. The duty to protect potential victims is more important than the doctor-patient confidentiality.

So, as this case evolved, we now generally recognize that physicians have a primary duty to provide care to their patients and keep any information they learn about them confidential, but they also have a duty to warn the public about potential harm from the patient as well as potential risks to which they may be exposed. It is not ethical for physicians to only "see patients." They also have an obligation to members of the community, so that they too may benefit from their vast knowledge. If the patient is sick, treat the patient; if the community is sick, treat the community.

Prevention is the best strategy for public health. Need I remind you that only 50 years ago, dentists only did fillings, pulled teeth, and replaced them with false teeth. As things evolved, we did a public health thing by adding fluoride to our drinking water; we encouraged everyone to schedule dental check-ups twice per year, and most importantly, "Colgate Toothpaste" made a great deal of money convincing people to brush and floss twice per day to prevent tooth decay and bad breath. Where have all the dental labs gone? It's a rare dentist who extracts teeth. My children are between 36 and 50 years old and not one of them ever had a toothache and will die with all their teeth intact. Teeth are built to last. When archaeologists recover 10,000-year-old cadavers, their teeth are still intact.

Please notice that we now have a registry for sex offenders. We are very good at taking dangerous criminals from our streets. If someone has an infectious disease, they will be isolated and treated. There are lots of alerts (weather and otherwise) that warn us of impending dangers. I would like to sound the alarm about how we are being buried in plastic that cannot be recycled and never deteriorate —ever!

In a busy pediatric practice (ZÖe Pediatrics); Dr. Stephanie Kong will never pass up an opportunity to educate the community. Whether there are two or three or thousands, she will take the time and make the effort to accept invitations to speak at churches, schools, day care centers or homes. She authored a book, *"A Minute for Your Health"* and for two years wrote a weekly pediatric column in *The Upson Beacon*. She is partnering with our health department on a telemedicine project and is always ready to address issues concerning clean water, clean air, and advocate for a conducive environment for kids to roam. Her mission statement is: "Children Do Not Have to Be Sick to Get Better."

While we are fortunate that Thomaston is a great place for children to grow into healthy, contributing members of society; we don't need to worry about the quality of our air and water; we just bought a million-dollar fire truck that is at our beck and call. I am very proud of that. There are no polluting industries, and fish and wildlife are abundant. We even have beautiful sunrises, sunsets, flowers, and flowering trees everywhere. We have good schools and plenty of opportunities for making a contribution. Can you tell I love this place that has been home to us for eight years? But don't become complacent. We have an obesity epidemic on our hands and the rate of heart disease, cancer and strokes continues to accelerate. We should be alarmed. So much more can be done to prevent disease.

Do you know how to boil a frog to death without protest? You start him off in cold water and increase the temperature one degree per day. He will not notice when the pot boils over and kills him. That is how risk factors become diabetes, heart attacks and strokes.

The point of this column is that we have so many resources that we are underutilizing. We have about 30 doctors in Thomaston. In addition to providing good care for their patients, they are all ready, willing, and able to do their civic duty to engage people and share their knowledge and experience. They can all identify the earliest signs of danger, causes of injury, and illness before they harm patients. Are we ignoring global warming at our peril? All our doctors subscribe to Ezekiel 33:2-4:

> Son of man, speak to the sons of your people and say to them, 'If I bring a sword upon a land, and the people of the land take one man from among them and make him their watchman, and he sees the sword coming upon the land and blows on the trumpet and warns the people, then he who hears the sound of the trumpet and does not take warning, and a sword comes and takes him away, his blood will be on his own head'.

163.
Are Community Churches Facing Extinction?

October 3, 2019

Fewer people are attending churches—even in the Bible Belt! Several people spoke to me about wanting to understand the issue more fully. It turns out that less than 25% of Americans now attend church at least once per month. Churches are valuable institutions that make a positive impact on our communities. This cannot stand. Where will you turn when the pillow of the community is not there for you?

Here are some relevant data primarily from Aaron Earls (Lifeway Research) from his article "Are Churches growing or declining" (2019) While mega churches have increasing attendance, the opposite is happening in community churches.

1. Most protestant churches had more than ten new people join in the past year and most of them join, attend for a while, and don't come back.
2. Most churches have fewer than 100 members. Only 10% have more than 250 in attendance weekly.
3. Collections are declining. The faithful few are not stepping up to compensate for fewer members. Congregants gave more (as a percent of their income) during the depression than today.

4. While 70% of Americans identify themselves as Christians, only 2% of young people show up regularly when they are not coerced to attend by their parents. Apparently, they believe in God and try to live by Christian principles, but they are not joining and buying into the regular church attendance habit when they become emancipated.

5. Fewer children are being dedicated, baptized, or christened; fewer marriages and funerals are taking place at places of worship under the supervision of a religious leader.

6. Regarding attrition, about 2% of church members either are not physically able to attend or meet their maker each year. Many more just stop going.

7. There are some who only turn to God when they are sick, arrested, lose a job, or are otherwise in desperate straits and don't go to church when everything is going well for them.

The canary in the coal mine is England, that is now one of the most irreligious countries on earth, with only 30% of its citizens calling themselves "religious" and less than 2% attending weekly services. While attendance shoots up at Christmas and Easter, in the last 10 years, the number of people attending services has fallen by 12% and less than half the levels of the 1960s.

We struggle to attract young people. Is it weekend sports? Stores open seven days per week? Schisms? Conflicts over politics, gay rights and the role of women, sexual abuse of children by church leaders, dictatorial bullying tactics, and too much harassment to increase collections, demand of inflexible members who only want "old time religion" and always criticizing weakening Biblical authority and traditional teachings? Some like whooping and shouting in the pulpit and some don't.

Young people are more mobile and accustomed to traveling long distances for experiences that are customized to their needs and wants, and they are more willing to leave their "home church" where the family attended. But none of those phenomena account for the increasing number of people who count themselves "spiritual" or even explicitly Christian but are part of the swelling ranks of the "unchurched." They want "authenticity." Would you tolerate a restaurant that claims to have "authentic" southern BBQ and instead serves yogurt and watercress sandwiches? No, because you know what barbecue is supposed to taste and look like. Maybe you would substitute chicken for the ribs, but it would still be barbecue. Everyone expects the church to stand up for the brotherhood of man, taking care of the least of these, morality, integrity, truth telling, honesty, kindness, and belief in Jesus Christ. On this there should be no compromise. My experience is that our young people are smart and not afraid of doing some hard thinking. Do the leaders in your church mostly offer criticisms and judgment instead of empathy and support?

Churches must make sure that when people make the effort to attend, they leave believing that their time and effort, training, and assets wouldn't more fruitfully be spent on something else. Many are very comfortable with being "political," just not partisan. They would have marched with Martin Luther King. They would have hidden Anne Frank. The church must not be mealy-mouthed about standing up to institutional racism or entrenched generational poverty or rampant violence or environmental degradation just because it doesn't endorse a candidate or a particular party. The Jesus that drove the traders from the temple would not want a defanged and neutered church, too polite to talk politics.

A week has 168 hours. If Sunday service is just two hours, how is your church reaching people for the other 166? "Religion—imperfect, troubled, always changing, conflicted, always surviving, always under assault—still manages to hang on." (Andrew Greeley) We need a renewal program. How about a revival or even a resurrection?

164.
Nature Versus Nurture: Both Matter

October 10, 2019

Believe it or not, there is a wonderful lady who has lived in Thomaston (on Goshen Road) all her life and excels at growing Bonsai trees. What is that you ask? It is taking an oak tree (or any tree for that matter) that should grow to be over 100 feet, keeping it alive but stunting its growth to less than three feet in over 100 years. In Japan, they are passed down from generation to generation for hundreds of years.

Thanks to my friend, Robert Gallman, for introducing me to Ms. Harolyn Castleberry. I enjoyed making her acquaintance as well as the opportunity to see the

Bonsai trees she has nurtured for 15 years. As a horticulturist, she went to a show at the Atlanta Botanical Gardens in 2005 where there was an exhibit of Bonsai trees. She was hopelessly hooked, got excited about it, bought a "how to" book and now has about 20 intricately beautiful Bonsais under her care. My favorite is her giant redwood that is two feet tall—absolutely beautiful! It even has a bird's nest in it! I would love for everyone in Thomaston to see these beautiful creations.

Ms. Castleberry's hobby brings into focus the old question of what is more important, nature (your genes) or how and where you grow up? In Jamaica, it is described as your *"broughtupsy."* If you encounter a family and for generation after generation, they are all obese (trait heritability), is it because they are genetically disposed or that the meal preparation and portion size was passed down from one generation to the next?

It takes a great deal of skill and knowledge to fool Mother Nature. Ms. Castlelberry must have an understanding of how a tree grows and be careful not to kill the tree, prune it back and feed it with just the right amount of nutrients. You may have thought Bonsai (planted in a container) originated in Japan, but it was China that first started this art form. You should see the results of their bioengineered goldfish!

I learned from my brother (Earl) who is a forester in Washington state that there is a great deal of effort going into developing "Super Trees" that grow faster, taller and live longer. So, while the Bonsai aficionados are dwarfing trees, there are those who are busy trying to grow 300-foot giants that may reach the sky. Genetic engineering and nutritional components nurture or impede development. For human beings, environmental conditions will have a significant influence on athletic performance, as well as height, weight, and strength. Will a particular child become the star or fail to thrive—A Bonsai or a super tree? Why is Jack Nicklaus the greatest golfer of all time and his sons cannot make it on the PGA tour? It is all well and good that your children have doting parents and grandparents, in order for your eagles to soar, they must also have doting pediatricians.

I made the point in previous columns that at the moment of birth, just by knowing the parents and where they live, I can predict what a child will become 30 years later. I can easily predict the language and dialect, the foods (grits and barbeque), the clothes and whether s/he will bless the food before meals, how much formal education s/he will earn, how tall, shoe size and how gracious, healthy, or sickly? So, is this a result of what s/he came into the world possessing or his/her experience after she arrives? Nature is acquired by genetic or hereditary influences (biological determinism). Nurture on the other hand is those things that are influenced by the environment. I will contend that every person you encounter and every meal you eat has an influence on you.

There are families that produce most of the criminals, violent and hostile people in society. Their children fail to thrive, and they all have short life expectancies. Other families produce geniuses, scholars and people of distinction who live long meaningful lives. How come? Sometimes one member of the family does the unexpected. Why?

The real issue isn't nature versus nurture, but how nature and nurture interplay to produce the diversities and uniformities of human beings.

Matt Ridley (an English anthropologist) believes that all human beings have the capacity to learn and adapt to the society in which s/he is raised. Cultural behavior is learned but always subject to modifications and even individual experiences. Our temperaments, dispositions, and personalities, regardless of genetic propensities are developed within one's social group and determine who we become. But we all know families where all the children are "totally" different and then there are other families who enjoy the same traits and personalities. *"Yes, he acts just like one of them, Hightowers."*

165.
Spirit Of the Heart Awards Banquet 2019

October 17, 2019

I am feeling "big up," proud and elated by being awarded the 2019 Spirit of the Heart Legacy Award at a banquet (with 500 in attendance) at the Intercontinental Hotel in Los Angeles on Saturday, Oct. 12. Others who were honored included Lamar Rucker (actor and advocate), Shaquille O'Neal, Lee Elder (professional golfer) and Dr. Karol Watson (distinguished cardiologist), UCLA. That is pretty good company. In her introduction, Dr. Elizabeth Ofili, chairman of the board, said the following:

"The Legacy award goes to Dr. Waine Kong in recognition of his exceptional commitment to the mission and vision of the Association of Black Cardiologists who made extraordinary contributions to reduce cardiovascular disease in minority communities. Dr. Kong is currently the president of the Heart Institute of the Caribbean Foundation and CEO emeritus for the Association of Black Cardiologists.

Dr. Kong graduated from Simpson College in Indianola, Iowa where he attended on a track scholarship and earned his MA in educational psychology from American University in Washington DC, He went on to earn an advanced graduate specialist (A.G.S.) certificate in special education from the University of Maryland and a PhD from Walden University. Later, he would attend the Dickinson School of Law and after graduating, joined the Georgia Bar.

He was an assistant professor of Human Development at the University of the District of Columbia, the vice president of Provident Hospital in Baltimore, the executive director of the Urban Cardiology Research Center in Baltimore and was the CEO of the Association of Black Cardiologists for 22 years before his retirement in 2008. He and his wife, Dr. Stephanie Kong, opened ZÖe Pediatrics in 2012 in Thomaston, Georgia. and along with ten other pediatricians, now serve 200 children per day from six locations.

Dr. Kong has visited over 100 countries and is an avid golfer who recently shot even par (four better than his age). He served as president of Kiwanis (Thomaston) for two years. He is a member of the board of trustees for Gordon State College (Barnesville, Ga.) and has been a weekly columnist for three years for The Upson Beacon. He is also a deacon at Greater Mount Zion Baptist Church and director of education for Alpha Phi Alpha in Columbus, Ga.

Dr. Kong is a great advocate for increasing the training of minority cardiologists. Under his leadership, ABC introduced its signature Seven Steps to a Healthy Heart. This campaign centered on research-supported steps individuals can take to reduce the development of cardiovascular disease and other health issues. For nearly two decades, this highly requested resource remains available in English, Spanish, print and digital formats.

ABC's most recognized campaign, "Children Should Know Their Grandparents," is the brainchild of Dr. Kong. This campaign, initiated in 2001, is still referenced today [18 years later]. It was designed to enlist family members to fight against heart disease in the African American community. The tools used to support this initiative included "*A Guide to A Healthy Heart*," a 30-minute educational video starring actor Robert Guillaume, and a 44-page companion guidebook. "Children Should Know Their Grandparents" captured headlines in nine target markets and generated more than 9,937,562 impressions. More than 50,000 visitors logged on to ABC's website and viewed the "Children Should Know Their Grandparents" video. ABC fielded over 100 requests for the video and guidebook program to be sent to local libraries and community centers. *The Journal of American College of Cardiology* wrote an editorial about the program, commending ABC for its ongoing commitment and said, "It is a different kind of program because it addresses the needs and culture of the African-American community."

One of ABC's most enduring programs is its community outreach. Dr. Kong and ABC founding member and past president, Dr. Elijah Saunders, pioneered ABC's community health programs beginning in the late '70s. With a five-year grant from the NHLBI in 1979, they started training volunteers from hundreds of churches in Maryland to monitor blood pressure of the churches' members and make appropriate referrals. In 1980, as a way to more directly reach African American men, they used leftover equipment and literature to organize 20 barbers in six barbershops as high blood pressure control centers as well. This innovative approach paved the way for proliferation of church-based, barbershop and beauty salon programs throughout the U.S. Over a period of more than two decades, Drs. Saunders and Kong worked as a team to further develop and expand the reach of church and barbershop programs through ABC and establish scholarships around their efforts. Though it now bears its signature name, "Spirit of the Heart," it has evolved and expanded since its early beginnings, extending its reach to schools, corporate wellness programs and even an outreach on Capitol Hill for Congress.

Today, he and his wife own "ZÖe Pediatrics" in Middle Georgia. They have four children and are grandparents to six grandchildren. Dr. Kong continues to work to increase the life expectancy of people with or at risk for cardiovascular disease, diabetes, and stroke in his role as president of the Heart Institute of the Caribbean Foundation headquartered in his native Jamaica and ZÖe Pediatrics Foundation in Thomaston, GA.

The Association of Black Cardiologists is proud to honor Dr. Basil Waine Kong with the 2019 Legacy Award."

166.

Loyalty Never Ends: Is Loyalty Important to You?

October 24, 2019

Do you only show loyalty when it is benefitting you? A friend of mine confessed that for him, "loyalty" is the most important characteristic of his relationships. "I put a high premium on loyalty. You betray me and I am done with you! How can you overlook someone not standing by you when you are depending on them? When two people pledge their fealty, allegiance, and loyalty, you should be able to count on that person through thick and thin. What I expect from friends and family is honesty, support and to meet their obligations." "The strength of a family, like the strength of an army, is in its loyalty to each other" (Mario Puzo).

The Japanese value loyalty above all else. On our visit to Tokyo 10 years ago, I was introduced to "Hachiko", the statue of a dog who walked his master (a professor) to the Shibuya Train Station and would wait for his master to return each evening so they could walk back home together. His master died at work and his faithful dog would not leave the station, eat, or drink until he died. Statues of Hachiko can now be found beside his master's grave, at Shibuya, as well as the National Museum of Science in Ueno, a very popular site for visitors, symbolizing their commitment to loyalty.

The Samurai took an oath of loyalty (bushido) to their lord (Daimya) and country by duty and honor, and they readily and willingly gave up their lives in the service of their master. "Where the battle rages, there the loyalty of the soldier is proved." (Martin Luther) When I am being abandoned by everybody else, a loyal friend will stand by me and never, never, never throw me under the bus. I show the same loyalty to family and friends. The sensation of belonging never goes away and they always inspire me to be my best self.

I have lived in a lot of places and seen a great deal of this country and nowhere is loyalty more pronounced than in Georgia, epitomized by President Carter and his wife Rosalyn. They have staying power because they are so loyal and faithful to each other. No doubt, many people betray the oaths of their marriage but while it may be forgiven, it is never forgotten. Whenever I have conversations about loyalty, I seem to recall an interview with a Nascar driver who was asked why he still drank Sanka coffee when there are so many other options now available, and he replied that his hero and mentor always drank Sanka and it is out of loyalty to him why he continues to drink Sanka.

When I share a meal with a loyal friend, it doesn't matter what the meal is, my taste buds are heightened, and everything tastes wonderful. When I take a walk in the company of those who have proven their loyalty, my hearing is enhanced, and the songbirds are glorious. Whenever I spend time with people who treat my relationship with them as a priority and will always be there for me as an advocate and defender, "God is in His Heaven, and all is right with the world."

Ruth 1: 16-17

> Entreat me not to leave you or to turn back from following you. For wherever you go, I will go and where you lodge, I will lodge. Your people shall be my people and your God my God. Where you die, I will die and there I will be buried.

167.
The Fragility of Life

October 31, 2019

It is early morning, and I am writing this column from Plantation, Florida. I am visiting a family friend who is not at her best. A year ago, she was diagnosed with cancer, and it has become progressively worse. In fact, we fear the worst as medical science has run out of options that could improve her prognosis.

When I arrived, her husband greeted me with a long bear hug and tears as we fell into each other's arms, and we continued to have our arms around each other as he directed me to where his wife was uncomfortably resting. I gave hugs and kisses for the patient as I sat beside her to offer whatever comfort I could. She is not despondent, as her husband tells me that people around the globe have been praying for healing. I believe in intercessory prayers, so I also held her hands and added my own prayers. In fact, my wife and I have been praying unceasingly since we learned about her deteriorating condition.

I am having difficulty seeing the strong, beautiful, vivacious, athletic woman I admired as she has no hair, and she could now be described as "skin and bones." I tried to relieve her back pain with a message but mostly, we talked about the "good old days" when she beat me at golf in Mombasa, Kenya (with elephants and monkeys for neighbors) and the dozen or so amazing overseas trips we took together. I suspect she forgot about pain while we were laughing and reminiscing about the good times. Do you understand why it is so important to visit the sick?

We moved from Sacramento to Miami while hurricane Andrew ravaged South Florida in 1992. So, when we arrived, the house we had rented was severely damaged, but their home was intact. So, their good fortune was also our good fortune. We stayed with them until the house we rented in Kendall was repaired. The hospitality was wonderful and harmonious.

Have you seen the movie, "Ghosts in the Dark" with Michael Douglas? It was based on the book "Man-eaters of Tsavo." It described the building of the railway through the jungles of Kenya. When they reached Tsavo, a pride of lions feasted on the workers daily and the railroad project was in serious jeopardy of being abandoned as the workers ran away out of fear of the lions. The Michael Douglas character was hired to kill the lions which he did very dramatically. Do you recall the cave with the bones of about 100 men? In any case, while we were visiting Tsavo (not to kill lions but to take pictures of the amazing animals), we all took the opportunity to read this famous novel. So, at breakfast one morning, Tessa announced that she had added a chapter to the book. You may need some help deciphering this.

On another occasion, her husband (a wonderful storyteller) who often regaled us with curious adventures, asked the group if they had ever heard of the "Hellawee" people? We had not, so he went on to tell us that they are structurally very short people but unfortunately lived in high bush country, so they frequently ask each other "Where the Hell are, we?" "Where the Hell are, we?" So, I was trying to tell this joke to my "know it all" auntie. But, as soon as I asked, "Have you heard of the Hellawee people? She immediately responded that she knew them very well and proceeded to tell us about their culture, their dance, and the art they produced. My wife looked at me with an incredulous stare that said, "Don't you dare finish that story." I couldn't.

As much as my wife and I love to dance, Laurie and Tessa were the first on the dance floor and the last to leave it. Her laughter was infectious. They were very happy as a couple, and we were all cheered by their presence. We mistakenly believed we were indestructible and never thought we would fall short of our expectations. As he once studied for the priesthood, Laurie was a great philosopher. After ravishing shrimp rotis for dinner and his wife had gone to sleep, we did what we always did when we got together—stayed up all night drinking Scotch and contemplating the great questions—never feeling tired or sleepy. The plethora of subjects we discussed included trying to come up with more accurate and scientific ways to say "sunrise" and "sunset." After all, the sun doesn't actually come up and down. In fact, "sunrise" and "sunset" has nothing at all to do with anything the sun does while the earth revolves. But the discussion was futile and all our attempts to describe this phenomenon more accurately was very unromantic and even silly. Sometimes science gets in the way. So, we decided it was okay to continue saying "sunrise" and "sunset."

This is most likely the sunset of my friend's life. While I have had bouts with my own demise, my fervent hope is that she will just vigorously jump out of her bed (cancer free) and be made whole again. Oh, how I would love to see that. So, I pray for a miracle. Children deserve to know their grandparents and husbands should have their life companions—forever. We love you, Tessa!

The point is, life is fragile, so, while we can, say "I love you" a lot! (Jim Taylor)

168.
The Fragility of Life Again?

November 7, 2019

The moon has waxed and waned a hundred times since you opened your door and welcomed my wife and me here. When I explained how fortunate we were to locate here to old friends, especially the ones I ran into on my visit to Los Angeles to pick up my "Legacy Award" a few weeks ago, my friend Malcolm said to me: "Waine, what do you get when you mix cream with lemonade? A small southern town will never fit the lifestyle of someone who traveled the world and experienced the best that life has to offer." I responded that, "Actually, my wife and I are very happy living in Thomaston."

Malcolm then said, "Actually Waine, you are at the sweet spot in your life, you retired with plenty of life in the old boy; you made a miraculous recovery from your heart attack; your wife and kids are dedicated to you; you are playing the best golf of your life; your children are successful—and your six grandchildren are beautiful and let you spoil them. The Lord is blessing you son. It wouldn't matter where you live. My theory about how people decide when and who they marry has a lot to do with who they are with when things are going good for them. If you are healthy and happy, you are inclined to appreciate everything about your life. If you are sick and miserable, you are going to complain. When you eat fish, if you are happy, you spit out the bones. If you are unhappy, you choke on them." Well, maybe!

Thomaston is an incredible place! No, we don't have a symphony, a museum, a zoo, amusement parks, nightclubs, fine restaurants, upscale shopping, access to a beach and someone just pointed out that someone can grow up here and never ride an escalator! But we also don't have crooked politicians, traffic jams, pollution, paid parking, crime, and hostility. Our playgrounds and parks are the best. Weatherwise, we are in the goldilocks spot (never too hot or cold) but just right most of the time. Natural disasters we have none. When we want a city experience, Atlanta, Macon, and Columbus are just an hour away.

What's not to love about Thomaston? I just had a great workout at our fabulous Wellness Center where I ran into Frank and Jack and picked up "free" pecans along the way. Our Archives, TUAC and the Historical Society do a good job promoting our history, culture, and the arts. I can buy jackfruit, papaya, mangoes, avocadoes, and fresh seafood anytime of the year. I love to wander the local stores and pick up things I don't need. As I wrote in several previous columns, my favorite time of the year is spring, when the wisteria bloom, but I enjoy the entire year, except when it doesn't rain. I can play golf 350 days per year. I am embraced by tall Georgia pines, flowers all through the year and abundant songbirds. While my tomatoes didn't do so well last year, several people offered me free vegetables from their garden.

Thanks to the house Ms. Sylvia built with great attention to detail, we live in a fabulous house in Johnston Heights that my wife has decorated with great care. Whether it is church (Greater Mount Zion Baptist Church where I am a deacon), Thomaston Kiwanis, playing golf with the Raintree Rascals, sitting in on a board meeting at Gordon College, I enjoy making a difference as well as the company of friends. I have a substantial life. When my wife and I take our morning walks along Nelson Drive looking at the woodland across the babbling brook, we often see a herd of deer grazing. As much as I hate them for eating my vegetables, they look absolutely amazing with the morning dew.

The one thing that gives me pause is how helpful, intelligent, and engaging the people of Thomaston are. So why is there so much fervor for Donald Trump? I just cannot explain that one. I am totally baffled. You hate lying and obscenity. You have integrity and treat your neighbors as you would have them treat you. You believe in equality and justice for all. You treat children like precious gifts from God and loyalty to family and friends is sacred. So, why? When everybody thought the world was flat it was still a big ball. Do you count yourself among the people who are happily sitting on the railroad track ignoring the signs that the train (global warming) is bearing down on us?

While I await my true home in Heaven, there are so many nice people here in Thomaston, I am just as happy to live here until it's time to set down my burdens and be with my Lord. We have a wonderful city. I certainly enjoy southern charm and hospitality. Don't you?

169.
Atonement, Justice and Grace

November 14, 2019

President Abraham Lincoln tells the story of a dying man who, encouraged by his wife, invited his lifetime enemy to visit so that he could make amends, bury the hatchet, and hopefully die in peace. All went well and through laughter and tears forgave each other for a lifetime of hateful conduct, embraced, but as the old rival made his way out, the dying gentleman shouted: "I hope you know that if I recover, I am taking back everything I just said, you no good piece of ..." We have all fallen short of what our better selves would have us to do. So, you were young; maybe high or drunk; you just lost your mind; used bad judgment; you were just a jerk; you were in bad company; you were in the heat of passion, or you were just plain evil, and the Devil made you do it. You did something awful. Somebody needed you and you didn't help. You were offensive. You may have even done something illegal and should have been rejected by society, locked up and otherwise punished for your misdeeds, but it was never reported.

Now you are older and wiser, you sincerely regret what you did, and the remorse is killing you. You are sorry and want to apologize. You listen to "In the Air Tonight" and you think it's about you. You cannot sleep and you have had no contact with the person you offended. Is there hope for forgiveness or mercy for your sin sick soul?

After apartheid ended in South Africa, Nelson Mandela and Bishop Tutu organized "Truth and Reconciliation" committees. To quote the great musical innovator John Lennon, "You say you want a revolution." But up until then, revolution had meant busting out the guillotine and rolling heads. The deal in the new South Africa was, if you did horrible things, instead of the legal route (arrest, trial and imprisonment or execution), you could confess your sins to the committee, show remorse and contrition to the people who suffered from your crimes and be forgiven if you promise to go forth and sin no more. There were reparations, but they were designed to help the aggrieved person, or their survivors get back up on their feet, and not enough to crush the offender. I believe the program was a success even if many believed that some of these crimes were so heinous that they were unforgivable, and the perpetrators should have paid with their own lives.

Yom Kipper (Jewish Day of Atonement), an annual day of fasting, introspection, and repentance, was celebrated in October this year and signifies a day when Jewish people are to confess their sins, ask for forgiveness from God as well as those they have offended, and make reparations. The ancient Hebrew tradition also calls for a periodic "jubilee" in which all ledgers, both tangible and moral, are reset to zero—a universal absolution of all debts. This is a reminder that score-keeping among our fellow humans may have its uses on a day-to-day basis, to allow finance and savings, but in the sight of God, is only useful to the degree that it makes us and our society better and can pass to the next generation.

Among Catholics, the faithful would flagellate themselves (beat themselves up) with a whip in order to pay for their sins as well as their "continued sin, depravity, and vileness in the eyes of God" (Sarah Osborn). By the way, the word "discipline" comes from the same root word as "disciple" and is the name of a whip made with seven cords representing the seven deadly sins with three knots in each representing Jesus Christ dying and the number of days he remained in the tomb for the sins of mankind.

The Amish have no capacity for revenge. Regardless of the crimes against them, they immediately and readily forgive the perpetrators.

To be forgiven is a universal human need. Some have lost their minds because of the burden of sin. When we do wrong, it offends our conscience. Fortunately, God sent his Son to pay for our sins; so, we can confess, ask for and receive complete forgiveness and live life to the fullest regardless of what we may have done. What an amazing promise.

I am thinking of John Newton, the captain of a slave ship who for years perpetrated suffering on thousands of people who then found God and composed the hymn "Amazing Grace." God can use you even if you are guilty of horrendous crimes. "If your brother sins, rebuke him, and if he repents, forgive him" (Luke 17:3).

If you ask others to forgive you, you must be willing to forgive those who trespass against you. When we screw up and offend others, one can feel remorse and make a genuine apology and not be forgiven if the victim is not ready to forgive. One may also not ask for forgiveness and still be forgiven and the victim may want to let bygones be bygones regardless of what the perpetrator did. Wounds heal and you don't need permission from the perpetrators to forgive them.

"Forgiveness has nothing to do with absolving a criminal of his crime. It has everything to do with relieving oneself of the burden of being a victim--letting go of the pain and transforming oneself from victim to survivor." (C.R. Strahan)

170.
Avoid the Temptation to Dismiss Scholars

November 28, 2019

As opposed to our traditional value for education and the respect of those with terminal degrees, I am sensing lately, a deprecation and dismissal of education and science in particular. "No matter what these know-it-all scientists say, (notwithstanding the fact that Venice is flooding), there is no global warming." I suppose it started with the questioning of Biblical "facts" and creationism by scientists who could state with certainty that the sun is much older than the earth even if the Bible says the opposite.

One out of four Americans still believe the sun revolves around the earth and will not be told otherwise. The earth is over five billion years old. The emergence of human beings didn't take place until less than two million years ago. In other words, our species didn't exist on the face of the earth for 99.9% of earth's history. We are 'Johnny come lately' and were definitely not around when the dinosaurs roamed the earth. So, typically, the anti-intellectual response is, "What do they know? That is ridiculous! These educated fools are replete with book knowledge but no common sense. Everyone knows that in seven days, God created the earth, the firmaments and everything in it—just like it says in the book of Genesis."

Anti-intellectualism can be extreme. Sensing a threat to his power from those who would question his crazy ideas, the Pol Pot regime systematically killed everyone (killing fields) in their country who was college educated. Francisco Franco killed 200,000 for the sin of having studied at a university. The other Tribes in Nigeria banded together and almost wiped out their Igbo brethren because they were the intellectuals who provided electricity, water, infrastructure, and a government. Did they care that after the Civil War they didn't have electricity or water?

In the United States, we require schools to be open 180 days per year (six hours per day). Japan requires 220 days (eight hours per day). How do you think our graduates will compete with their Japanese counterparts? Do you really want to suppress the educational ambitions of our children? The Amish, fearing that educated children would abandon their culture and lifestyle, got the Supreme Court to make an exception so their children could not be required to go to school after grade six. In a few countries, Muslim girls put their lives on the line just because they want to go to school. Do you 'poo' your children's ambition for an education and still want them to compete in the world economy?

Academic elitism is the other view that if you are not 'learned' you don't know anything and are not worthy of respect. "It is better to be considered a fool than to open your mouth and remove all doubt." Some even believe that educated people (the elite) should control education and make all political decisions for our country. This is an even greater sin.

Obviously, we all know stupid educated people as well as very bright and intuitive people who have very little formal education. It is also worthy of note that very few of the billionaires in the United States are college educated—John D. Rockefeller, Henry Ford, Tiger Woods, and Bill Gates. There is obviously something stifling about being educated. How many doctors, lawyers and professional people have a net worth of over $1 Billion? None! To understand this concept more thoroughly, read: *Rich Dad; Poor Dad* by Robert Kiyosaki. His father was a nuclear physicist who died in debt. His uncle was a high school dropout and became a millionaire.

A hundred years ago the literacy rate (people who can read and write) was less than 20%. We did such an amazing job that now three quarters of people around the world are literate mainly through the efforts of missionaries and religious organizations.

When evangelicals were the salt of the earth, they founded educational institutions like Harvard, Princeton, Yale, Dartmouth, College of William and Mary and Rutgers University. Scholarship was the top priority for the evangelicals in years past. I attended Simpson College, a Methodist college in Indianola, Iowa where George Washington Carver (invented peanut butter and a hundred other uses for the peanut) also attended. The recent denigration of science in no way reflects the fervor for scholarship pioneered by these early evangelicals.

According to Rosie Beal-Preston in her book, *How the Christian Hospital Movement Changed the World*, "The religious revival sparked in England by the preaching of John Wesley and George Whitefield was part of an enormous unleashing of Christian energy throughout the 'Enlightenment' of Western Europe. It reminded Christians to remember the poor and needy in their midst. They came to understand afresh that bodies needed tending as much as souls."

The point is, if you are a parent, support your child's learning activities and motivate them to achieve as well as provide the environment that will facilitate their educational pursuits. In fact, all the children of our community would benefit from your support of an enriched educational experience. More importantly, whatever your political persuasion happens to be, do not belittle your children's interest in science and scientists. Without our scientists, we would not have the internet, antibiotics, GPS, improvement in our healthcare and weather forecasts. If you are enjoying a good quality of life, thank a scientist. We risk enormous catastrophes if we ignore their findings and prescriptive remedies. Let's change the narrative.

171.

I Would Rather Have Jesus than Power, Silver or Gold

December 5, 2019

I read recently that the world's oldest post office, after 700 years of service (Sanguhar, Dumfries) is closing shop—another casualty of the internet. This mournful occasion got me to thinking that there must have been a time when there was a first post office. Ah, but where would that office send mail? Did they sell stamps? And from where would it receive mail? How useful is it to have one FAX machine or one telephone? If Bell calls Watson and Watson doesn't pick up, has he made a call? Who owned the first radio or television set? Just like you cannot clap with one hand or have a one-ended stick, we need other people to do most things. While musing on these questions made me chuckle, it actually was kind of sad because we need to be connected. There is a whole world out there. We are increasingly siloed like this woebegone post office.

The musical band "Manhattan Transfer" had a catchy song that imagines trying to put a call through to Jesus. The operator questions and she replies, "My mother used this number/ When I was very small/ And every time she dialed it/ She always got the call." While I never get a busy signal, evangelicals today are like that singer trying to put a call through and they don't know how. I blame political power that has had a corrupting effect. Is there a rebellion against God? Until recently, evangelicals were about conversion, devotion to an infallible Bible and encouraging believers to know God and to bring their lives into conformity with truth.

The evangelicals that my mother faithfully followed, and I admired (Harold Ockenga, Billy Graham, Oral Roberts, and Charles Swindoll), taught the Word and enriched the lives of their congregants (including mine) but more importantly, to correct, teach and guide us home. But then the IRS challenged Bob Jones University's tax-exempt status over segregation. And Roe v Wade legalized abortion. And the Christian Right organized into a political force and the taste of that power was so sweet, and so addicting, that they have been chasing that high ever since.

Are evangelicals surrendering their advocacy for God's Word for worldly influence? I have been marveling at how they twist themselves into pretzels to accommodate the behavior of President Donald Trump, Alabama Senate Candidate Roy Moore, and Jim Beck from Georgia, who was indicted for stealing millions of dollars. My repeated reading of the Book says a great deal about fidelity to one's spouse, truth-telling, integrity and extending kindness toward our fellow travelers on planet Earth. Can we have Christianity without Christ? I note we don't even use the term "family values" or the "moral majority" in the public sphere anymore, knowing what a mockery we've made of these terms. Where is the justification for adulterers who boast about their sexual exploits?

So, here comes Trump and Moore and Beck, who deliberately violated Christian values but received the full support of evangelicals through some kind of intellectual duplicity and spiritual surrender. The Good Book says, "Shun immorality and all sexual looseness" (1 Corinthians 6:18). Circumscribing the word of God is perilous and we become no better than clanging cymbals.

So, I finally found the Biblical underpinning, authority, and logic for their stance. It's all there in the story of Noah and the Great Flood. That is the one Biblical story that never made sense to me. While my Sunday school teacher was talking about cleansing the earth of sinners, I was more focused on the millions of people—men, women, children, babies, and the animals who drowned while Noah and his family sailed off into the sunset. I wonder what Noah fed the lions, tigers, and hyenas for 40 days?

Is this the inspiration for evangelicals? Should the bounty of the world serve only the select few and to literal hell with everyone else? Build a wall around our country, stop immigration from those countries, discontinue foreign aid, separate children from their mothers at our border and ignore the pleading from the rest of the world. Ladies and gentlemen, every human being has worth and is cut from the same cloth—all made in the image of God. But according to modern evangelicals, as long as we are doing well, who cares what becomes of everyone else. Do you think for a minute that this is pleasing to God? His patience is not limitless. He is not invested in just the success and prosperity of some of His people but all of his people.

The better model for me is the story of Daniel, Shadrach, Meshach, and Abednego. These four amigos took a stand, told it like it is and spoke truth to power, "If we are thrown into the blazing furnace, the God we serve is able to deliver us from it…but even if He does not, we want you to know that we will never serve your gods or worship the image of gold you have set up." And after much drama, power yielded to them and instead of the king converting them, they converted the king and his people. Truth can rescue a sliding foot if worship is practiced with integrity. "The prayer of a righteous person is powerful and effective." (James 5:16) So, "Let your light shine before others that they may see your good deeds and glorify your father in Heaven." (Mathew 5:16) We are to submit to the Word even when our political inclination and ambitions want to point us in other directions.

We must know who we are. That is, we must know "whose" we are and to whom we belong. The power of the Word will continue to transform believers. "Scripture is God-breathed and is useful for teaching, rebuking, correcting, and training in righteousness, so that the servant of God may be thoroughly equipped for every good work. (2 Timothy 3:17) I would rather have Jesus because every good and perfect gift comes from above.

172.
The Attack on Women: Train Your Children to Be Respectful

December 12, 2019

A misogynist is a person who hates or doesn't trust women. Other than brute force, I cannot think of any field of human endeavor where women do not excel. You may have seen their dominant presence on television recently regarding the impeachment hearings. While you may not be a chauvinistic pig, it appears to be fashionable to talk and act menacingly to and about women these days. Put downs are on the rise. Evidence of disdain, abuse and marginalization of women seems to pop up with more regularity. You may have to tolerate it with certain politicians, but not have to suffer in silence from misogynist friends, family, and co-workers. You need to be particularly vigilant with your children. Degrading any woman with derogatory and degrading names, limiting their access to demanding occupations, discounting their options by interrupting or belittling their opinions and insisting that they shut up and do what they are told is no longer tolerable.

My grandson is a martial artist. Many of his colleagues have sought to use their achievements in fitness to pursue careers in stunt work, modeling, and acting. It has been eye-opening watching how reliably the show business world wants to take empowered, strong, young women and package them as kittenish pin-ups gazing over their shoulders with big eyes. And it's no better for the young men, who are marketed as meathead hunks, smoldering with a hint of danger. These are people we know—thoughtful, accomplished, complex young people who work together as companionable colleagues in a meritocracy that preaches and practices respect—flattened out and caricatured for easier commodification and sold back to us as inoffensive lowest common denominator consumables. What we have here, as so often when we talk about the sexes, is a failure of imagination.

My granddaughter is in grad school majoring in theoretical math—a field where very few women participate. Really, one would be hard-pressed to think of a less 'sexually charged' field of endeavor. And yet, many of her colleagues in STEM fields find themselves on the losing end of a disturbing level of sexual politics, shut out of research positions because the professor might fall in love with them, or fired because he did. The promise of an environment characterized by objectivity and rational thinking remains elusive and we lose out on the contributions from our best and brightest because of it. Again, a failure of imagination.

My younger grandchildren are learning their Bible stories. I am surprised to learn that *The Garden of Eden* is still essentially taught as a patriarch's fantasy:

> The man ruled and owned all he surveyed, and his wife (the little woman) neglected her needs to focus on his every whim. Yes, she might have lied about her romance with the evil serpent but otherwise, she was the "helpmate" and all his for the taking. She willingly did what she was told, except for the little issue about eating fruit from the tree of good and evil.

Maybe the plan is to be taught the broad outlines of the story now and introduce the subtleties when they are older, but this casual framing of the story is just bad theology. There are a hundred interpretations of the foundational story of our faith besides making Eve a naughty wife. Again, failure of imagination.

Ladies and gentlemen, we need to recognize that this is the 21st century. Can we treat each other as equals? Women's work is hard, not because they can't do it, but because men get in the way and make it harder. If you want women to respect and trust you, I hope you know that respect and loyalty cut both ways.

Whether it is my wife, my daughters and my daughters-in-law, mothers, aunts, and cousins, I have come to believe that the women in my family are to be respected for their opinions, skills and knowledge. They are equally valuable and deserve the same respect as men. My wife is the very effective CEO and president of our company, and our daughter-in-law is the head of our ABA Center that treats children on the spectrum.

Learning respect for each other starts at home. We need good role models. How do the men act toward their wives and female children? Apples do not fall too far from the tree. When disrespect of women occurs, adult males need to step in.

Here are some suggestions offered by Drs. Brian Johnson and Laurie Berdahl ("Will Your Boys Grow Up to Respect Women?" *Psychology Today*):

1. Talk about shared good qualities of genders (skills, intelligence, character, personality, strength, kindness) and promote these in both boys and girls. For example, praise boys for their kind heartedness and girls for assertiveness and taking on challenges.

2. Equally support boys' and girls' interests and activities, despite whether or not they are typical for a child's gender.

3. Support gender equality by sharing home and child responsibilities, and by rotating chores so boys and girls do equal amounts and types of work.

4. Adopt a zero-tolerance house rule of no sexism in your home.

5. Model respectful, kind behaviors you would like to see children around you exhibit toward others. Emotional or physical abuse by women in boys' lives can also be an underlying factor in future disrespect and abuse of women.

6. Men can support gender equality by not objectifying women: not talking about them sexually, about their looks or body parts, or calling them objects (e.g., "piece of tail"). Objectification is part of the harmful sexualization process being forced onto our girls.

> *When people respect someone as a person, they admire her.*
> *When they respect her as a friend, they love her.*
> *When they respect her as a leader, they follow her.*
> (John Maxwell)

173.
A Baby Can Make All the Difference in the World

December 19, 2019

Thomaston is a Christmas place. The memories being created will live with the children of this city for all their lives. Thanks to the Christmas parade, the Empty Stocking Fund, singing on the square, amazing Christmas plays, concerts and cantatas, Christmas Lane, the awesome decorations on every home and office, the hugs and warm greetings, the exchange of presents and even the cake and punch we are offered on our visits to family and friends. And more importantly, we do not ignore the needs of those less fortunate. It is just a nice place to celebrate Christmas. While the most popular Christmas song this year is "I don't want to go home for Christmas," if you grew up in Thomaston, I am certain you look forward to coming back. There is no place like home.

For over 20 years, we have been sending a Christmas letter outlining past year's activities and accomplishments that I want to share with you. The bottom line is, God continues to bless our family.

The highlight for 2019 is that I SURVIVED A TRIPLE BYPASS! There was really no warning as I developed symptoms on my way back from a golf vacation in Jamaica. I was able to get off the plane in Atlanta on a Wednesday and had my bypass on the following Monday. To show you how God works, the cardiologist who did my cardiac cath knew me and reported that the cath revealed 100% occlusion of my circumflex and 90% occlusion of my RAD and LAD. The surgeon, Dr. Omar Lattouf, was also a seat mate of mine on a flight from an American Heart Association conference and he remembered our conversation. He performed the bypass without using the bypass machine. I was up and walking on the same day and my recovery has been remarkable.

Nine months later, my memory has improved, and I am playing the best golf. I now walk and carry my golf bag for 18 holes. I was able to watch our first grandchild (Mackenzie) graduate from Harvey Mudd College, our oldest grandson Brooks graduate from high school and take the trip Stephanie and I planned to Spain, Portugal, Morocco, and Gibraltar. I am reminded that "His eye is on the sparrow, and I know He watches me." Stephanie and I are blessed beyond measure and she says the BEST blessing this year is that she is not writing our annual Christmas message alone.

Our oldest daughter Jillian and her husband Brian who live in Phoenix are empty nesters! I am reminded that we started our annual Christmas message tradition with the birth of Mackenzie in 1997. She is now a graduate student at the University of Maryland and Brooks is a business major at Arizona State University. How time flies. Jill continues in her law practice and Brian continues his IT work for CIGNA and they now follow Brooks around the world as he hones his skills as a Taekwondo master.

Our oldest son Freddie and his wife, Tracy, moved to Columbus and are growing their respective lines of business with ZÖe Center for Pediatric and Adolescent Health and ZÖe ABA. We are blessed to be able to work with the two of them and get to know them on a whole other level. They are both creative and talented professionals. Mr. Kai is officially a preteen and growing like a weed. He is excelling in soccer and is quite the avid artist. Ms. Hailie continues to channel her grandmother Stephanie and loves the arts and gymnastics. We are still Pop-Pop and Nana and are thrilled that we have at least one set of grandchildren we can see on a regular basis.

Our youngest daughter Melanie and her husband, Don (Portland), are preparing to launch their daughter, Audrey! She will graduate from high school and be off to college. They and Mr. Vincent will adjust to being the Three Amigos as Audrey takes flight. Melanie has finished her consultant role with Play Connections and looks forward to taking a year off to figure out what to do next. They all came to Columbus to celebrate Thanksgiving with us and what a glorious time we had! She described Don as the rock of their family, and he is that. Mr. Vincent is interested in the theater. He is exploring what it means to be a teenager and has very understanding parents.

Our youngest son Aleron (Atlanta) continues to write full time and was recently rated as the 48th best-selling author on Amazon both in written and audio books in the Lit RPG genre. He has now published eight books and sold more than one million copies. He has turned into an amazing icon. He travels with his significant other and whatever the future holds for him he sits down every day happy. He mentors young Alpha Phi Alpha brothers and has joined me at Alpha meetings in Columbus. It is great to be able to share the A-Phi-A experience with my son. He is still single, which my wife continues to harass him about, as well as his decision to retire from medicine at 36 years old.

It has truly been an amazing year. Stephanie and I have gone to another level in our relationship. We have so many shared memories and our lives are so intertwined we not only complete each other's sentences; we truly complete each other. We continue to obediently follow God's lead and take comfort in the fact that with the challenges managing 100+ staff and our schedules, He will see us through. I publish my weekly column, served on the deacon board at Greater Mount Zion Baptist Church and the board of trustees at Gordon College. I received the ABC Lifetime Achievement Award in October along with a special recognition from the City of Los Angeles and unbeknownst to me, my children created a large endowment in my name with the Association of Black Cardiologists to benefit medical students.

I hope you don't overlook the reason for the season. We are celebrating the 2019th birthday of our Messiah who came to establish a new order of love for us. Pray for our nation and pray for peace. We don't know what the future may hold, but I am alive and know the ONE that holds the future. He has the whole world in His hands.

174.

Does It Take a Great Sinner to Make a Great Saint?

January 9, 2020

The word 'evangelical' means good news but has come to mean the zealous preaching of the redemptive power of Jesus Christ so that all human beings can, by God's grace and mercy, be born-again, receive salvation, and through a direct relationship with the Almighty, prosper in love and fellowship with each other. Believing that people have a spark of divinity and a disposition to benevolence (that should be cultivated), we celebrate the glory of God's creation and advance His kingdom by redeeming lost souls to the cross.

While all Christians subscribe to this mission, at its extremes, Fundamentalists believe in the inerrant Bible that is true in every detail and the church reigns supreme as the arbiter of morals, the social order, and the truth of the Gospel. On the other hand, new evangelicals are members of congregations who believe the Bible to be an inspiration and a guide—but not to be taken literally. For example, Fundamentalists believe the six-day creation story and that the first man was formed from clay by the hands of God who infused him with the breath of life—fully grown. Others subscribe to Darwinism, or some version of how human life came into being.

Under the assumption that democracy without God is as empty as morality without religion, the blurring of the lines between religion and politics probably started with declaring that President Eisenhower was a political leader as well as our spiritual leader.

In an attempt to put in motion fierce winds before which enemies will be blown away, evangelicals, under a plethora of outspoken leaders have opposed Communism, forced busing, illegal immigration, exploitation of labor, the sale of alcohol (temperance), tobacco, dancing, gambling, family planning, same sex marriages as well as advocates for the care of the poor, personal morality, prayer in schools and social justice.

Over the years, there were obvious and open disagreements regarding slavery, school integration, whether women could serve as preachers, the place of women in the family (women should surrender their lives to their husbands), global warming, gun ownership and whether the church should even assert themselves in politics. Rev. Jerry Falwell nevertheless proclaimed that President Reagan was the greatest president of all time and in order to achieve a spiritual-moral revival in America, the faithful must become Republicans and bring God and morality back to government. The National Religious Broadcasters Association also passed a resolution to the effect that God appointed President George W. Bush to serve as our president. *Christianity Today* responded that: "George W. Bush is not the Lord. The American flag is not the Cross. The Pledge of Allegiance is not the Creed. 'God Bless America' is not Doxology." *The Grand Rapids Press* also wrote, "Your deeds, Mr. President— neglecting the needy to coddle the rich, desecrating the environment and misleading the country into war—do not exemplify the faith we live by."

During the 2016 election season, candidate Donald Trump promised to appoint conservative anti-abortion judges and take a strong stance on illegal immigration and became the evangelical's standard bearer. They overlooked his many shortcomings and became a strong part of his base. Eighty percent of evangelicals voted for him.

On the heels of Pat Robertson claiming that he had a vision and saw Donald Trump seated "at the right hand of God" and anointing him, President Trump accepted the mantle offered by the evangelicals and proclaimed himself to be "the Chosen One."

When I brought up this blasphemy to an evangelical, he said: "Trump may be the Chosen One. We were not trying to elect a Pope. We have a President that we know is flawed. We are not blind to the fact that he is a liar and a user who is willing to throw wives, cabinet members, politicians, and his own lawyers under the bus. His relationships are transactional, and nothing is sacred to him. I know you have a great deal of respect for Martin Luther King, but Ralph Abernathy revealed that MLK was involved with other women outside his marriage. Do you think less of him because of that? Jimmy Carter was a good, God-fearing man, and he was the worst president we ever had. If God only used perfect people to do his work, we would never get anything done." However, according to Mark Galli, editor-in-chief of *Christianity Today* (a magazine started by Billy Graham):

> The reason many are not shocked about this is that this president has dumbed down the idea of morality in his administration. He has hired and fired a number of people who are now convicted criminals. He himself has admitted to immoral actions in business and his relationship with women, about which he remains proud. His Twitter feed alone—with its habitual string of mischaracterizations, lies, and slanders—is a near perfect example of a human being who is morally lost and confused.

Trump's evangelical supporters have pointed to his Supreme Court nominees, his defense of religious liberty, and his stewardship of the economy, among other things, as achievements that justify their support of the president. We believe the impeachment hearings have made it abundantly clear, in a way the Mueller investigation did not, that President Trump has abused his authority for personal gain and betrayed his constitutional oath. The impeachment hearings have illuminated the president's moral deficiencies for all to see. This damages the institution of the presidency, damages the reputation of our country, and damages both the spirit and the future of our people. None of the president's positives can balance the moral and political danger we face under a leader of such grossly immoral character.

175.
Let's Go for a Walk

January 16, 2020

Whether it is my wife, my children or someone I want to know better, my modus operandi is to invite them to go for a walk with me. And when we go off together in the woods, the park, by a stream or just following a road or around the block, my first rule is to shut up. I wait for my company to initiate and carry the conversation. I learned over the years that using these walks to lecture, berate, bring up unpleasant subjects leads to:

You have bad news.

What is it now?

I hate when you ask me to go for a walk because you only do it when you need to criticize me for something or other.

Number one rule: Shut up and listen. Be known for your thirsty ears. Just be present. Practice empathy.

This came up this week when a friend sent me the suicide note from a friend's 15-year-old daughter:

...I know that you and mom loved me but I did not feel loved. You provided me with more than I ever wanted, took me to places that most of my friends have not even heard about. Despite what you thought was a good life, my heart was longing for love. I needed someone to love and accept me for who I was. I needed someone who would reach to the depth of my soul and feel the vacuum there. The material things you provided could not do that. I felt alone. Didn't you wonder why I was spending so much time alone in my room? There were so many things I wanted to tell you, but you were so busy with everything going on in your own lives. It pains me to empty the contents of this pill bottle. Goodbye Mom and Dad. I love you.

When I shared this sad story with my wife, she reminded me that the key to maintaining a good relationship with our four children as well as our grandchildren was frequent walks. It is good for body and soul. All my children have loving memories of our walks and I believe it was an important ingredient for their successful careers and family life. They have even continued the family tradition I started with their own children. When they visit me, they always invite me to go for a walk with them so we can talk.

Talking has long been recognized as therapeutic but walking and talking is even better. If you don't feel like talking, you are walking and enjoying the great weather and landscapes we have in Thomaston, so there is no pressure to keep up the conversation. I wrote before about our human need to have 24 strokes per day to feed our self-esteem needs. A stroke is any recognition by someone else that you exist, you are important or that you are valued. These are expressed with a smile, a nod, a verbal greeting, a hand wave, a handshake, a hug, a kind word, a compliment, or something even more intimate. Dr. Eric Berne, in his book, I am OK; You are OK, determined that one other person (spouse) can only supply about a quarter of our daily stroke needs. Apparently, man was not meant to be alone, and loneliness has become the curse of our time. We are programmed to interact, to meet, greet, work, and play in groups and sing the "Happy Birthday" song to each other. I hope you never have to find out what it feels like to not have anyone remember that it is your birthday.

You are all aware that I am passionate about golf, it is not only fresh air, green grass, trees, and sunshine but I value the jokes, the conversation, the harassment, the sharing of our experiences and opinions about current events and how to improve our golf skills and the golf experience. It is the greatest game ever invented. I am told that our President (as busy as he is supposed to be) has been playing golf about every three days.

My friend, (Dr. Malcolm Taylor) tells me that he is NEVER too busy to miss a family event: births, deaths, birthdays, anniversaries, weddings, Christmas, and Thanksgiving. It is important to him to feel connected to his extended family and they should all know that they can all depend on him as well. He is fond of saying, "If you have God, family and friends, you may stumble, but you will never hit the ground."

Once, when I visited my mother, she grinned and said, "Since you are always asking me to take a walk with you around the block, as a surprise, you don't even need to ask me today because I am ready." She then took a child's wooden block from her pocket, placed it on the floor, took my hand and said, "Let's go!" She was a funny lady.

According to an (ipsewilder-ness@gmail.com) blog:

> I had a friend at school who swore that I had worn a dent in her shoulder by resting my hand there perennially as we perambulated the school grounds, sharing gossip and teenage woes. But the zeitgeist is such that getting outside, away from screens and technology and into nature is being recognized as not just a nice idea, but a mental health strategy. If during the restorative and

calming walk we also get to chat and share something about what's going on and how we are feeling, then surely the psychological benefits will be compounded. Thankfully, walking and talking therapy for mental health is flourishing and the time is absolutely ripe.

While the Australians call it a "walk about," I came by it honestly from my Jamaican roots. One of our folk songs that captures this sentiment goes like this:

This long-time gal, I never see you,

Come let me walk and talk

This long-time gal, I never see you. Come let me walk and talk.

Bald-head John Crow sitting on the treetop,

Plucks off the blossom,

Let me walk and talk gal

Let me walk and talk.

176.
Meet Mr. Dannie Smith, a Renaissance Man

January 23, 2020

According to Wikipedia, a renaissance man is a very clever person who is good at many things. Leonardo da Vinci (painter, scientist, engineer, and mathematician), Michelangelo (sculptor, architect, poet), Albert Schweitzer (theologian, musician, philosopher, doctor) and Benjamin Franklin (author, printer, politician, scientist, inventor, and soldier) epitomize these multi-talented, multi-dimensional bigger than life personalities.

Thomaston is blessed to have our own renaissance man in the person of Mr. Dannie Smith. To know him is to love him as well as appreciate his talents, gifts, and skills. While physical therapy is his profession, he is just as gifted as a chef, singer, musician (who plays multiple instruments), and a public speaker on multiple topics. He also distinguishes himself as a civic leader. He is equally at home on a golf course or a tennis court as well as a hot shot at board and card games. What he has more than most is a big heart and compassion for his fellow travelers on our planet.

As a frequent user, one of the landmark contributions that I am eternally grateful for is the Wellness and Cardiac Rehabilitation Center at Upson Regional Medical Center. Dannie was the chair of the committee that planned, built, and furnished the center in partnership with Rev. Al Simmons. Aren't you happy that you have people with vision in our community? If you were one of the thousand people who heard the fabulous Christmas concert at First Baptist, you probably noticed Dannie, Director of the Orchestra, moving from instrument to instrument and sharing his musical talents. I even enjoyed the style he put into the "bells" rendition.

Dannie was born in Flint, Mich. and when he was seven years old, his family moved to Los Angeles. In 1971 he met his future wife, (Vicki) a Thomaston native with a heavenly voice, traveling with the Continental singers playing trumpet, as he admired and watched her nightly performances.

After a whirlwind romance, they married two years later and moved to Atlanta so he could attend physical therapy school and Vicki could start her career as a music teacher. (Thanks for bringing him back to Thomaston Vicki!). In 1977, Dr. Lanier Allen invited Dannie to move to Thomaston to start up a physical therapy program at Upson Regional Medical Center. The department opened in 1978 and over the next several years, initiated therapy programs in the area nursing homes and home health agencies. He was also instrumental in starting the cardiac rehab program and the wound center. Dannie is now retired from URMC but continues with a specialty nerve testing practice with his daughter at URMC, Crisp Regional Hospital and Ortho Georgia in Macon. Vicki and Dannie have two daughters (Emily and Amanda) and three grandchildren (Eleanor, Mariana, and Samuel).

Dannie has participated in numerous short-term mission trips in medicine and music, recognized the sacrifices long-term missionaries make and was determined to find ways to support them. He chose "Righteous Rides" as the vehicle for his new mission.

Do you know that transportation is the number one concern and need for international missionaries when they return to the United States? So, having invested in sharing God's word abroad and helping to improve the quality of life for the less fortunate, because these missionaries have been out of pocket for several years, they have no credit or the resources to purchase or rent a car. Sometimes they don't even have a ride from the airport. Righteous Rides to the rescue!

The ministry started with one van 11 years ago in St. Louis and now has 150 vehicles—seven of which are located in Thomaston under the supervision of Dannie and Vicki. Their operation requires that two vehicles go to the airport, meet the family of the returning missionary, and turn over one of the vans (clean, insured, maintained and a tank full of gas) to the family while Dannie transfers to the second van for his ride back to Thomaston—extremely satisfied that they are doing God's work. This operation is repeated weekly with the help of over 20 volunteers, Tire and Auto Master, and JM Paint and Body Shop. To the delight of these families, Righteous Rides even include hugs all around and a welcome home goody bag for each member of the family. Often bewildered to be back in the United States, the children especially enjoy the welcome and the company of friends.

There are obviously more needs that can be met with their current resources and you can help. First and foremost, you can volunteer and experience the joy of giving your time to this worthy cause. They will also accept used vehicles that can be upgraded and of course, contributions are appreciated, regardless of how large. Can you think of anything more worthy of your support? Additional information is available at righteousrides.org or you may wish to contact Dannie personally (706/656-5000).

I am fortunate to call Mr. Dannie Smith a friend: Thomaston's Renaissance man is also a righteous man!

177.

My Brother Left Us Too Soon (Reflections: Earl DeCarlton Kong)

January 30, 2020

Having survived a triple by-pass less than a year ago, I have been thinking about the heart—this muscle that quietly powers our lives, supplying its rhythm and pace. My brother's heart stopped on Jan. 23, 2020. He was 75 years young. I was mistaken because I thought the muscle that powered his heart on long hikes up mountains, fighting forest fires, fishing and hunting was no regular heart. I thought it was some iron man kind of heart, but it quit on him, and I am shaken to the core.

Although my brother lived in Washington State, and was a year and a half younger, he was a lifetime companion. While our teachers tried to civilize us by having us memorize poems, play acting, singing, and reading the Bible, Earl preferred to hunt birds with a slingshot, climb trees to feast on fruits in season and hang-out with the farmers who always had a pot boiling on a wood fire with yam, dasheen, cartwheel dumplings, saltfish or corn pork. They predictably offered him some of their vittles served on cocoa leaves. Eating with a stick, he used to jab each tasty morsel for the trip to his mouth. Even though he was younger and shorter, he was scrappier and kept the bullies from his nerdy brother.

We grew up in the countryside of Jamaica and got our *broughtupsy* from our dear sweet grandmother (Ms. Rosie). We shared a bed, took baths together in a wooden tub as well as made pocket money from the peas, cabbage, and carrots we planted. We also raised rabbits, a delicacy that we sold in the open-air market. Throughout our childhood, we never missed Sunday school or church as well as Sunday afternoon picnics at our Aunt Myra's house to eat homemade ice cream, coconut drops, grater cake and drink cane juice that Mass Claudie made with a homemade apparatus. After the playing, screaming, dancing, eating, and drinking was done, cousins (Monica, Melvis, Donovan and Carlen) and other members of Aunt Myra's household would walk us home, singing and telling duppy (ghost) stories. After we got back to our house, it was now dark, and we had to walk them back. But obviously, we wouldn't be expected to walk back to our house without company, so they walked us back again. We would finally agree to bid each other adieu at some arbitrary halfway point.

Our personalities were different. He was very curious. He took our gramophone apart looking for the people making the music and destroyed our entertainment. He also dismantled the alarm clock to find out what made it tick. I tried to make up songs and poems and hang-out with others playing board games and rehearsed for elocution contests and plays. He was masterful at playing marbles and his pockets usually bulged with marbles and cashews. We did perform together at a talent show acting out comedic routines as Mutt and Jeff.

We migrated from the Jamaican countryside to New Jersey where we were introduced to a stepfather (Arthur) and two other brothers (Robbie and Kevin). We both attended Morristown High School in 1959. While we struggled with the academic work, I predictably excelled in choir, participated in plays as well as track and cross-country. We both joined the wrestling team. We weighed in at 114 and 122 pounds and the Kong Brothers racked up impressive records including a district championship. When we graduated from high school, two unlikely scholars went off to college, me to Iowa and he to New York where he was a frequent visitor to Uncle Elton and Yvonne McKenzie's house. He later joined the Air force and met his lovely bride on an evening out from base in Corvallis, Oregon.

After completing a tour of duty in Taiwan, he returned to Corvallis where he earned a degree in forest management from Oregon State University in 1975. He then completed an internship with the Bureau of Land Management studying forests, insects and diseases and was then employed by Washington State Department of Forestry for 40 years. His usual routine was that he traveled to his job site on Mondays, worked in the woods Tuesdays, Wednesdays and Thursdays and traveled back to his wife and two sons (Devin and Aaron) on Fridays. He told me he loved the routine because he just loved communing with nature. I accompanied him on one of his workweeks and while exhausted from hiking, I just loved his company and enjoyed the great outdoors. He assured me that we wouldn't get eaten by bears or attacked by snakes while in our sleeping bags. I must admit that he scared the hell out of me driving recklessly on logging roads.

He was an expert fisherman and a marksman with various guns he used for target practice and hunting. So, we bagged deer, picked berries and fruits and even flowers for the missus. One of the activities I particularly enjoyed was taking geoducks (delicious!) from the Puget Sound where he lived. His family could almost live off the land. He also made the most amazing smoked salmon salad with a homemade smoker. My brother was a rugged intellectual. He could name the genus and species of every animal, fish, bird, insect, and rock. He had also become a star gazer who could pick out and name stars and constellations and was a talented water-color artist. I was not only in awe; I prize the dozen pieces of his art that hang on my walls. When we hit golf balls on the beach, we only needed one ball as his dog (Popcorn) brought back the ball from wherever it went.

As bookish as I thought I was, I finally came to the realization that my younger brother was the true Thoreauvian scholar. After he retired, he wrote articles on ecology and published a book on tree safety, *The Hazard Tree Handbook*, with the intent of reducing accidental deaths from falling trees. He spoke to me about the Gaia hypothesis and the planet's ability to heal itself. He also became a consultant to the Tlingit people in Alaska to help them manage their forests. When his wife (Carol), my wife (Stephanie) and I accompanied him on one of his trips, it turned out to be a truly amazing experience.

On our flight from Juneau on a six-seat bush plane to Kake, we meandered between mountains and whenever the pilot spotted whales or glaciers, he would circle back to give us a closer look. When we landed, the pilot had to buzz the runway to scatter the wild animals as there was just a runway, no fencing, no hangar, or any other buildings and no one to greet us. We disembarked and the pilot took off again. Transportation from our hotel arrived and we made our way to our living quarters that were literally on the water, flooded with salmon trying to make their way to spawn and die. They would ride the high tide to the top, lay their eggs and are left high and dry. It was a feast for our eyes as well as the bears and birds. When we visited the caviar factory, they invited us to eat all the fish eggs we wanted. I was in heaven.

We met the carver of totem poles, visited Eskimo families Earl had befriended and one man with a yacht, took us out fishing (caught some large halibut) and saw Orcas, sperm whales, sea lions, porpoises, and eagles. My wife did not accompany us when we went out tracking bears and other wildlife.

On a previous trip to Australia, we had a conversation with two Aboriginal men who told us that the goal of life was to sit down happy whether it is the end of a job, a day or a lifetime. Earl, you can sit down happy. After your humble beginning and fractured early education, you excelled. You were a great success leaving behind a dedicated wife, two wonderful sons and a gaggle of grandchildren and great grandchildren who will not only celebrate the contributions you made to their lives but also to mankind. You were an inspiration to this brother who will miss your jokes, horsing around, the adventure and fun that followed in your wake as well as your great intellect. The Lord just uttered the familiar words, "Welcome to your permanent home, good and faithful servant, come in and claim your reward."

Since Earl's death, I have been raising awareness about heart disease by participating in panel discussions and various other community related activities on the topic. While preventable, heart disease claims too many of us prematurely. The life you save may be your own.

178.

Was Christianity a Secret Society in its Early Days?

February 6, 2020

One of my simple pleasures is to browse bookstores—a kind of storehouse of knowledge that is disappearing. I walked up and down isles of Barnes & Noble in Atlanta last week for something to catch my fancy and for some reason I was drawn to *Secret Societies* by John Lawrence Reynolds, who promised in the subtitle to take me "Inside the Freemasons, the Yakuza, Skull and Bones, and the World's most Notorious Secret Organizations." It was also for sale—50% off! So, I bought it along with a half a dozen other titles I look forward to reading.

I spend part of everyday listening to Rachmaninoff, laying back on my duvet, reading with a drink close by. A teacher once told me that as long as you love to read, you will never be bored. I am not often bored. It is a message I pass on to everyone but it appears to be a losing cause as I find that so few people read these days. We seem to spend so much time on social media and looking at screens to pick up a book or even a newspaper. Let me assure you that reading is a free and accessible indulgent pleasure.

On one of our trips to India, 15 years ago, we had a four-hour layover at Vnukovo International Airport in Moscow with nothing to read. I had exhausted all the reading material I brought with me, and I walked the entire airport searching and found nothing in English to read. I panicked and ended up reading the schedule of flights in and out of Moscow. That was as boring as it gets.

So, I just completed the book on secret societies and learned as the author concluded:

> We want so much to be roused from our humdrum lives…Secret societies prosper when their believers can coalesce around some individual whose unique powers of perception serve as a beacon to his followers." Carl Sagan warned that "Sooner or later this combustible mixture of ignorance and power is going to blow up in our faces. When governments and societies lose the capacity for critical thinking, the results can be catastrophic, however sympathetic we may be to those who bought the baloney."

My surprise was learning that:

The story of early Christianity exemplifies the complexity of secret societies and the reactions to them. On one hand, Christians were part of the secret cult, with beliefs and practices far from mainstream Rome. On the other, they had to remain hidden because, although they posed no threat, they faced grave danger. The result was the most vicious of cycles. The more they were persecuted, the more they stayed secret—and the more they stayed secret, the more they were feared and persecuted.

When we visited the Catacombs of Rome 15 years ago, we were told the origins of the word 'underground', where a group organized in secrecy promoted concerted resistance with the expectation of liberation at some time in the future. Early Christians certainly 'fit the bill'. Admitting that you were a Christian was a death sentence. Roman citizens thought they were depraved, hated them, and wanted every last man, women and child killed because:

1. Driven by the belief in a resurrection, they believed in burials (inhumation) in a sacred ground instead of the usual practice of cremation.

2. The communion ceremony (Eucharist) represented the blood and body of Jesus Christ in secret rituals as directed by Jesus. "This is my body, which is for you; do this in remembrance of me." (Bread and wine) but the word on the street was that early Christians were cannibals.

3. The usual practice for getting rid of unwanted babies in Rome was just to discard them to die from hunger or the elements. The early Christians found this practice deplorable, so they rescued and nurtured these babies, but the word got around that they were ritualistically eating these babies.

4. They preached "brotherly love" which the authorities translated to mean sexual orgies between brothers and sisters.

5. They "met in clandestine locations, avoided contact with respectable society, and identified themselves by flashing the image of an instrument of torture (the cross) when they met."

6. They would not worship the emperor and were converting others to resist the authorities.

7. Instead of a defense against discovery and harassment, the general belief was that anything that is good should not be kept secret and anything that is kept secret cannot be good and their motives were suspect.

As a result, these early Christians became 'outlaws' and fair game to be hunted down, tortured, and killed. Peter was crucified upside down. Andrew was crucified preaching until his last breath. James was also crucified and then sawed into pieces. John was boiled in oil but survived to write Revelations on the Isle of Patmos. Phillip was hanged. Bartholomew was flayed (cut to pieces). Doubting Thomas was killed by a spear and Thaddaeus was killed by an arrow and on and on.

I thank God for the sacrifices of these saints and celebrate the fact that I can declare my faith openly without fear of torture and death.

"The arc of the moral universe is long, but it bends toward justice"
(Martin Luther King).

179.
Why Does the Flu Virus Spread in Winter?

February 20, 2020

The Crazy Flu by Debra L. Brown

There once was a girl named Sue.
She came down with a case of the flu.
She let out a sigh,
My temperature is high, what ever shall I do?
Oh my! Oh my!
I think I will die.
What ever shall I do?
So, she stumbled out of bed. "I know I'll take some meds. If this the flu,
I take an aspirin or two.
Then I'll drink some broth and some juice.
Oh my! Oh my!
she began to cry.

I think this is acute.
So, she grumbled back to bed
and pulled the covers over her head.
She let out a sneeze,
a cough and a wheeze.
"Won't someone help me, please?
Oh my! Oh my!
Will I survive
the case of the crazy flu?
So, she finally fell asleep. She slept and slept for a week.
She tossed and turned,
her symptoms have passed. Her temperature is normal at last.
Oh my! Oh my!
I think I survived
this case of the crazy flu.

Yes, it is true that the flu virus thrives in the cold of winter and there is virtually no flu in countries with tropical climates. According to Dr. Peter Palese (professor and chairman of the microbiology department at Mount Sinai School of Medicine in New York) who studied this phenomenon in his laboratory with guinea pigs:

> Transmission was excellent at 41 degrees. It declined as the temperature rose until, by 86 degrees, the virus was not transmitted...The virus was transmitted best at a low humidity, 20%, and not transmitted at all when the humidity reached 80%.

Please note that we are talking about how the flu virus is transmitted, not the cause. Nothing about getting wet, going from a hot environment to a cold environment, washing your hair and going outside can make you sick without being exposed to a germ.

What we have abbreviated to the flu or "influenza," is Italian for "influenza di freddo," or "influence of the cold" dating back to 300 years ago. It is commonly characterized by a cough, sore throat, stuffy nose, fever, cold sweats, aches, weakness, fatigue, vomiting and diarrhea. You may have one, some or all of these symptoms.

It is highly contagious. Just like every seed has the potential of a forest and one candle can light a million candles, an infected person can spread the virus to an infinite number of other people. They can infect others one day prior to the onset of symptoms and up to seven days after symptoms appear. More than 200,000

Americans are hospitalized each year because of the flu, and about 36,000 die—mostly the elderly or anyone who has a compromised immune system. It is spread by direct contact when you touch surfaces that have been touched by someone with the virus or shake hands with someone who is infected and then touch your own nose and eyes. Flu viruses are also spread by microscopic airborne droplets when someone sneezes and their particulates are then inhaled by others in a room.

180.
What Does the LORD Require of You?

March 12, 2020

To act justly and to love mercy and to walk humbly with your God."
(Micah 6:8)

On Feb. 4, 1968, Rev. Dr. Martin Luther King, Jr. said the following at Ebenezer Baptist Church in Atlanta:

> If you want to be important, wonderful. If you want to be recognized, wonderful. If you want to be great, wonderful. But recognize that he who is the greatest among you shall be your servant. That's a new definition of greatness. And this morning, the thing that I like about it is that by giving that definition of greatness, it means that everybody can be great because everybody can serve. You don't have to have a college degree to serve. You don't have to make your subject and verb agree to serve. You don't have to know about Plato and Aristotle to serve. You don't have to know Einstein's theory of relativity to serve. You don't have to know the second theory of thermodynamics in physics to serve. You only need a heart full of grace, a soul generated by love. And you can be that servant.

This is not to say that we don't appreciate and celebrate excellence and achievement. We are drawn to athletes breaking records; scientists bringing us marvelous breakthroughs, doctors miraculously treating diseases that would have been inconceivable in the past. We admire the skyscrapers that define the skyline of every major city in the world. Fine art elevates our spirits. And not just highbrow art. Even a well-made suit, a clever turn-of-phrase, and a catchy tune are accomplishments. Yes, even the trappings of wealth and celebrity, such as social media "likes," spacious mansions, vintage cars, and so on. The word "idol" no longer conjures the idea of a blaspheming wayward nation and instead just means a popular TV personality.

We are even impressed with religious leaders whose eloquence and knowledge of the word is flawlessly preached to millions. And why not? But we should not be blinded to the fact that the teachings of our Lord and Savior are not about achievements and certainly not about material possessions, but an invitation to serve. If you are a Christian, you have a mandate to selflessly serve. Selfless service should be offered and provided out of a genuine and deep desire to help and be of service. The fortunate should always help the less fortunate. Service to others can be offered in numerous ways including financial assistance to direct physical help, hugs, holding hands, visiting, intercessory prayers, advice, support for those being bullied, healing and teaching. If you are devoted to God, regularly attend church and pray unceasingly. It is all worthless if you don't help others when your help is required. From everyone who has been given much, much will be demanded; and from the one who has been entrusted with much, much more will be asked (Luke, 12:48).

It will destroy our happiness if we compare our lives with what we perceive the lives of celebrities to be. While not discounting great achievements in every field of human endeavor, no matter how much wealth and fame you accumulate, fleeting worldly success will never get you to true happiness. You will most likely end up feeling unfulfilled and inadequate. Whatever your starting point in life and whoever you have become, we can all achieve true greatness right here in Thomaston by serving others—being a good husband or wife, father or mother, a good son or daughter, uncle, or auntie and most importantly, a good neighbor—even for the least of these. While this will not bring you the adulation of the world or personal gain, rest assured that you will earn favor and be exalted in the sight of God. "He that is greatest among you shall be your servant" (Matthew 23:11).

According to Wikipedia, writing about John D. Rockefeller, America's first billionaire: In his 50s Rockefeller suffered from depression and digestive disorders. During a stressful period in the 1890s he developed alopecia, the loss of body hair. By 1901 he wore a toupee. His doctors gave him a year to live. So, with this death sentence, he figured that he might as well give away his money before he died. He became active in church, taught Sunday school and helped mold the lives of all those he encountered physically, socially, and spiritually. He built amazing hospitals, colleges, medical research centers and in the process was responsible for wiping out hookworms and yellow fever across the country. It seems to be the cure for whatever ailed him, and he went on to live an amazing life—98 years old. The well-being of others became his mantra and the more he gave away, the more he received in return. Mr. Rockefeller could sit down happy and rightfully claim his place among the angels.

My personal experience and my testimony are that my daily tasks of service and caring for others give me the personal satisfaction that I could not have received doing something else—no matter how important my obligations may be. My commitment is to lighten the load of others. Selfless service should be offered out of a genuine desire to help. When we help somebody, we should thank them for the opportunity to serve them. Our ethics should be grounded in this compassion for others.

In a selfish dog-eat-dog, every man for himself world, mankind will perish under the pursuit of power, fame, notoriety, greed, avarice, gross materialism, egocentricity, and self-gratification. All religious and service organizations: Kiwanis, Greater Mount Zion Baptist Church, My Lodge is summed up in the mission statement of Alpha Phi Alpha fraternity, "First of all, service to all, we shall transcend all." I believe the most beautiful, sublime and profound feeling human beings can experience is knowing that we have unselfishly helped someone along the way— (especially damsels in distress).

My pastor once asked me, "Waine, what do you own?" I replied, "My house, my automobile, my clothes, money in my bank account." And then he said, "If I asked you the same question 50 years from now, how would you answer?" Only what we do for others will survive.

And if you think that death will help you escape this mandate to serve, think again, when every knee must bow and every tongue confess, you will be judged for your eternal life and I hope you will not be found wanting because you have lived a selfish life. You still have the opportunity to live a life of service to others.

"Do nothing out of selfish ambition or vain conceit,
but in humility consider others better than yourselves." (Philippians 2: 3)

181.

Transitions: What a Difference A Day Makes!

March 5, 2020

What a difference a day made. Twenty-four little hours. Brought the sun and the flowers Where there used to be rain. My yesterday was blue, dear. Today I'm part of you, dear, my lonely nights are through, dear. Since you said you were mine.
(Dinah Washington)

Now you see it, now you don't. One day Mount St. Helens was there and the next day it wasn't. One day, the stock market is roaring and the next day it falls. One day we are poor, the next day we are rich or vice versa. One day we are single and the next day married. We crossed the stage, received our diplomas and became graduates. We had our first kiss, and we definitely will not be the same afterward. Maybe we boarded a plane and took off in one country and landed in another—different dress, language, customs, political systems, etc. How do you cope? The second hand of a clock crosses over past midnight and we are in a new year. We were on a cruise once when the captain decided to celebrate New Year's twice. So, he crossed the international date line and crossed it again.

One day, you may have been unemployed and living on the generosity of others. Now you have a job, you buy clothes, a new pair of shoes and an automobile. So, instead of slouching with your head bowed, you now have pep in your step. One day nobody loves you and the next someone thinks you are the bee's knees, and you wake out of your depression. Your lonely days are over. One day, you are on top of the world with family, friends and the next you are depressed because your spouse wants a divorce. That is devastating as family, friends and even acquaintances chose sides. One day, you are part of the workforce and the next you are retired—that may not be good. So, how do you plan to spend the next 30 years?

We cannot vote and then we can. We are too young to go to a bar one day and can drink as much hard liquor and beer as we want the next. One day you were well and hardy and today you are in a wheelchair. One day you were a sinner with no redeeming social value and now you are a born-again Christian with hope for living a Christian life. And one day you will be no more. One day you are behind bars thinking that your only problem is the bars that fenced you in, then you are released and discover that your problems multiply. What a difference a day makes. Some changes bring joy, some bring heartache and pain. For every day you live without trauma, shouldn't you be grateful?

My grandmother is fond of saying, "Don't get upset over spilled milk, losing a treasure, destruction of property or the death of a loved one. If something or someone exists, at some point it will not exist." The Upson County Medical Center building may be a solid and imposing structure but someday, maybe 100 or 1,000 years from now it will not exist. We have the nuclear capacity to destroy the world over 100 times, will we always be restrained? Even the sun has an expiration date.

The opposite of this fact is that within everyone is the promise of a dynasty. Within every acorn is the promise of a forest. My grandmother has now spawned over 100 children, grands, great-grand and great-great grands. Adam and Eve spawned seven billion people.

One thing is certain, change. Life is mercurial—a series of ups and downs. You cannot step into the same river twice.

> To everything there is a season, and a time to every purpose under the
> heaven: A time to be born, and a time to die; a time to plant, and a time
> to pluck up that which is planted; A time to kill, and a time to heal; a
> time to break down, and a time to build up; 4 A time to weep, and a time
> to laugh; a time to mourn, and a time to dance; A time to cast away
> stones, and a time to gather stones together; a time to embrace, and a
> time to refrain from embracing; 6 A time to get, and a time to lose; a time
> to keep, and a time to cast away; A time to rend, and a time to sew; a
> time to keep silence, and a time to speak; A time to love, and a time to
> hate; a time of war, and a time of peace...every man should eat and
> drink, and enjoy the good of all his labor, it is the gift of God.

(Ecclesiastes 3)

182.
Regarding the Novel Coronavirus and COVID-19

March 19, 2020

On March 11, the World Health Organization declared the coronavirus a pandemic. It is present in more than 100 countries (including the United States, where more than 3,700 people are infected so far and 70 have died.) There are 121 confirmed cases in Georgia and one death. The United States Congress physician predicted that somewhere between 70 to 150 million will be infected and more than a million will die if it continues on this present trajectory. Johns Hopkins University is predicting an even more dire situation for the country.

Worldwide, 6,500 have died and 162,392 have been infected. Ten percent of those infected will become seriously ill. The 2% death rate will be mostly among the elderly, particularly those living in nursing homes, prisons, and group homes. The most vulnerable are those families who have refused immunizations over the past dozen years.

To put this into perspective, every year the world experiences a pandemic it is called the influenza virus or flu. We have tests for the influenza virus and while it is not a cure, we have antiviral medication that stems the tide of symptoms. The cure for the flu and any virus including the novel coronavirus and COVID-19 is YOU. Just like the flu, a healthy body will be able to ride out the symptoms until your immune system wipes it from your body. Having survived the infection with the flu or novel coronavirus, you will have some immunity going forward.

The most important thing to do in protecting yourself, your loved ones and our community is to practice community mitigation strategies (actions that we can take to slow the spread of respiratory virus infections.) and common sense. As Tom Hanks stated on a posting, he and his wife are in Australia and had some nasal congestion, a low-grade fever and some chills. They decided to do the responsible thing and got tested. It was a positive result for COVID-19. They are self-quarantining and coping. No hysteria.

The capacity of our healthcare system in Thomaston is adequate for the foreseeable future. Remember, the hospital cannot treat the virus but can treat you if you have conditions made worse by the virus. This column is meant to give you some strategies to protect yourself, your loved ones, and the community at large. If the number of cases increases rapidly, we will not have the capacity to take care of everyone who is sick.

Our protocol at ZÖe Pediatrics is to use universal precautions. All our locations have sick and well waiting rooms so we can segregate kids from each other. We are working with LabCorp to increase testing. However, LabCorp has only a limited amount of testing reagents. What we tell staff and patients is the following:

1. If you are not feeling well, coughing and have a temperature, stay home, and reduce the risk of infecting others.
2. All employees should sanitize their workstation, phones and chairs as often as needed but especially when changing shifts.
3. Wear a mask.
4. Cough into our elbows.
5. Sanitize each exam room before and after each patient visit.
6. Instead of our customary handshakes and hugs, clasp your hands as if in prayer and say: "Namaste" which has been used in India for centuries. It just means "God Bless you" or "I will keep my germs and thank you for keeping yours." Some are bumping fists, elbows, hips, and feet. It's all good.
7. It is a respiratory disease so you cannot be infected from what you eat. It is transmitted primarily through your eyes and nose so avoid touching your face after coming in contact with someone else.
8. Frequently wash hands with soap and water for at least 20 seconds. If soap and water are not readily available, use hand sanitizer with at least 60% alcohol. Rum and other liquor in your cabinet is not likely to be more than 40% alcohol.
9. If you insist on having church or participate in community meetings, please ask the elderly or frail not to attend. They are the most vulnerable.
10. We ask children to maximize the use of facetime and not visit their grandparents and great-grandparents for a while. In fact, it may be a good idea for the elderly not to receive visitors.
11. Nothing comes from nothing. If you have been home and no one has visited, you do not need to wipe down surfaces. The recommended precautions are for after you have had contact with potentially infected people or things such as money, packages, toys, phones, pens, doors, and doorknobs.

We cannot wait for this to be behind us so we can get back to handshakes, kissing and hugging once again. COVID-19 is taking away a lot of our joy. But pray unceasingly. This too shall pass.

183.
Being A "Know It All" President Is Not Helping

March 26, 2020

"I know more than the Generals." "I know more than the lawyers." "I know more than the Scientists." "I think nobody knows more about campaign finance than I do, because I'm the biggest contributor." "I understand social media. I understand the power of Twitter. I understand the power of Facebook maybe better than almost anybody." "I know more about courts than any human being on Earth." "Who knows more about lawsuits than I do? I'm the king." "I understand politicians better than anybody." "Nobody knows more about trade than me." "I know more about renewables than any human being on Earth." "I think nobody knows more about taxes than I do, maybe in the history of the world." "I'm the king of debt. I'm great with debt. Nobody knows debt better than me." "I understand money better than anybody." "As a builder, nobody in the history of this country has ever known so much about infrastructure as Donald Trump." "Technology — nobody knows more about technology than me."

When you know it all, you reject input from others, spend most of your time in self-promotion endeavors rather than on the agenda at hand and, never wanting to look weak or not knowing something, you turn meetings into lectures, make up stuff to fill in what you don't know and fire people who disagree or criticize. You surround yourself with yes-men who are advised that if you are going to survive in this administration, don't think. Just do what I tell you to do. I am predicting that Dr. Anthony Fauci will be the next victim. While he has been cautious, he must also be true to himself and the American people.

Albert Einstein, the most brilliant scientist that ever lived, mused that he was the most ignorant person in the universe because he knew what he didn't know. You become a know it all because you do not know what you don't know. The epitome of this is a teenager who knows more than his parents and his teachers. According to Mark Twain, when he was 15, his parents were the most stupid and ignorant people in the world. It surprised him greatly how wise they became by the time he turned 21.

With all the expert advice available to our President, "Relax. We're doing great. It will pass." was not helpful. Asking the American people and the people of the world not to pay attention to the fake-news fear mongering about the coronavirus, characterizing it as political hype and offering false assurances, was not helpful either. For the record, contrary to President Trump's assurances, the virus has not been "contained" and testing is not available to everybody who wants it, and Google does not have an app for everyone to find where they can receive testing. More importantly, 30,000 have now been infected and 350 Americans have died. Globally, there have been 316,000 cases and 14,000 deaths. We should have seen this coming.

As of today, Americans are on lockdown, sports and political events are cancelled, schools, churches, restaurants, and bars are shutting down and everyone is advised to stay home to flatten the curve so that health care facilities are not overwhelmed. Most notably, the stock market has tanked. We are short of hospital beds, medical equipment, masks, ventilators, and inhalers and most importantly, medical personnel.

According to Beth Cameron:

> When President Trump took office in 2017, the White House's National Security Council Directorate for Global Health Security and Biodefense survived the transition intact. Its mission was the same as when I was asked to lead the office, established after the Ebola epidemic of 2014: to do everything possible within the vast powers and resources of the U.S. government to prepare for the next disease outbreak and prevent it from becoming an epidemic or pandemic. One year later, I was mystified when the White House dissolved the office, leaving the country less prepared for pandemics... The job of a White House pandemics office would have been to get ahead: to accelerate the response, empower experts, anticipate failures, and act quickly and transparently to solve problems... We were to prepare for and, if possible, prevent the next outbreak from becoming a pandemic.

From its founding in 1946, the CDC has been a highly trusted and effective agency fighting diseases worldwide. However, funding for the CDC has been cut to a level where it cannot function effectively, and important members of staff left. Even the liaison officer from the CDC to the China CDC was called back at a crucial time when we could have learned a great deal from their experience in China. We even intentionally left ourselves vulnerable by eliminating our $30 million crisis fund.

The result is that we were unnecessarily caught unprepared. Local communities must rely on the federal government to address crises like this. The response has been inadequate, and lives are being un-necessarily sacrificed.

184.

Surviving the Pandemic (Everybody Needs Everybody)

April 2, 2020

The virus is spreading to small towns. The number of confirmed cases in Albany, GA is now up to 500, primarily because many of them attended a funeral together. Sixty patients in Phoebe Putney Hospital in Albany have tested positive. While Upson County is not a hot spot like Albany, we now have at least five confirmed cases with every expectation that things will get progressively worse. There are now 142,537 confirmed cases across the country and over 2,510 deaths. The prediction is that small towns (like Thomaston) will be severely affected. So, brace yourselves.

In addition to an infected person sneezing, coughing, yawning, or breathing and their tiny droplets being inhaled by others, our scientists tell us that COVID-19 is usually transmitted from an infected person touching their nose and then touching a surface, and then that surface is touched by others who then place their hands (that picked up the virus) to either their noses or eyes. You have nothing to worry about if you were not in the presence of an infected person, even if you touch a contaminated person or a surface, if you wash your hands thoroughly or use a hand sanitizer or avoid touching your face you will decrease your risk. In any case, the best advice is to assume that you and everyone else is infected and act accordingly.

Different surfaces can maintain the virus for different lengths of time. A hard surface like a door handle or door to a public bathroom or countertop is more of a risk than paper or money. *The New England Journal of Medicine* published a study that tested how long the virus can remain stable on different surfaces within a controlled laboratory setting. Materials made from copper - four hours; cardboard - 24 hours; plastic and steel - 72 hours. Cleaning with good old-fashioned soap and water is actually just as effective as alcohol-based sanitizers, bleach, and other disinfectants.

I am thinking about the elderly who cannot receive visitors, go to church, visit the senior center and are not able to hug their grandchildren. On the other hand, without the opportunity to be held and touched by family and friends, babies can suffer from developmental delays and cognitive impairment. Isolation is deadly for the elderly as well as the young. Children will be greatly stressed by threats to their health and the financial well-being of their families.

I am also thinking about teenagers who cannot hang-out, attend club meetings, compete in sports, will not be able to attend proms, visit colleges, or go to the beach for spring break. Their graduation ceremonies will be cancelled. How will young men hone their skills and the art of seduction when they cannot come closer than six feet of those to whom they are attracted? Maybe they will have to learn how to write love letters and poems like we did in the good old days!

As schools are closed, the worst of all is that they have to be cooped up with their parents and siblings 24/7. There may be arguments and even fights. I hope we can be patient with each other. In addition to anxiety over the virus, teens are most likely to feel frustrated to the extreme and prone to act out. So, make an effort to add structure to your children's lives by making a schedule of activities and sticking to it.

Whenever I have unworthy thoughts, I think of the village of Eyam in England. I read about Eyam some time ago and I regard their citizens as public health heroes. You see, the bubonic plague that was decimating London was shipped to Eyam in a bolt of cloth to a dressmaker in Eyam from London. As the deaths mounted, they were all thinking about relocating but that would only infect wherever they went. So, under the leadership of their religious leaders, they decided to hunker down and quarantined themselves within the boundaries of their village. Over the course of a year almost all of them died but none left to infect other villages.

Thankfully, COVID-19 is not as deadly as the plague and wherever you are domiciled is more comfortable than what the people of Eyam endured during this reign of terror in the 1660s. If they could do it, so can we. The future of our species requires us to be considerate and supportive of each other and to make sacrifices. Joy comes in the morning when we can put this behind us and celebrate our resilience. We will go to church once again, but in the meantime, mail in your tithes and offering. The expenses of the church continue, and the CARES package will not benefit religious entities.

As we cannot have funerals or wakes, how will we honor our fallen heroes and sheroes? This is not a good time to die when so many are dying. As churches cancel services, the Evil One must be celebrating. He has caused all of us to stop coming together to worship but we can pray unceasingly. I pray that we will call out to our God, like Elijah did, to show God's power and be examples of what it means to truly believe.

We are predisposed to addictive behaviors during times of stress. My prediction is that isolating people in their homes will lead to obesity as we cannot resist the urge to open the refrigerator 100 times per day. It may lead to alcoholism and drug dependence, separations, and divorces. Everyone will be bored and exercise less and watch more television and otherwise spend most of our time looking at screens. With the cancellation of professional sports, we will be watching reruns, depressing news, movies, and game shows.

Sigmund Freud once remarked that the goal of life is to love and to work. I would suggest that even as we are not working, we should find meaningful work to do. You can write your novel, paint a masterpiece, build, invent something and even compose a symphony. This could be a remarkably creative period in American history. Most of all, love, and care for all the members of your family and be patient with them. As for me, I love my wife's company when I read and write. I have promises to keep and miles to go before I sleep and miles to go before I sleep.

Through it all, there is a bright side. I read a poem from a gentleman from China who marveled that he heard some birds singing and didn't recognize it at first because it was a long time since the hum of traffic and factories drowned them out. He said he could also see the stars and the sunset because there was no pollution.

On the home front, Democrats and Republicans worked together to pass the CARES Spending Bill. I was even shocked when I read Alan Landers' column last week. In the three years that I have been writing this column, I have NEVER agreed with ANYTHING written by Alan Landers and found myself agreeing with Everything he wrote two weeks ago, (March 26). Is it possible we share a few things in common? Great column, Alan.

The virus closed casinos and bars, brought families together and we are just a little kinder and more tolerant of each other. We are praying more fervently and examining what is important and what is not important to our lives. I am enjoying the fact that our children are checking in with us almost daily just to make sure we are OK. Love is in the air, let's pass it along. Thank a health care provider and our first responders for their dedication!

185.
The Looming Crisis: Welcome to the World of Microbes

April 16, 2020

In 1945, when Alexander Fleming, the father of penicillin, received the Nobel Prize for Science, he pointed out that microbes evolve and would soon develop resistance to available antibiotics. He warned us to be extremely vigilant as microbes could be our doom. He was prophetic.

Modern medicine is now facing this dilemma. The options for treating evil microbes are going down and their number and severity are going up. We unwittingly consume a great deal of antibiotics not only from prescriptions but increasingly from what we eat—fruit, beef, chicken, and pork). As a result, some antibiotics have no therapeutic value against evolving "superbugs" increasing the rate of death from infectious diseases. Even before the appearance of COVID-19, methicillin resistant staphylococcus aureus (MRSA) has been killing 700,000 people per year and we have nothing to treat the carbapenem-resistant *enterobacteriaceae* (CRE). The forecast is that microbial infections will be the cause of death for 10 million people per year worldwide.

Our bodies are home to trillions of microbes and most of them are surprisingly good for us. Only a tiny number of them make us ill. But they are, nonetheless, the cause of a third of all deaths in the world. Microbes make up about 10% of our diet and break down what we eat so it can be digested from the 20 or so digestive enzymes permanently residing in our gut.

While we are spending time sheltering at home, my wife and I are catching up on movies. So, we just watched "War of the Worlds" and guess what saved the world? A virus! This is not only true in movies but could be our savior in real life as well. No doubt you are also watching "Outbreak," "World War Z," "Black Death," "The Andromeda Strain," "The Last Man on Earth" and "Contagion."

The lesson is that we have to be proactive. Why is it that we preach that "Prevention is better than a cure" to our children and don't practice what we preach? Our country could have been so much better off today if we had not disbanded the "Medical and Bio-defense Preparedness Office, not reduced the budget for the Centers for Disease Control (CDC) and ignored the warnings from multiple informed sources. There was not enough work being done finding out how microbes affect us. There is so much more to learn and so little time to get it done. While it is hard to wrap our minds around a microscopic organism causing the demise of mankind, it has that potential. Just like it only takes one seed to produce a forest, or one candle to light every other candle in the world, it only takes one infected person to infect the entire planet.

1. Microbes consist of bacteria (bubonic plague, cholera, and pneumonia), fungi (mushrooms, yeasts, molds, and athletes' foot), viruses (COVID-19, AIDs, SARS, EBOLA, smallpox, the common cold and flu, measles, mumps, chicken pox, hepatitis, herpes and polio) and protists (amoebas, algae, protozoa, archaea and slime molds). If you made a pile of all the microbes on earth it would be greater than all the animals. There are also more microbes in our bodies than cells.

2. Viruses are tiny microorganisms and mostly invisible. If you blow one up (as we have been doing with the COVID-19) to the size of a tennis ball, the human from which it was extracted would be five hundred miles tall.

3. Microbes even live in the ocean. A quart of sea water contains 100 billion viruses. After hurricanes, as a result of the widespread sea water, it is usually accompanied by vibrio infections—one of the superbugs.

4. Of the hundreds of thousands of viruses identified so far, only a few hundred affect humans either for good or evil.

5. Microbes produce the gas that occasionally escapes from our bodies as they convert what we eat (particularly beans) to methane.

6. Passionate kissing accounts for the transfer of one billion bacteria from mouth to mouth—including herpes.
7. The varicella-zoster virus that causes chickenpox can be in-active for 50 years before springing back as shingles.
8. Viruses cannot propel themselves and have no means of locomotion. We have to go out and get them from surfaces, door handles, money, handshakes and inhaling it. But once they get into a cell, they explode with activity.
9. About 40,000 species of microbes live in and on us (on our skin, our nostrils, and lungs, in our mouth and stomach). You can soak yourself in alcohol and wash your hands for an hour and never rid yourself of all of them. But you don't want to; again, most of them are beneficial.
10. While minorities are at greater risk because they have suboptimal health care, COVID-19, is an equal opportunity infector although infections in children are relatively uncommon.

As citizens of Mother Earth, this pandemic should have taught us that we are all in this together. Where are you going to run? Where can you hide? There is no escape. Viruses can bide their time until they are ready to cause havoc. What effect will global warming have on new viruses that have been dormant for millions of years with the melting of the glaciers or the opening of new farmlands in ancient rainforests?

186.

Making Good Decisions

April 30, 2020

I had lunch at my favorite deli today and made ten decisions before I walked out with my tuna sandwich on Italian bread with tomato, lettuce, peppers, and sweet onion dressing. It turns out that each of us make over 1000 decisions per day. In the larger scheme of things, it really didn't matter whether I had a turkey sandwich.

We minimize our decisions by adopting routines and fall back on what Mama told us. If you live in Georgia, we like biscuits, grits, eggs, bacon, ham, and Brunswick stew. In Japan, they have soup for breakfast. In Jamaica, they have dinner for breakfast—in other words, whatever was left over from dinner. I am decisive and economical when I make non-consequential decisions but force myself to deliberate and contemplate every scenario with the important ones like who to vote for or whether I should hit a six or a seven iron when I am 150 yards away.

Some decisions are just more consequential. Should I drop out of school? When and to whom should I marry. When and how many children should we have? Should I quit my job? Which car should I buy? Where should I live? Should I join the service or a service organization? How do you know when you have a good deal so you can pull the trigger?

Over the course of my life (77 years) the many mistakes (bad decisions) I made were usually because I wasn't deliberate and contemplative; I allowed my emotions to get the best of me; didn't have enough data; I didn't ask enough of the right questions; I didn't have access to people in the know; I didn't interrogate the "facts" or look beyond what seemed intuitive or obvious. People who disagreed or took issue with my plans (sometimes obnoxiously) were valuable in contributing another point of view. If I had responded emotionally and rejected their input because of how they expressed themselves, I would have made many more ill-informed decisions. It is sobering to realize that because no one can predict the future, regardless of how deliberate we are, some of our decisions will still produce bad outcomes. I recognized long ago that to reduce bad decisions, I should include several points of view. One person cannot possibly have all the answers to make consistently good decisions.

At the very least, don't let emotions make your decisions. Emotions distort clear thinking, logic, and good sense. When you are emotional (angry, in love, excited, feeling sorry for someone and just being passionate), force yourself to chill out before committing. In other words, do not rely on what your heart or what your gut tells you. For good or bad, make the best of your decisions or as my grandmother told me, "Once you make a decision, kill the other options."

187.

Force Majeure:
When Circumstances Are
Unforeseeable and Unavoidable

May 7, 2020

While "The dog ate my homework" will not excuse a student from homework assignments, traditionally, war, terrorism, fires, earthquakes, hurricanes, embargoes, orders by a court or governmental entity and epidemics have justifiably been used to excuse parties from their contractual obligations. In other words, occurrences that were outside the control of a contractor that could not have been anticipated, prevented or mitigated by mere mortals. The *Force Majeure* provision in contract law is commonly found in contracts that potentially free someone from obligations if an extraordinary and unavoidable event prevented one or both parties from holding up their end of the bargain. These events must not be the result of the defendant's actions, hence they are considered "acts of God." But if expert witnesses determine that others in similar circumstances were able to deliver the goods, then the defendant would be judged by this standard.

With the great San Francisco fire of 1906, the government could establish a state of emergency and take people's homes, set them on fire and take whatever actions they needed for the public good. During the spread of a tree virus, or in an animal epidemic, the government has the authority to come on a farmer's property and destroy the trees and kill all his cows. While a jury will most likely decide, cases often turn on whether they believe it could have been helped.

Unexpected and one in a million chance occurrences is a common clause in contracts that release both parties from obligations when an extraordinary event or circumstance took place that was clearly beyond the control of the parties. Increased cost of raw materials and labor will not be an excuse from fulfilling obligations and delivering the goods. Before satellites, a rainstorm during an outdoor event was unforeseeable. With advances in technology and forecasting, what was once unforeseeable can now be anticipated and mitigated—if you pay attention.

My wise grandmother was fond of telling me that the future belongs to those who anticipate and take steps to mitigate potential disasters. In other words, she advised me to plan ahead. The Boy Scouts captured the same sentiment with the five Ps: "Poor planning is the cause of piss poor performance." By failing to prepare, you are preparing to fail and even an act of God will not excuse the consequences.

On the other hand, no amount of planning will save us from an act of God or a true *Force Majeure*. If we are hit by a meteor, no amount of planning could have helped. I wonder what the courts will decide when students sue their institutions that did not provide the educational experience for which they signed up and paid for?

188.

Being Grief Stricken

May 14, 2020

My grandmother Rosie was fond of saying, "Son, we didn't come here to stay. Our permanent home is with our Lord." Life is mercurial. Here today, gone tomorrow. The horrible grief you may be suffering is not permanent either.

As the COVID-19 sicknesses and deaths increase, it also takes a toll on the survivors. In just the past three months, the number of Americans who have died from COVID-19 is approaching 100,000. In its wake are grieving family and friends. We are robbed of the opportunity to lean on each other and celebrate their time with us—no wakes, no funerals, and no comforting hugs. It can be debilitating and even paralyzing. I am sorry, online ceremonies are no substitute.

Interestingly enough, grief is not a universal experience. Among the Maasai warriors (Kenya), when a comrade dies, there is no sense of loss. He was somebody (a father, son, and comrade in arms) and now he is a nobody—equivalent to a piece of stick that they leave in the forest for predators. They are actually amused at the fuss Christians make over a "dead body."

According to Dr. Elisabeth Kübler-Ross, the emotional trajectory from learning that you have a terminal illness or learning that someone important to you passed is denial (It's not true, she will be home soon.), anger (How could you abandon me?), bargaining (I will do anything to undo this), depression (being overwhelmed and sad), and if you don't get stuck on one of these stages you arrive at acceptance and recovery (ready to put things behind you and move on). Life is for the living. The key to recovery is to know where you are in the grieving process and assure yourself that this too shall pass. But don't be surprised that years later, you can become sad again. Here is my remedy: Stay six feet away from the refrigerator (don't binge) but talk about it often to everyone who cares to listen. Talking it out helps, especially with a grief counselor.

Part of the grieving rationale is thinking I could have prevented this. If I had prayed more; if I were kinder; if I had made sure he saw a doctor sooner; if I had only… Why didn't God take me instead? The older I get, the more I question the grieving process.

I want my children to be healthy, wealthy, and wise, not to be burdened with grief. I worked my entire life so they can be happy and then I become the cause of their depression. I will continue to live my life to the fullest, playing golf, reading, writing, laughing with my family and friends and enjoying the hugs of my grandchildren. But I really mean it when I tell them not to be sad at my passing. Dying before they do will be a blessing. So, when I show up for my appointment with the cemetery, I don't want anyone to cry for me. Continue to live well.

189.
An Open Letter to Alan Landers. Is it time to give up on "The Great Agitator?"

May 21, 2020

Over the years, as much as I disagree with your public expressions regarding your unwavering support for President Trump, I have secretly admired your dogged public advocacy. I respect anyone who can muster improvised and imaginative defenses for what you believe is a noble cause even though they are mostly indefensible. I admire how creative you can be to justify your support. I know it's not always easy, but damn it, come hell or high water, you love the man so he must be inerrant—until now.

This is the 40th anniversary of the Mt. St. Helens eruption in Washington state. I had enjoyed my climb there the year before with my brother Earl who was a forester, as well as our visit to Spirit Lake. But this morning on "CBS Sunday Morning" a woman who owned a hotel was angrily objecting to the road closers, saying, "This is a horrible hoax. Nothing is happening on this mountain. They don't know what they are talking about. How do they expect us to make a living?" But, as the scientists predicted, a few days later, (May 18, 1980) the volcano blew away the mountain killing 57 people, destroying 47 bridges and 185 miles (298 km) of highway.

The warnings and weather forecast for the impending COVID-19 'hurricane' that would devastate our country was predicted by our scientists. Piercing alarm bells sounded even within the President's cabinet and security briefings. All of it was ignored, minimized, and characterized as a hoax. We are now faced with an enemy that renders our armies, battleships, rockets, drones, and fighter jets impotent. We have been preparing for the wrong war. COVID-19 required preparation and effective execution by the CDC, but our president fired the great leaders at the CDC, gutted their budget, shut down the pandemic's office at the White House, recalled our CDC liaisons who were working with the Chinese CDC and continues to minimize the impact of the virus. Our stockpiles of equipment and supplies to help our hospitals were outdated, unmaintained and depleted. We have not done well catching up. Most importantly, President Trump still thinks he knows better than the scientists.

Thousands of our neighbors are suffering and dying each day. The current projections are 150,000 casualties. For all of his failures, President Trump is trying to switch the blame on past administrations, the Democrats, the World Health Organization, and the Chinese. He recently came out against testing as this will only increase the number of cases.

I see more and more Republicans are distancing themselves from President Trump. I hope you will be one of them. We deserve better.

190.

My Ignorance is to be Respected as Much as Your Knowledge

May 28, 2020

Some years ago, I was playing in a golf tournament where I was assigned to play with partners I never met. I don't usually discuss politics or religion on a golf course but when one of my playing partners said, "Even though I never went to college, I am smarter than stupid Obama." I pointed out that President Obama graduated at the top of his class from Harvard School of Law. He responded, "I am still smarter." "So, why is Obama so stupid and you so smart?" "Because we all agree that he is stupid." "So, let me be clear, facts don't matter, everything boils down to your subjective perspective. If two plus two is four and you don't like it, you can take a vote and decide that it is five. The majority rules. If you don't like the facts, can you and your friends make up alternative facts? Is that right? "That's the way it is," he responded. "So, it's kind of if you like someone, they can do no wrong, but if you hate someone, they can do no right." "That's right," said my adversary. "So, there is no global warming?" "That's right."

Now, there are many ways to be intelligent and our culture is full of stories of people who were bad fits for higher education but expressed genius otherwise. I think we can all agree that sometimes intellectuals lose track of lived reality. It may be that this golfer felt that he had more horse sense than the egghead Obama. Where would we be without the pilgrims who defied the priests or the slaves who learned to read upside down to confound the master?

I am thinking of the Spectrum ads. In one, a brave soul is designated to cross the river to bring goods to market. He suggests that instead of taking this tortuous path, they could build a bridge so they can safely cross back and forth. The majority, however, told him to just get on with it and he is eaten by a creature. In the second, the man who is about to be sacrificed in a volcano so it will rain, asks if it wouldn't be better to create an irrigation system, but the crowd persuades him to take the plunge. The poor guy jumps, and the leader puts out his hands expecting rain. At some point, it stops being populist or inspired and becomes willful ignorance. When you reject ideas proposed by scientists, progress is not possible.

In Plato's *Allegory of the Cave*, he envisions a tribe of people who spend their entire lives in a cave. They assume that the reflected shadows on the walls of the cave are reality. But eventually, someone escapes from the cave and, while he initially marvels at the amazing fantasy of trees, rivers, and rocks, as he hits his head on a tree and stubs his toe on a rock, he comes to realize that his people have been living a lie. He returns to tell them "the truth" and they respond: "Boy, you don't know what the hell you are talking about. Listen to your elders." And when he persists, they execute him.

While there are certainly many educated fools who are detached from ordinary folk, should we really rile against scientists and intellectuals? Between 1975-1979, the Khmer Rouge killed everyone who graduated from a college (the killing fields) because Pol Pot, the party leader, didn't want anyone to challenge his lies.

When up is down and down is up, it's probably good practice to let The Bible have the last word:

"Walk with the wise and become wise, for a companion of fools suffers harm?"
(Proverbs 13:20)

191.
Eating Our Young:
An Open Letter to Police Chief
Mike Richardson

June 4, 2020

I learned today that a fine young man (22-year-old Officer Walter Navarro) who served honorably as one of our police officers with an outstanding record for two years was terminated due to a silly Snapchat post. I saw the photograph in which officer Navarro's girlfriend was giving the young man a facial. She must have been a very persuasive girlfriend as I have never had a facial. As the facemask was black, she jokingly puckered her lips with the caption, "I date a black man" and took a picture.

The young officer sent it out on Snapchat. Ladies and gentlemen, it was a joke. The fact that this silly encounter made it into the public domain and became the cause for public outrage and his dismissal doesn't sit right with me.

In this race-charged time we live in, any incident that smells of racism looms large with a few members of our community (in their infinite wisdom) acting chagrined and mortally wounded. But over what? Two young people having fun with each other. It was a private joke, folks. No reason to mortgage their souls. By insisting on putting his head on a platter we are "eating our young." While we find "black face" characterizations abhorrent, this is not that—not even close.

Officer Navarro came to the United States 12 years ago, he worked hard to become a United States citizen and became one three years ago. He is young, and if we do not help him now, he will be lost in a country he worked hard to become a part of.

Chief Richardson, I have known you since you arrived in town and you enjoy my trust and respect, but by acting so harshly to something so silly is an outrage. It doesn't deserve the attention it got, and I protest the firing. I don't believe for a minute that Officer Navarro had any intention of offending anyone. Let's have a meeting with those who feel offended and return this fine young man to duty. In the two years in which he served this community, you admitted that he enjoyed your confidence and there has NEVER been a complaint filed against him—he's a good apple.

In your public letter you stated that:

> Officer Navarro is a Latino American police officer who made an extremely poor decision that had serious consequences. He served the department well, and during his two years on the job had never received a single complaint regarding conduct, rudeness, racial bias or unprofessional behavior or the mistreatment of others of any nature. Regardless, in the end, we serve the public and if the public trust is broken, I have the responsibility to fix it. We cannot do our job effectively without the support and confidence of the community we serve.

I do not share your belief that the public's confidence has been broken by this silly post. He deserves our mentoring —not our boot.

Let us not hijack the promising future of these young people or remain asleep with our eyes wide open. Let us not blame our actions on the complaints of a few people, as well-meaning as they may be. While I have never met the gentleman, if that post or photo is all we are going on, I recommend that we reinstate Officer Navarro immediately. There was no crime.

192.

A Pandemic of the Soul

June 18, 2020

This is a check-up. How are you? I mean, how are you really? With all our unprecedented challenges, are you OK? The virus lingers, a storm is brewing, and Black Lives Matter protestors continue to demonstrate. Some police officers are showing their colors with how unnecessarily brutal they can be. How could they have shoved that elderly man to the ground and as he laid there bleeding with brain injury, they just walked on without assisting? I was appalled at this callous treatment for a citizen who they vowed to serve and protect. This is why I am taking stock. Are you OK?

The stock market is volatile, unemployment is incredibly high, food bank lines are long, and our government is printing lots of money and giving it away. Can this level of indebtedness be sustained? Do we really want to burden our grandchildren and great grandchildren with so much debt? With so much uncertainty, how are you? Prayers help, soul searching is timely, but we used to find solace at club meetings and at church., We haven't heard a reassuring word from our pastors or had a hug from Sister Prather or seen Deacon Patrick in three months. To me, social media is absolutely no substitute. So, how is it going with you?

The adults I know are anxious to get back to work and I am even hearing that kids are begging to go to school and to visit with Grandma and Papa. When was the last time you hugged your grandchildren or got some baby therapy? Our teenagers have been social distancing without an end in sight. What good is being a teenager without hanging out with friends? Saturday nights with family must be torture. For those graduating this year, it's been anticlimactic—no senior day, no prom, and no graduation. I hope they at least got the traditional presents and money from church, family, and friends. How many times a day do you hear: "Mama, Mama? The incidence of domestic violence and child abuse are way up. What's happening in your world?

My grandmother was fond of saying, "Don't be too concerned about the pain in your leg, many people have no leg." We are still blessed. We are blessed that most of us still have our health and strength. A check from a job or from our government arrived, but are you OK?

While we must focus on putting out the fires that are threatening to consume us, we all need to recognize how incredibly difficult it is to be sequestered for an extended period of time. While we should try not to lament and feel sorry for ourselves, the better option is to find creative things we can do to mitigate this cramping of our lifestyles. So, how are you feeling today?

I have fallen in love with nature: sunshine, sunrise and sunsets, clouds, rain, birds, flowers, the wind on my face. Just because we cannot go to ball games, concerts, and parties, doesn't mean we cannot enjoy nature. Even though I hate them for eating up my garden, on our walks next to a creek in our neighborhood (Johnston Heights) we look forward to seeing the herd of deer. Looking at pictures on screens doesn't help. How is it where you live?

I recognize that I need human contact. This is me reaching out to you. I hope you are well.

193.

Lessons I Learned from My Mother

June 25, 2020

When I migrated to the United States in 1959, I was 15 years old. My mother was diligent about teaching me about life in the United States. I was left in the care of my grandmother in Jamaica when my mother went off to this great land of opportunity. So, she preceded me here by ten years. She had even become active in passing fair housing legislation in New Jersey and I participated in these meetings in our living room after my arrival. Here are the rules of survival that she taught me:

1. I pray for God to put a hedge of protection around you. Pray unceasingly.

2. You are black and don't forget it. While it may not be obvious to everyone, be true to yourself.

3. Get an education. Your path to financial independence and respectability is education. You either work hard now and live well later or waste your youth and suffer for the rest of your life.

4. Avoid the police at all costs. It never goes well. So, when they are approaching you, take evasive action. Try desperately to work out whatever issue you have with someone without involving the police. Don't give them a reason to even talk with you. Don't jaywalk, have marijuana on you or break the law in any way to give them an excuse to abuse you.

5. Don't patronize any business that doesn't have black employees. This goes double for restaurants. If there are black employees, they will make sure your food is OK. Banks, lawyers, doctors, car dealers and other businesses are less likely to take advantage of you if they have black employees.

6. Don't burn bridges. Even when you are being fired, be respectful. Enemies one day, best friends another day and vice versa. Be careful of friends who hang-out with people who wish to harm you. A friend of your enemy is also your enemy. Avoid hateful people.

7. If the egg falls on the rock, too bad for the egg. If the rock falls on the egg, too bad for the egg. This is an important calculus. In life, you should always judge whether you are a rock or an egg. If you are approached by a gang that is intent on beating you up, that is not a good time to stand your ground. Choose your battles carefully and don't feel like you have to take on everybody.

8. When you point your finger at someone and accuse them, just recognize that there are three fingers pointing back at you. Don't be so focused on the speck in someone else's eye and ignore the huge one in your own.

9. Have integrity and treat others as you want them to treat you. Don't get arrested, don't get any girl pregnant until you are married and avoid illegal drugs. This is a great country with wonderful opportunities, but you increase your chances of failure carrying around baggage.

10. Don't ever try to outsmart or pull a fast one on anybody. Just have integrity and outwork them.

I am now 77 years old and much has changed. Did I teach my own children the same lessons? Yes. Racism lingers. We actually elected a Black president, but racism lingers. God brought my family to Thomaston ten years ago and it has been a wonderful experience for us, but racism lingers. What is the future we want? Enlightened self-interest should tell us that we can only enjoy God's bounty if we promote justice for all.

194.

Change is Gonna Come

July 2, 2020

God is doing a new thing in our country, and we need to catch-up with Him. After 250 years of slavery, the vice president of the Confederacy (Alexander Stephens) promoted the myth of white supremacy by proclaiming:

Our new government foundations are laid, its cornerstone rests upon the great truth that the Negro is not equal to the white man and subordination to the superior race is their natural place.

This blasphemy was the rallying cry of the South during the Civil War and continues to haunt us. Even after Jim Crow laws, mass imprisonment, convict leasing (peonage), unemployment, inferior schools, lynchings, red-lining and flooding drugs to the Black community, we continue to excel. And yet we rise!

After the *Emancipation Proclamation*, Black people forged a thriving city called Greenwood, Okla. White racists (who resented these upstarts), in a paroxysm of violence, killed 300, left 8,000 homeless and burned every building to the ground. When the police were called, the police joined the rioters, and no protection was offered. And yet we rise. Please recognize that these previously enslaved people, whose starting blocks were back in the weeds, are now excelling in every field of human endeavor. Once again, what's the difference between a white horse and a black horse?

In Isaiah 43:18, it says: "Do not remember the former things, nor consider the things of old. I am about to do a new thing. Now it springs forth." There is no mistaking our charge. We cannot discover new lands if we are not willing to turn our backs on what is familiar, just like a monkey won't be able to move to the next branch if he is unwilling to let go of the branch he is holding on to.

If you felt at home with the rhetoric from the White House, I suspect you have finally become disappointed and forlorn because honest scrutiny (taking off your blinders) should have impressed on you that President Trump is stuck in an antiquated narrative. Is "MAGA" a restatement of Alexander Stephens' cornerstone proclamation? Is he trying to put Black people back in their place? Thanks to cell phone cameras, we are now witnessing (in living color) the abuses resulting from his rhetoric.

As Blacks and Whites march together proclaiming "Black Lives Matter," it should awaken an ethic based on respect for human rights and a commitment to universal justice. If there is any hope for lasting peace and prosperity in the land, it will come from people of good will holding responsible parties to account for their abuses and excesses. Together, we can create a new future. The Lord is reaching out to redeem our country. Will you take His hand? I just learned that after the French Revolution, they not only punished enemies, but also those who stayed silent during the siege.

With an open mind, you may finally recognize that Black people are peaceful and patient people who preserved our dignity in the face of marginalization, humiliation, and disenfranchisement by clothing ourselves in the armor of God—hoping, yearning, longing and working for a better future. Isn't this what you hope for as well? "Everything Has Become New" (Corinthians 5:17)

195.
Meet Colonel Bill Anderson: One Tough Marine and Vietnam Veteran

July 23, 2020

I first met Bill when I started playing golf with the Raintree Rascals in 2012. We often had side conversations about what I wrote in my columns—sometimes he agreed and sometimes he disagreed but "I will defend your right to write whatever the hell you want to say." I must have made an impression because he invited me to give a talk at his church (First Presbyterian Church). Rev. Gilstrap and everyone I met were most gracious and as we exchanged points of view, I hope a good time was had by all. As a follow-up, Bill and Kathy invited me to visit them in their home out on Pickard Rd. We have become friends.

Their home is out in the country on about 20 acres of land—lovely, fruited trees, flowers, a barn with a horse and lots of cardinals feeding at bird feeders. After a few beers, I am delighted to hear his life story and his 20 years in the Marine Corps. He was such a killing machine Hanoi Hanna singled him out on the radio to announce a $10,000 bounty on his head. So, I said: "When I was in Nam, I also went up the Mekong Delta and Danang." "Which years were you there?" "Well, I went there on a cruise five years ago." We had a good laugh. But I asked him if he knew why Vietnam is now the largest producer of shrimp? "I have no idea." Well, after we bombed the hell out of them, and left thousands of craters and they filled up with water. They seeded the ponds with shrimp and now it's a major source of income. "Well, when they give you lemons, make lemonade."

Bill's father was a handy man who fixed farming equipment, built barns, truck bodies and anything else that needed building or fixing. He was born in 1938 and grew up working side by side with his father. He learned to drive a tractor when he was 12, a car when he was 13 and logging trucks at 14. He was pulled over by the police for broken taillights and given a warning. The police didn't even ask for a driver's license because he knew he didn't have one. I asked him if a Black kid would have been treated with the same consideration and he said: "Probably not."

He met his wife in his senior year of high school. Once he got over his bashfulness to ask her out, they became a couple, being together for almost 70 years and the proud parents of Mark, Lance, and Karen. Both Bill and Kathy graduated from the University of Wisconsin. Interestingly enough, my wife was also a Badger for both undergraduate and medical school.

In the rough and tumble life of Bill Anderson, he gravitated to boxing and therein lies a thousand tales. He was friends with a boxing legend (Sargent Percy Price) who defeated Mohamed Ali during the Olympic trials. The only reason Ali went to the Olympics was because Percy injured his leg. He also met John Wayne. When JW tried to squeeze Bill's hand, Bill squeezed back and when JW let go, he said, "Damn Colonel, you have a good grip."

Bill and Kathy moved to Thomaston in 1993 to work at the mill as an engineer under Bill Davis and retired in 1998. On his retirement, he started playing golf with the Raintree Rascals but now retired from golf as well.

According to Bill: "I have always been aggressive and couldn't back down from a fight. From time to time, I have been a SOB, but I was a good one." Just keep being you, Bill!

196.

The Courage of
Cordy Tindel (CT) Vivian
(1924-2020)

July 30, 2020

On the same day last week, two of my heroes passed. While Congressman John Lewis received the lion's share of accolades and honors, my wife and I knew C.T. Vivian personally and losing him was very emotional. C.T. was an assistant pastor of Providence Missionary Baptist Church (Atlanta), pastored by Rev. Gerald Durley, where I was a deacon.

Part of the history of the Civil Rights Movement pits a burly 220-pound Sheriff Jim Clark of Selma, who strongly opposed the right to vote for Blacks, against the slender Black preacher who probably weighed 150 pounds. Sheriff Clark and Bull Conner became symbols of the struggle of African Americans' right to vote. Sheriff Clark represented institutional racism in the South and C.T. represented the will of Black people to participate in our democracy. Sheriff Clark directed the use of cattle prods and nightsticks against civil rights demonstrators. C.T. Vivian used non-violence - a David and Goliath confrontation.

Martin Luther King gave C.T. the title of "Field Marshall" and after leading sit-ins at lunch counters, boycotts, and endless marches, following the passage of the Voting Rights Act of 1965, Dr. King assigned C.T. the task of leading the first group of Black citizens to register. Sheriff Clark was pictured in the movie "Eye on the Prize" standing on the top of the stairs leading up to the courthouse with his hands folded as C.T. left the group at the bottom of the stairs and advanced toward his tormentor. Sheriff Clark told C.T. that he would not be allowed into the courthouse and C.T. points his finger at Sheriff Clark's face and informs him that it is now legal for Black people to vote and stopping them was illegal. Sheriff Clark reaches back and with his right fist, hits C.T. squarely in the face sending C.T. flying down the marble steps. Bloody but unbowed, C.T. runs back up the stairs and demands entry and low and behold, Sheriff Clark withdraws, and the first group of Black voters registered to vote in the South. When I saw the movie, I was in awe that he could get back up after a blow to the face and stay on task. So, inquiring minds wanted to know, wasn't he in pain? How could he have summoned up so much courage to run back up those steps? C.T. told us he was on a mission and never felt pain, even though he was bleeding.

CT received the Presidential Medal of Honor, and while he never stopped preaching the gospel of equal rights, among his many innovations was the creation of a federally funded "Upward Bound" program to enrich the educational experience of high school students to help them succeed in college. Upson-Lee adopted the program that currently serves 53 students providing summer and after school enrichment in English, mathematics, foreign languages, and science.

He became president of the Southern Christian Leadership Conference and dean of the Shaw University Divinity School in Raleigh, N.C. His life was well lived, and his legacy is revered. And the Lord said: "Come in good and faithful servant and claim your reward. You can sit down happy."

197.
Ex-Urban Migration: Living Off the Grid

August 6, 2020

Thomaston, are you ready to be invaded? Both young and old are finding it desirable to live in small towns and some are headed for Thomaston.

In response to a report on television that millennials are moving out of cities, my friend (Ms. Bertha Ziegler) responded: "You mean they are going to live off the grid?"

According to the Census Bureau, there was a net migration of 76,000 millennials out of New York state in 2018 and 50,400 millennials out of New York City in 2018. Why are they moving south? It could be our great weather, flowers, peaches, and giant firs. While there are numerous individual reasons, here are a few:

1. Cost of living. In urban areas, houses, taxes, and utilities have dramatically increased. Moving south can be particularly attractive to young families.

2. A desire to make meaningful contributions to the improvement of a community. These opportunities are rare in urban settings.

3. Working from home. Technology has now made it possible for people who want to live in rural areas to still stay connected with work, educational opportunities or friends. More companies are relocating to rural areas, offering good jobs.

4. Less congestion means fewer opportunities to be infected (COVID-19) It is always healthier in the country.

5. Government services. When you call, they come? And where else will they pick up big, discarded items from in front of your house? I never heard of that before I moved here.

6. Low crime, wonderful houses of worship, honest and fair politicians, and law enforcement, and don't forget, free parking.

7. When I lived in Atlanta and other cities, I had to make a tee time a week in advance. In Thomaston, I can go to Raintree anytime and play, no reservations required.

Cities are obviously more efficient and offer more variety of restaurants, golf courses, museums, educational institutions, theaters, intellectual pursuits, and entertainment in general. High end healthcare is certainly more accessible. Infrastructure and transportation are more convenient. It's easier to provide services when people live closer together creating a large tax base. I suspect it is easier to find a date or at least have more choices (not necessarily quality) of partners. But Atlanta, Macon and Columbus are only an hour away.

Migration from metropolitan areas to small towns has become an area of emerging interest. Isn't this something our political leaders should alert us about? Is this something we should encourage? Would our quality of life be enhanced by a doubling of our population? What are the consequences that an increase in the number of young people have on our economy? I am also hearing that retirees are deciding that a quiet, affordable life of small towns is something they want. My wife and I were ahead of the curve and can wholeheartedly support the notion that Thomaston is a great place to live for both young and old.

198.
Mathematics: The Language of God

August 13, 2020

When I studied sociology in college, I read William Cameron's 1963 text *"Informal Sociology: A Casual Introduction to Sociological Thinking."* He was sharing his enthusiasm for the new computing machines that promised to hasten discoveries because it was now possible to quickly manipulate big data. "It would be nice," he mused, "if all of the data which sociologists require could be enumerated because then we could run them through IBM machines and draw charts as the economists do. However, he warns, "not everything that can be counted counts, and not everything that counts can be counted."

My oldest granddaughter (Mackenzie) is on such a mission as a graduate student at the University of Maryland doing pure math. While she has a keen interest in artificial intelligence, she believes that "truth" and all the rules of nature can only be deduced from logical reasoning and quantitative calculations. It is the foundation for all sciences, computer hardware and software. By the way, she did not get this penchant from her Pop-Pop. While I love pie, I had trouble calculating Pi and while she excelled in calculus, special relativity and God knows what else, Algebra II was as far as I ventured. I have trouble making change and adding up the numbers on my golf card.

Say I have four sons, three able-bodied and one unable to work, and four daughters, two of whom are married, and I want to provide for each of them and their children and children I may yet have. And I do not know how large or small my fortune will be when it comes time to inherit. Well, for the proportions, I would consult the formulas in the book *"Kitab al-Jabr"* written in the 9th Century by Muhammad ibn Musa al-Khwarizmi for just these very questions. The term "algebra" comes from the book's title.

The Romans did not have a concept of zero. It took some smart people in India to invent it and yes, "0" is an even number. Other names for zero include nought, nil, zilch, zip and even love in tennis. We ended up with 60 seconds in a minute and 360 degrees in a circle because the Babylonians did math in base 60 instead of ten as we are prone to do.

COVID-19 is increasing at a rate of 60,000 cases per day. We are less than 5% of the world's population, but we account for 25% of the cases. President Trump boldly asserted that this was due to our expanded testing and then with over 150,000 deaths told us to not believe the numbers. Does this mean that you are not pregnant if you don't get a pregnancy test? We could eliminate diabetes, high blood pressure and cholesterol disease by just not testing anyone. If we didn't have police to catch speeders, there would be no speeding.

199.
All are Welcome to Thomaston

August 20, 2020

While we are being bountifully blessed, it is important to recognize that we owe it to the Great Architect of the universe to be righteous. Let us not take it for granted. We should earn it by our deeds, or we do not deserve it. I believe the promise is that as our good works and praises go up, blessings rain down. As tragic as it is, the casualties of COVID-19 are low compared to the rest of the country and as I mentioned in several columns, we are sheltered from hurricanes, earthquakes, forest fires, floods, tsunamis, and live in a community were the crime and preventable deaths are low. We have clean air and plenty of clean water.

For God's sake, we now own a million-dollar fire truck. Have you stopped to give thanks for how clean our streets are and how well maintained our highways and byways are? We have a lot for which we should be grateful. We are indeed blessed—free from hate and violence. Inclusion is important to attracting and retaining industry and employment—especially health care employees. Thankfully, it is not hard to attract good doctors, dentists, and nurses to Upson County. If Thomaston is to continue being a healthy community, we need doctors and nurses who feel at home here. Even during a pandemic, everyone can receive quality health care and a good education. All things considered, we get along and enjoy a wonderful quality of life.

If we are to receive our daily shower of blessings, we owe a debt of gratitude. So, in case you are wondering, here is what is required.

Save the post office. So many people depend on its services through wind, rain, and snow. Treat each other with brotherly love and reach out and help someone in need. I feel gratified handing out boxes of fruits and vegetables to people in need at Greater Mount Zion Baptist Church on Thursdays from six to seven.

I can shout it from the mountaintop or the rooftop. The message is clear: no matter what you look like, where you come from, who you love, or what you believe, you will be treated with kindness in Thomaston. Everyone is invested in the community and believes we belong—a right to life, liberty, and the pursuit of happiness. I am soooo glad God brought us to this place. Thank you one and all for your many kindnesses.

I will leave you with some inspirational thoughts from Martin Luther King:

> Now there is a final reason I think that Jesus says, "Love your enemies." It is this: that love has within it a redemptive power. And there is a power there that eventually transforms individuals. Just keep being friendly to that person. Just keep loving them, and they can't stand it too long. Oh, they react in many ways in the beginning. They react with guilty feelings, and sometimes they'll hate you a little more at that transition period, but just keep loving them. And by the power of your love, they will break down under the load. That's love, you see. It is redemptive, and this is why Jesus' dominant and frequent messages were about love. There's something about love that builds up and is creative. There is something about hate that tear down and is destructive. So, love your enemies. (From "Loving Your Enemies") Martin Luther King Jr., a Knock at Midnight: Inspiration from the Great Sermons of Reverend Martin Luther King, Jr.

200.

Global Warming: The Pandemic X 1,000 Percent

August 27, 2020

We have vacationed in Death Valley and have many snapshots making light of the famous sweltering heat, such as pretending to crawl to an oasis gasping for water or jumping headlong into a swimming pool fully clothed. But, last week, Death Valley lived up to its name by registering the highest atmospheric temperature ever on the earth—130 degrees. I also read a report that 28 trillion tons of ice melted from our glaciers since 1994, largely due to greenhouse gas emissions.

Are you listening and observing what is going on around us: extreme weather, record hurricane sizes and speeds, record number of forest fires, floods, islands disappearing into the ocean, ecosystems around the world nearing collapse and over a million animal species facing extinction? Whether it is on land, in the seas, in the atmosphere, we are having a devastating impact on our environment.

We should take this thing seriously. If we don't, it will no longer be a question of if but when Mother Earth will become uninhabitable. We just cannot continue to treat our planet with such utter disregard. This is not just a blip, but a significant departure from the patterns of earth's history.

While nuclear wars and pandemics are our most imminent threats, in time, with nowhere to hide and nowhere to run, global warming will likely be the cause of human extinction—an existential threat: no more life on our planet and we will only have ourselves to blame.

That is a roundabout way to let you know that I have decided to install solar panels on my roof. It makes sense. I can then buy an electric car and have zero operating expenses and stop burning fossil fuels and reduce carbon emissions. We can all do our part. When fossil fuels spill, that's an environmental disaster, but when there is a huge spill of solar energy, that's just a nice day.

Our insatiable need for plastics is producing a mountain of waste. Plastic pollution has increased ten-fold since 1980. Where will it all go? When I was a hospitalized patient, I counted five bags of plastic gloves, gowns, bedding, masks, tubing, and syringes leaving my room each day. A plastic straw, garbage bag and golf ball are forever. Add to that, plastic tees, and clubs. Every year we dump 300-400 million tons of heavy metals, solvents, toxic sludge, and other wastes into the waters of the world.

Prof. John Spicer from the University of Plymouth wrote: "Climate change is certainly one of the greatest threats that face humankind... The current situation is desperate and has been for some time."

I hope the coronavirus pandemic has taught us that we cannot just wish it away. We need to trust the scientists and instead of continuing on a path of destruction, we must do more to restore our environment. We can waste less and invest more in renewables—solar, wind and hydroelectric. Only then will we leave future generations a sustainable planet.

201.
The Roots of Our Discontent

September 3, 2020

England is the size of our West Coast (California, Oregon, and Washington). How did this island once rule the world? I was born in Jamaica in 1943 and grew up under English rule. We were not alone. At some point in history, the sun never set on territories ruled by England (Canada, China, India, Australia, New Zealand, Iceland, most of Africa, most of the West Indies, South America and yes, until the *Boston Tea Party*, the territories we now refer to as the United States of America. Maybe (by extension) they are still running things. We got our language, our laws, the King James Bible, education, values, rituals, and traditions from Mother England but we also got racism and slavery.

It all started with a lie. As they were the first to create a map of the world, they purposefully drew England to be twice the size that it is to claim a more robust place in the world. Having turned gunpowder that was being used for fireworks in China into killing machines, they set about conquering the world and then using the men from conquered territories to conquer and control other territories. They then set about concentrating enormous wealth in England (gold, diamonds, art and artifacts and talent—rum, sugar, bananas, and starch from Jamaica). They were the envy of the world and even after 300 years of brutal slavery, most Jamaicans still want to be English ladies and gentlemen—refined, learned, mannerly, sophisticated, and well groomed—perhaps even with a walking stick and a taste for whiskey like Johnny Walker.

Perhaps the architect of racism was Sir Francis Bacon. Around the time the Bible was translated, and William Shakespeare was having his way with the English language, Bacon preached that white men were endowed with superior values, intellect and resolve that made them the only ones capable of running the world or anything else for that matter. So, they should not be reluctant to assume their rightful place as rulers, while all others (including women) should also just assume their rightful place as slaves, servants and accept being treated like children. That is our inheritance, and even in the face of hundreds of years of evidence to the contrary, some of us still cling to this myth. So, in light of the Black Lives Matter movement in the United States, there have been protests over several British traditions including their national hymn. "Rule, Britannia! Britannia rules the waves! Britons never, never, never will be slaves." On the one hand, they have been proudly singing this hymn since 1740 and many pledged that they will never stop singing their beloved lyrics. They complain that their culture is being hijacked to conform to a progressive agenda where insults are suspected in everything. Should we really judge traditions by our current values? The opposite view is that the lyrics are vulgar, inappropriate patriotism, boastful and xenophobic (fear of anything different, foreign, or strange). According to Catriona Lewis: "Do those Brits who believe it's OK to sing an 18th century song about never being enslaved, written when the UK was enslaving and killing millions of innocents, also believe it's appropriate for neo-Nazis to shout, "We will never be forced into a gas chamber... Slavery was Britain's holocaust."

Should they change these lyrics?

202.

Projecting Our Deficits onto Others: Are You Talking About Me or Yourself?

September 10, 2020

A father who is feeling that his life has been a failure tells his son that he is going to grow up to be a big fat nothing. A mother who has difficulty controlling her own sexual impulses accuse her daughter of running around. "You are nothing but a ...." If a man is embarrassed by his obsession with a woman, one of the predictable defenses is to accuse the woman of coming on to him. "Look at how she carries herself and the clothes she wears." If an otherwise moral and upstanding woman is contemplating stealing something, she will broadcast to everyone who will listen that people are always stealing her stuff. "Why can't people leave other people's property alone?" A habitual liar is forever accusing others of spreading lies—fake news. The person who constantly gossips is the very person who will complain about people who gossip and will even accuse others of gossiping about him. The entertainer Flip Wilson was famous for saying, "The Devil made me do it." If a man is caught stealing, his defense might be that it's the fault of the property owner that she didn't do a better job of protecting her stuff or my parents didn't raise me right.

Ladies and gentlemen, if you have a fragile ego and you cannot stand to admit fault, you will project your faults (that have the potential of making you feel bad) by pointing your finger at someone else rather than admitting that YOU are really the guilty one. Can you see how we may be formulating a sense of who we are from other people's projections? When you point your finger at your neighbor, there are three more pointing back at you.

According to Psychology Today, "Projection is the process of displacing one's feelings onto a different person... attributing one's own unacceptable urges to another." In other words, all of us from time-to-time project our feelings onto others so we don't have to face the music (our undesirable deficits and unresolved issues). We deny that we have these bad traits in ourselves and attribute them to others, falsely accusing them of things of which we are guilty.

Sigmund Freud's greatest achievement was his work popularizing the unconscious. When we react to everyday events, who is really pulling the strings? Our thinking at the moment or the stuff in our unconscious? To Freud, everything we experience in life has been recorded and stored and we tend to repress and suppress the embarrassing stuff, but some things just want to get out and if we don't like what that says about us, we project it onto others and tell ourselves that it is the other person's problem. We can then continue to believe we are perfect. I am OK but you are not so hot. Thoughts, desires, and feelings that we find difficult to accept are attributed to someone else. Look at all the problems you have? Do you see how we attribute difficult feelings or wishes to someone else to avoid confronting them in ourselves?

> *"You hypocrite! First take the beam out of your own eye,*
> *and then you will see clearly to take the speck from your brother's eye."*
> (Matthew 7:5)

> *"Do not taunt your neighbor with the blemish you yourself have."*
> (Babylonian Talmud)

203.
Responsive Reading for Churches

September 17, 2020

Leader: O LORD God of hosts, how majestic and magnificent is Your name.

Congregation: Our father, strong and mighty, incline Your ears and hear our prayer.

Leader: We stand in awe of Your miraculous creations, particularly the splendor of the community we call home. You are our light and salvation.

Congregation: In our distress, we cry unto You because our souls are hungry for Your wisdom, guidance, and intervention.

Leader: Trouble is everywhere, and we are consumed with grief. Too many have died in our country from this virus we call COVID 19.

Congregation: All night long those who have lost loved ones flood their beds with weeping and our eyes grow weak with sorrow.

Leader: Deliver us quickly out of this torment and declare Your glory Almighty God.

Congregation: Bring us out of our distress. Have compassion on those afflicted and deliver us Almighty God, we put our trust in You.

Leader: You keep your promises Almighty God, and You said the needy will not be forgotten, nor the hope of the afflicted perish. You are a refuge for those who suffer, the ever-present help in times of trouble.

Congregation: Your promise is a lamp unto our feet, and a light unto our paths.

Leader: You promised that You would never ignore the cry of the afflicted and that those who know Your name will never be forsaken.

Congregation: We shall wait on You and not be weary. We shall be of good courage as we lift our hands to You in supplication. Let not this evil triumph.

Leader:: Forsake us not O Gentle Savior. Teach us to do Your will and lead us into uprightness, integrity, and truth so that sinners will walk from darkness into the light and become gracious and full of compassion for our fellow citizens.

Congregation: Defend us from this virus. Place a shield and hedge of protection around us and restore glory on us so we can live with good health and prosperity.

Leader: We lay our requests before You and wait with expectation.

Congregation: Weeping may remain for a night but rejoicing comes in the morning.

Leader: If You be for us, who can be against us? If we trust in You, who and what shall we fear?

Congregation: We will give thanks and sing praises to You, our LORD Most High, for You have kept Your promises and provided bountifully for us.

Leader: We come before You with thanksgiving. Your mercy is everlasting; and Your truth endure forever.

Congregation: May the words of our mouths and the meditations of our hearts be forever pleasing in Your sight O Lord, our rock and our redeemer.

Leader: Save Your people and bless our inheritance. Feed us until we want no more. Turn our mourning into dancing.

Congregation: Let Your mercy, O LORD, be upon us.

All: From everlasting to everlasting, thou art God. May Your mercy endure forever, Hallelujah! Hallelujah! Hallelujah! Amen. Amen. Amen.

204.

What Would it Take for You to Stand Against a Tide?

September 24, 2020

If you were there when they crucified our Lord and Savior, would you have taken up the cross or waited until it was safe to celebrate his victory over death?

If you were there when the disciples were hunted down and killed, would you have stuck out your own neck to save them?

If you were present during slavery, would you have fought against it?

If you were present at the lynching of Black men, would you have spoken up?

If you were there when Hitler was sending Jews to the gas chamber, would you have risked protecting a Jewish girl in your attic?

If you were present at the integration of schools in Arkansas, would you have tried to protect the Black students or objected to school integration and yelled racist epitaphs at them?

You were a witness to a white police officer choking a Black man to his death, did you support the Black Lives Matter movement, or did you turn a deaf ear?

Do you perpetuate injustice or stand up against it or worse, just ignore it? Could you be silent if you knew that someone was being raped or observed acts of cruelty against a neighbor?

Are you willing to be banished and fall into disfavor by those whose approval you crave?

Are you willing to transcend your fears, endure hate, disapproval, and scorn to stand up for what is right?

"First, they came for the socialists, and I did not speak out—because I was not a socialist. Then they came for the trade unionists, and I did not speak out—because I was not a trade unionist. Then they came for the Jews, and I did not speak out—because I was not a Jew. Then they came for me—and there was no one left to speak for me." Pastor Martin Niemoller (Berlin, 1836)

205.
Standing Positive and COVID-19 Negative

October 1, 2020

It would clearly be an understatement to say that these are trying times. We may be avoiding the virus but look at all the unprecedented things that confront us. We are under constant bombardment with negative news and attack campaign ads. California is burning and Texas is flooding. I am sorry but listening to church service on YouTube and Zoom meetings don't do it for me—poor substitutes for shaking hands and hugging the members of my church and seeing the smile on their faces that says: "So glad to see you. How have you been?" I don't know about you, but I have a hunger for singing together, prayers and meditation, listening to Sister Goochs' solos and thoughtful sermons by Rev. Reeves.

At this critical time in our children's lives, they are not able to play with friends, check their reality with each other or just walk together. Home school? Who has the patience for that? My granddaughter (Audrey) graduated from high school this year with no fanfare—no walk across the stage to receive her diploma with her grandfather loudly expressing his pride, no prom, no senior day. It gets worse. Child abuse and domestic violence are at an all-time high and it follows that a lot of relationships are going south.

On the election front, there is no more civility, the most outrageous myths are being treated as facts. We are at each other's throats. The television ads are vicious and cruel with no respect for truth. At a time when the death toll continues to rise and frustration and anger are spilling over in the streets and even your faithful worry that we may never return to a life without these avoidable deaths and destruction, we continue to believe with all our hearts Almighty God, that if we just trust and obey You, You will make a way. As it says in Matthew 6: "Do not worry about your life… but seek first His kingdom and His righteousness… do not worry about tomorrow." Thank you, Father God, for loving us and taking care of us in these traumatic days. Even the darkest night will end, and the sun will rise. Yes. Misery may last a night, but joy comes in the morning. Let us pray for victory over the virus and a return to civility.

In addition to our gratitude to You first and foremost Father God, we thank all those who reached out to others in need, whether they were hungry, sick, or even dying. We ask Your favor for the first responders, nurses and doctors who unselfishly dedicated themselves in the service of others.

We pray for the many souls who are on their way to glory. We ask You to comfort the broken-hearted and to strengthen all who are struggling from this trauma. We implore You to reach out to those vulnerable people living in nursing homes, prisons, and group homes. May we all use our time to do beneficial things for others. Make each one of us a vessel of hope and good works. Let us be united for the common good.

"God of our weary years, God of our silent tears, thou who hast brought us thus far on our way. Thou who hast by Thy might, led us into the light. Keep us forever in the path." This we pray.

206.
The Wages of Sin: You Reap What You Sow, the Harvest can be Hard to Bear

October 15, 2020

In my column a few weeks ago, I made the point that a good night's sleep is an excellent commentary on your health, the quality of your life, and the life you have lived. Guilt and restless nights are part of the wages of sin. Even though you may get away with your crime, your conscience (that tells you whether something is morally right or wrong) will weigh heavily on you for the rest of your life.

Someone pointed out that "sound sleep" is also a quick test of whether someone is marriage material and whether he or she can be trusted to be honest and live up to their commitments.

It is happening more frequently these days that someone with racist inclinations is caught on camera doing despicable acts, getting fired, ruining their careers and their family's standing in the community, and sometimes sent to prison. Just imagine the reception they will have when they get there.

So, what's the lesson? Is it wise to teach your children hate and violence? Is there any future in it? Whether it is family, friend, or foe? I know if I hung around hateful people who abused others, as much as they were my friends and bosom buddies today, it will only be a matter of time before that bile will be turned on me. So, why would you want to be part of a group that preach or practice hate? And since this should be obvious to everyone, do you understand why people who are hateful and practice violence don't have trustworthy friends? Friends and comrades today, enemies tomorrow.

There is a tragic story in the news about a sheriff in Arizona who contracted COVID-19 and suspecting that he would die, transferred the ownership to his home, his car, and all his assets to his son. He recovered only to learn that his son had liquidated all his assets and he didn't have a home to return to. Where did his son learn these values? Apples do not fall too far from the tree.

Frank Ancona was an Imperial Wizard with the KKK who was killed by his son. Edgar Ray Killen, a member of the KKK who killed James Chaney, Andrew Goodman and Michael Schwerner died inside the Mississippi State Penitentiary while serving three consecutive 20-year sentences. James Fields, a young man with a promising future, joined his neo-Nazi comrades in Charlottesville and was convicted in the death of Heather Heyer and will serve the rest of his life in prison.

The secret of raising successful children is to teach them to respect and treat others with kindness and brotherly love. If they learn this one lesson, they will be a delight to know and do business with. He or she will also marry a fine mate, get a good job and reward you with wonderful grandchildren.

According to Quotabulary:

Most of one's personality traits are acquired during childhood. The way one thinks, and acts is shaped by the way he has been raised, which is why parents have a very important role to play in a child's development. Parenting is about teaching children to differentiate between the right and the wrong, making them capable, and supporting their emotional, social, and intellectual development. For the children's upbringing to be healthy, the parents need to dedicate enough time to them, adopt the right ways of teaching or guiding them and create an environment conducive to the children's development.

207.
Suicide Threat from COVID-19 (The Number of People in Crisis is Increasing)

October 22, 2020

There is a mental health crisis accompanying the COVID pandemic and unfortunately, it is intensifying. Disrupted routines, unable to meet everyday responsibilities and the guilt from not being able to care for our loved ones is taking a severe toll on our well-being.

Center for Disease Control Director Robert Redfield recently said: "Suicides and drug overdoses have surpassed the death rate for COVID-19 among high school students." He could have added alcoholism, obesity, sleeplessness, child abuse, domestic violence, loneliness, boredom, worry and frustration accompanied by short tempers.

Dr. Redfield is alerting all of us that isolation causes anxiety that has a very negative impact on the mental health of all of us, but especially young people. Stress is a relatively new experience in children and they may respond more severely and more unpredictably. The overwhelming fear for children is the risk of losing their parents. What would become of me?

Human beings are social beings (especially when they are young) and we cannot singularly focus on preventing the spread of COVID-19 to the detriment of our mental health and social needs. The reason for being a child is to play. If they cannot play and have access to peers, they become frustrated, forlorn, and hostile.

In adults, in addition to social isolation, absence of intimacy, unemployment, lack of sleep, death of friends and relatives, insecurity about the future, everything being out of their control, we often feel like we are going crazy. A single friend confided in me: "I cannot take the chance of being with anybody, so I haven't had a date in over six months. What am I going to do?"

While we need to be cautious about opening our schools, there must be creative ways to meet the needs of our youth other than have them watching screens all day.

"What I have seen recently, I have never seen before. I have never seen so much intentional injury," said a nurse from John Muir Medical Center referring to the plight of children.

The number of calls to the Colorado Crisis Services increased 48% in 2020 over 2019. In Cook County, Illinois, the number of suicide deaths is already higher than for all of 2019. In Yakima County, Washington, the suicide rate has risen 30%. In Albany, Georgia., Dougherty County coroner Michael Fowler claimed, "Suicides have increased during the pandemic. With 11 or 12 suicides in 2020 so far -- the county's typical average for an entire year -- the number is likely to increase between now and January."

Every threat of suicide is a warning sign that should be taken seriously. Take time to talk calmly and reassure children about what is happening in a way that they can understand and assure them that their needs will be met no matter what happens. I urge churches to have a calling tree that checks in on all their members. I believe it is important for everyone to know that they are being thought about and connected to the community.

Please everyone, schedule a weekly family Zoom call, just to see and hear how your extended family is doing and be patient at the craziness that is going on around you. Take genuine interest in each of your children and monitor what they are doing for signs that they are not OK. Most importantly, be kind and give generously and even sacrificially to those in need.

As for yourself, pray unceasingly and if you don't have a pet, get one. It will soothe the savage beast in you. While you must socially distance and wear a mask when you are around others, read and play games instead of just watching TV. Interact with others as much as you can. Stay six feet away from the refrigerator and go outside for walks, play golf, tennis, pickleball, or just appreciate the gifts of nature. We will get through this together.

208.

Where Does It End?
(Do Not Be Overcome by Evil,
But Overcome Evil with Good
(Romans 12:21)

October 29, 2020

In these troublesome times of identity politics, not even Martin Luther King, Abraham Lincoln, and Nelson Mandela are sufficiently virtuous to satisfy the inexorable demands of some members of the Black Lives Matter movement. This purity standard has spiraled into supporters or enemies, us and them, angels and the damned - a search for enemies.

If we insist on our heroes being pure, the list will be extremely short. It is a defining moment of political upheaval when we may be tempted to abandon the extremely valuable contributions of less honorable and perfect individuals.

When we become fixated on a single value, just recognize that the implications have significance beyond our moment in history. During the French Revolution and the Crusades, in their feeding frenzy, it was "off with their heads" for anyone who did not pass the test.

If the statues and names on buildings of Confederate generals must fall under the pretense that they were racists, so was Jefferson, Washington and even Mahatma Gandhi, who believed that people from India were smarter than African Americans.

What is the litmus test? By what standard do we put a shine on some and blot out the others? And why stop there? Let us rid ourselves of arguing for the removal of statues based on whether these individuals believed in white supremacy. While I am at a loss for the rationale for putting Confederate generals on pedestals, I, for one, will never give up on Abraham Lincoln and Thomas Jefferson.

In our zeal to dismantle the existing social order, should we also abandon all the innovations, inventions, creations, works of art and surgical procedures that were brought to us by evil actors. We must be careful that we do not throw the baby out with the bath water.

I will never stop singing "Amazing Grace" because the author (John Newton) was the captain of a slave ship. Maybe the evilest of all was Dr. Marion Sims, the "father of gynecology," who performed experimental surgery on enslaved Black women, without anesthesia, but greatly advanced medical procedures. What about Nazi doctors who performed the most inhumane and diabolical experiments on Jews as a shortcut to medical breakthroughs - significant advances in medicine.

What do we do with that knowledge? Should the source of these innovations be considered?

209.
Arrogant Boastful Know-It-Alls: Do You Have All the Answers?

November 5, 2020

When our group was traveling on a Safari in Kenya, our friend, Laurie Watkins, passed the time by telling one of those long-drawn-out jokes; and he really sold it.

He began earnestly telling us about a tribe of people called the Hellawies who supposedly lived nearby, explaining in vivid detail their lifestyle. I mean, this guy could really tell a joke. He had us all—hook, line, and sinker, and then came the punchline: they are very short people who live in the high bush country and when they went hunting, they were forever asking, "Where the hellawie? Where the hellawie?" We had a good laugh.

On my return, I tried to tell my know-it-all auntie the story. I barely got the name of the tribe out of my mouth before she volunteered that she knew them well. She described their style of dancing, their art, and their customs. I looked at my wife and she shook her head in that way that let me know I couldn't dare finish the joke.

My stepfather grew up among dirt poor farmers on other people's land. Delivered from a provincial life by joining the Army in WWII, he survived his ordeal and collected war stories and enough skills that qualified him to make a good union wage at a Ford Motor plant. He compensated for a spotty education with bluster.

His braggadocio enabled him to keep his pride in the Jim Crow South and a North that turned out to have just as many unwritten rules to keep him in his place. It made him ornery and tiresome. Famously suspicious of intellectuals, he was forever quoting Bible passages and Benjamin Franklin as a guide for all occasions.

Before we had GPS, we wasted a lot of gasoline. What he is best known for was getting lost because he knew what he was doing without consulting a map or seeking the advice of someone who knew the area.

The smartest man who ever lived (Albert Einstein) said he was the most ignorant because he knew what he didn't know.

As teenagers learn a little, they can become argumentative, and it can be difficult to engage them because they know just enough to be dangerous. They know everything because they haven't learned enough to know what they don't know. They have what is regarded as an "illusion of knowledge."

I used to say that if you had lived during the Renaissance, it would have been possible to have read all of the books, every single thing anyone had ever written down in Latin or Greek. There were a finite number of books. I'm sure some Albizzi or Medici could boast that he knew everything worth knowing in all of Christendom. But if that was ever true, it's certainly demonstrably false now. We are living in an age of infinite knowledge when it is not possible for anyone to know even 1% of the world's knowledge.

In Luke 6:43-45, Jesus tells us:

> No good tree bears bad fruit, nor does a bad tree bear good fruit. Each tree is recognized by its own fruit. People do not pick figs from thornbushes, or grapes from briers. A good man brings good things out of the good stored up in his heart, and an evil man brings evil things out of the evil stored up in his heart. For the mouth speaks what the heart is full of.

Jesus is telling us that if a person walks the earth humbly, open to new experiences and the wisdom of other people, then he "stores" these and they become his repertoire, the cache from which he can draw his insights and revelations. Conversely, if he stores soundbites and gossip, boasts and roasts, then those are the meagre provisions he will draw on when he goes to speak.

210.

Discrimination Hurts Everyone (Whether You are the Victim or the One Dishing it Out)

November 12, 2020

On the topic of birdwatchers, consider the curious case of Christian Cooper, a birder doing his thing in Central Park (NY). Concerned for the wildlife in the park, he asked a nearby dog walker to leash her dog, per the park's rules. A common conflict, but the dog walker was a white woman and the birder a Black man and she knew that if she called the police, they would be likely to see him as the aggressor. Fortunately, he knew his rights and was armed with a video recorder. This woman did not get her way. But what if she had? What if Black men like Mr. Cooper were driven out of birding by such encounters? History tells us that the field would be poorer for it.

When I welcomed Mack Salter's (Tree man) work crew to cut down a big oak in my yard, to my surprise, two of his crew members were women. No doubt many women and minorities know their way around a tractor and a chainsaw, but I have to admit, I have never seen a Black woman in that role. Mack is not only a tree expert, but I also give him props for that little glimpse I got of him as a man who doesn't do things the old-fashioned way. I got to see him as that rare specimen: an equal opportunity employer. He was able to calculate the height of my tree and dropped it in the precise spot to avoid destroying things that were potentially in its path. I was impressed. It got me thinking about equal opportunities.

You see, I dream of a time when everyone's ambitions are nurtured, and every student can prepare to become all he or she can become, unhindered by racism. Tiger Woods made golf the focus of the world with his unbelievable talent. What if Blacks were still barred from the Masters? Baseball was enriched when Jackie Robinson joined the Dodgers. Tennis became exciting when the Williams Sisters emerged as stars and Dr. DeGrasse Tyson became the best-known astrophysicist, cosmologist, and planetary scientist in the world. Do you receive medical care from a non-white doctor?

Because of our general commitment to universal brotherhood, I have never met anyone who openly admitted that discrimination was good and that he or she was a racist. Almost all of us proclaim our support for eradicating prejudice, but our actions refuse to live up to our commitment. My point is, whether we express or practice racism conscientiously or unintendedly, it hurts all of us. If you insist on keeping your knee on my neck, we are both hindered from doing what needs to be done to support ourselves and our families. Racism hurts everyone. I lament those who squander their wealth on guns and ammunition as well as most of their valuable time training to kill people when their children are ignored at home and do not have the resources to develop their talents.

Competition is the hallmark of American democracy. Ideally, it means that everyone should have equal access to opportunities and be given a fair shot at success. While it is reasonable to put your selfish interests first and vigorously compete, it does not give you the right to illegally thwart the ambitions of others. I compete enthusiastically with my competitors on the golf course, but I wish them well, help them find their wayward balls, advise them about distances, tell them about new equipment and tips I picked up from a pro, magazine article, or TV program. I applaud their good shots, but I will never let them get away with not abiding by the rules. At the end of each round, we shake hands and I wish them well. I love this game and it has been a source of amazing thrills and agonies over a lifetime.

The cure for various viruses, hunger, pain, cancer, diabetes, and heart disease is potentially within the capability of every child, so we do ourselves a disservice to half-heartedly commit to the upbringing, education, and opportunity of every child. Just consider how much of our human potential is wasted with this racial nonsense. Given half a chance, there is a whole world of unlimited human potential in our young people. During the opening ceremonies of the Olympic games, the Japanese contingent represents Japan, the Chinese squad represents China and Kenyans represent Kenya, but when the American team arrives, we represent the whole world, and we win! I love our diversity. According to Wikipedia:

> Educational inequality is the unequal distribution of academic resources, including but not limited to; school funding, qualified and experienced teachers, books, and technologies to socially excluded communities. These communities tend to be historically disadvantaged and oppressed. More times than not, individuals belonging to these marginalized groups are also denied access to the schools with abundant resources. Inequality leads to major

differences in the educational success or efficiency of these individuals and ultimately suppresses social and economic mobility.

What have you done to increase access to a quality education for the children of Upson County? Can we (in our own way) try to rid the world of racism. We can all resolve to never miss an opportunity to speak out when some within our orbit are denied equal access to opportunities. The scientific and technological ingenuity that will inevitably result will fuel new discoveries, social progress, and maximize our potential. We all benefit from the contributions of all segments of our society.

211.

Let Women Stay at Home and Hold Their Peace ("Seven against Thebes" Aeschylus, 467 B.C.)

November 19, 2020

More recently, according to Bella Abzug: "This woman's place is in the house - the House of Representatives." And the boss proclaimed that her husband is the boss.

As the number of COVID-19 cases spike and we are all spending more time in the safety of our homes, we are paying much more attention to homemaking and home improvements. Perhaps, with less disposable incomes and the threat of social unrest, we are taking another look at self-sufficiency and liking the idea of doing for ourselves. It is this background that I have taken to reading "Gone with the Wind" by Margaret Mitchell (1936).

While I have seen the movie several times, I never read the book. So, in my quest to understand Southern traditions and values, I am making my way through this amazing novel. Ms. Mitchell is a very gifted writer and a keen observer of the people in her time and place. She was also an apologist for and promulgator of myths about The South.

I imagine that some people who read this book treated it as a manual for daily living and a time that they remember fondly whether or not it ever truly existed. Here are some telling passages:

"She never saw her sit down without a bit of needlework in her hands. Scarlett could not imagine her mother's hand without her gold thimble."

This is an image of womanhood that manages to be both industrious and also ornamental, as needlework adds value but never has gotten its due as meaningful work. It is the perfect metaphor because the loop of a stitch is the easiest thing in the world – not strenuous or brainy at all – but the elaborate embroidery of the time demonstrates deliberation and art. Similarly, Mitchell's women are ruthless and strategic as generals, with a handle on the minutiae of finance and the broad sweep of history while also being prized for being pretty but insubstantial with no real thoughts or even bodily functions:

Before marriage, young girls must be, above all other things, sweet, gentle, beautiful and ornamental, but, after marriage, they were expected to manage households.

Ellen's life was not easy, nor was it happy, but she did not expect life to be easy, and, if it was not happy, that was a woman's lot. It was a man's world, and she accepted it as such.

The man owned the property and the woman managed it. The man took the credit for the management, and the woman praised his cleverness. The man roared like a bull when a splinter was in his finger, and the woman muffled the moans of childbirth, lest she disturb him. Men were rough with speech and often drunk. Women ignored the lapses of speech and put the drunkard to bed without bitter words. Men were rude and outspoken, women were always kind, gracious and forgiving…unfailingly thoughtful of her husband's pleasure.

She wanted him, and she had only a few hours in which to get him. If fainting, or pretending to faint, would do the trick, then she would faint. If simpering, coquetry, or empty headedness would attract him, she would gladly play the flirt and emptier headed than even Cathleen Calvert. And if bolder measures were necessary, she would take them. Today was the day.

She was so full of food and so tightly laced that she feared every moment she was going to belch. That would be fatal, as only old men and very old ladies could belch without fear of social disapproval.

What Melanie did was no more than all Southern girls were taught to do - to make those about them feel at ease and pleased with themselves. It was this happy feminine conspiracy which made southern society so pleasant.

It goes without saying that the women thus depicted are a very privileged few. Obviously, there were many women in the antebellum South whose lives were more frank, closer to the bone. Enslaved women, of course, but also women who ran shops and farms with their families, and other women who worked for wages, who ran machines or made art.

People like Mitchell, their mythmaking made such women invisible. We have to use our common sense and deduce that they were there. Wherever there is butter, we have to remember that it means somebody is milking a cow, somebody is churning cream. Wherever there are linens, we have to remember that there is somebody bleaching and boiling and hanging and ironing the linens. Yes, even the linens of the highborn ladies who are supposedly out here mutely birthing children and never belching.

In 2020, the place for all of us is the home. There is perhaps something to Mitchell's observation of a "happy feminine conspiracy." Women knew that when men are content, uncontradicted and safe, home was likely to be a very pleasant place for everyone. So, from the cradle to the grave, women strove to make men pleased with themselves because satisfied men delighted in repaying lavishly with gallantry and adoration. Who doesn't want to live in a peaceful home?

So, there is something to this homemaking after all. It is simply time that we all pitch in as well as giving credit for the work.

I maintain that women are not possessions. They are equal intellectually and should be where they choose to be. As a society, we lose when everyone is not allowed to be all they can be.

212.
Hold on, Help is on the Way

November 26, 2020

The world as we know it will never be the same. Most of us have never lived through a pandemic, but if you are reading this article, you can say that you lived through the pandemic of 2020. School-aged children will be talking about this into their adulthood as the news of the coronavirus overwhelms our daily activities.

Twelve million Americans have been infected and 260,000 have lost their lives to this virus. America has, by far, the highest rate of infection in the entire world and our death toll is approaching the number of Americans lost in WWII.

Even with the promise of a vaccine, as the spread of COVID-19 escalates (seemingly like a forest fire), the frustration of losing direct contact with family, peers, and colleagues as my personal space shrinks, I feel at times trapped by the pandemic. I am emboldened though by the words of Dr. Anthony Fauci - Hold on, help is on the way.

Our work, our information, education, and recreation are now on a screen. My travel to explore the world or to frolic in the sea on distant shores is reduced to what I can access on my computer. So, the time I spend looking at a screen grows exponentially at the expense of the world unexplored, meals not shared with family and friends, ceremonies and rituals neglected, hugs and handshakes not received.

The prospect of not having my family around during Thanksgiving and Christmas is almost inconceivable. As much as that sucks, it is worse to become infected. My condolences to those who have lost family members. When a grandparent dies, an entire library and a wonderful source of nourishment goes up in flames.

As I rise each morning, I stretch and when I realize that 'all systems go', I check with my wife and she is well. I feel joy that we have survived another day, another night without a life-threatening infection and we thank the Great Architect of the universe that He has blessed us for another day. So far, my family has been spared.

As I drove by First Baptist Church this week, I saw long food lines. Other parts of our country from California to Texas are experiencing the same thing. Cars line up for miles to access their daily bread. As businesses go bankrupt in unprecedented numbers, about 12 million Americans will lose federal unemployment benefits at the end of the year if Congress fails to pass new legislation, I will remember to hold on because help is on the way.

All Americans have been affected by this virus. We have worried together how to keep our mortgages paid, how to keep our children safe, and moving forward, how to protect our loved ones. Keeping body and soul together has become stressful for us all, causing a deterioration of our mental and physical health. Domestic violence, obesity, addiction, and suicide are on the rise. These negative effects are long-lasting, not only for those who are immediately affected, but for our entire country. But hold on, help is on the way!

As we move forward as a nation and look forward to celebrating the birth of Christ, I am reminded that as fractured as we have become, I still see folk helping each other and encouraging each other. Regardless of your political affiliation, the freedom we all enjoy in the greatest country of all time is testament that we are stronger together than we are apart. It's a good time to help each other out. This can be a great way to feel better. We are not in this alone.

Find a family to help. A bag of groceries anonymously left on a doorstep will bring a smile and hope to the lucky family. During this crisis, these gestures are important.

And do think of the children who are stressed out and losing sleep over what to expect? Will they starve? Will their parents die? Why can't I play with my friends? One of my convictions is that I never bet against these United States of America. We have the resources and the resolve to get through this.

Joy comes in the morning. Keep yourselves safe and never forget that HELP IS ON THE WAY!

213.

The Contributions of Immigrants (Confessions of an Immigrant)

December 3, 2020

"Then they brought every kind of illegal immigrant labor into Georgia to take what little jobs were left, plus they allowed the federal government to pay for the illegal immigrant housing and healthcare while Georgians were left trying to feed their families and fighting to stop foreclosure on their homes."

Apparently, some people still believe that immigrants are a drag on our economy, they unfairly compete for jobs, and are mostly criminals and drug dealers.

While I readily admit that immigration is a complex issue that does not lend itself to simple solutions, apparently, there always was and always will be an audience in Georgia for those who peddle a false narrative. And the fact that immigrants are many and varied means the attacks on them shift with the wind. We are lazy but at the same time stealing your jobs. We don't share your values but are reinvigorating your religious institutions and holding the line on culture wars. We are lawless and yet drawn to the military and law enforcement. We are buzz-killing bookworms while also bringing the spice to your food, music, dancing, and culture. This is contrary to the upward mobility of immigrant families and please do not discount the contributions that the children of immigrants make to our country's long-term strength.

As an immigrant from Jamaica in 1959, I take great pride in the contribution I have made to this great country in gratitude for providing me with amazing opportunities to excel in my career as well as raise amazing children and grandchildren who will continue to contribute to our further advancement. Even so, when it comes to inventing new products, creating innovative technologies, paying taxes, serving in our armed forces, and helping to make us a dominant force in science, music, and winning gold medals at the Olympic games, we owe a great deal to immigrants. While new immigrants are 12% of the population, we are an integral part of the United States.

In many respects, I am very much a typical immigrant. I arrived at 15 and while attending high school, worked as a dishwasher and busboy in addition to caddying at a country club where I learned to play golf. I then attended college on a track scholarship but in those four years, I also worked as a dishwasher for 75 cents per hour, got promoted to janitor for $1.50 per hour and in my senior year, I worked on a bridge building crew for $2 per hour. I would eventually obtain a Ph.D. in educational psychology and become a member of the Georgia Bar (lawyer).

I got married in my senior year of college and we both went on to graduate school. We have four amazing children. And the beat goes on as our grandchildren are showing promise of even more accomplished careers. Through it all, I adhered to the lessons I learned from the grandmother who raised me: Trust in God, treat others as you want to be treated, and don't try to outsmart people - outwork them!

The Small Business Administration reports that immigrants are more likely to start a business. In fact, recent immigrants founded 45% of the Fortune 500 companies and make up 17% of business owners and CEOs including Intel, Sun Microsystems, eBay, Google, Apple, Amazon, Office Depot, Merck, Tesla, and Yahoo. More than 50% of the employees in the science/technology sector are immigrants. Immigrants have more formal education, especially in medicine, science, and engineering. Immigrant workers are a source of affordable and available employees in farming, construction, childcare, cleaning services, and landscaping. The crime rate is lower for immigrants who, for the most part, are productive workers. Continued improvement in our economy will depend on whether or not we attract, welcome, train and retain the best future workforce from around the world - we gain at the expense of the countries where they came from. The cost of training a doctor, nurse, pharmacist, or engineer consumes a great deal of these countries' budgets and then they migrate to the United States. Children born to immigrant families are upwardly mobile, promising future benefits not only to their families, but to the U.S. economy overall.

Most of our fruit, grain, vegetable, and meat production are supported by immigrants, and without them, these industries would have a hard time hiring workers. If these workers can no longer come to work in the United States. It would be difficult to replace them. There is a 30% shortage of nurses in the United States. I also heard a watermelon farmer lament that he could offer American workers $50 per hour and have no takers. A third of workers in the farming, fishing, forestry, building and grounds cleaning, maintenance workers, hotel workers, and home health care workers are immigrants. Employer demand for low-skilled labor remains high. There are still many unfilled jobs for low-skilled employees. Who will take care of the baby boomer generation in our retirement years?

I contend that immigration has been and will continue to be a positive force for our country.

214.

The Young Black Woman Who Developed the COVID-19 Vaccine Platform Technology

December 17, 2020

I have been monitoring (with alarm) the toll this virus has been unleashing on our communities as we passed 300,000 deaths in the United States. This, by any measure, cannot be passed off as a hoax. My heart leaped for joy with the news that a vaccine against COVID-19 was being fast tracked by the FDA - not by politicians, but by scientists. The ingenuity of scientists in America, France, and England cracked the code and gave us the relief we so badly needed.

At my age and risk factor profile, (open heart surgery in 2019) I would like to be as close as possible to the front of the line to receive this life saving vaccine that promises immunity against this deadly virus. While I may experience a fever and fatigue for about 24 hours, I would no longer have to worry about succumbing to this virus and I can enjoy a better quality of life with family, friends, and neighbors. It will do wonders for our economy if we cooperate with the guidance provided by our scientists.

Some clarification is in order. The COVID-19 vaccine is a little different than the vaccines we are used to hearing about. There is no expired virus that will be injected into any of us. In fact, the technology that has given us this vaccine is actually not a virus at all. The vaccine is made from what is termed a messenger RNA molecule. This particular messenger will fool our immune cells into thinking that they are seeing the true coronavirus, when in fact the messenger RNA is a harmless imposter. The messenger is actually priming our immune systems to start trolling for the coronavirus and attack it if we get infected. The messenger is helping our bodies create immunity without becoming infected. What a wonderful mechanism to protect us from this nasty little virus.

It turns out that the scientist who discovered the messenger (mRNA 1273) vaccine platform technology is Dr. Kizzmekia Corbett. As a senior fellow at NIH, she was assigned to lead a team to study coronaviruses in 2014. When the interest in this virus waned at NIH, Dr. Corbett continued to work on the theory that a mRNA model could effectively provide immunity in a human host and this research interest has resulted in the production of this therapeutic vaccine and the eventual expedited manufacturing of vaccines that have proven to be 95% effective in clinical trials.

Dr. Corbett was born on Jan. 26, 1986, in Hurdle Hills, N.C. Her mother (Rhonda Brooks) is a schoolteacher. She grew up in a household with step siblings and foster children. In the fourth grade at Oak Lane Elementary School, her teacher (Ms. Myrtis Brasher) thought she was the brightest student she ever encountered and encouraged her mother to provide enrichment classes and experiences which the young future Dr. Corbett relished. Dr. Corbett earned a bachelor's degree in biology/sociology from the University of Maryland and a Ph.D. in viral immunology at the University of North Carolina. After earning her Ph.D., she was appointed by NIH as a senior fellow and was assigned by Dr. Anthony Fauci and Dr. Barney Graham to lead a team to continue to work on corona viruses - and the rest is history.

This young woman will be responsible for curbing a pandemic that has killed millions of people and devastated economies. She was not born out of wealth and privilege, nor did she go to Ivy League colleges or universities. She is a public servant who used her curiosity and mind to help save mankind. I am predicting that she will win the Nobel prize for science and a movie will be made of her life. Instead of lauding her, however, the right-wing media is using its influence to minimize her accomplishments because of tweets she shared with her "girlfriends." These tweets are very typical for an unmarried 30-something woman and reflect the sentiments of other 30-something professionals most recently portrayed on the popular sitcom, Friends. How are her personal tweets relevant - her work contributed to saving the world's economy? Are we going to judge her for this accomplishment or some sophomoric tweets?

Our society has been degraded to sound bites. This is so very sad. Is the fabric of America now reduced to sound bites? Our forefathers and foremothers of every ethnicity, religion, and economic class worked tirelessly to make us the nation we are. We are a nation of great thinkers and until recently were revered by both allies and foes. Our greatness is the result of our diversity, and my prayer is that we can all work our way back to that.

Prejudice is more deadly than the coronavirus. When you confront it, be like the messenger RNA developed by Dr. Corbett. If you are piling on and trying to denigrate her because of her gender, race or tweets, be a messenger for the good this woman has done. Your message may be just the one that convinces someone to take the vaccine who otherwise may not have done so because it was invented by a Black woman. Black people have contributed a great deal to our nation. She stands on the shoulders of great African American scientists like George Washington Carver. Peanut butter anyone? Your race, gender and color don't determine the content of your character or your contributions. We certainly have had numerous examples.

I am sure you have heard the phrase, "A rising tide lifts all boats." I live by that mantra. My wife and I truly believe that by helping others we help ourselves and our great country. In Dr. Corbett's case, the tide she has created will lift the lives of billions of people. Why a few very small-minded people want to focus on trivial tweets is beyond me. As a society, I hope we are better than that.

215.
Christmas In Jamaica When I Was 14

December 24, 2020

As soon as we said goodbye to November, the Christmas breeze would start blowing in Woodlands, Jamaica. Our father had abandoned us, and mother migrated to the United States, so we were being raised by our grandmother. Throughout the month of December, everybody's gotten into the Christmas spirit with broad smiles and started greeting each other with "Happy Christmas" and the predictable response was, "When it comes."

It's a time of cleaning up the yard and house so my brother and I would set out to cut the grass with our machetes. Unfortunately, with a swing of the cutlass, it took a glancing blow off a stone and cut me just below my left knee. I am bleeding profusely but Granny just washed the blood off and tied it with some chickweed and a piece of cloth and in less than 10 days it was all healed up again but leaving a scar that I still have. We got back to painting the first three feet of the coconut trees in our yard and brought in red poinsettias for the table.

The raisins and currants that had been soaking in ovenproof rum for several months would now be stirred into the batter and baked in a delicious fruit cake. Since we didn't have an oven, Granny would put the batter in our Dutch pot and pile red hot coals on top as well as under the pot and we took turns blowing the coals to keep the fire going. When the cake came out, Granny would holler: "Hell on top, hell on the bottom, but hallelujah in the middle."

She also prepared roast beef and ham along with our red Christmas drink we call sorrel with plenty of ginger and white rum. Granny got down on her knees, not only to pray, but also to polish the floors. Everything had to look spick and span for company.

When company came, they took a stone and knocked on our gate and Granny would enthusiastically holler: "Push the gate and come on in. I am so glad to see you. Happy Christmas." My brother and I would sit on the wooden sofa in our living room listening and watching the adults laughing as they ate the roast beef, ham, cake and sorrel. The palaver would go on for hours, but children were never allowed to interrupt grownups unless we were asked a question or asked to perform.

Granny would ask us to show off by spelling a difficult word, recite a Bible verse or a poem. My favorite word to spell was Mississippi because I would spell it "M I crooked letter, crooked letter I, crooked letter, crooked letter I, humpback, humpback I" and my favorite poem was "Spanish Needle" by Claude McKay.

> Lovely dainty Spanish needle
> With your yellow flower and white,
> Dew bedecked and softly sleeping,
> Do you think of me tonight?

Family would unpredictably drive up with presents and new clothes and enjoy the Christmas vittles. I say unpredictable because we had no telephones or any means of communicating so we were always prepared for company. If the food was not enough, Granny would add more pepper so each person would eat less.

When the long-awaited day arrived, at the crack of dawn, we would be awakened by firecrackers. Like African drums, they would explode in one part of the village and an answer was required from another area and back and forth it would go for about an hour.

Both of us gave Granny a flask of brandy and she got us clothes. I gave Earl a bag of marbles and he gave me something I did not recognize in a paper bag. So, I said it looks like the bladder of a pig. He said it was, but it was also a balloon. He showed me how he tied one end of the stomach and put a straw in the other end and blew it up. So, we had many hours of fun blowing up a pig's bladder, letting out the air and blowing it up again. Later, we would cut it up, fry it with garlic and onions, and eat it with hard dough bread - great Christmas present!

Granny would give us our Christmas money and we would then dress up in our new clothes for the community picnic. Our favorite event was the donkey races. My rough and tumble brother was convinced that he could win the race but as soon as he jumped on, the donkey kicked up his rear legs and threw him to the ground.

He wasn't breathing and I thought he was dead, but he just got the wind knocked out of him. Two men carried him to the shed and placed him in a makeshift bed and two ladies fanned him. After about an hour he emerged to declare: "I am as good as new," to great applause.

He came back just in time for the maypole dance. So, he took a ribbon and in and out he went around the maypole with 20 other people. And when it was all tied up, they unwound it again.

After a full day of dancing, talking, and laughing, eating jerk pork, roast beef, curry goat, scotched fish, Christmas cakes, grape nut ice cream and drinking sorrel and cane juice, everyone agreed that this was the best Christmas ever. Too bad it only comes once a year.

216.

Verily I Say unto You: "When You Save a Child, You Save the World"

December 31, 2020

My wife (Dr. Stephanie Kong, ZÖe Pediatrics) became a pediatrician because she was inspired by that simple mandate. She is the most dedicated person I know who works 12-hour days trying to save children. "How many do you want to save?" "The next one." "But", I would argue, (when I often see her exhaustion): "you cannot save them all." And she will dutifully reply: "Maybe, but I want to save this one."

It is Christmas Day, and the alarm goes off at 4 a.m. and as she is leaving our bed, I plead: "Darling, it's Christmas. Can you just rest today?" She turns off the alarm and returns to our bed. I close and pump my fist and do the "Yes!" gesture. We are snuggling but an hour later she says: "I can't. Duty calls." And she is off to work on her computer reviewing the care her patients are receiving by the other nine doctors and sending them notes.

This woman is driven. Even when I persuade her to take a vacation, she will still wake up at 4 a.m. to review charts and throughout the day, even sitting on a beach with a computer, she looks in on each office, checking on wait times and calling whoever may be slacking. That is her way of staying ahead of her demanding responsibilities. She hates surprises and can only relax when she feels that she has everything under control.

She once told me the fable of the woman who was walking on a beach and saw several dozen starfish that had washed up on shore and was dutifully throwing them back into the ocean when someone shouted: "You cannot save them. There are too many." She replies: "But I can save this one. We are only commanded to do what we can." My wife daily repeats the prayer: "God, grant me the serenity to accept the things I cannot change, courage to change the things I can, and wisdom to know the difference."

What if King Herod had his way and Jesus Christ, our Lord and Savior, had been killed as the soldiers scoured the land seeking out and killing all firstborn male children? Can you even imagine the state of mankind if He didn't live to walk among us and forgive us our sins?

Matthew 2:13-16 says, "And being warned of God in a dream that they should not return to Herod, they departed into their own country another way. And when they departed, behold, the angel of the Lord appeareth to Joseph in a dream, saying, arise, and take the young child and his mother, and flee into Egypt, and be thou there until I bring thee word. For Herod will seek the young child to destroy him. And when he arose, he took the young child and his mother by night and departed into Egypt: and was there until the death of Herod: that it might be fulfilled which was spoken of the Lord by the prophet, saying, out of Egypt have I called my son. Then Herod, when he saw that he was mocked of the wise men, was exceeding wroth, and sent forth, and slew all the children that were in Bethlehem, and in all the coasts thereof, from two years old and under, according to the time which he had diligently enquired of the wise men."

"Suffer little children, and forbid them not, to come unto me: for of such is the kingdom of Heaven." (Matthew 19:14) The condition for claiming your reward is to receive the kingdom of God as a humble child. So, do what it takes to rescue children from despair, wipe away their tears and nurture them for a bright future. You will be judged by the many kindnesses you extended.

Typically, Maasai warriors of Kenya greet each other with "How are the children?" They recognize that if the children are weeping and not doing well, the village will fail, but if they are strong and healthy, so is the village, and it takes the entire village to raise each child. Please consider carefully what you are feeding our children.

Happy New Year! Joy comes in the morning.

217.
My Tribute to
Dr. Lemuel Julian Haywood

January 7, 2021

Last week, COVID-19 robbed the world of another giant, a true world changer. He was Professor Emeritus of Medicine at the University of Southern California who published over 600 scientific articles over his lifetime related to pioneering work in high blood pressure, cardiac arrhythmias, sickle cell disease, and computer applications in cardiology. He was the first Black cardiologist appointed a full professor of medicine at a majority institution.

You may recall that in the old days, patients who were critically ill would require a nurse sitting at the patient's bedside (24/7) and constantly monitoring blood pressure, pulse, heart rhythm, and breathing regularity. Dr. Haywood made it possible to monitor patients from the nurse's station and the intensive care unit (ICU) was born. The concept has since been adopted in every hospital in the entire world. In 1969, it was described as the first computerized system for real-time heart arrhythmia detection.

He was Born in Reidsville, N.C. in 1927. His father was a physician and his mother a teacher. He served in the Army and at the end of the war earned a B.A. in biology from Hampton University in 1948 and an M.D. from Howard University School of Medicine in 1952. After a two-year fellowship in cardiology at White Memorial Hospital in Los Angeles, he returned to the county hospital as a member of the Loma Linda University faculty. In 1963, he was a traveling fellow at Oxford University, under Regius Professor Sir George Pickering. The Coronary Care Unit at the Los Angeles County Hospital-USC Medical Center, which he established in 1966, was renamed "The L. Julian Haywood Coronary Care Unit" in 2016.

I knew Dr. Haywood for 40 years, always the gracious host and inspiring friend. In 2018 when I received the "Lifetime Achievement Award" from the Association of Black Cardiologists (ABC), he not only attended, but was generous with his praise for my accomplishments as the CEO of the ABC for over 20 years. He also reminded my son (who he inspired to become a physician) about their game of chess when we were guests at his home in Los Angeles when Aleron was a high school student.

With all his accomplishments, Dr. Haywood was a humble man who was always ready to give advice to cardiologists in training as well as anyone else who sought him out. And what a generous soul! I don't believe he ever said no to any request for financial assistance from family, charities, churches, friends, and educational institutions. He even paid the full cost of a city park in the town of Warrenton, N.C. as a memorial to his parents in 2018.

When we were traveling in Australia about ten years ago, we met with some Aboriginal men and I inquired about their ambitions. One gentleman replied that their goal was to sit down happy. Whether it was the end of a job, a project, a day, a year, or a lifetime, they do what they do because they are motivated to sit down happy with pride in what they accomplished. Dr. Haywood, you can sit down happy.

218.
Organizing a "White House Conference on Children" in 2022

January 14, 2021

Dear President Biden:

In 1971, as a professor of human growth and development at the University of the District of Columbia, I participated in the White House Conference on Children that was spearheaded by President Lyndon Johnson as part of his War on Poverty. He was ably aided by Mr. Stan Salett, his national education policy advisor. Many innovative educational strategies emerged from this conference, not the least of which were *"Sesame Street"* and the "Carnegie Corporation Children's Television Workshop."

I was fortunate to serve on a committee with Ms. Marianne Wright-Edelman, who would go on to establish the Children's Defense Fund in 1973, as well as Ms. Jules Sugarman, who had started the Head Start Program in 1965. While the idea Ms. Sugarman pioneered was a catch-up summer enrichment program, it showed great promise to change the course of the lives of poor children. Because it received such great acclaim at the conference, the "Head Start Act" was signed into law in1981" making Head Start enrichment programs available to every community in the country that served one million children per year.

When wealthier families saw the success of the program in preparing infants for school, they demanded the same opportunity for their children. As it has evolved, ALL children are able to receive the nurturing, nutrition, and age-appropriate education to thrive. Again, in 1975, I served as a consultant that evaluated the parent involvement component of local Head Start Programs in Pennsylvania.

It's been 50 years since the promise of hope to equalize disparities was launched. There is data to suggest that the results have not lived up to expectation. Childhood obesity is on the rise. Educational disparity gaps are increasing.

Does that mean that the concepts of these programs were faulty? I would argue no, and it's not time to throw the baby out with the bath water. So, is it time to sanction and plan for the 2022 White House Conference on Children under the Biden/Harris administration?

Obviously, many of the same issues continue to plague our society and several (obesity, inactivity, autism, violence against children, cyber bullying) are relatively new. We need to take advantage of the great minds in this country by bringing them together to address these problems.

In the wealthiest nation on earth, some of our children are denied the opportunity to fulfill their potential. We NEED to start planning for the 2022 White House Conference immediately. I suggest we invite Michelle Obama to chair this initiative. Just as the 1971 conference led to great innovations, this proposed conference will lead to programs to assure our youth a bright future.

Please do what you can to bring this conference to fruition. Great ideas emerge from the collaboration of great minds. Let the planning begin. I am available to serve in any capacity you deem worthwhile.

Sincerely,
B. Waine Kong, Ph.D., JD, President
ZÖe Pediatric Foundation, Inc.

219.

If You Aspire to Be Happy, Strive Not for Fame and Fortune but To Have a Servant's Heart

January 21, 2021

As we celebrate Martin Luther King's birthday, what comes to mind was his commitment to live a life of service. "Whoever wants to become great among you must be your servant." (Mark 10: 43)

According to his now deceased wife: "Martin Luther King, Jr. Day is not only for celebration and remembrance, education, and tribute, but above all, a day of service. All across America, on the holiday, his followers perform service in hospitals and shelters and prisons and wherever people need some help. It is a day of volunteering to feed the hungry, rehabilitate housing, tutoring those who can't read, mentoring at-risk youngsters, consoling the broken-hearted, and a thousand other projects for building the beloved community of his dream."

So, it now becomes a day on, not a day off.

Dr. King was also my fraternity brother (Alpha Phi Alpha). We all dedicate ourselves to be "servants of all." My wife is fond of reminding me and her colleagues that service to her means giving her best to her patients, family, colleagues, friends, community, and country. I honor my ancestors by finding opportunities to serve and to be kind to mankind.

To me, service means showing my best self to everyone I encounter. We are all so dependent on each other. Just by walking by someone who is infected with COVID-19 could mean the death of us. Life can be so fleeting. So, what are we waiting for? Let's get cracking and give our best to our fellow travelers on this planet.

If I can help somebody along the way, please educate me about it and I will see what I can do. I thank everyone who is willing to accept help from me because that is the only way I get my blessing. "Lean on me when you are not strong and I will help you carry on, for it won't be long before I will need somebody to lean on." (Bill Withers)

I wish you and your loved one's health and success in 2021.

"If you want to be important, wonderful. If you want to be recognized, wonderful. If you want to be great, wonderful. But recognize that he who is greatest among you shall be your servant. That's a new definition of greatness. And this morning, he thinks that I like it: by giving that definition of greatness, it means that everybody can be great, because everybody can serve. You don't have to have a college degree to serve. You don't have to make your subject and your verb agree to serve. You don't have to know about Plato and Aristotle to serve. You don't have to know Einstein's theory of relativity to serve. You don't have to know the second theory of thermo-dynamics in physics to serve. You only need a heart full of grace, a soul generated by love." (Martin Luther King, 1968)

220.

Paradise Lost: An Epic History of the World

February 4, 2021

I believe Milton is the greatest English poet of all time. His most famous works are the 12 books (10,000 lines) he wrote under the general title of *"Paradise Lost."* The concept is that before creation, there was Heaven occupied by God and his angels. God's main man (Lucifer), the most beautiful, charismatic, and ambitious of all His angels, ("equal to the highest in Heaven") but a seditious upstart, is hell bent to "subdue The Omnipotent… dispossess God and himself to reign." So, he persuades a third of the angels to join him in his treachery against God Almighty.

The plot does not succeed. When Lucifer and his followers lose the Angelic wars, God confronts Lucifer and is prepared to throw him out of Heaven along with his fallen angels.

Faithful, now proved false! But think not here to trouble rest; Heaven casts thee out from all her confines… How hast thou disturbed Heaven's blessed peace, and into nature brought misery, uncreated till the crime of thy rebellion! How hast thou instilled thy malice into thousands who were once upright?

This results in three worlds: Heaven, Earth (Paradise), and Hell - where "peace and rest can never dwell… condemned to waste eternal days in woe and pain… in perpetual agony." Before condemning them all to hell, God grants Lucifer one concession, that when he creates the world and propagates it, He would give humans "free will," affording Satan the opportunity to tempt mankind to sell their souls and turn against God.

On the one hand, Lucifer is convinced that he could be a powerful persuader, convincing humans to give in to selfish ambitions, seducing them with false promises to forfeit their souls, while God fully expects that mankind would not be ingrained, but grateful for all the great and wonderful things He has done.

> This paradise I give thee. Count it thine to till and keep and of the fruit to eat: Of every tree that in the garden grows. Eat freely with a glad heart… thy realm is large." Live in peace with each other, "reaping immortal fruits of joy and love, in blissful solitude." By worshiping in spirit and truth, "Man shall find grace.

Eve, "the mother of the human race," would become Lucifer's first victim. While God gave mankind free will, God has programmed them to strive to improve their condition and a passionate nature so they will populate the earth (be fruitful and multiply), risking the unintended consequences. Human beings are born free and free they will remain. They must want to serve me. So, the history of the world became a struggle between good and evil, with God and Satan fighting for our souls.

So, Lucifer (now Satan/Devil and the evil one) speaks:

> All is not lost - the unconquerable will, and study of revenge, immortal hate and courage never to submit or yield… our labor must be to pervert that end… Farewell, happy fields, where joy forever dwells! Hail, horrors, hail, infernal world! And thou, profoundest Hell, receive thy new possessor - one who brings a mind not to be changed by place or time. The mind is its own place, and in itself can make a Heaven of Hell, a Hell of Heaven… Woe to the inhabitants on earth… The Almighty hath not built here for His envy, will not drive us hence: Here we may reign secure; and, in my choice… live in hatred, enmity and strife… high passions, anger, hate, mistrust, suspicion, discord… guilt and shame, perturbation and despair, anger, obstinacy, hate and guile… havoc, spoil, and ruin are my gain… To reign is worth ambition, though in Hell: Better to reign in Hell than serve in Heaven… Heaven's fugitives… Awake, arise, or be forever fallen! What can be worse than to dwell here? All good to

me is lost; Evil be thou my good... with revenge enlarged, by conquering this new world, compels me not to do what else, thou damned, I should abhor... to ruin all mankind.

The poem is long and arduously written in the old style of English and it's an epic on the nature of human beings. The preceding paragraph is but a few lines. I enjoy reading them aloud. Are you tempted to read all 12 books?

Finally, you may have heard the story of the passing of a gentleman of goodwill who had qualified to enter the pearly gates of heaven, but he had second thoughts. "I am a party person. I don't want to spend eternity with boring people who thought a good time was going to church. I don't like either milk or honey!" So, St. Peter made him an offer: "Would you like to check out hell before finally deciding?"

On his arrival in hell, he was greeted most graciously by many of his old friends, given the most lavish banquet in his honor, as well as the freedom to do whatever he liked without consequences. This is not so bad, he thought, and informed St. Peter that he decided to stay in hell. "Is this your final answer?" "That is my final answer."

As soon as he made his decision, he was thrown into the fiery furnace and the hell's angels set about torturing his soul.

So, he inquired: "What about yesterday, you were so nice to me." To which the Devil answered: "Just good public relations! But now that you decided to spend eternity with us, you are mine through eternity. Ha."

221.
Value of Rethinking, Joy of Being Wrong

February 11, 2021

My grandmother was fond of telling me that it is not what you don't know that will hurt you, but what you know, that isn't so. We long ago seized on ideas that we thought were compatible with the beliefs of our family and resisted all attempts to change. Once an idea is settled in our brain, we are going to defend it come hell or high water. We prefer hanging onto what we were taught as children rather than trying to grapple with new ideas. Physicians tend to write the prescriptions and hold on to practices that their mentors recommended when they were in training rather than try new treatments and new perspectives on disease.

According to Adam Grant in his book, *Think Again*, "We become so wrapped up in preaching that we're right, prosecuting others who are wrong, and politicking for support that we don't bother to rethink our own views."

Questioning our long-held beliefs makes the world unpredictable. Generally, we prefer order in our universe. It requires a lot of soul searching to admit that what we grew up believing was wrong or that facts may have changed. Reconsidering or questioning our assumptions can threaten our identities, throw us off center or cause us to flounder.

While we regularly update our clothes and cars, our belief system is another matter entirely. We tend to stick to our guns or fall on our swords when it comes to what we believe. If you have been a Christian for your entire life, you are not likely to even listen to anything a Muslim, Jew, or Buddhists have to say. Are there only Christians in Heaven?

We tend to listen only to data (facts) that reinforce our beliefs, make us feel smug that we are on the right side of an issue, and avoid anything that may upset the apple cart. We are usually set in our ways and our thinking. We favor the comfort of our convictions over the discomfort of thinking about it, second guessing, and doubting.

Do you stick to your routines when your fellow employees are being fired? Do you ignore the fact that your partner has become distant? Do you still stop to ask strangers where the Johnsons live or use your GPS? Do you remain quiet when your friends and family are abusive to others? Do you prefer to feel right than to be right?

During the last days of World War II, the leader of Japan called on all loyal citizens to fight a Holy War in the tradition of the Bushido warrior code. All citizens were asked to die rather than surrender. "If the whole people will march forward with death-defying determination, devoting their entire efforts to their own duties and to refreshing their fighting spirit, I believe that we will be able to overcome all difficulties."

Ota Masahide, a survivor, and Okinawa historian wrote that Premier Suzuki distributed hand grenades to the civilian population as the means to commit suicide with their loved ones. Those that survived the grenades "worried" about being alive and found other ways to kill themselves with other weapons such as scythes, razor blades, ropes, rocks, and sticks.

Military propaganda had warned the civilian population that if they were captured, the Americans would torture, rape, and murder them. As the mayhem unfolded, they found all sorts of ways to kill: Men bashed their wives and parents bashed their children, young people killed the elderly and the strong killed the weak, Masahide said. "What they felt in common was the belief that they were doing this out of love and compassion."

Convinced that only the nuclear bombs could force a surrender, the United States bombed Hiroshima and Nagasaki.

The belief in the emperor as a living God or the Chosen One, prompted many to die for him. On Jan. 1, 1946, when General Douglass McArthur forced the Emperor Hirohito of Japan to go on the radio and admit that he was just a mortal man and the emperor's divinity was a myth, rather than accept the truth which was entirely at odds with what they grew up believing, thousands of true believers chose mass ritual suicides (shudan jiketsu).

The big lie had been carefully constructed. The commentaries on the Constitution of 1889 said, "The Emperor is Heaven descended, divine and sacred… He must be reverenced and is inviolable… the law has no power to hold him accountable."

But the world belongs to people who adapt to changing facts and circumstances. Progress is impossible without change. We live in a time of rapidly changing facts and opportunities. Are you still holding on to your flip phone or have you adopted the new technology?

If happiness, prosperity, and living without regrets are your objectives, I invite you to let go of knowledge and opinions that are no longer serving you well. And if you cannot be flexible, at least be willing to rethink your opinions. Wisdom is knowing when to abandon sacred beliefs. There is joy in being proved wrong because you are now more enlightened.

222.

How Will We Enjoy a Prosperous Future Living in the Past?

February 18, 2021

In Margaret Mitchell's *"Gone with the Wind"* (p. 466) Scarlett is quoted as saying, "It hurt too much. It drags at your heart till you can't ever do anything else except look back. That's what's wrong with Ashley. He can't look forward anymore. He can't see the present, he fears the future, and so he looks back. I never understood it before. I never understood Ashley before. Oh, Ashley, my darling, you shouldn't look back! What good will it do? I shouldn't have let you tempt me into talking of the old days. This is what happens when you look back to happiness, this pain, this heartbreak, this discontent…"

She rose to her feet, her hand still in his. She must go. She could not stay and think of the old days and see his face, tired and sad and bleak as it now was. "We've come a long way since those days, Ashley," she said, trying to steady her voice, trying to fight the constriction in her throat. "We had fine notions then, didn't we?" And then, with a rush, "Oh Ashley, nothing has turned out as we expected."

"It never does", he said. "Life's under no obligation to give us what we expect. We take what we get and are thankful."

On the other hand, instead of nostalgically trying to squeeze a few more years out of the good old days, there are those who are haunted by painful memories of loved ones who perished or were abandoned, family wealth and privilege that was squandered, physical abuse and mental torment they suffered, who cannot let go and forgive - who wish they could move on like trees in winter, letting go of their leaves so new ones can sprout in the spring. Others use the hard times and bad luck to motivate them to strive for a better tomorrow. In Jamaica, we say, "Better Must Come." Here is God's promise: "Weeping may last for a night, but joy comes in the morning." (Psalm 30: 5)

Should we let the past dictate how we live in the present? Some of us like to live in the past because it's familiar, it's comfortable, it's pictures on the wall of the old country and our ancestors, it's the pretty dresses and ice-cream socials, it's

Thanksgiving and Christmas every day. What's there not to like about that? Comfort foods and happy times are good times.

Do you still delight in telling the tales of being the captain of your football team and the steak dinners you and your team enjoyed after a big win? Are your best days behind you? Do you feel like you are losing it? My wife's favorite quote is: "Yesterday is gone, tomorrow is not promised, and that's why today is a present."

Embrace it. Enjoy it. In fact, let us be glad about it! When you fill up your life with things of the past, you leave little room to enjoy your present.

One of my favorite places to visit is Egypt. It is home of Cleopatra, Nefertiti, the great pharaohs and their pyramids, the mystic sphinx, mummification, the first alphabet, the marvelous inventiveness of their ancestors in medicine (Imhotep), astronomy, agriculture, and irrigation. They once ruled the world. So, they got stuck at some point in their past glory. We have enjoyed magnificent tours - a golden sea of memories. I have been on a mission on each visit (without success) to find any evidence of present achievements. So, it has become a nice place to visit but a terrible place to live.

Whether your past is painful or full of longing happiness, it doesn't even matter that you are old and only have your memories and nothing to look forward to, you can still move on from the past to make tomorrow great - even if it's just one more day. It is time to stop blaming and repeating, "If it wasn't for… we would be so much better off."

Some of us may believe we are living in the present but still being drawn back to the past. But the past is only a steppingstone that can fuel our ambitions, it is not a milestone. According to Stewart Stafford: "I don't believe in yesterday; I believe in tomorrow. Whether it's positive or negative, the future is a new experience and not a ghostly replay of a time that was and can never be again."

223.

Crossing the Rubicon: Doing the Right Thing is Always the Best Thing

February 25, 2021

Ladies and gentlemen, we are at a crossroads. Do we want to live in a country where people do the right thing, or do we plan to do what we want without a moral compass? Are we a country of laws or can some people get away with murder? I dare say that our democracy (and our world) will only survive if each of us is committed to doing the right thing.

In response to Republican Senator Pat Toomey explaining that he had voted his conscience when he voted to find President Donald Trump guilty for his incitement of the insurrection and was committed to do the right thing, to my shock and disdain, Mr. David Ball, chairman of the Washington County GOP in Pennsylvania, proclaimed: "We did not send him there to do the right thing."

He then voted to censor Senator Toomey, a long-time loyalist to the Republican agenda. Having a conscience and doing the right thing seems to have been irrelevant to Mr. Ball's political expediency. Have we crossed the Rubicon?

Sen. Toomey thought differently and explained that when President Trump's legal challenges failed to turn the election in his favor: "President Trump summoned thousands and inflamed their passions by repeating disproven allegations about widespread fraud... He urged the mob to march on the Capitol for the explicit purpose of preventing Congress and the Vice President from formally certifying the results of the presidential election. All of this to hold on to power despite having legitimately lost."

Does Mr. Ball have a spouse, children, friends, business associates, and relatives who depend on him to do the right thing? If you are not a person that lives by upright principles, I certainly would not want you anywhere in my life.

When did we lose our focus on honesty and integrity? As Americans, aren't these principles at the core of what we hold dear? At what point did Mr. Ball think he had the monopoly on how a man or woman thinks and acts? The Bible teaches that as a man or woman thinks, so are they. Does this then mean that Mr. Ball is a man without a conscience; does it also mean that those who voted with Mr. Ball are also without a moral compass?

We all had grandmothers, parents, teachers, pastors, friends, and neighbors who impressed on us not only to treat everyone as we want to be treated but to "always" do the right thing (honorable and just) - don't lie or steal and make your word your bond.

> So, whoever knows the right thing to do and fails to do it, for him it is sin." "Do not be deceived: God is not mocked, for whatever one sows, that will he also reap." "Do not grow weary in doing good." "Seek the LORD and his strength; seek his presence continually!" "Repay no one evil for evil but give thought to do what is honorable in the sight of all." "If your enemy is hungry, feed him; if he is thirsty, give him something to drink; for by doing so, you heap burning coals on his head." "For what shall it profit a man, if he shall gain the whole world, and lose his own soul?

Where have all these lessons gone? When does doing the right thing become a cause for derision?

I am dismayed to say that many people like Mr. Ball think we are in an America that is waging a "zero sum" war within. That is to say for me to win, you must lose. Our better angels are calling for all of us to learn to live with the differences among us that made this country great. A zero-sum mentally ensures that we all lose.

> Now, the effects of the corrupt nature are obvious: illicit sex, perversion, promiscuity, idolatry, drug use, hatred, rivalry, jealousy, angry outbursts, selfish ambition, conflict, factions, envy, drunkenness, wild partying, and similar things. I've told you in the past and I'm telling you again that people who do these kinds of things will not inherit God's kingdom. But the spiritual nature produces love, joy, peace, patience, kindness, goodness, faithfulness, gentleness, and self-control. (Galatians 5:19-23)

Even though we often fall short of these rules of the road, we all subscribe to them. Step back from the line. Let us not cross the Rubicon.

224.

Guess Who is Playing Nice... Luke Combs

March 11, 2021

In celebration of the country singer:

I love country music - especially the lyrics. So, while I loved Luke Combs lyrics, I detested the fact that his concerts were wrapped in the Confederate flag, which I found offensive. He had always told himself that he was just expressing his proud Southern heritage, but finally came to recognize that the Confederate flag was a painful reminder of slavery and the Jim Crow South. So, he recently pronounced:

> As I've grown in my time as an artist, and as the world has changed drastically in the last five to seven years, I am now aware how painful that image can be. I would never want to be associated with something that brings so much hurt to someone else... I'm trying to learn. I'm trying to get better. I know that I'm a very highly visible member of the country music community right now. And I want to use that position for good, and to say that people can change, and people do want to change, and I'm one of those people trying.

I was delighted that he has grown as an artist and a decent human being who recognizes how painful it is for so many when we see the Confederate flag flying from a rooftop, yard, or pickup truck. I can now publicly admit my affection for his lyrics:

> I can't turn it off once I turn it on," "It takes one hand to count the things I can count on." "Taste the salt on the rim, feel the sand on your skin." "Even though I'm leavin' I ain't going nowhere." "I got away with you. And somehow, I still ain't been found out. It's the crazy truth. Like I strolled out the gates of Alcatraz. And walked in the Louvre. And the Mona Lisa's hanging in my house. I bust out of Buckingham Palace with the crown jewels. And I got away with you." "The moon went into hiding. Stars quit shining. Rain was driving, thunder, lightning. You wrecked my whole world when you came. And hit me like a hurricane." "I was the one phone call when my brother went to jail. Pawned my guitar just to pay his bail. No, I'll never get it back. But I'm okay with that." "I'm one number away from calling you. I said I was through, but I'm dying inside. Got my head in a mess, girl I confess. I lied when I said:

I'm leaving and not coming back." "I like a sunrise, duck blind. Birdie on a par five. Miller Lite before noon. I like two-door old Ford. Wood board back porch. Three cords and the truth." "I love the way she ride." and "Nothing picks me up like a beer can.

Ladies and gentlemen, those are right up there with, "If I said you had a beautiful body, would you hold it against me?" and "I am the only hell my mama ever raised." and my favorite: "You are the reason my kids are ugly."

Luke was born in 1990 in North Carolina. He has been performing since he was a child and dropped out of college to pursue a highly successful singing career in Nashville, with several hits including the number one on the hot country songs chart, "The Way She Rides." He won two Grammy Awards, five CMA awards, two iHeartRadio music awards, and a host of other accolades. He is an amazing performer. And now I can proudly proclaim my admiration.

Good on you mate!

225.

A Thing of Beauty is a Joy Forever

March 25, 2021

I had plans to write something insightful, informative, and even creative this week, but a funny thing happened on my way to the computer. On a beautiful spring afternoon, playing with the Raintree Rascals at Raintree Golf Club on Monday (March 15, 2021), I shot a 70!

Can you imagine? I have not shot under par in 25 years. This was two under par - four birdies and two bogies. I am now thinking that maybe I should sign up for senior "Q" school and try the senior tour. Just kidding. As you can tell, I am very pleased with myself - a remarkable personal achievement.

I will be 78 years old this coming July so just shooting my age would have been an accomplishment. This was eight shots better. And that included missing three putts shorter than five feet. It could have been a 68! (Golfers always think this way.

But I should have also missed several long ones that found the bottom of the cup). The Lord giveth and the Lord taketh away, blessed be the name of the Lord.

In addition to my 38 points, my teammates (Billy Stringer, Bill Cook, and Johnny Davis) all made their points with the Stableford Scoring System we use (bogies=1, pars=2, birdies=3, and eagles=4) for a total team score of plus 27! A record for our club. In the old days when birdies were four points, I would have made 42 points! I don't expect to repeat that performance ever again in the few years I have left. I give credit to swimming for an hour each day. I am feeling very fit (for my age). This could be the fountain of youth.

Golf is a remarkable game. The memory of my fabulous round is indelibly imprinted in my fond memories. It was a thing of beauty. Here is what Allan Berman wrote about our game:

ODE TO GOLF

In my hand I hold a ball. White And Dimpled, Rather Small.
Oh, How Bland It Does Appear. This Harmless Looking Little Sphere.
By Its Size I Could Not Guess, The Awesome Strength It Does Possess.
But Since I Fell Beneath Its Spell, I've Wandered Through the Fires of Hell.
My Life Has Not Been Quite the Same, Since I Chose to Play This Stupid Game.
It Rules My Mind for Hours on End, A Fortune It Has Made Me Spend.
It Has Made Me Yell, Curse and Cry, I Hate Myself and Want to Die.
It Promises A Thing Called Par, If I Can Hit It Straight And Far.
To Master Such A Tiny Ball, Should Not Be Very Hard At All.
But My Desires The Ball Refuses, And Does Exactly As It Chooses.
It Hooks And Slices, Dribbles And Dies, And Even Disappears Before My Eyes.
Often It Will Have A Whim, To Hit A Tree Or Take A Swim.
With Miles Of Grass On Which To Land, It Finds A Tiny Patch Of Sand.
Then Has Me Offering Up My Soul, If Only It Would Find The Hole.
It's Made Me Whimper Like A Pup, And Swear That I Will Give It Up.
And Take To Drink To Ease My Sorrow, But the Ball Knows…I'll Be Back Tomorrow.

Please come out and play the greatest game that was ever conceived. Little children play it. Very old people play it. Blind people play it. One handed people play it. You too can enjoy it.

You know how good it feels when it's your birthday and family and friends gather around to sing the birthday song? In golf, when it's your turn to hit the ball, you are the focus of everyone's attention and if the shot is good, you are applauded and if it's bad, your playing partners commiserate and help you find your wayward balls.

It's a game like no other. I really enjoy the camaraderie, the sunshine, the acres of green grass, the birds singing, the trees blooming, the reflection of the sky and clouds in the lakes, the exercise and occasionally, a really memorable round. What else could you be doing that offers so much?

226.
Sherry Farr, R.N.
A Nurse on a Mission

April 1, 2021

I am a great advocate for nurses. I have been advising students that if they have an opportunity to be trained as a nurse - go for it. No other profession offers the opportunity to travel to any country of the world and get a job the next day. Doctors, lawyers, dentists, teachers, pharmacists, and physical therapists cannot do it because of training/licensing requirements. When nurses are certified in one country, they can work anywhere. It turns out that the criteria for nursing certification is the same the world over. If you like to travel, this is the profession for you.

Countries around the world have a nursing shortage and will welcome any nurse who wants to live and work with them. They will welcome you with open arms. While the salaries will not match what is usual and customary in the United States, Canada and Europe, some countries will make up for it with free housing, transportation, and meals.

There are 2.7 million nurses in the United States, and we are short by 20%. When I was a patient at Emory Midtown, the 12 nurses who looked after me were from ten different countries. Each year, we import thousands of nurses and still come up short. I know of one hospital that advertises in Jamaica that if you are a certified nurse, sign up at their recruitment center and they fill a chartered plane and bring them back to Atlanta where they provide a good salary, medical coverage, housing, and meals. In the meantime, Jamaica fills their nursing needs by recruiting from India.

We have a shortage because of increasing population growth and especially the aging of our baby boomers, coupled with not enough nursing schools graduating nurses to accommodate the increasing need (particularly for specialized nurses). Many of the nurses are also retiring because of burnout from their stressful lifestyle. We should be concerned. Who will provide the loving tender care for our over 80 population? I am anticipating an adverse impact on our healthcare system. In other words, be generous with your appreciation for the nurses you know. They are the backbone of our healthcare system. Gordon College has an excellent nursing school whose students are volunteering to help administer the COVID-19 vaccines.

In the tradition of nurse Lillian Wald who founded the Visiting Nurse Service and the Children's Bureau in 1912, an advocate for women and children and lobbying to end child labor, our own Sherry Farr (a native of Thomaston and honor graduate from Brookwood School) has been a public health advocate since her graduation from the Medical College of Georgia in Augusta in 1983. After stints at the Monroe County Hospital in Forsyth, the Putnam General Hospital in Eatonton, and Macon Northside Hospital, she returned to work at Upson Regional Medical Center in 2000 as a med/surg charge nurse.

She found her true calling in 2016 when she was offered the nurse manager position at the Upson County Health Department. Being certified in CPR and Child Safety Seat technician, she transferred to the Lamar County Health Department in Barnesville as the county nurse manager, where she is currently in charge of their public health initiatives.

Ladies and gentlemen, no one takes their responsibilities more seriously. She started the Lamar County Family Connections Collaborative; she is active with the Rotary Club and is an advisor to the Lamar County 4H program. Most notably, as a member of Ramah Primitive Baptist Church, she is the medical team leader for Discipling Ministries International.

Her honors include the First Humanitarian Award (1999) from Macon Northside Hospital, the Lamar County Career Woman of the Year (2013), and the Ruth B. Freeman Nursing Award for Population Health Practice (2016) from the Georgia Public Health Association.

According to Dr. Charlaya Campbell (ZÖe Pediatrics, Barnesville): "Sherry is a dedicated public health nurse. We work closely to assure the children of Lamar

County receive superb medical care. As a physician, I am concerned about individual patients while she is focused on general public health. If the patient is sick, you treat the patient; if the community is sick, you treat the community. Right now, we have several public health priorities that include COVID-19, obesity, low birth weight newborns, and domestic dysfunction. Sherry is forever thinking about what she can do to help us address these issues. She is a true champion for the residents of Lamar County. Please help us help you and contact her at the Lamar County Health Department to get your COVID-19 vaccination."

227.

Jealousy: The Ugly Emotion Known as the Green-Eyed Monster

April 8, 2021

Why did Cain kill Abel?

According to the Bible, the cause of the murder had nothing to do with anything Abel did except Cain was jealous because God favored Abel, which gave rise to the green-eyed monster or "Mankind's greatest flaw" that leads to recklessness and bad mindedness in the one who envied, and possessiveness in the envied – a poisonous snake around your ankle.

A falling out between siblings and family members and friends always seems to be about envy – making an otherwise good and loving relative want to destroy a rival and themselves in the process because they are favored by a parent.

I wrote in a previous column about people who win the lottery getting poisoned and hated for their good fortune. Maybe siblings don't mind their brothers and sisters succeeding, each of us just wants to be better than the rest of them. We would much rather be the cousin that is bombarded with appeals for help than the one asking for the loan.

According to Eric Berne, those who feel like they are in a one down position lie in wait until the person who they feel jealous fails, giving them sweet revenge. "Now

I got you, you SOB! What right did you have to be better off than me?" They shout it from the rooftops: "How low the mighty has fallen!"

According to the dictionary, envy is a feeling of discontented or resentful longing aroused by someone else's possessions, qualities, luck, painful or resentful awareness of an advantage enjoyed by another, joined with a desire to possess the same advantage. When you want what someone else has, a covetous feeling arises toward another person's attributes, possessions, or status.

Envy is triggered when you believe you are shortchanged in some way and will go to great lengths to overcome your inadequacies. So, this can be accomplished by cutting those that are better off down to size, put them down in some way, putting them in their place, or work hard to bring yourself up so you will no longer feel inferior. We need to feel some perceived level of success or at least to measure up. Of course, it is much easier to bring the target of your envy down than to elevate yourself.

When envy is triggered and you become unhappy, you will likely feel hatred toward the object of your envy and disappointment within yourself but also be motivated to compensate for, or eliminate the source of your envy to level the playing field.

Is your attraction, high regard, and admiration for someone an idealization of their desired qualities or possessions activating envy? Do you suspect that what you want (wealth, education, talent, status, cars, and material possessions) can be had from associating with them so at least hope that some of it will rub off on you and bring you happiness and fulfillment? Sounds like a formula for happiness.

According to "Envy: The Emotion Kept Secret" in *Psychology Today* (March 15, 2011): "Your ideal self is what you aspire to be; the best that you think you could or should be, and often this ideal comes from social comparisons. Your sense of self is constantly measuring itself against your ideals and coming to various conclusions. If you measure up, you feel good, excited, and even elated. If you don't measure up, you may feel depressed, or ashamed. Self-esteem is determined to a great degree by your own comparison of your sense of self to your ideal self. However, it is sometimes easier to project that ideal onto someone else in the form of envy.

The values against which yourself is measured are likely to change as you mature and as you learn to evaluate your potentialities and accept your limitations. If you have realistic ideals and can generally live up to them, your self-esteem will not be threatened. If your ideals are exaggerated and you cannot reach them, your

good feelings from successes may be short-lived and you may feel that you are never good enough and will envy others."

So, when you envy someone else, you are giving them a compliment. Maybe we are all guilty of envy, calling it "keeping up with the Jones." In the final analysis, we probably all want to be smug about how others view us with a little envy – maybe not enough to encourage assault and battery as we flaunt and show off spouses, successful children, cars, boats, airplanes, big houses, makeovers, and clothes.

Don't compare yourself to anyone. You are incomparable!

228.

Happiness and a Good Life is Built on the Quality of Your Relationships

April 15, 2021

I was playing a very competitive round of golf at Raintree yesterday (April 8) and I was just delighted in the balmy spring weather, feeling strong, playing well and just having a jolly good time with Randy, Calvin, Dannie and Willie-Bee. The trees were in bloom, the bees spreading pollen and making honey, birds singing their hearts out and we had the course all to ourselves. We were all in good spirits, telling jokes and laughing hysterically. When I made an amazing 30 Ft. putt for birdie on 12, I felt so happy in that moment, I was tempted to kneel right there on the green to thank the Almighty for blessing me with this wonderful life. What a mighty God we serve and what a mighty life I am able to live right here in Thomaston.

This week, I hired someone to dig up the roots of the vines that are growing on the trees in my yard and explained to the young man that if you destroy the roots, the vines will wither and die. "Son, you need roots in your family and community to thrive. In Jamaica, when a child is born, the father will take the child's navel string (placenta) and plant a tree over it and the child will be reminded throughout his or her life where their roots are. Wherever you may roam, your tree will always anchor you to the place of your birth. So, when my daughter joined us 50 years ago, I asked the doctor for the placenta so I could follow the tradition and he confessed that he had never had that request. I persisted.

Whatever your station in life, just about everyone wants to be rich and famous. Obvious, isn't it? Or is it? It turns out that meaningful bonds with significant others is the secret sauce and far more important for our well-being and happiness than silver and gold. But it turns out that quality relationships with trustworthy, kind, and considerate people can only be achieved if you are also trustworthy, kind, and considerate. You then become a magnet for other trustworthy, kind, and considerate souls.

Holding grudges, being selfish, childless, isolated, suffering in silence and living with conflict, greed and hate are ingredients of a short, tortured life, while being satisfied in relationships that are warm and protective leads to a long meaningful life. Everyone suffers setbacks, failures, disappointments, and tragedies, but they are magnified if you do not enjoy supportive relationships. The most resilient are those who have family and friends they can rely on. Think on this the next time you decide to blow up bridges in your wake.

I am reminded of the story of the most hateful man in the valley who died after a short, sad, and miserable life but the pastor insisted that he could not release the man for burial until someone said something kind about him. "Come on people, someone must have witnessed his generosity or any act of kindness. Please come forward and speak up." After a long pause, one of the Deacons finally came forward and said: "Pastor, his brother was worse."

Failure and social rejection can be crippling for everyone. Obviously, succeeding at something is a good start. You cannot be happy being dependent on the goodwill of others, especially your parents. You got to pay your bills. It is a miserable existence if you are forever being tormented by bill collectors and denied credit. You don't have to be rich, but must be able to meet your financial responsibilities. In a land of opportunity, you have to really try to fail like getting hooked on drugs, committing crimes, being hateful, having babies you cannot support and a bad reputation. None of us is without sin and we have fallen short of expectations, and nobody is perfect or without vulnerabilities. But being willing to help out a friend in need so you will have a friend to lean on when it's your turn goes a long way to keep you upright. I have repeated Dr. Malcom Taylor's words: "If you have God, family and friends, you may stumble but you will never hit the ground." Yes. We need each other. I invite you to lean on me when you are not strong, and I promise to be your friend.

Social media has a way of convincing us that everyone else is leading perfect lives while we struggle. Please don't compare yourself to others. Let me introduce you to Richard Cory:

"Whenever Richard Cory went downtown, we people on the pavement looked at him. He was a gentleman from sole to crown, clean, favored, and imperially slim. And he was always quietly arrayed, and he was always human when he talked, but still he fluttered pulses when he said: "Good morning," and he glittered when he walked. And he was rich. Yes, richer than a king—And admirably schooled in every grace. In time, we thought that he was everything to make us wish that we were in his place. So, we worked, and waited for the light, and went without the meat, and cursed the bread; And Richard Cory, one calm summer night, went home and put a bullet through his head" (American poet Edwin Arlington Robinson, 1897).

Yes, because we all strive for inclusion, belonging, feeling special and even to be honored and applauded, social exclusion is painful. But as desirable as fame and fortune may be, it's the quality of our relationships that guarantees us a long meaningful life. It is worth the occasional hassle.

According to Mark Twain:

There isn't time, so brief is life, for bickerings, apologies, heart burnings, callings to account. There is only time for loving, and but an instant, so to speak, for that.

Acknowledgements

I am grateful first to my wife for being my fiercest critic but always inspiring me to be my best self and providing the environment of us to live well---always dreaming up ways to enhance both the quality and quantity of our lives. I will never forget nor will I fail to appreciate the ten nights you spent in a very uncomfortable sofa beside my bed while I was in Emory Hospital after my triple by-pass surgery. It greatly comforted me. Wives of writers, columnists, comedians, and public speakers get used to being a convenient target and my wife in particular has had a great deal of her private life revealed to the public—without her permission. Thanks darling, for your ever-present love and support.

My editor (Debbie McClain) was particularly helpful in giving us access to all my columns and supported my wish to publish this volume.

Finally, my children (Jillian Kong-Sivert, J.D., Freddie Kong, B.A., Aleron Kong, M.D., and Melanie Kong-Shaw, M.A., B.C.B.A.) provided a great deal of inspiration and particularly your willingness to recommend books, articles, data and news items---and most valuable of all, you could all be counted on to give me honest feedback and to bounce ideas around. I love you guys. Thanks for our great memories and mutual support on our life's journey. I am certainly willing for my character to be judged by the success of my children. I am so proud of all of you!

Other Books by the Author

**Bad Boy from Jamaica:
The Garnett Myrie Story**

Basil Waine Kong

ISBN 978-149-90104-1-1 (Paperback)

**The Hero of Fern Gully
and Other Jamaican
Short Stories**

Basil Waine Kong and Glen Laman

ISBN 978-1-7353069-4-0 (Paperback)
ISBN 978-1-7353069-5-7 (Hard Cover)